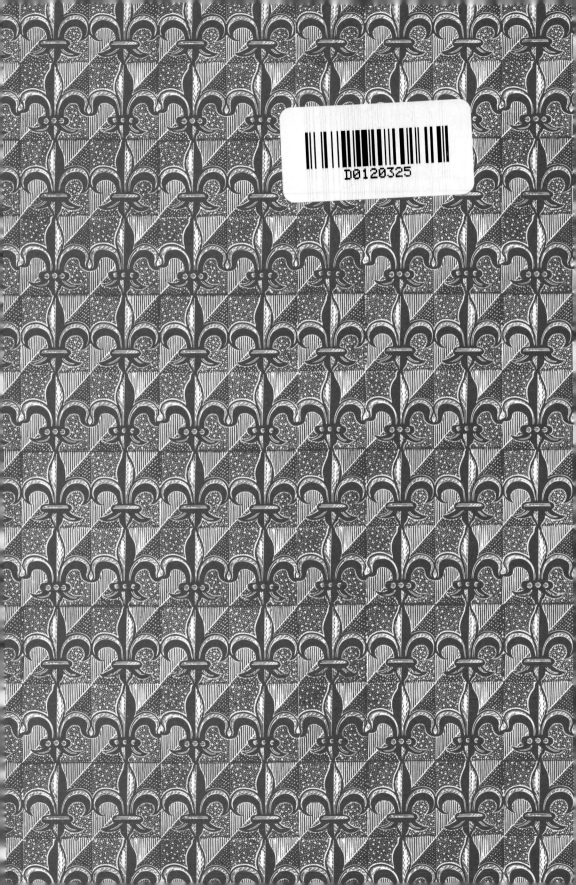

Best of Enemies

ROBERT GIBSON

BEST OF ENEMIES

Anglo–French Relations
Since the Norman Conquest

SINCLAIR-STEVENSON

To my sons
Ian, Graham and Robin

First published in Great Britain in 1995
by Sinclair-Stevenson
an imprint of Reed Consumer Books Ltd
Michelin House, 81 Fulham Road, London SW3 6RB
and Auckland, Melbourne, Singapore and Toronto

A CIP catalogue record for this book
is available at the British Library
ISBN 1 85619 487 6

Typeset by Deltatype Ltd, Ellesmere Port, Cheshire
Printed and bound in Great Britain
by Clays Ltd, St Ives PLC

We prided ourselves on our prejudices: we blustered and bragged with absurd vainglory; we dealt to our enemy the monstrous injustice of contempt and scorn; we fought him with all weapons, mean as well as heroic. There was no lie which we would not credit. I thought at one time of making a collection of the lies which the French had written against us and we had published against them during the war; it would be a strange memorial of popular falsehood.

W. M. Thackeray, *The Four Georges*

Do you wish to escape from your nationalistic illusions? Then consult foreigners: what they think of you today is what posterity will think in the future.

Joseph de Maistre, Cinquième paradoxe
in *Lettres et opuscules*

Contents

List of Illustrations

Acknowledgements

My main debt of gratitude is to the works and authors listed in the bibliography at the end of this book. They are not the only authorities I have consulted but they are the ones to whom I feel most beholden. To a greater or lesser degree, their earlier quarrying provided me with most of the fragments from which my mosaic has been constructed.

For valuable pointers along my way, I am particularly grateful to Alan Cameron and to the following professorial friends and colleagues: Leslie Davis, Robert Lethbridge, Ian Macfarlane, the late Vivienne Mylne, Peter Rickard, Michael Screech, the late Robert Shackleton and Michael Sheringham; and for what I learnt through teaching them, two of my research students, Claire Garnier and Joanna Hair.

I am indebted to Eve Hurste for so expertly typing the first draft of what was originally a much longer hand-written version of this book, to Justine Clements who so competently helped me recast it into its present form and to Roger Cazalet whose work as editor has been quite exemplary.

I am grateful to the University of Kent for granting me periods of study leave in which to pursue my research and to the staff of its library for their assiduity in helping me track down texts long since out of print.

Most of the cartoons reproduced here come from the rich and impressively organised archives of the Centre for the Study of Cartoon and Caricature at the University of Kent at Canterbury. For their help in locating and selecting them, I wish particularly to thank its archivists, Jane Newton and Rob Edwards, and for the speed and skill with which they made the prints therefrom, my thanks are due to James Styles and Spencer Scott of the University's Photographic Unit.

For permission to reproduce cartoons still under copyright, I wish to thank the following: the *Daily Mirror* for 12b; Ewan Macnaughton Associates (agents for the *Daily Telegraph*) for 16b; Express Newspapers plc for 10c, 13a and 16a; the *New Statesman* for 13b and 14b; *Punch* for 15a; Solo Syndication (agents for the *Evening Standard*) for 11c, 12a and 15b.

For permission to quote from books still under copyright, I wish to thank the following: Curtis Brown Ltd and the Estate of Sir Winston Churchill for the quotations from the speeches and writings of Sir Winston Churchill; Macmillan Publishers Ltd and the Estate of Charles Morgan for the quotations from the writings of Charles Morgan.

Finally, I would like to acknowledge all that I owe my wife, who for over forty years now has stayed with me with flagons, comforted me with apples and kept the world at bay. When all is said, it is to her that I owe the most.

Robert Gibson
Canterbury and Sidmouth, 1995

I : *The Growth of Nationalism in the Middle Ages*

From this period, we may date the commencement of that great animosity which the English nation has ever since borne to the French, which has so visible an influence on all future transactions and which has been, and continues to be, the spring of many rash and precipitate resolutions among them.

David Hume, *History of Great Britain* (1754–7)

The notion of nationhood is a relatively modern concept. The term *natio* was by no means unknown in the Middle Ages – indeed it occurs in Cicero, Caesar and the Latin Bible – but it did not then have the resonance it unfailingly has today. Self-awareness and self-importance are now essential components: pride in a common descent, a common history and a common culture. Scale too is significant: the size of the community claiming nationhood is impossible to quantify but must surely be considerable. None of this was true of the medieval *natio*: it could denote an entity as small as a city state, a district or even a group of University students from the same geographical locality. At the University of Paris in the Middle Ages, there were four such 'nations': the French, the Normans, the Picardians and the English. The present-day rue des Anglais, in the fifth *arrondissement* of Paris, commemorates where once they were housed, though in medieval times, the University English 'nation' also included Scots, Irish, German, Scandinavian and Slavonic students.

Medieval man was clannish, his horizons were literally limited and his loyalties were strictly circumscribed. The community which commanded his allegiance had to be small, tangible and immediately accessible. He would regularly have been enlisted to fight on behalf of his local overlord but not for a cause as vague as his country. The present-day entities of England and France took centuries to forge. In the early medieval period, England was sub-divided into many kingdoms, fighting as fiercely amongst themselves as they were obliged to do against waves of rapacious invaders from over the North Sea. Across the Channel, the political situation was equally fissile but somewhat more advanced. In Roman Gaul, there had been Franci from the third century. They played the leading part in destroying the old Roman Empire and they dominated the new order, with Frankish kings and Frankish warriors. Francia came to designate that region of their greatest strength. In the period of its greatest power, under Charlemagne (742–841), Francia designated all the Cisalpine provinces of ancient Gaul, from the marches of Brittany in the west to beyond the Rhine in the east. When the Carolingian Empire broke up in the tenth century, the eastern provinces passed over to the German kingdom while western or Gallic Francia, the nucleus of modern France, designated the Paris basin together with some outlying districts to the south and the west. Brittany became a separate kingdom as were Toulouse, Poitou, Aquitaine and Normandy, all immensely powerful and jealous of their independence. How and why France and England fought intermittently for five hundred years to secure mastery of those provinces will be the subject of this chapter.

Before the Norman Conquest, England had only the most perfunctory of relations with the European mainland. For the inhabitants of England, there was neither the incentive nor the means to make the Channel crossing in significant numbers. To the inhabitants of what had once been Gaul, England remained what it had long since been, the remote island of Albion, so-named because of the white cliffs that rose on the horizon of the forbidding grey sea. England became embroiled only when William, Duke of Normandy, insisted that he was the rightful heir of the childless Edward the Confessor, and resolved to secure his inheritance by force of arms. This was the traditional way in which the Normans settled disputes. From the time of their first incursion into the Seine valley in the second half of the ninth century, when they laid siege to Paris and burned and looted churches, the Northmen acquired a formidable reputation as ferocious fighters and able administrators. The standard account of the creation of Normandy (Northmannia) is that in 911, to win peace and counter the threat of adjacent Brittany, Charles the Simple gave his daughter to Rollo the Ganger and ceded him lands in the lower Seine. By the middle of the tenth century, Normandy had become established as an independent state with well-defined borders and its own administrative organization. It was from its Channel coast, after the most careful planning to which the Bayeux Tapestry bears testimony, that Duke William launched his invasion in October 1066.

When Edward the Confessor died on 5 January 1066, there was no clear-cut successor to his throne. Of the six contenders, those with the strongest claims were Harold, the Earl of Wessex, son of the Earl Godwin, the most powerful magnate in the kingdom, and William of Normandy, whose great-aunt Emma had married two English kings, Ethelred the Unready and Canute. From the outset, the succession was bitterly contested by the rival claimants and by contemporary chroniclers. With his dying words Edward commended his Queen and country to Harold's protection. But William maintained that the English crown had been promised to him both by Edward and by Harold when he was released from imprisonment after being shipwrecked on the Breton coast.

The Battle of Hastings, on 14 October 1066, was desperately close run and the outcome remained in doubt till the end. It is by no means certain that Harold was killed by an arrow through the eye. In some accounts the blinded Harold is hacked to pieces by William in person; in another, his devoted Edith Swan Neck finds Harold's mutilated body, recognizing it by marks only a lover could have known, and his old mother, Earl Godwin's widow, is said to have offered to buy the corpse from William for its weight in gold; in yet another, Harold survives, goes first to Denmark and then on a religious pilgrimage whence he returns to spend the last ten years of his life as a hermit in a cave within the cliffs of Dover. Be all of that as it may, William certainly won the battle, proceeded to crush the spirited resistance with characteristic ruthlessness, and had himself crowned King of England just over two months later on Christmas Day. In so doing, he became a real English king, enjoying the same rights and privileges as his West Saxon predecessors.

It was a spectacular personal victory for William rather than for

France. In the event, Philip I of France was not best pleased that the kingdom of England had now been amalgamated with the duchy of Normandy. Because Normandy was a fief of France, William was technically Philip's vassal, bound to pay him homage and sworn to do his bidding. William's victory locked England into the French feudal system and effectively started a time-bomb ticking that was to set off a chain of explosions over centuries to come.

After the Conquest, England became the very model of a feudal military hierarchy. As absolute suzerain at the apex of the intricate power-structure, William claimed the whole of England as his own. His henchmen were rewarded with vast estates but they remained his tenants and his vassals, pledged to provide him with military support whenever he required it. That support was certainly needed in the years immediately following the Conquest as England was forcibly pacified and effectively colonized. Between the victory at Hastings and the compilation of the Domesday Book in 1086, while more than 200,000 Normans settled in England, at least 300,000 English people perished either through William's ferocious campaign of repression or through starvation following the seizure of their land and livestock. The massive Norman castles that still stand at key-centres across the length and breadth of England provide enduring testimony to the thoroughness with which the invaders were determined to defend the fruits of their victory.

On the overall effect of the Conquest on English life, English historians have notably failed to agree. Some insist on the basic continuity of English society and see the Norman occupation as an interlude of little consequence; others maintain that England's consecutive political history must be dated from 1066. Symptomatically, Sir Frank Stenton, one of our foremost authorities on the subject, contradicted himself. In 1908, he claimed that before the Conquest, England had no administration worthy of the name and that to liken it to contemporary Normandy was to compare decadence with growth. Two world wars later, his views had radically changed. He now found the Normans 'a harsh and violent race . . . the closest of all western people to the Barbarian strain in the continental order. They produced little in art or learning and nothing in literature that could be set beside the work of Englishmen.'

This is surely too censorious a judgement. A direct consequence of the Conquest was the form of the French language that became current in Great Britain and Ireland over the two centuries that followed. It was used by the ruling classes and the literature and the authors who wrote in it are still classified as Anglo-Norman. The range of works is extensive, including historical subjects, translations of Biblical books, bestiaries and tales of the knights of the Round Table. Among the more noteworthy works are the *Chasteau d'amour*, a poem in praise of the Virgin Mary by Robert Grosseteste (1175–1233), Bishop of Lincoln and the first Chancellor of Oxford University, the important mystery play *Le Jeu d'Adam* and the *Lais* of the twelfth-century poetess Marie de France.

The equally eminent Professor T. F. Tout preferred instead to stress the positive consequences of the Conquest. In his view, the Normans superimposed on England a French dynasty, French nobility, Church notables and a French-speaking ruling, writing and trading class. They effectively bridged the moat between England and the Continent, which had kept them divided in spite of the best endeavours of Caesar, Agricola, St Patrick, Boniface and Canute. After the Norman Conquest, Britain became an integral part of Western civilization, receiving and responding to every movement radiating from France. If imposing castles were built, so too were hundreds of churches, and work was begun on new cathedrals on a scale grander than ever before envisaged. Great monasteries were founded by all the leading French orders and pious Norman conquerors bestowed rich English lands on their own favoured monasteries in France. Although scholars are likely to continue debating the extent to which the Normans imposed their administrative and cultural models upon the English, and how far English traditions and institutions absorbed the Norman conquerors, the impact itself of the encounter was staggering – the more so since within a hundred years of the Battle of Hastings, the Normans had ceased to rule.

William's family dynasty was remarkably short-lived. When he died in 1087, his rich estates were divided between his three sons. Robert 'Curthose' inherited Normandy, William 'Rufus' became King of England and Henry 'Beauclerk' was given a large sum of money and told to get himself a large fief. In the event, Henry did better still. In 1100, when William Rufus was killed by a stray arrow while hunting in the New Forest and Robert was away crusading in the Holy Land, Henry seized the English throne. And in 1106, at the Battle of

Tinchebray (Orne), he defeated his brother Robert, imprisoned him for the rest of his life and proceeded to rule England and Normandy as though they were the provinces of a single kingdom. On the death of Henry in 1135, the throne passed to Stephen, grandson of William the Conqueror whose ninth child, Adela, had married Stephen, Count of Blois. With Stephen's death in 1154, the crown passed to another French dynasty with all the ferocious energy of William the Conqueror's and with lands stretching from the Channel coast to the Pyrenees. This change was to usher in the richest of all periods in Anglo–French relations and at the same time to unleash the conflicts that ended with their calamitous destruction.

★

The leaders of this new dynasty are known variously as the Angevins, because they hailed originally from Angers, capital of Anjou, or as Plantagenets, after their progenitor Geoffrey of Anjou, who married Henry I's daughter Matilda. Geoffrey was passionately dedicated to hunting, and to improve ground cover would carry sprigs of broom in his helmet, which he would plant whenever he came upon a likely place. The Latin for sprig is *planta* and for broom, *genista*, hence Geoffrey's nickname, which was subsequently applied to the whole of the royal house that occupied the English throne from 1154, when Henry II became king, to 1485, when Richard III's crown was plucked from a bush at Bosworth by Henry Tudor. The name of the line could be said to have ended as it began, out in the field.

Henry II, the first Plantagenet King of England, was also Count of Anjou. His wife, Eleanor, was Duchess of Aquitaine in her own right. He took over the government of Brittany and also the great county of Toulouse. It was Henry's hereditary right to rule England and Normandy, and to rule Anjou, Touraine and Maine in accordance with the customs of his Angevin ancestors; with Scotland, Wales, and Ireland also under his rule, his was indeed a considerable empire.

Members of the ruling class lived in harmony, moving easily from one region to the other. As well as sharing the same tastes in sport, hunting and love-making, they were all French-speaking. In the thirteenth century, the international vernacular was French: it was the language both of Crusaders and Western European traders. In this period, Western Europe was, in many respects, conspicuously cosmopolitan. To the medieval mind, unfamiliar with jealously guarded national borders, Western Europe was one. The religious orders of monks and friars transcended nations and ranged across the continent. Intellectual solidarity was reinforced by a shared inheritance of ancient Roman literature and the universal use of Latin, the common tongue of all University students. The spirit of that age is encapsulated in this love lyric from the beginning of the fourteenth century:

De Amico ad Amicam

A Celuy que pluys eyme en mounde,
Of alle tho that I have founde
Carissima,
Saluz od treyé amour
With grace and joye and alle honoure,
Dulcissima.

Sachez bien, pleysant et beele,
That I am right in goode heele
Laus Christo!
Et mon amour doné vous ay,
And also thine owene, night and day
In cisto.

Ma tres duce et tres amé
Night and day for love of thee
Suspiro
Soyez permanent et leal;
Love me so that I it fele,
Requiro.

A vois jeo suy tout donné
Mine herte is full of love to thee
Presento;
Et pur ceo je vous pry,
Sweting, for thin curtesy,
Memento.

Jeo vous pry par charité
The wordes that here wreten be
Tenete;

And turne thy herte me toward
O à Dieu que vous gard!
Valete!

When a student moved from Oxford to Paris or Bologna, he heard the same sort of lectures, in the same tongue, that he had listened to in the College whence he came: the same subjects, the same technique, the same viewpoint, the same ethos. He might even find that the famous professor at whose feet he sat had originally come from his own shire or village. Stephen Langton, Roger Bacon, William of Ockham and John Duns Scotus are the most famous of the British scholars who taught in Paris: there were many others. Church officials of England and France were readily interchangeable. Thomas à Becket was the son of a humble Norman merchant who was born in Rouen and prospered in London; John of Salisbury was elected Bishop of Chartres in 1176; a Scot, John Kirkmichael, was Bishop of Orléans at the time of Joan of Arc. And in the political world, too, there were no nationalistic constraints: the barons who wrested Magna Carta from King John called in Louis, heir of the French monarchy, to save English liberty from an English tyrant; the party of opposition to England's Henry III enthusiastically endorsed the leadership of the Frenchman Simon de Montfort; a century later, the Anglo–Burgundian alliance came close to destroying France as a state of stature. But for all that, though the cosmopolitan spirit in medieval Europe was real and strong, the forces of nationalism generated against it were to prove even stronger.

Those forces derived in the first instance not from the people but from their kings. When he found himself overlord of a vast region, the ruler came to need a justification more compelling than that of mere possession. National monarchs began to emerge when the king became the symbol of cultural unity, when the king of England or of France ruled over a community of people who spoke uniquely the English or French tongue. In the course of time, France absorbed what had been autonomous principalities because there was no unsurmountable linguistic barrier between the new ruler and his recent acquisitions. The same was not true of the English king and his continental subjects: the linguistic gulf between them was no less important than the Channel.

The watershed was the loss of Normandy, conquered for France by Philip II in 1206. Since before the Norman Conquest, the kings of France had seen themselves as the overlords of Normandy, and in 1206,

King John was obliged formally to recognize that the French lands he had inherited in 1200 were fiefs held in trust from the French crown. Philip II proved to be a king of great sagacity (his sobriquet was *l'Auguste*), who became the scourge of the Plantagenets. The struggle between him and his heirs against the sons of Henry II has sometimes been called the 'first' Hundred Years War. It ended in victory for the French at Bovines in 1214 and the expulsion of the Plantagenets from all their ancestral domains in France, except for some fragments of land along the coast of south-west France, variously known as Aquitaine or Guyenne. To retain even these, the King of England had to do liege homage to the King of France, solemnly acknowledging that he was his vassal.

During the long reign of John's eldest son, Henry III (1216–72), there was little open hostility between England and France. Henry's mother and wife were both French, and Henry himself was French rather than English in his artistic preferences. Many French admirers were attracted to his extremely cultured court, some of them impecunious but high-born adventurers in search of an earldom, a bishopric or a well-to-do heiress. Each of these brought with them from France a retinue of servants and clerks. In Henry III's own court, there were always many French-speaking officials, and for eighteen years in succession the King's Wardrobe, the central household office, was placed in charge of a Frenchman. One sign of incipient nationalistic feeling is that the native-born English came to resent these foreign incursions. They were fiercely denounced by Henry's outstanding chronicler, Matthew Paris, in his *Historia Anglorum*, and this fomented an outcry against the *alienigenae*, which led to their expulsion with the Barons' Revolt of 1258.

In 1259, in signing the Treaty of Paris, Henry formally renounced his claim to Normandy, Maine, Touraine and Poitou but not, significantly, to Aquitaine where, nonetheless, he acknowledged his status as the king of France's vassal. Aquitaine, thereafter, was to become the focus of an increasingly bitter dispute, one of the prime causes of the Hundred Years War.

The French kings had always wished to reduce Aquitaine to the same state of vassalage as all the other great fiefs held of the French crown. It had special significance for the English too. It had been anglicised since 1152 and its highest administrative offices – the Seneschal of Guyenne, the Constable and Mayor of Bordeaux, the Seneschal of Saintonge, together with the captains of most of the *bastides* or border-fortresses – were traditionally English. If there were few English land-owners, many of the important Guyennais *seigneurs* owned estates in England. Aquitaine, the 'land of the waters', was also the land of wine. Wine was to Aquitaine in the Middle Ages what wool was to England – its principal source of revenue. The money levied in Bordeaux on wine regularly equalled, and sometimes surpassed, the total annual revenues of the English crown. In the fourteenth century, wine flowed into England in vast quantities and grain, wool, leather and salt were exported in return. The whole region had considerable economic as well as historic importance to the English and there was never any possibility of their yielding it without a bitter struggle.

Anglo–French antagonism intensified under Henry III's son Edward I, who ruled from 1272 to 1307. He tightened the administrative and economic links between England and Aquitaine: most of the officials in his English household were Englishmen and Englishmen administered Aquitaine for him. His English wardrobe-clerks set up country houses on the Garonne or in the Dordogne, while French-style *villeneuves* were built at Winchelsea and Kingston-upon-Hull. The most eminent of his generals was Captal de Buch, the chief of the leading Gascon family. While he strove to unify Britain, Edward also maintained a lively interest in continental affairs. He was reluctant to surrender an inch of land allowed him by the Treaty of Paris and this led him into war with Philippe III (*le Hardi*) and Philippe IV (*le Bel*). In 1295, in his summons of the English bishops and abbots to Parliament, his fiery denunciation of the French anticipates the century-long war that was to follow and reveals how far nationalism had advanced: 'It has now gone forth to every region of the earth how the King of France has cheated us out of Gascony. But now, not satisfied with this wickedness, he has beset our realm with a mighty fleet and army and proposes, if his power equal his detestable purpose, which God forbid, to wipe out the English tongue from the face of the earth.'

Edward I's need to defend the English 'tongue' is particularly interesting: for all his Gallic sympathies, his own father, Henry III, had been the first to convene Parliament with a proclamation in English in 1258. The connection between nationalistic aspirations and pride in a common language could scarcely be clearer.

Although there had been intermittent conflicts between the Plantagenet and the Capetian kings in the course of the thirteenth century, the
start of the so-called Hundred Years War is normally located in the third
decade of the fourteenth. The roots of the conflict were several and
intertwining. There were economic issues: England's need to safeguard
its wine trade with Aquitaine, its wool trade with Flanders and its salt
trade with Brittany, all regions on which the French kings cast covetous
eyes. There were political tensions between the Plantagenet Empire,
which allowed for a fair measure of local autonomy and provincial self-
expression, and the French urge towards central control inherited from
the Roman *imperium*. More specifically, there was the vexed question of
who was best qualified to succeed to the French throne, left vacant in
1328 when Charles V, the last of the Capetians, died without leaving a
direct heir. Edward III of England maintained that his was the strongest
claim. His mother was the late king's sister; his grandfather was Philippe
le Bel; and French was his native language, because for all his
grandfather Edward I's expressed concern for the English tongue he had
proceeded to marry a French princess, and his children and grandchil-
dren had subsequently to be *taught* English as part of their childhood
education. In the event, the French throne was seized by Philippe de
Valois who had himself crowned in 1328.

War between the two rival claimants did not break out immediately,
indeed in 1329 Edward paid homage to Philip for Gascony. There was
sporadic fighting in Flanders and Picardy between 1337 and 1340 and it
was only then that Edward III assumed the title 'King of France'. This
was chiefly to please his Flemish allies, who wished to be absolved from
the charge of fighting against their lawful king. That same year on 8
February, Edward ordered a proclamation to be displayed on the doors
of churches throughout France, insisting that his cause was just:

> Edward, by the grace of God king of France and England and lord of
> Ireland, to all prelates, peers, dukes, counts, barons, nobles and commons of
> the kingdom of France, of whatever estate they be, these are the true facts.
> It is a well-known fact that my lord Charles, of happy memory, formerly
> king of France, died legally in possession of the kingdom of France, and that
> we are the son of the sister of the said Lord Charles, after whose death the
> said kingdom of France, as is well-known, came and devolved upon us by
> right of succession; further, that Sir Philip Valois, son of the lord Charles's
> uncle, and thus more distantly related than we, seized the kingdom by

force, against God and justice, while we were younger in years, and still holds it wrongfully.

We have now, after good and mature deliberation, and placing our faith in God and the good people, taken up the title to the government of the said kingdom, as is our duty. We are firmly intent upon acting graciously and kindly with those who wish to do their duty towards us; it is not in any way our intention to deny you your rights, for we hope to do justice to all, and to take up again the good laws and customs which existed at the time of our progenitor, St Louis, king of France; nor is it our wish to seek our gain and your prejudice by exchanges and debasement of the coinage, or by exactions, or by raising taxes which were never due; for, thanks be to God, we have sufficient for our state and the maintenance of our honour. We also wish that our subjects, as far as possible, should be relieved, and that the liberties and privileges of all, and especially of holy Church, be defended and maintained by us with all our power. We wish further, when dealing with the business of the realm, to have and to follow the good advice of the peers, prelates, nobles and other of our wise and faithful subjects of the said realm, without doing or initiating anything with undue speed and only to satisfy our whim. And we tell you again that our greatest desire is that God, working through us and the good people, should grant peace and love among Christians, and especially among you, so that a Christian army may go in haste to the Holy Land to deliver it from the hands of wicked men; this, with God's help, we aspire to do.

Philip VI promptly countered with a proclamation of his own, giving tongue to a refrain that has been voiced throughout French history ever since: the English are perfidious and their word can never be trusted.

We know for certain that, through inducement and very wicked and false counsel, the king of England, mortal enemy to ourselves and our kingdom, scornfully using the most wicked deceit and malice, has caused to be written many letters, sealed with his seal, in which are contained falsehoods, lies, treason and things injurious to us, to our kingdom and to our subjects, the which letters he plans to send, or has indeed already sent, to important places in our said kingdom so as to turn the people against us, if he is thus able. And because it is our firm intention that our said people shall never see nor hear the very great fraud, malice, lies and wicked intent of the said king of England, we wish . . . in order to counter his evil design, to have it proclaimed and solemnly made known that whoever shall find any persons, of whatever estate or condition they may be, bearing letters from the said king of England or other of our enemies, shall take and arrest them and bring them in custody to have them submit to such sentence and punishment which it shall be appropriate to pass upon persons bearing false and fraudulent letters.

The first great battle of the war was a ferocious naval engagement off the coast of Sluys on 24 June 1340. A large French fleet had been assembled there, reinforced with many crusading ships from the Mediterranean, and in smashing it as comprehensively as he did, Edward III not only cleared his passage into Flanders but eliminated the threat of a cross-Channel invasion. Thereafter, on land as at sea, in the course of the next hundred years there were remarkably few major set-piece battles. The most outstanding of France's military commanders during the Hundred Years War, the Breton Bertrand du Guesclin (1320–80), deliberately avoided pitched battles and based his campaigning on the strategy of persistent harrying and skirmishing. The three most celebrated battles that were fought – at Crécy on 26 August 1346, at Poitiers on 10 September 1356 and at Agincourt on 25 October 1415 – all took a similar course: a retreating English army, overtaken by vastly superior French forces, each time won a shattering victory by fighting on terrain that enabled it to exploit the long bows of its archers with devastating effect.

Of the many accounts of these battles, the most vivid are those by the French chronicler Jean Froissart, who spent most of his life in one royal court or another including that of Edward III and Queen Philippa, who, like Froissart, hailed from Hainault. In Froissart, the stress is always on the dramatic, the colourful and the chivalrous, as in his description of how the sixteen-year-old Black Prince fought at Crécy:

> The battle, fought on that Saturday between Broie and Crécy, was indeed deadly and very bloody; yet, there were done many fine deeds of arms which were never recognised, for it was already very late when the battle began. This fact hindered the French more than anything, for many of their men-at-arms, knights and esquires, because of the dusk, lost their lords and masters; they wandered about the fields, often coming across the English whom they fought and by whom they were at once killed, for the enemy took no prisoners and spared the lives of none; they had decided to act in this way only that very morning, when they had heard of the great number of French who were pursuing them.
>
> Many said that if the battle had begun in the morning, rather than in the late afternoon, the French would have been able to demonstrate great feats of arms, which in fact they did not. Yet certain lords and knights and esquires on the French side, in addition to certain Germans and Savoyards, did actually break through the archers in the Prince of Wales' division, and came up against his men-at-arms, whom they attacked with swords, man to man, with great valour, and in this fighting many fine deeds of arms were

done, for there were on the English side those splendid knights, Sir Reginald Cobham and Sir John Chandos, and many others, too, not all of whom I can name; for all the flower of English chivalry was there around the Prince. Thereupon the earls of Northampton and Arundel, who had charge of the second division and were holding themselves in the wings, came to bring help to the Prince, who was having to fight very hard; and those who had charge of the Prince, seeing the danger, sent one of their knights to the king, who was further up the slope on the mound of a windmill, in order to seek his help. He approached the king and said: 'Sire, the earls of Warwick and Oxford, and Sir Reginald Cobham, who are in the Prince's company, are heavily engaged, and are fighting off the French very fiercely. They seek your help, and that of your division, to get out of danger, for they fear that if the pressure is maintained much longer, your son may have too much to do.' The king, in reply, asked the knight (whose name was Sir Thomas Norwich): 'Sir Thomas, is my son dead, fallen or so wounded that he cannot help himself?' 'No,' replied the knight, 'if it is God's will, but he is in the thick of the fighting, and may need your assistance.' 'Sir Thomas,' replied the king, 'go back to him and to those who sent you, and tell them, on my behalf, not to seek my aid again for fear of what could happen so long as my son is alive; and tell them, too, that I order that the lad be allowed to earn his spurs, for it is my wish, if God so allows it, that the day be his, and that the glory of it belong to him and to those in whose charge I have entrusted him.' Having heard these words, the knight went back and reported to his commander what you have heard. They were all greatly encouraged and reproached themselves for having sent [Sir Thomas]; they now fought more manfully than before, performing many fine deeds of arms, as is recounted, so that the field remained in their hands with honour.

The opening stages of the Hundred Years War were fought in a remarkably regulated way. Challenges would be exchanged between heralds inviting opponents to agree the time and place for battle. During the frequent truces, English knights could travel freely throughout France and socialise with their sometime enemies. The ingrained sense of what was proper was demonstrated when Count William of Hainault, brother of the Queen of England and nephew of King Philippe of France, continued to serve as Edward III's paymaster until the English army reached the borders of France, which at that time did not extend to many of the great outlying provinces. With Edward's consent, he withdrew his forces because it was not felt to be seemly for him to fight against his uncle and his liege. Further testimony to the chivalric spirit of the age can be gauged from the fact that when, a year after Crécy, the widow of the Earl Aymer of Pembroke founded

Pembroke College, Cambridge, she was able to stipulate that preference on all appointments should be given to Frenchmen over English.

While war for the ordinary soldier was, once battle was joined, as ferocious as close combat has ever been, for the mounted aristocrat it was an exciting sport. If death occurred, it was all in the day's work. Should a knight be captured, he was treated with the deference due to his rank as Froissart describes in his account of the aftermath of the Black Prince's brilliant victory at Poitiers, where among the many aristocratic prisoners was the King of France himself, Jean II (*le Bon*).

That same day of the battle, at night the prince made a supper in his lodgings for the French king and for most part of the great lords who were prisoners. The prince made the King and his son, the lord James of Bourbon, the lord John d'Artois, the count of Tancarville, the count of Estampes, the count Dammartin, the count of Joinville, the lord of Partenay to sit all at one board, and other lords, knights and squires at other tables; and always the prince served before the king as humbly as he could, and would not sit at the king's board for any desire that the king could make, but he said he was not sufficient to sit at the table with so great a prince as the king was. But then he said to the king: 'Sir, for God's sake, think no evil and be not dismayed, though God this day did not consent to follow your will; for, Sir, surely the king my father shall bear you as much honour and friendship as he can possibly do, and shall agree with you so reasonably that you shall ever be friends together hereafter. And, sir, methinks you ought to rejoice, though the day did not go as you would have had it, for this day you have won the high renown of prowess and you have surpassed this day in valour all others of your party. Sir, I say this not to mock you, for all that are on our side, that saw every man's deeds, are plainly agreed by true sentence to give you the prize and the crown.' Therewith the Frenchmen began to whisper and said among themselves how the prince had spoken nobly, and that by all estimation he should prove a noble man, if God send him life and allow him to persevere in such good fortune.

For all of this regal entertainment, there was literally a price to pay. After prisoners of rank were captured they were released only on payment of a ransom. In the case of King Jean II, the ransom was so vast, three million gold crowns, that the two countries were left to haggle over it for decades to come. King Jean was held prisoner in London, but released after promising that the ransom would be paid. However, important hostages were retained to ensure that the promise would be kept. They included his son Louis, Duke of Anjou, and, when Louis broke his parole and absconded, such was King Jean's sense of honour, that he returned voluntarily to England in 1363, reaching Dover towards evening, on 4 January, two days before Twelfth Night. Froissart describes what followed:

> News of their arrival was brought to the King and Queen of England who were at Eltham, a very fine royal manor about seven miles from London. Some of the household knights, Lord Batholomew Burghersh, Sir Alan Buxhull and Sir Richard Pembridge, were immediately sent down to Dover, where the King of France had remained since his arrival. They greeted him with all possible respect, telling him that King Edward was delighted he had come. The next morning King John mounted his horse and rode with all his followers to Canterbury, which they reached at dinner-time. Entering the Cathedral of St Thomas, the King paid humble devotion to the body of the Saint and offered it a rich jewel of great value. After spending two days at Canterbury, he rode on towards London and, travelling in short stages, came to Eltham where the King and Queen of England were waiting to receive him with a great company of knights and ladies. He arrived on a Sunday in the afternoon, and between then and supper there was time for much dancing and merriment. The young Lord de Coucy in particular took great pains to dance and sing well when his turn came. He was much applauded by both French and English, for whenever he did a thing he did it well.
>
> It would be impossible for me to record all the honours with which the King and Queen of England received King John, but finally he left Eltham and entered London. There he was welcomed by people of all conditions who came out in companies to meet him, greeting him with the greatest respect. Amid a great playing of musical instruments he was escorted to the Palace of the Savoy, which had been got ready for him, and where he was lodged with the members of his family and the French hostages . . .
>
> King John spent the rest of the winter there cheerfully and sociably. He was visited frequently by the King of England and his sons, the Dukes of Clarence and Lancaster and Lord Edmund. They held several big entertainments and parties together, dinners, suppers and so forth, either at the Savoy or at the Palace of Westminster situated near by, to which the King of France went privately whenever he liked by boat along the Thames.

King Jean fell ill and died at the Palace of the Savoy in London in April 1384. His eldest son, the Duke of Normandy, Charles V (*le Sage*), succeeded to the throne. It was against this king's son, Charles VI (*le Bien-Aimé*), that the young Henry V of England went to war.

On 16 September 1415, before he began his march through Normandy, while stationed at Harfleur, Henry V issued a personal challenge to the Dauphin, offering to settle their differences in single combat:

> Henry by the grace of God King of England and of France, and Lord of Ireland, to the high and puissant Prince, the Dauphin of Vienne, our Cousin, eldest son of the most puissant Prince, our Cousin and Adversary of France. From the reverence of God, and to avoid the effusion of human blood, We have many times, and in many ways, sought peace, and notwithstanding that We have not been able to attain it, our desire to possess it increases more and more. And well considering that the effect of our wars are the deaths of men, destruction of countries, lamentations of women and children, and so many general evils that every good christian must lament it and have pity, and We especially, whom this matter more concerns, We are induced to seek diligently for all possible means to avoid the above-mentioned evils, and to acquire the approbation of God, and the praise of the world . . .
>
> We offer to place our quarrel, at the will of God, between Our Person and Yours. And if it should appear to you that you cannot accept this offer on account of the interest which you think your said Cousin your Father has in it, We declare to you that if you are willing to accept it and to do what we propose, it pleases us to permit that our said Cousin, from the reverence of God and that he is a sacred person, shall enjoy that which he at present has for the term of his life, whatever it may please God shall happen between Us and You, as it shall be agreed his council, ours and yours. Thus, if God shall give us the victory, the crown of France with its appurtenances as our right, shall be immediately rendered to us without difficulty, after his decease, and that to this all the lords and estates of the kingdom of France shall be bound in manner as shall be agreed between us. For it is better for us, Cousin, to decide this war for ever between our two persons, than to suffer the unbelievers by means of our quarrels to destroy Christianity, our mother the Holy Church to remain in division, and the people of God to destroy one another.

The offer was declined. What was meant to be a triumphal march through Normandy soon became (like Edward III's long march in 1346) an increasingly desperate search for an escape route to the Channel coast. It culminated in the muddy field of Agincourt in conditions described by the contemporary French chronicler Jean de Waurin. In his eyewitness account, the combatants are significantly less chivalrous than those depicted by Froissart. The battlefield was too constricted and the terrain too muddy for the French cavalry to charge. They were slaughtered not by their aristocratic opposite numbers but by plebeian English foot-soldiers, who cut them down in swathes with arrows from their longbows and slaughtered the survivors with swords and axes:

> It should also be stated that, while all this was going on, the English had captured a certain number of valuable French prisoners.
>
> Then came the news to the English king that the French were attacking his people at the rear, and that they had already captured some of his baggage and other stores. This was done under the leadership of one Robinet de Bornoville, who had with him Rifflart de Plamasse, Ysembert d'Azincourt and certain other men-at-arms, as well as about six hundred peasants, who stole the said baggage and several horses from English hands while their guards were busy in the battle. The king, Henry, was much troubled by the loss, but it did not prevent him from pursuing his victory, nor his people from taking many good prisoners who would bring them riches, taking from them nothing but their head armour.
>
> At this moment, when they were the least expecting it, the English experienced a moment of very great danger, for a large detachment from the French rear-guard, among them men from Brittany, Gascony and Poitou, having grouped themselves around some standards and ensigns, returned and, in good order, advanced with determination upon those holding the field. When the king of England saw them coming, he immediately ordered that every man who had a prisoner should kill him, something which they did not willingly do, for they intended to ransom them for great sums. But when the king heard this, he ordered a man and two hundred archers to go into the host to ensure that the prisoners, whoever they were, should be killed. This esquire, without refusing or delaying a moment, went to accomplish his sovereign master's will, which was a most terrible thing, for all those French noblemen were decapitated and inhumanly mutilated there in cold blood, and all this was done on account of his worthless company of riff-raff who compared ill with the nobility who had been taken prisoner, men who, when they saw the English preparing to receive them, just as suddenly turned in flight, so as to save their lives; several of them, in fact, managed to get away on horseback, but there were many killed among those on foot.
>
> When the king of England saw that he was master of the field and had overcome his enemies, he graciously thanked the Giver of Victories; and he had good reason to, for of his men there died but about sixteen hundred of all ranks, among whom was the duke of York, his great uncle, which was a great blow to him. Then the king called together those closest to him, and asked them the name of the castle which was close by; and they told him, 'Agincourt'. To which he replied: 'It is proper that this our victory should always bear the name of Agincourt, for every battle should be named after the fortress nearest to which it has been fought.' When the king of England and his army had stood there, defending their claim to victory, for more

than four hours, and neither Frenchmen nor others appeared to challenge them, seeing that it was raining and that evening was drawing in, the king went to his lodgings at Maisoncelles. The English archers went out to turn over the bodies of the dead, beneath whom they found some good prisoners still alive of whom the duke of Orléans was one. And they took away many loads of equipment from the dead to their lodgings.

The battle of Agincourt proved a particularly rich source of literary inspiration both immediately afterwards and over the centuries to come. For the English, it was, of course, a victory divinely inspired and, as such, fit subject for a religious celebration.

The Agincourt Carol

Deo gracias, Anglia,
Redde pro victoria.

Our King went forth to Normandy
With grace and might of chivalry;
Ther God for him wrought mervelusly;
Wherfore England may call and cry
    '*Deo gracias*'.

He sette a sege, the sooth for to say,
To Harflu town with royal aray;
That town he wan and made afray
That France shal rewe til domesday:
    '*Deo gracias*'.

Then went our King with alle his host
Through France, for all the Frenche bost;
He spared no drede of lest ne most
Till he come to Agincourt cost [hill]:
    '*Deo gracias*'.

Then, forsooth, the knight comely
In Agincourt feeld he faught manly.
Thorough grace of God most mighty
He hath both the feeld and the victory:
    '*Deo gracias*'.

There dukes and erles, lord and baròne
Were take and slain, and that wel sone;
And sume were ledde into Lundòne
With joy and merth and gret renone:
    '*Deo gracias*'.

Now gracious God He save our King,
His peple, and alle his wel-willing;
Yef him good life and good ending,
That we with merth mowe savely
  [may confidently] sing
    '*Deo gracias*'.

For the French, it was the occasion for lamentation. The contemporary poet Robert Blondel spoke for France when he grieved:

> O day full of tears, day cursed by France which has lost all the flower of her knighthood. You have robbed us of all our games, all delight, all our sweet songs and our learning. You have chosen to inflict on us tears and lamentation. Across the whole of France, there isn't a road nor pathway, town or hamlet, however small, which doesn't feel the pain . . .

It was largely out of that common experience of suffering and the need to assuage it, that the French forged their national identity.

★

While the aristocrats on either side were, for the most part, chivalrous towards each other, the civilian populace were rather less fortunate. From the start, the English invaders waged total war against them. The countryside was systematically ravaged through the process known as the *chevauchée*: mills, barns, haystacks, wine-vats were destroyed, cottages were set ablaze, livestock and villagers slaughtered, men were tortured, women raped, pregnant women disembowelled. In 1355, the Black Prince, so chivalrous in his treatment of his royal captives, could report on his *chevauchée* from Bordeaux into the Languedoc: 'We took our road through the land of Toulouse, where many goodly towns and strongholds were burnt and destroyed, for the land was rich and plenteous.'

And four years later, the French chronicler Jean de Venette described the effect of another such *chevauchée*:

> The loss by fire of the village where I was born, Venette near Compiègne, is to be lamented, together with that of many others near by. The vines in this region . . . were not pruned or kept from rotting by the labours of men's hands. The fields were not sown or ploughed. There were no cattle or fowls in the fields . . . no lambs or calves bleated after their mothers in this

rapacious gullet with green grass instead of rams. At this time rabbits and hares played freely about in the deserted fields with no fear of hunting dogs, for no one dared go coursing through the pleasant woods and fields . . . No wayfarers went along the roads, carrying their best cheese and dairy produce to market . . . Houses and churches no longer presented a smiling appearance with newly repaired roofs but rather the lamentable spectacle of scattered smoking ruins to which they had been reduced by devouring flames. The eye of man was no longer rejoiced by the accustomed sight of green pastures and fields charmingly coloured by the growing grain, but rather saddened by the looks of the nettles and thistles springing up on every side. The pleasant sound of bells was heard indeed, not as a summons to divine worship, but as a warning of hostile intentions, in order that men might seek out hiding places while the enemy were yet on the way. What more can I say? Every misery increased on every hand, especially among the rural population, the peasants, for their lords bore hard upon them, extorting from them all their substance and poor means of livelihood. Though there were few flocks or herds, those who owned any were forced to pay their lords for each animal, 10 solidi for an ox, 4 or 5 for a sheep. Yet their lords did not, in return, repel their enemies, or attempt to attack them, except occasionally.

The aim of the *chevauchée* was to destabilize the enemy's country by depriving the Royal exchequer of much-needed taxes and by demonstrating that the King was incapable of defending his subjects. This policy was reinforced by the practice known as the *pâtis*, a cynical and highly efficient protection racket. Every village or hamlet had to pay dues, in money, livestock, food and wine, to troops of the local stronghold. Failure to pay was punished by arbitrary executions and ritual burnings at the stake. Road-blocks and toll-gates were set up and travellers compelled to pay for safe conduct. Profits were pooled: soldiers paid one third of their booty to the garrison commander, who remitted one third to the king together with one third of his own profits. In time, the *pâtis* were extended throughout English-occupied France and England became deluged with plunder. Froissart reported that 'England was glutted with French spoils: not a woman but wore some piece of jewellery or had in her press some splendid linen or goblets sent over as booty from Caen or Calais'. Another chronicler, Thomas Walsingham, could report fifty years later: 'There were few women who did not possess something from Caen, Calais or another town over the seas, such as clothing, furs and cushions. Table cloths and linen were seen in everybody's houses. Married women were decked in the trimmings of French matrons and if the latter bemoaned their loss the former exulted at their gain.'

Many great English houses were paid for by booty won in France: Cooling Castle in Kent, built by Lord Cobham in 1374; Bodiam Castle in Sussex, built by Sir Edward Dallingridge, Captain of Brest, in 1388; Caister Castle in Norfolk, built by one of the most successful of all the English *entrepreneurs*, Sir John Fastolf. However, not all the outstanding English buildings dating from this period were founded on plunder. In 1438, All Souls College, Oxford, was founded by Henry VI and Archbishop Chichele, to pray for the souls of all the faithful, especially those who fell in the wars against France. For the French themselves, the lasting legacy was bitterness, not only against the predatory invaders but against their own lords who seemed unable or unwilling to protect them. Honoré Bonnet observed in his treatise on medieval warfare, *The Tree of Battles*:

> God well knows that the soldiers of today take from their prisoners great and excessive payments and ransoms without pity or mercy, and this especially from the poor labourers who cultivate lands and vineyards, and, under God, give sustenance to all by their toil. And my heart is full of grief to see and hear of the great martyrdom that they inflict without pity or mercy on the poor labourers and others, who are incapable of ill in word or thought; who toil for men of all estates; from whom Pope, Kings, and all the lords in the world, receive, under God, what they eat and drink and what they wear.

Each of England's great warrior kings spent less time on the battlefield than they did besieging cities. It was an activity that proved costly in time and in human lives, the besiegers as vulnerable to disease as the besieged were to starvation. Edward III laid siege to Calais for the whole of 1347. The siege was finally lifted when six of the town's most prominent burghers emerged, by prior arrangement, with their heads and their feet bare, halters round their necks and the keys of the town and castle in their hands. Edward was all for beheading them without further ado but, according to Froissart, was dissuaded from doing so only after an impassioned plea for mercy by his heavily pregnant wife. All the town's inhabitants, men, women and children, were ordered to leave immediately, leaving behind their houses with all the contents, and Edward proceeded to 'repopulate Calais with pure-blooded English people . . .'

At the siege of Limoges in 1370, Edward's son, the Black Prince, was more ruthless. The sack of the defeated city is described by Froissart:

> On the next day, as the Prince had ordered it, a large section of the wall was blown up, filling in the ditch at the place where it fell in. The English saw this happen with pleasure, for they were all prepared, armed and drawn up in their ranks, ready to enter the town when the moment should come. The foot-soldiers were able to enter this way with ease: on entering, they ran to the gate, cut the supporting bars, and knocked it down, together with the barriers. And all this was done so suddenly that the townspeople were not expecting it. Then the Prince, the duke of Lancaster, the earl of Cambridge, the earl of Pembroke, Sir Guiscard d'Angle and all the others, together with their men, rushed in, the pillagers on foot, all prepared to do harm and ransack the town, and to kill men, women, and children; for this is what they had been ordered to do. This was a most terrible thing: men, women and children threw themselves on their knees before the Prince crying 'Mercy, gentle sires, have mercy.' But he was so enraged by hatred that he heard none of them; thus none, neither man or woman, was heeded, and all were put to the sword, as and wherever they were found or come upon, men and women who were in no way guilty. I do not understand how they could have no pity upon the poor people who were not cut out to commit treason; but these were the ones who paid the penalty, and paid it more dearly than did the leaders who had committed this crime. At Limoges, at that time, there was no heart so hard, who had faith in God, who did not weep bitterly at the terrible mischief thus perpetrated, for more than three thousand persons, men, women and children, were killed and executed on that day. May God receive their souls, for they were certainly martyrs.

Henry V's exploits as a besieger of French cities were recorded no less vividly by the chroniclers who succeeded Froissart. Holinshed's description of the siege of Harfleur in 1415 provided the basis for two examples of Shakespeare's most fiery rhetoric: the 'Once more unto the breach' proclamation in Act III, Scene 1 and the bloodthirsty speech to the town's citizens in Act III, Scene 3 when they are threatened with the direst consequences if they refuse to surrender. Two years after Agincourt, Henry was back in France, laying siege to Rouen, and the whole campaign, from first to last, was graphically recorded in a rhyming chronicle by one of the serving English soldiers, John Page. He paints a vivid picture of the English and French notables preparing to negotiate for the surrender of the city, and the poorer citizens cast out by the French soldiers because there were no provisions to feed them and prevented by the English soldiers from passing through their lines to the open countryside beyond:

> Early on the morrow, our king ordered marquees to be pitched, one for the English and the other for the French – both were sited in Gloucester's lines – so that however bad the weather they could all negotiate dryheaded. When both tents were erected the negotiators got down to business. They were Warwick (that wise and worthy earl) who was the leader for our side, Salisbury (that earl so true) and also the Lord FitzHugh and Hungerford, steward to the king – I can't remember the other names. From the city there came to meet them twenty-four distinguished citizens.
>
> It was a solemn sight for both sides to see – the marquees in all their panoply, the citizens crowded on the city walls, our soldiers outside parading round in great numbers, and the brilliant heralds who went from one tent to the other. The king's heralds and pursuivants displayed their appropriate blazonries – the English, a leopard; the French, a lily; the Portuguese, castles and towers; the others, the various insignia of their several lords. Their costumes glittered with gold as bright as the sun which shone on them.
>
> But this was a bitter sight for the poor folk in the fosse who were nearly dead of sorrow and pain. They had scarcely a few rags to cover their nakedness, and a few tatters on their backs to protect them against the weather; it had rained during the whole period of their agony. There one could see a piteous spectacle – one could see wandering here and there children of two or three years of age begging for bread, for their parents were dead. These wretched people had only the sodden soil under them, some unable to open their eyes and no longer breathing, others cowering on their knees as thin as twigs. A woman was there clutching her dead child to her breast to warm it, and a child was sucking the breast of its dead mother. There one could easily count ten or twelve dead to one alive, who had died so quietly without call or cry as though they had died in their sleep.
>
> Here were two contrasting sights – the one of joy the other of sorrow; as though Hell and Heaven had been shared between them – these were the happy ones, those the wretched. No king, however ruthless, could look on such a scene without emotion. He only had to glance about him to turn sorrowful and pensive. There men might learn what it is to fight against the right. For while our enemies were in their strength they were truly cruel, God knows, and showed no pity until they were forced to ask for it on their own behalf.

When, after a truce of eight days brought no French army to rescue the Rouennais, the city was forced to surrender:

> The eighth day, to tell you the truth, was the feast of St Wulfstan – it was a

Thursday. On that day our king, seated like a conqueror, took his place in his ceremonial royal robes inside the Charterhouse to receive the keys of the city. Sir Guy le Bouteiller and a company of the burgesses brought the keys to the king, and begged him to receive their allegiance. Our sovereign king ordered Exeter to accept the keys, and to become the captain of the city. He charged him to take possession of that rich city and enter it in his name that same night, taking with him many knights as escort . . . And as they went through they shouted loudly, 'St George, St George! Hail to our king's own right.'

The French people of the city were gathered in their thousands to see them pass by, and they all shouted, 'Welcome; enter safely now, and please God we shall have peace and unity.' It was a pitiful sight to see the people. Many of them were mere skin and bones with hollow eyes and pinched noses. They could scarcely breathe or talk. Their skin was dull as lead, like the dead rather than the living; they looked like those effigies of dead kings that one sees on tombs. There one could realise how lack of food destroys people. In every street were corpses, and hundreds of citizens crying out for bread. For many days afterwards, they died – quicker than the carts could carry them to burial. May God guide them to his Holy House that they may live in bliss; Amen.

While the mainland of France bore the brunt of the devastation in the Hundred Years War, England did not escape entirely unscathed. In the years following the deaths of the Black Prince in 1376 and Edward III in 1377, towns along England's south coast had been devastated by raids from Franco-Castilian galleys. Raiding was resumed at the beginning of the fifteenth century and a graphic eyewitness account of this activity is provided in Thomas Walsingham's *Annals of Henry IV*. The first raid he describes took place in 1403:

The Armorican Bretons, with their allies the French, came to the town of Plymouth at this time with a big fleet, and bursting in by night, attacked the unwary townsmen and oppressed them, and burnt the town and plundered the whole night, until 3 o'clock the following day with no one coming to help. This disaster was the result of the wickedness and pride of the townsmen, who, trusting in their own strength, refused the aid of neighbours. For when the hostile fleet was seen to approach, the patriots ran to the town, wishing to defend it. But the men of Plymouth, as if unworthy of so much kindness offered to them, soon doubled the price of victuals in the town. When the patriots asked why they did it, they replied that they had no need of such help, and had sufficient resources of their own. When they had been given such an impudent answer, those who had come to help went away again . . . And so it happened that the enemy

despoiled the town with impunity, and quietly took to the ships whatever
they wished to carry away.

An aged Breton lord warned the raiders that the English would hit back.

> And so it happened as the Armorican lord had prophesied, that Brittany
> would mourn what England had lost; for William de Wilford, with sailors
> from Dartmouth, Bristol and Plymouth sailed to Brittany, and took six ships
> off the fortress of Brest; and on the morrow of his arrival, his men took four
> ships laden with iron, oil and tallow. When this was done, they crossed to
> Belle Isle, where they took thirty vessels, filled with wine from Rochelle, to
> the number of 1,000 casks. Leaving them, about 4,000 of his men landed at
> Penare, and burnt farms and estates, penetrating inland six leagues. On their
> return to the sea, they destroyed 40 vessels, great and small, by fire (the
> village of St Matthew was also burnt to ashes) . . . The Captain of Brest, the
> Sieur de Castellis and many other Breton leaders . . . sent a serjeant at arms,
> to ask if William de Wilford was prepared to make satisfaction for the
> damage he had done to the region. To which our admiral replied that he
> wished to burn half of Brittany for his satisfaction, and that they should have
> no other recompense . . . So they came back home . . . bearing joyful news
> to that country, and leaving Brittany sad.

The following year, the Sieur de Castellis sought revenge.

> The Sieur de Castellis . . . thought in his rashness that there was no one
> equal to him, until he climbed up to land at Dartmouth, where he was
> beaten by the rustics, and killed by those whom he most despised . . . The
> common people . . . who lived round about saw a great fleet anchor for
> several days off the port of Dartmouth, and thought rightly it was an enemy;
> so at night they flocked into the town, to stop the ascent of the foe. The
> Sieur de Castellis, and those who were with him, imagined that the town
> lacked defenders, because they could see no one moving about to prepare
> resistance; so after six days they landed. (The countryfolk came out of
> hiding and after fierce fighing, in which the women joined valiantly, the
> Sieur de Castellis and many of his countrymen were slain.) Many were
> killed by the countryfolk because they were ignorant of their language,
> although they offered great sums for ransom. The countryfolk, misinter-
> preting them however, thought that they were threatening when they
> were really begging for their lives.

What is noteworthy about these raids is that they were not carried out at
the behest of some land-hungry royal commander. They took place at a
much more parochial level and the degree of animosity involved

provides a graphic indication of the growth of nationalistic antagonism. The full flowering of this nationalistic feeling in France meant that while the English won the most spectacular of the battles they finally lost the war.

Periodically, it looked as though the French cause was irretrievably lost. Edward III's effective campaigning in the 1350s led to the Treaty of Bretigny in 1360, which assigned vast territories to England together with an exorbitant ransom for King Jean II. After the turn of the century, France's cause continued to look hopeless as long as the country was riven by internecine conflict between factions as bitterly opposed to each other as the Armagnacs and the Burgundians. The consequences of the conflict are vividly recorded in the anonymous *Journal of a Parisian Bourgeois*. The following extract for the year 1419 is typical:

This damned war has caused so much misery that I believe France has suffered more in the past twelve years than she had done in the previous sixty. Alas! First, there is Normandy entirely ruined. Almost all of them, the men who used to have the land tilled, each dwelling in his own place with his wife and his household in peace and safety, merchants and merchant-women, clergy, monks, nuns, people of all walks of life, have been turned out of their homes, thrust forth as if they were animals, so that now those must beg who used to give, others must serve who used to be served, some in despair turn thief and murderer, decent girls and women through rape or otherwise are come to shame, by necessity made wanton. God Almighty knows how many monks, how many priests, how many ladies of the religious orders and other gentlewomen have been forced to abandon everything and surrender bodies and souls to despair! Alas! how many children have been born dead for lack of aid, how many men have died without confession, through torture or otherwise, how many dead lie unburied in forests and out of the way places! How many intended marriages have been abandoned, how many churches burned and chapels, hospitals, and infirmaries, where once Our Lord's holy service and works of mercy were done, of which now only the sites remain. How much wealth is hidden that will never do any good, and the churches' relics and jewels too and other things that will never be any use except perhaps by chance. In short, I do not think that anyone, not the most brilliant, could enumerate all the unhappy, appalling, monstrous, and damnable sins that have been committed since the disastrous and damnable appearance in France of Bernard, Count of Armagnac, Constable of France. Ever since France first heard the names of 'Burgundian' and 'Armagnac', every crime that can be thought or spoken of has been done in the kingdom of France, so that innocent blood cries for vengeance before God. It is my sincere opinion that this Count of Armagnac was a devil in the shape of a man, because I cannot see that anyone who wears his sash ever obeys the law or the Christian faith. On the contrary, they behave towards all those over whom they have power like men who have denied their creator, as is perfectly plain throughout the kingdom of France. I am sure that the King of England would never have dared to set foot in France in the way of war but for the dissensions which sprang from this unhappy name. Normandy would still have been French, the noble blood of France would not have been spilt nor the lords of the kingdom taken away into exile, nor the battle lost, nor would so many good men have been killed on that dreadful day of Agincourt where the King lost so many of his true and loyal friends, had it not been for the pride of this wretched name, Armagnac. Alas, never, I think, since the days of Clovis, the first Christian King, has France been as desolate and as divided as it is today. The Dauphin and his people do nothing day or night but lay waste all his father's land with fire and sword and the English on the other side do as much harm as Saracens. It is better, though, much better, to be captured by the English than by the Dauphin or his people who call themselves the Armagnacs.

What amounted to civil war between the French themselves, together with Henry V's outstanding ability as a military campaigner, led to the Treaty of Troyes of 1420 by which France's Charles VI made Henry his heir and gave him his own daughter Catherine in marriage. Henry's triumph was short-lived. Two years later, in the course of his six-month siege of Meaux, he contracted dysentery, the scourge of so many besiegers before him. He died in August 1422 aged just thirty-five. His son, the infant Henry VI, was promptly crowned in Paris as King of France and England and was acknowledged as such by the bourgeoisie and the University of Paris. England's course still seemed set fair when, in 1424, his uncle and Regent, the Duke of Bedford, won yet another outstanding victory for his country at Verneuil, but the tide was about to turn and would flow so inexorably against the English as to sweep them out of France.

Charles VI's son, the Dauphin, had refused to accept the terms of the Treaty of Troyes. Somewhat diffidently at first, then with increasing conviction, he became both the symbol and the rallying point for all those who wished to oust the by now detested English invaders. His cause was given dynamic impetus when the seventeen-year-old Joan of Arc emerged out of total obscurity and proceeded to transform the course and character of the war. Entirely emblematic of her character and style is the challenge she issued on 22 March 1429 to the commanders of the English army besieging Orléans. It was written by Joan herself and, as was customary, delivered by a herald.

> King of England, and you Duke of Bedford, calling yourself Regent of France, you William Pole, Count of Suffolk, you John Talbot and you Thomas Lord Scales, calling yourself lieutenants of the said Duke of Bedford, do right in the King of Heaven's sight. Surrender to the Maid sent hither, by God the King of Heaven, the keys of all the good towns you have taken and laid waste in France. She comes in God's name to establish the Blood Royal, ready to make peace if you agree to abandon France and repay what you have taken. And you, archers, comrades in arms, gentles and others, who are before the town of Orléans, retire in God's name to your own country. If you do not, expect to hear tidings from the Maid who will shortly come upon you to your very great hurt. And to you, King of England, if you do not do thus, I am a chieftain of war and whenever I meet your followers in France, I will drive them out; if they will not obey, I will put them all to death . . . I am sent here in God's name, the King of Heaven, to drive you body for body out of all France . . . You will not withhold the Kingdom of France from God, the King of Kings, Blessed Mary's son. The King Charles, the true inheritor will possess it, for God wills it and has revealed it through the Maid and he will enter Paris with a good company.

The siege of Orléans was duly lifted. A string of French victories followed and, on 17 July, the Dauphin was crowned in Rheims Cathedral as Charles VII. While his sobriquet soon became *le Victorieux*, Joan's own life and career did not last much longer. On 23 May 1430, she was captured at Compiègne by the Burgundians and handed over to the English. A year later, she was tried by a French ecclesiastical court as a heretic, found guilty and burned by the English secular arm on 28 May. The French King chose not to intervene. The English were branded as Joan's butchers and from then on, after the young Henry VI assumed royal power in 1442, their fortunes in France declined rapidly.

By the early 1430s, it was proving more and more difficult to raise money in the English Parliament for military campaigning in France. In 1435, the Duke of Burgundy transferred his allegiance from the English to the French and the outstandingly able Duke of Bedford died. Henry VI turned out to be a gentle, saintly, scholar, totally incompetent as an administrator, and his marriage to the passionate and indomitable Margaret of Anjou – yet another French princess who became an English queen – did little to restore amity between the nations.

When, after a series of ineffectual truces in the 1440s, full-scale war was resumed between England and France in 1449, little went right for the English. That the coast of England itself was no longer secure emerges from Margaret Paston's letter to her husband John, written from Norwich on 12 March 1450:

> There ben many enmys ayens [off the coast of] Yermowth and Crowmere [Cromer], and have don moche harm, and taken many Englysch men and put hem in grett destresses and grettely rawnsommyd hem; and the seyd enmys ben so bolde that they kom up to the lond and pleyn him [disported themselves] on Caster [Caister] sondys and in other plasys as homely [familiarly] as they were Englysch men. Folkys ben rythgh sore aferd that they wol don moche harm this somer, but if [unless] ther be made Rytgh grett purvyans [measures] ayens them.

On the mainland of France itself, the English armies were well enough led but they were undersupplied. Their once fearsome longbows were no match for the by now well-developed French artillery and in 1453, the Anglo-Gascon army, together with its doughty veteran commander Talbot, was blown to pieces at Castillon. The English were driven out of France and of all the rich domains over which their kings had ruled intermittently down the centuries since the Conquest, only Calais remained. Their departure was celebrated in a ballade by Charles d'Orléans, one of the most graceful French poets of the century. A nephew of Charles VI, he was taken prisoner at Agincourt and transported to England where he remained in captivity for twenty-five years:

> How pleasant a sight to see the English so discomfited! Noble land of France, rejoice as you see how they are hated by God. Their courage and their power are now no more. They thought in their presumption that they could overcome you and enslave you and they sought to dispossess you of your heritage. But now it's clear that God is fighting on your side and supports you in all you do. He has totally shattered their overweening pride and Guyenne and Normandy have been restored to you.

Although the Hundred Years War is normally presumed to have ended in 1453, English kings continued to cast covetous eyes on France till the century ended. Between 1455 and 1485, the Lancastrians and the Yorkists were embroiled in a conflict as ruinous as that between the

Burgundians and Armagnacs in France. For all that, in 1474, England's Edward IV, born in Rouen and son of a Lieutenant of France, still felt strong enough to claim the French throne and, with a handsome grant from Parliament, he invaded France in alliance with his brother-in-law, the Duke of Burgundy. In 1475, Louis XI bought him off with the Treaty of Picquigny, which provided him with a lump sum of 75,000 gold crowns and an annual pension of 50,000 gold crowns for the rest of his life. Henry VII, who spent his formative years as an exile in France, fought his only continental war against the French. It ended in 1492 with the Peace of Etaples, which brought him an indemnity of 750,000 crowns. No great battles were fought, few lives were lost. The threat of overwhelming force was enough to secure plentiful booty, more than adequate consolation for the elusive French crown.

*

The most momentous and most durable consequence of the Hundred Years War was the ultimate destruction of all the dreams of Anglo–French family unity and the creation of two separate nations. To be sure, rivalry between the two entities had expressed itself soon after the Conquest, as when Philippe I became convinced that William Rufus coveted the French crown and the Abbot of Saint Denis commented: 'Because it is neither permitted nor natural that French should submit to English or English to French, events will set his evil hopes at naught.' There was renewed tension in 1116, when Louis VI (*le Batailleur*) ordered Henry I to hand back Normandy and challenged the English king to combat man-to-man. However, dynastic disputes in that age and on that scale were more like family quarrels than wars between nations in arms. With the Hundred Years War, the map of Europe and the minds of its inhabitants were radically transformed. As Professor T. F. Tout succinctly observed in 1922: 'the two countries entered the war as kinsfolk and neighbours and emerged with the tradition of national enmity'. Nearly a hundred years earlier, in a particularly eloquent passage of his Inaugural Lecture at the Sorbonne in 1834, the great French historian Michelet declared:

> In France, the English had lost Normandy, Aquitaine, everything, in fact, except Calais . . .
> Normandy, an image of herself, an English land in the way it looked and

because of what it produced, which filled her with yearning whenever she looked across the Channel and saw it; Aquitaine, her French Eden, with all the bounty of the South, olives, wine and sun.

Almost three centuries had passed since England had married Aquitaine and Eleanor – not merely married, had really *loved*, sometimes placing it above herself. The Black Prince felt at home in Bordeaux; in London, he was like a foreigner.

More than one English Prince had been born in France, more than one had died there and asked to be buried there. That good Regent of France, the Duke of Bedford, was buried at Rouen. The heart of Richard the Lionheart was left with the nuns of Fontevrault Abbey.

The English had lost far more than territory. They lost the best of their memories, two or three hundred years of endeavour and of wars, ancient glories, new glories. Poitiers and Agincourt, the Black Prince, Henry V . . . Up till then, it was as though these illustrious dead had lived on through their victories. Only now did they truly die . . .

The English have left few traces of their occupation of the Continent – other than ruins. In the course of their long occupation, these grave and politically mature people founded virtually nothing. For all that, they have done an immense service to our country it would be all too easy to under-estimate.

Until the English invasion, the French way of life had carried on in much the same way as it did everywhere else in the Middle Ages: there was nothing specifically French about it. It was feudal and Catholic before it was specifically French. England forced France brutally back into herself, forced it truly to concentrate. France searched, dug deep, descended into the very depths of the lives of her own people. And what did she find there? She found France. Thanks to her enemy, she discovered herself as a nation . . .

France owes the English a great debt. It was England who taught France to know herself . . .

In the course of this same period, England, too, acquired awareness of itself as a distinctive nation. Significant portents are manifest in Froissart when he records that Richard II, who married Princess Isabeau, daughter of France's Charles VI, was resented for being too sympathetic towards the French: 'For ye be always inclined to the pleasure of the Frenchmen and take with them peace, to the confusion and dishonour of the realm of England . . .'; and 'The people of England . . . said how Richard of Bordeaux would destroy them all if he be let alone. His heart is so French that he cannot hide it, but a day will come to pay for all.'

The growth of nationalistic feeling is clearly discernible from early in the Hundred Years War in the populist poetry of both sides. The most eloquent, not to say most rabid, of the English poets was Laurence

Minot, who composed most of his works between 1333 and 1352, but it effectively demonstrates how, even in medieval times, an out-and-out patriot could combine uncritical adulation for his king with total contempt for all foreigners. His French counterpart is Eustache Deschamps (1346–c.1407), technically a more accomplished poet with a much wider range, but single-minded in his Anglophobia. In poem after poem, he attacks the English for devastating France and looks forward to the day they will be forcibly expelled and England itself totally destroyed. A less gifted but more humorous populist French poet was Olivier Basselin, who owned a fuller's mill beneath the walls of Vire to the south-west of Caen in the Calvados. He was the leader of a group of Norman merry-makers whose drinking songs came to be known as *vaux-de-vire*, which became corrupted to *vaudeville*. In one of his characteristic lays, he exhorts his compatriots to join with him in expelling the English from France:

> Come now, you village folk who love the French king, be of good cheer, all of you, in our fight against the English. Each of you take a hoe and you'll find it easier to uproot them. If you find they're staying put, then at least pull faces at them. Don't be afraid. Go and fight those *Goddams*, beer-guts every one of them, because every single one of us is worth four of them – well, *three* of them anyway . . .

After his death in the second decade of the fifteenth century, reputedly hanged by the English for inciting resistance, an unknown friend wrote a simple dirge in his honour:

> Alas, Olivier Basselin! Shall we hear from you no more? The English have done for you now, you who could sing so gaily and lived such a joyous life. With your good companions, you used to wander all over Normandy, all the way down to Saint Lo in the Cotentin. There has never been such a pilgrim. The English have thinned the ranks of the companions of the Vaux de Vire. Never again will we hear the songs you taught to those who sang them so well. With all our hearts we'll pray to God and to the gentle Virgin Mary. May she bring the English to a sticky end! And may God the Father curse them all!

Though England was never subjected to the same brutal devastation as France, expressions of national feeling became increasingly frequent in English popular poetry too. Concern is expressed for 'oure England', 'oure Englysshemen' and 'oure Englyssche marchauntes'. After a military victory 'Englonde may calle and cry *Deo gracias*'; after defeat, 'Englonde may say and syng Allas! Allas!' However, the growth of nationalistic antagonism was a gradual process and for a considerable time it did not encompass the whole of the entities we know as 'England' and 'France'. At no stage of the Hundred Years War could it be said that English victories were purely English: under Edward III, almost as many Frenchmen were fighting for him as against him; the ranks of the Black Prince's army at Poitiers included a formidable Gascon contingent led by their brilliant commander the Captal de Buch; in the fifteenth century, the Burgundians made a massive contribution to the victories on which the English failed to capitalise.

The gradual growth of nationalism can be more clearly seen in the university world. In the Treaty of Calais (1360), it was expressly stated that all the subjects of England and France who wished to study in the lands of the 'enemy' should retain all the privileges and liberties they enjoyed in peacetime. But when, in the second decade of the fifteenth century, Henry V had conquered Normandy, the University of Caen was founded to prevent his Norman subjects from attending the University of Paris; and a Gascon university was established at Bordeaux expressly to weaken the University of Toulouse, which remained loyal to France.

The growing divergence between the two countries was also made manifest in the exchanges between English and French delegates attending the Council of Constance in 1414. The French claimed that 'France contains many more and more notable provinces, many more episcopal churches, many more notable universities'. They further asserted that their towns and cities were larger, and that the numbers of their dioceses, clergy and people were ten times greater than those of England.

The English retorted that they had more counties, more parish churches, more ancient and noble kingdoms and claimed 'Britain itself is so broad and spacious that distance from its north to south, even if one travels a straight road, is, we all know, about eight hundred miles or forty legal days' journey.' France, they argued, was not so vast. The French nation was in no wise superior to the English, 'whether a nation be understood as a race, relationship, and habit of unity, separate from others, or as a difference of language, which by divine and human law is the greatest and most authentic mark of a nation and the essence of it'.

In the last stages of the Hundred Years War, the English and French began to theorise as to the reason for their rivalry. In the middle of the fifteenth century, some of the principal arguments on either side were set down in *Le Débat des Hérauts d'Armes de France et d'Angleterre* (c. 1455). The English and the French heralds debate the relative merits of their countries before Dame Prudence. The Frenchman sings the praises of his country's wine and reproaches the English for squandering so much of their corn harvest on the production of an inferior drink such as beer. The Englishman lists the many battles his country has won; the Frenchman retorts that the English are notorious boasters and that they are better at starting wars than ending them.

A somewhat bizarre argument for his country's superiority was advanced by Sir John Fortescue, one of England's leading constitutional lawyers, in his treatise *On the Gouvernance of England*: 'there bith . . . mo Men hanged in Englond in a Yere for Robberye and Manslaughter than there be hangid in Fraunce for such manner of crime in seven Yers.' His point was not that the French were more law-abiding: it was that they were not manly enough to commit violent crime.

Over the course of the Hundred Years War, the English became characterised in the French national consciousness as brutal invaders, and such stereotypes as had existed before the conflict were radically transformed. Writing in the twelfth century, when Anglo–Norman culture was in full flower, Richard de Cluny observed: 'England is full of joy. It owes none of this to the French. On the contrary, it's to England that France is indebted for all it knows of gaiety and love.' In the tales of chivalry that entertained courtly readers in the thirteenth and fourteenth centuries, England was depicted as a land of mystery and romance; English lords were famed for their prowess at ball games and archery, while English ladies were renowned for their beauty and their gracious manners. In the eyes of early medieval French commentators, however, joy in England was not unconfined. Froissart was only one observer to discern a marked melancholy streak. He described the English as 'enjoying themselves in sad fashion as is the custom in their country'. This was believed by some to be the consequence of England's being an island and there being an inherent quality in the element of water that induced melancholy and dreaminess. For many other writers, a more significant factor was heavy drinking, which was both a symptom and a cause.

John of Salisbury, who was present in Canterbury Cathedral when Becket was murdered and became his first biographer and most erudite classical scholar of his time, declared, 'You know from experience that the English are noted among other nations for their devotion to drink.' Medieval proverbs agree: 'The Auvergner sings, the Breton writes, the Englishman drinks'; 'The Norman sings, the German guzzles, the Englishman boozes'. In a snatch of dialogue in one of Eustache Deschamps' poems an Englishman sneers, 'French dogue, all you do is drink wine', to which the Frenchman replies, 'True enough, but you drink ale brewed in Hell.' Coupled with the Englishman's reputation for heavy drinking was his notoriety for profanity. In medieval French popular literature, English characters regularly swear. In *Le Roman de Renart*, Reynard the Fox, pretending to be an Englishman, begins his speech with the expletive 'Godehelpe'. In *Le Mystère de Saint-Louis*, every speech uttered by an English character is prefaced with an apostrophe to the Almighty or to a Saint:

> By St Gorg! St Joan ! Bigot [By God]!
> Burlare [By our Lord]

So commonly used was the expression 'God dam!' that the term *Godon* became the standard popular term for 'an English soldier'. It was to prove a particularly long-lived term in France: more than three centuries after the end of the Hundred Years War, on the eve of the French Revolution, Beaumarchais' Figaro declares that the one word Goddam is all a traveller needs to know when he goes on a visit to England.

To untravelled French folk in the Middle Ages, the English were notable for one other attribute: they all had tails. The gibe *Anglois coué* was widely used from the twelfth century onwards. A Latin example of *caudatus Anglicus* may be dated as early as 1163. In one version, the inhabitants of Dorchester are given tails for having shown disrespect to St Augustine; in another, the tails are attributed to the inhabitants of Rochester, on the main highway to the Continent. This may not be without relevance since the legend seems to have taken root and spread widely at the time when England's Angevin kings were seeking to extend their dominions in France.

When Henry V overran Normandy in the second decade of the fifteenth century, Olivier Basselin rallied local resistance with the age-old gibe: 'Hey! you surely don't think I'm taken in and that I'm prepared to go and live in England? They all have long tails over there!' It is a time-honoured practice to denigrate the members of another tribe or district, even in times of peace. In times of armed conflict, the colours with which the enemy is painted become distinctly more sinister in significance. So it was to prove during the Hundred Years War.

Because the official English strategy of the age was to plunder and destroy, their soldiers soon won a reputation for brutality and ferocity. 'The more blood they shed,' declared Froissart, 'the crueller and more ruthless they become . . . They're fiery and furious, they quickly grow angry and take a long time to calm down.' He perceived a direct connection between their urge to kill and their appetite for booty: 'They greatly covet the wealth of others, they're all too ready to go to war against people greater and wealthier than themselves and they're prepared to take great risks for the sake of the rich pickings.' He conceded that the English gentlefolk with whom he had consorted at Court 'are upright and loyal by nature', but 'the ordinary people are cruel, perfidious and disloyal . . . They will not allow [the upper classes] to have anything – even an egg or a chicken without paying for it.' And, in his view, the English mercantile classes were no better: 'They are extremely covetous of the possessions of others and are incapable by nature of joining in friendship or alliance with a foreign nation. There are no more untrustworthy people under the sun than the middle classes in England.'

The French conviction that the English were not to be trusted took root very early in their relationship. *Coué*, the medieval adjective for 'tailed', was identical in pronunciation with *couvé*, meaning 'hatched'. Some Frenchmen, not understanding the allusion to tails, took the expression to mean that the English were prone to brooding or scheming. This chimed appropriately with various French proverbs: 'England? Fine soil but bad people'. 'The English smile sweetly when they promise – but they don't deliver'. A list of things you'd be unlikely ever to see in a long day's march included 'The pity of a Lombard, the hard work of a Picardian, the humility of a Norman, the patience of a German, the generosity of a Frenchman, the trustworthiness of an Englishman'.

Historical reasons for the French belief in English perfidiousness are not hard to find. Initially, it doubtless had much to do with the rebellious attitude of English kings to their feudal French overlords, paying due homage to them at one moment, going to war against them the next. Treachery was not confined to felonious activities overseas. Within the confines of their own land, the record of the English was far from spotless: the treachery of the English barons to their overlord King John; or the murders of Edward II and Richard II. The Anglophobic Eustache Deschamps was quick to seize on this and proclaim: 'Alas! that England should live with such acts of treachery. England, today you are the most hated of all nations because of your evil deeds.'

From the twelfth century onwards, the French were suspicious about English standards of fair play in sport: while the English were renowned for their prowess at wrestling, it was felt that they often won by *un tor de Englois*, a crafty throw that took the opponent by surprise. Different attitudes to chivalry were another factor in moulding French opinion. Regularly in the fifteenth century, the English were accused of lack of sportsmanship, backing out of tournaments for no good reason, quibbling about the weapons to be used, refusing to acknowledge defeat after they had been fairly beaten. It was also observed that the English would not hesitate, if the occasion warranted, to disregard the rules of war, one of the more notorious instances being in 1449 when, during a period of formal truce, the troops of an Aragonese captain in the pay of the English seized the Breton town of Fougères, plundered the houses and churches, raped the women and killed any men who resisted. The perpetrators went unpunished and the action inspired a famous ballad beginning:

> Englishmen, Englishmen, for shame, for shame,
> You promise one thing – and you do another.

The poet ends by reminding his readers of the ultimate fate of Carthage and Troy, a comparison that French Anglophobes would make with England for centuries to come.

The Hundred Years War laid down a particularly luxuriant seed-bed of nationalistic prejudices. The English came to regard the French as their natural prey and developed feelings of hatred and contempt for them. It was not long before they transformed their victorious military commanders into great national heroes. Writing in 1485, to summon

England's faltering knighthood back to the ways of chivalry, Caxton urged them to study the exploits, not only of Lancelot, Galahad, Tristram and Gawain, but also of 'Edward the First and Third and his noble sons . . . Read Froissart . . . And also behold that victorious and noble king, Harry the Fifth and the captains under him . . . whose names shine gloriously by their virtuous nobleness, and acts they did in the honour of the order of chivalry.' The great English leaders in the Hundred Years War were secure in the national pantheon with King Arthur and the knights of the Round Table.

The reaction of the French was rather different. They could not readily forget that it was across their countryside that the *chevauchées* had raged and that their villages and cities had been besieged and plundered. For years afterwards, indeed for centuries, French writers brooded over the consequences of defeat and the iniquities of the English invaders. In 1828, at the age of twenty-three, Alexis de Tocqueville wrote from Normandy to a friend about the Hundred Years War.

> It was then that began the most heroic, the most brilliant and the most unhappy time in our nation's story. Such, dear friend, was the first history book that fell into my hands and I cannot convey the impression it made on me: every event is engraved on my memory and that is the source of that often unreflecting instinct of hatred which rises up within me against the English. Time and time again when I come to those disastrous battles in which valour was always crushed by superior discipline, I have skipped the pages and jumped whole passages – to which, nevertheless, irresistible curiosity would later drive me back.

In 1943, to stir up hatred against the English for a recent raid on Rouen, a Vichy poster depicted British planes raining bombs down on a shattered city. The caption read: 'Criminals always return to the scene of their crime.' In the centre foreground was the anguished figure of Joan of Arc at the stake.

2 : *The Religious and Cultural Divide in the Sixteenth and Seventeenth Centuries*

Of all the Nations of Europe, the English and French should love one another best, as well for their vicinity as for the great commerce that is 'mongst them in time of peace, and for their consanguinitie, there being in this country thousands of families which are descended from the French, and as many more in France whose progenitours are English.

Guillaume Herbert, *Considerations on behalf of Forreiners which reside in England* (1642)

In the Middle Ages, wars between England and France had been essentially a series of disputes between members of an extended family about the ownership of land. After the accession of the Tudors, the stage was spectacularly enlarged and the issues grew progressively more complex. At the outset, Henry VIII's military and diplomatic style seemed to hark back to the age of chivalry. His father created him Earl Marshal at the age of three and had allowed him to joust publicly in 1508 when he was seventeen years old. When he acceded to the English throne a year later everyone rejoiced at Lord Mountjoy's pronouncement that 'Our king does not desire gold or gems or precious metals, but virtue, glory, immortality.' The surest way to attain such ends was war. War stimulated Henry VIII's intellect and fired his sense of honour. He aspired to be not merely 'the most valiant prince under heaven' but 'the most goodliest prince that ever reigned over the realm of England'. This meant vying with and, indeed, surpassing Henry V. It also meant, inevitably, war with France.

In 1513, a Latin biography of Henry V was translated into English to encourage Henry VIII 'to attain to like honour, fame and victory'. Englishmen and Frenchmen alike urged him to regain his French inheritance. His former tutor, the often outspoken poet John Skelton, hailed him

> As king most sovereign
> That ever England had;
> Demure, sober and sad,
> And Mars's lusty knight
> God save him in his right!

In the summer of that same year, 1513, he invaded France, convinced that his was a just war, and aware that to recover his inheritance would guarantee him pride of place on his country's roll of honour.

The campaign began auspiciously with Henry VIII himself leading the brilliant cavalry action of 16 August, which won the Battle of the Spurs. The French frontier town of Thérouanne and the fortress of Tournai promptly fell into English hands. These events inspired two outspokenly anti-English poems, *Le Courroux de la Mort contre les Anglais* and *La Folye des Anglais*. In the former, Death complains that she is being over-worked by the *millours* from England and she commands them and their tailed *godons* to depart from her sight. The author of *La Folye des Anglais* finds the English foolish for crossing the sea to France when they should have stayed behind to protect their own homeland against the marauding Scots (who, as events turned out, were crushed at Flodden Field on 9 September 1513). He gives voice once more to the French refrain that became all too familiar in the course of the Hundred Years War, the desolation left behind by the English armies:

> How many murders have you committed? How many of our maidens have been taken by force? How many of our people killed or ruined? How many poor widows left to carry such a heavy burden by your insane atrocities? Can you not realise that for all of this, you stand condemned for your infamy? Anybody who grows rich in such a fashion will, in the end, be made hungry by Time.

The same desolate note is sounded in another French poem

deploring the loss of Tournai, *The Loss of Tournai's Virginity, with her Tears and Lamentations Following her Deflowering*. Tournai herself speaks as a rape victim:

> I've been handed over to a bunch of pirates, to swinish *godons* drunk on beer. They've bound and gagged me. They'll end by cutting me into pieces. How I wish I were in my grave. I'm in despair at being in the clutches of men who know neither tenderness nor love nor honour, who are always so ready and so eager to pillage and rob, reduce people to poverty, indulge in acts of treachery . . . I'm at the mercy of Godless church-robbers, men more treacherous than Judas ever was. I must do their bidding but I do not believe their words or their promises. Their presence appals me. It stinks in my nostrils.

In the event, the English presence in Tournai was short-lived. Like his father before him, Henry VIII, for all his rhetoric on the subject of honour, was ready to trade off the elusive dream of recovering the throne of France for a handsome financial settlement. The French agreed to pay him a million gold crowns and to buy back Tournai for a further 600,000 crowns. For the English exchequer, this must have been welcome news but to any patriot concerned with national status, the true significance of these transactions should have been somewhat dispiriting. Between 1475 and 1550, the Valois Kings of France were quite content to pay for English quiescence with handsome subsidies. Their principal preoccupation was with the growing menace of the House of Habsburg, and in this larger context the military campaigning of Henry VIII was a side-show. It was preferable to have him as an ally than as an enemy, though, and to further that end, and to demonstrate that the age of chivalry was not yet dead, the French and English kings together staged their memorable meeting on the Field of the Cloth of Gold.

The meeting had first been mooted in October 1518, when France and England signed a treaty of 'perpetual friendship' and concluded a marriage alliance between the Dauphin Francis (then aged one year eight months) and Henry's daughter Mary (who was a year older). The meeting finally took place between 7 and 20 June 1520 in a vale between the village of Guines, in what was still the English 'pale' of Calais, and the village of Ardres, in neighbouring France. The fabric of the tents, pavilions and costumes of the participants was cloth of gold, hence the name by which it has ever since been known: *le camp du drap d'or*, the Field of the Cloth of Gold. The two leading performers were each at the height of their considerable powers. Henry, just twenty-nine, was still slim and handsome, a patron of the arts, a gifted musician, dancer, singer, able scholar, gifted linguist and vigorous athlete. Francis I, not quite twenty-six, was a Renaissance dilettante, schooled in the arts and manners of France and Italy, connoisseur of painting, student of architecture, handsome, courteous. It was a sumptuous occasion, a Summit Conference, Olympic Games, wine and food festival, even an architectural competition in which the English sought to outclass the array of glittering French pavilions with a vast temporary palace specially constructed for the occasion. The guest list was as glittering as the structures and the costumes: it included Henry's first queen, Catherine of Aragon; Francis I's queen, Claude of Brittany; the king's sister, Margaret d'Angoulême, who was later to write the *Heptameron*; Thomas More, already famous for *Utopia*; Cardinal Wolsey; William Budé, the leading Greek scholar of the age; and Clément Marot, who composed both a *rondeau* and a *ballade* for the occasion. In each, Marot pays fulsome tribute to the glory and the grandeur of the two kings, 'the fairest in all the world'. Over the glittering field, he sees proudly fluttering the banners of Love, Victory and Beauty; the Goddess of Love stands guard at the gate, denying access to Discord who carries the 'golden apple, which always means ruinous war'. Francis I claimed that he and Henry were two of the happiest princes in all the world. He wrote a letter to Henry in his own hand and called him his brother. The Queen Mother of France hailed Henry as her newly acquired son.

It did not take long for the gilt of the grand occasion to wear off. Between 1523 and 1525, Lord Berners, a former Chancellor of Henry VIII's exchequer who attended the king at the Field of the Cloth of Gold, translated Froissart's *Chronicles* from French into English. He was aware of 'the great pleasure that my noble countrymen of England take in reading the worthy and knightly deeds of their valiant ancestors' and, by and large, most of the deeds in question had been done against the French. In fact, disaffection between the English and the French became apparent rather earlier. No sooner had the guests departed than the French began to fortify Ardres against their English neighbours with the wood from the dismantled pavilions. Francis utilised the great tents, three of the pavilions and the regal chamber used at Ardres on his march through Champagne to fight his great rival, Charles V, ruler of the Netherlands and, since 1519, the Holy Roman Emperor. In 1521, Henry VIII's ambassadors shuttled between the two contestants, professing Henry's undying devotion to both. In 1522, he finally committed himself to Charles V. Skelton, outspoken as always, could not conceal his contempt for royal duplicity for 'so many trusys [truces] taken, and so lytel Perfyte trowthe' and waxed sarcastic over the shameless profligacy of the Field of the Cloth of Gold:

> There hath ben moche excesse
> With banketynge braynelesse,
> With ryotynge rechelesse,
> With jambaudynge thryfelesse,
> With spende and wast witlesse,
> Treatinge of trewse restlesse,
> Pratynge for peace peaslesse
> The countryng at Cales [Calais]
> Wrang us on the males [hurt our purses].

Wasting public money was not the only criticism contemporary English critics made of the Field of the Cloth of Gold. Fashionable English ladies who participated in the festivities felt inferior to their French counterparts who paraded wholly *décolletées*. When they sought to introduce the fashion in England, the chronicler Polydore Vergil tartly commented that they lost more in modesty than they gained in gracefulness. In his Chronicle of *The Union of the Noble and Illustre Families of Lancastre and York*, Edward Hall described how modish young noblemen returned to England 'all French in eating, drinking and apparel, yea and in French vices and brags, so that all the estates of England were by then laughed at; the ladies and gentlemen were dispraised, so that nothing by them was praised but if it were after the French turn'. Concern over the aping of French manners by some of the sprigs of the English nobility was so great that the Lord Chamberlain summoned Nicholas Carew and some other gentlemen of the Privy Council and banished them from the royal court. They had all recently returned from France where, it was alleged, one of their amusements had been to ride through the streets of Paris, along with the French king in disguise, 'throwing eggs, stones and other foolish trifles at the people'. It is from this age that frivolity and sexual licentiousness first begin to appear on the English bill of indictment against the French.

Confronted by what seemed to them Henry VIII's quite unwarranted diplomatic *volte-face*, the French renewed the traditional charge of English perfidy. In a poem entitled *A Defence against the Emulators, Enemies and Slanderers of France*, France herself declares:

> Everyone well knows that my son and my king, obeying the law, has always sought for peace, but the Emperor has broken his word. By their very nature, the English are treacherous and disloyal. They close their eyes to the truth. I am revolted to see how their treachery lies concealed in the hearts of such powerful kings who lay down the law and then pervert justice.

In another diatribe, *The Repentance of the English and the Spaniards*, the poet declares: 'Leave our land behind you, you lawless English. Drink your beer and eat your salt beef. You've crossed the water to wage your war in France. But, for all your power, you'll be sent packing, you'll certainly be sent packing.' While in the *Nunc dimittis of the English*, Henry is accused of being 'a false Pluto, who [at the Field of the Cloth of Gold] promised peace, love and total loyalty yet now reveal your great treachery since you've taken the side of my enemy . . .'

In the course of the sixteenth century, the English were fully prepared to trade insult with insult and to accuse the French of perfidy in their turn. In a letter from Paris on 8 June 1578, the English Ambassador, Sir Amias Poulet, observed, 'French doings are utterly uncertain and commonly fall out directly contrary to reason and good judgment.' On 23 June he commented:

> The cunning dissimulation and subtle treachery of the French have served them to good purpose in time past to advance their traitorous practices; and now I think they reap no less profit of the opinion which is generally conceived of their faithless dealing. They pretend to do this or that, and because they so give it out, no man believes them, and by this means they do what they will before it is believed that they intend it.

In transferring his allegiance, as he did, from Francis I to Charles V, Henry VIII was merely being true to the spirit of his age. It was indeed an age of contrasts. While it could, without any sense of impropriety, stage the Field of the Cloth of Gold, it was also the age of the mercenaries, soldiers who engaged in war as a profession and who were quite prepared to serve any master provided he paid promptly and in full. During the sixteenth century German princes consistently made handsome profits through supplying their *Landknechten* to any power prepared to pay for them. But the most feared and respected of all mercenaries were the Swiss. Their decision to desert Francis I on the eve of the battle of Pavia in 1525 was not unconnected with the fact that he lost the battle and was himself taken prisoner.

Soldiers of fortune had, at various times, posed a formidable social threat in the course of the Hundred Years War. Between 1338 and 1354, a force of international fighters nearly 10,000 strong terrorised France and ran the equivalent of a latter-day protection racket. Another group of *routiers* gathered in 1361 and operated under the command of the Englishman Sir John Hawkwood, who once declared, 'Do you not know that I live by war and that peace would be my undoing?'

At the beginning of the sixteenth century, the disturbing presence of large bodies of mercenaries was eloquently described by Sir Thomas More in his *Utopia* (1516):

> France, in particular, is troubled with another more grievous plague. Even in peacetime (if you can call it peacetime) the whole country is crowded and beset with the mercenaries hired because the French follow the train of thought you Englishmen take in judging it a good thing to keep idle retainers. These wiseacres think that the public safety depends on having always in readiness a strong and reliable garrison, chiefly of veterans, for they have not the least confidence in tyros. This attitude obliges them always to be seeking for a pretext to war just so they may not have soldiers without experience, and men's throats must be cut without cause lest, to use Sallust's witty saying, 'the hand or the mind through lack of practice become dulled'. Yet how dangerous it is to rear such wild beasts France has learned to its cost, and the examples of Rome, Carthage, Syria, and many other nations show. Not only the supreme authority of the latter countries but their land and even their cities have been more than once destroyed by their own standing armies . . .
>
> However the case may be, it seems to me by no means profitable to the common weal to keep for the emergency of a war a vast multitude of such people as trouble and disturb the peace. You never have war unless you choose it, and you ought to take far more account of peace than of war.

The problem remained unresolved towards the end of the century when the Kent magistrate William Lambarde bemoaned the fact that his country was the corner of the kingdom through which invariably passed all the soldiers going to and from the battlefields of Europe:

Since the time that our nation hath conversed with foreign people in the wars abroad, what Frenchman so garish and light in apparel, what Dutchman so daily drunken and given to the pot, what Irish more idle and thievishly disposed, what Scot more cowardly, sudden, and ready to stab, what Spaniard more insolent, fleshly, or blasphemous than be many of our own English, who have not only learned and transported hither all these vices of those other men, but are grown so perniciously cunning therein that they excel their teachers and teach it to others at home?

The age of mercenaries was also the age of Machiavelli (1469–1527) who claimed that terrorism and deceit were perfectly justifiable means to achieve the end of a peaceful and prosperous state. He also declared that 'war is just when it is necessary'. Like other rulers of his age and Lord Palmerston in the nineteenth century, Henry saw nothing perfidious in switching his support to whichever side best suited his nation, his dynasty and himself. Charles's allegiance was invaluable because he was King of the Netherlands as well as Holy Roman Emperor and because England's export trade had come increasingly to depend on the sale of cloth at Antwerp. Like Henry VII before him and Elizabeth afterwards, he needed to prevent the whole of Europe's western coastline from being controlled by powers hostile to England. The alliance with Charles V also offered Henry the prospect of being able to vie with Henry V: their secret treaty of 1523 would have given him the French crown, together with Paris and the north-west provinces of France, and restored the Lancastrian dual monarchy. These best-laid schemes, in the end, came to naught. In 1523, Henry's invading army came within reach of Paris but was forced to turn back because of the failure of Charles V's forces elsewhere. In 1544, Henry personally led another invasion, took Boulogne and was then abandoned by the Emperor, who chose to turn his back on France in order to crush forces opposed to him in Germany. The final balance sheet of Henry's military adventuring against France showed a considerable debit: he overestimated his opponents' weakness and he was overconfident in his own strength.

★

Discredited though Henry VIII's military balance sheet undoubtedly was, that of his sister Mary was significantly worse. After she became

Queen of England in 1553, she proceeded to marry Philip II of Spain. This ensured that England became part of the Habsburg combine against France and it was not long before she declared war on the traditional enemy as her brother had done before her. The pretext was that the King of France had pledged support to Thomas Stafford's claim to the throne of England. Stafford's grandfather, the Duke of Buckingham, had gone to the block for making the same claim in 1521 and for Mary, imperious as were all the Tudors, it was a challenge that could be countered only by war. The consequence was the loss of Calais, which had remained an English outpost in France since it had fallen to Edward III in 1346.

For the French the recapture of Calais was the occasion for unalloyed rejoicing. A large number of popular songs and poems were written. Du Bellay, who had earlier celebrated the retaking of Boulogne by looking forward to a total victory of the French on *English* soil, exalted that, after two hundred years, virtue was at long last triumphant. In his *Exécration sur l'Angleterre*, he consigned the English queen and her soldiers back to the depths of hell, from which they had all too clearly come. While Baïf, in his *Celebration of the Retaking of Calais and Guines*, waxed lyrical over the vengeance France had finally taken for the defeats at Crécy and Agincourt all those years before. The English response was more ambivalent. National pride was inevitably dented and considerable resentment was expressed that Philip II had not moved his army the mere twenty miles that separated him from the beleaguered English troops at Calais. Later historians, however, are agreed that its loss was one of the few benefits that Mary bestowed upon England. Calais had lost its importance as a trading centre, and the expense of maintaining it far outweighed its true worth. Posterity's verdict on Mary has consistently been harsh, exemplified in Dickens's pungent dismissal in his *Child's History of England*:

> 'When I am dead and my body is opened,' she said to those around her, 'ye shall find CALAIS written on my heart.' I should have thought, if anything were written on it, they would have found the words – JANE GREY, HOOPER, ROGERS, RIDLEY, LATIMER, CRANMER, AND THREE HUNDRED PEOPLE BURNT ALIVE WITHIN FOUR YEARS OF MY WICKED REIGN, INCLUDING SIXTY WOMEN AND FORTY LITTLE CHILDREN.

These were all Protestant victims of Mary's attempts to extirpate heresy, and reference to them at this juncture serves to make the point that in the rich brew that was sixteenth-century statecraft the religious issue was a particularly powerful ingredient. It helped significantly to sour relations between England and France.

As a consequence of the Reformation, the French could now add heresy to their ever-growing catalogue of iniquities perpetrated by the English. This did rather more than demonstrate once again that England was perfidious. It was believed, keenly by interested parties, to constitute proof positive that the Tudors had forfeited any right to the English throne. When Mary died in 1558, she was succeeded by Henry VIII's daughter Elizabeth. In the eyes of the Catholic Church, Elizabeth was illegitimate since, when she was born, to Anne Boleyn, in 1553, Henry's first wife, Catherine of Aragon, was still alive. The strongest claimant was the granddaughter of James IV of Scotland and Margaret Tudor, Mary Stuart who became Queen of Scots in December 1542, when she was just six days old. Her mother, another Mary, was a member of the Guise family, the most powerful and ambitious family in all France, which claimed direct descent from Charlemagne himself. Because of these regal connections, on both sides of the North Sea, the infant Mary became the most sought-after royal personage in Western Europe.

Henry VIII, Mary Stuart's great-uncle, was anxious to establish a friendly power on his northern flank, so, in the Treaty of Greenwich, drawn up in July 1543, he arranged for her betrothal to his son and heir, the sickly six-year-old Prince Edward. When the news reached Scotland, the public outcry was so intense that the treaty was never ratified. Henry's fury knew no bounds. In the spring of 1544, he sent an army across the Scottish border and ordered his soldiers to 'put all to fire and the sword. Burn Edinburgh town, so razed and defaced when you have sacked and gotten what you can of it, as there may remain for ever a perpetual memory of God lightened upon the Scots for their falsehood and disobedience.' His soldiers needed no second bidding. That summer, they devastated Edinburgh and set fire to the Abbey of Holyroodhouse where Mary's father, James V, had been buried a few months before. Next year, their medieval-style *chevauchée* took place at harvest-time when they set the crops ablaze in the Tweed valley and burnt the abbeys of Melrose, Jedburgh and Dryburgh. Brutal raids of this pattern went on till 1548. It was time to re-activate the Auld Alliance between France and Scotland.

This alliance was founded on military and political necessity rather than cultural or temperamental affinities. For centuries past, the Scots and the French had been sworn enemies of the English but there was never any unified strategic planning and each partner regularly made opportunistic use of the other. The French counter to Henry VIII's Scottish campaign was a case in point. When Henri II dispatched a fleet of over a hundred vessels to Leith in the summer of 1548, it was not out of humanitarian motives. It was because he proposed to betroth the infant Mary Stuart to his fragile four-year-old son and heir, Francis, and thereby scotch Henry VIII's dynastic plans. Accordingly, after the French troops had cleared the English from the market town of Haddington, a formal treaty was signed there on 6 July 1548, proclaiming that Mary, Queen of Scots would marry the Dauphin Francis 'to the perpetual honour, pleasure and profit of both realms'. To save Mary from harm, she was dispatched to the French royal court, leaving Mary of Guise behind to oversee her Scots inheritance. This was a move well worth taking. When, in April 1558, the terms of the painstakingly negotiated marriage contract were finally agreed in Paris, it was proclaimed that after the wedding ceremony, Scotland and France would be united and their citizens would enjoy dual nationality. There were, in addition, secret protocols in which Mary promised that if she were to die childless, her kingdom would pass to Henri II and that he would inherit her rights to the English throne.

1558 proved a momentous year. Elizabeth acceded to the English throne and Mary Stuart married the heir to the throne of France. After the wedding, the French king formally proclaimed Mary's right to the English crown and very shortly afterwards, her royal canopy, banners and silver plate all bore the arms of England quartered with those of Scotland and France. In that same year, to demonstrate that not every Scot was enthusiastic at the prospect of a Catholic take-over, John Knox published his *First Blast of the Trumpet against the Monstrous Regiment of Women*. For a brief time thereafter, Mary Stuart's prospects remained bright. In April 1559, when her father-in-law Henri II died after an accident while jousting, she became Queen of France; on 5 December 1560, her youthful husband Francis II died of an abscess on the brain after a mastoid infection and in July 1561, after agonized hesitation, she left her beloved France forever and returned to Scotland. Her beauty and her artistic gifts had made a marked impression at the French court and all the leading poets of the day, Du Bellay, Buchanan, Michel de l'Hôpital and Baïf, had each composed at least one poem in her praise. Her departure was mourned by Ronsard:

> Like a fair meadow bereft of its flower, like a painting deprived of its colours, like the sky robbed of its stars, the sea without water, a ship without sails, a field from which the corn has been harvested, a wood which has lost the leaves of its trees or a ring from which its precious jewel has been removed, so grieving France is now to lose its loveliest adornment as it sees departing the lady who was its fairest and brightest flower.

This being an age when any accomplished poet could pen a tribute to a royal personage as readily as he could emblazon the charms of his mistress, Ronsard did not take long to address an equally fulsome tribute to 'the most illustrious and most virtuous Princess, Elizabeth, Queen of England', in which he marvelled at the prospect of an island illuminated by two suns. But honeyed praise turned to bitter blame when it became clear that Elizabeth was not prepared to release Mary from her protracted captivity. Ronsard, for one, was indignant that the French had not taken up arms to rescue her:

> French people who refuse to take up your arms, you betray your ancestors Renaud, Lancelot and Roland, who were only too ready to do battle for their ladies, and would mount guard over them or ride to their rescue. You Frenchmen of the present day haven't had the courage to look at or to touch your armour to rescue so lovely a queen from servitude.

In similar terms, Edmund Burke was to mourn the death of chivalry two centuries later when none of his contemporaries took up arms to rescue Marie-Antoinette.

Protests and dire warnings issued from France during Mary's trial but she was nonetheless executed in February 1587. This provoked considerable indignation in France. Detailed accounts of the execution were widely circulated; there were various funeral orations; and, in response to an official English government tract justifying the trial verdict and the execution, a Stuart supporter produced a 492-page diatribe on *The Martyrdom of the Queen of Scots* in which Elizabeth was denounced as a child conceived and born in adultery and who had, in her turn, indulged in every form of vice. One more name could now be added to the list of illustrious people executed with all due ceremony by the English state: to go back no further than Joan of Arc, it included Sir Thomas More, Cardinal Wolsey, Anne Boleyn, on the deaths of each of whom French Humanists produced a rich array of poems and pamphlets. And a whole host of anti-English tracts was produced in France in the name of the Catholic cause, many written by English and Irish refugees, as the Protestants took control again in England and sought revenge for the victims martyred by Mary. It had long been accepted that the English were quite merciless whenever they invaded France; it was now all too apparent that they were just as ready to slay their own.

In point of fact, as Reformation was succeeded by Counter-Reformation, England proved to be no more bloodthirsty over religious matters than her neighbours. In the second half of the sixteenth century, the Inquisition in Spain became notorious for its brutal excesses, and for thirty years France was riven by religious civil war.

In March 1562, followers of the Duc de Guise attacked a Protestant congregation, and there were violent brawls in Paris and fighting at Montpellier when Huguenots attempted to hold open-air prayer meetings. By July, English Protestants were so incensed by reports of Catholic atrocities in France that Elizabeth I felt obliged to send a force of 6,000 troops into Normandy. She expressed 'great compassion to see the young King, our brother, so abused by his subjects', feared that the war in France might cause 'an universal trouble to the rest of Christendom' and complained that the Guise family were dealing in hostile fashion with her subjects resident in France. She added: 'And thereupon we could not forget how they were the very parties that evicted Calais from this crown; a matter of continual grief to this realm, and of glory to them.'

Elizabeth's intervention had little impact on the French civil war, which blazed up at intervals for years. The most notorious of many sanguinary incidents was the Massacre of St Bartholomew's Day, 24 August 1572, when Huguenots were systematically slaughtered throughout France on the orders of twenty-two-year-old Charles IX at the instigation of his mother, Catharine de' Médicis. The religious wars in France fascinated English observers in just the same way as English state executions of major personages preoccupied the French. It has been estimated that between 1561 and 1600 some 250 English works were written on the subject and it proved a fertile source of inspiration to English playwrights, Marlowe's *Massacre at Paris* and Chapman's *Bussy d'Ambois* being the best known. The outcome of the wars in France was a fascinating subject in its own right but the abiding English interest in it also expressed all too understandable fears of a Catholic take-over in England. Queen Elizabeth was still unmarried and there was no shortage of suitors.

Two of these suitors were French. The first was the Duke of Anjou, who had wooed her unsuccessfully before acceding to the throne of France in 1574 as Henri III. The second was his brother François, Duke of Alençon, whom Elizabeth nicknamed her 'Frog'. Although he was half her age, he pressed his suit so enthusiastically in the summer of 1579 that her subjects took fright. John Stubbs, a barrister from Lincoln's Inn, wrote a pamphlet: *The Discovery of a Gaping Gulf, wherein England is like to be swallowed by another French marriage, if the Lord forbid not the banns by letting her Majesty see the sin and punishment thereof.* He argued that it would be exceedingly dangerous for the queen, at the age of forty-five, to become pregnant. Clearly the courtship was all part of an evil French plot to make Elizabeth conceive and die in childbirth. Every young man seeking to marry a much older woman must have ulterior motives. 'How can we think otherwise in a young prince, heir apparent of France?' Stubbs demanded. 'It is quite contrary to his young appetites, which will otherwise have their desires.' Furthermore, since he was a Frenchman, Alençon probably had the pox.

The growing tendency for the English to associate the French with sexual licence has already been noted in connection with the celebrations at the Field of the Cloth of Gold. This preconception seemed well founded with the stories that circulated of Catharine de' Médicis' *escadron volant* of militant young females, sexual predators who were quite uninhibited in their behaviour and, allegedly, danced naked before the French queen immediately after the massacre of St Bartholomew's Day. Accounts of their activities are to be found in Brantôme's *Vie des dames galantes*, and a chaster representation of them in the Princess and her spirited young ladies who attend the court of the King of Navarre in Shakespeare's *Love's Labour's Lost*.

The longevity of the English association of the French with the more imaginative or more dangerous forms of sexual activity is expressed in all manner of words and phrases coined from the seventeenth century onwards: *French goods* or *French gout* = syphilis; *a blow from a French faggot-stick* = to lose one's nose through syphilis; *French tricks* = either fellatio or cunnilingus; *French prints* = obscene pictures. In the exchange of national insults, the French sometimes gave as good as they got. What we call a *French letter* the French call *une capote anglaise*, though we would seem to have no riposte to the expression *les Anglais ont débarqué* (literally, 'the English have landed'), which means, 'it's the wrong day of the month'.

Be that as it may, Elizabeth manifestly did not harbour such xenophobic sentiments. Like Henry VIII, she was highly educated, a gifted linguist, and something of a Francophile. When John Stubbs insulted Alençon as he did, Elizabeth was furious. On 27 September she issued a proclamation against 'such fanatical divinations', which, she declared, were nothing but 'forged lies against a prince of royal blood, as Monsieur the French king's brother'. She gave orders for Stubbs and his bookseller, Page, to have their right hands cut off. A less severe punishment was imposed on Sir Philip Sidney, who warned the queen against marrying the brother of the man who had authorised the St Bartholomew's Day Massacre. He had served at the French court, knew Alençon personally, and described him as a war-loving adventurer 'having Alexander's image in his head but perchance ill painted'. He was banished from the queen's court for a year and put his exile to good effect by beginning *Arcadia* and composing graceful love-sonnets, such as the following, which demonstrate that not all late-sixteenth-century Englishmen shared Stubbs's crude prejudices about the French:

Sonnet XLI

Having this day my horse, my hand, my lance
Guided so well that I obtained the prize,
Both by the judgement of the English eyes
And of some sent from that sweet enemy France;
Horsemen my skill in horsemanship advance [commend];
Townfolks my strength; a daintier judge applies
His praise to sleight which from good use doth rise;
Some lucky wits impute it but to chance;
Others, because of both sides I do take
My blood from them who did excel in this,
Think Nature me a man of arms did make

> How far they shoot awry! The true cause is,
> Stella lookt on, and from her heav'nly face
> Sent forth the beams which made so fair my race.

(First published, posthumously, in 1591)

In the last two decades of the sixteenth century, Counter-Reformation popes urged the Habsburg powers to mount a crusade against heretical rulers such as Elizabeth of England and Henri of Navarre. Philip II of Spain responded by launching his Armada against England in 1588. The year after it was defeated, and again in 1591, Elizabeth dispatched expeditionary armies to France to support Henri IV in his fight against the Catholic League. The most prominent volunteer in one of the English contingents was the Earl of Essex, who saw the spectacle of the French King battling for the Protestant faith against overwhelming odds as something of a *beau idéal*. His Protestant supporters must have been more than a little discomfited when Henri became a Catholic convert in 1594, allegedly commenting 'Paris is well worth a Mass', but he proved to be a wise and tolerant ruler, effectively bringing the French civil wars to an end with the Edict of Nantes in 1598, granting toleration to all his Protestant subjects.

In the meantime, in England, the sense of being beleaguered and the spectacular defeat of the invincible Armada unleashed a flood-tide of national pride and nostalgia for past military glories. In his essay *The True Greatness of Kingdoms and Estates*, Francis Bacon attributed England's military superiority over the French to the sterling qualities of the rural middle classes: 'England, though far less in territory and population hath been nevertheless an overmatch: in regard, the middle people of England make good soldiers, which the peasants of France do not.'

In *Description of England*, William Harrison warmly praised the rural yeomanry, a class peculiar to England, of which his contemporaries should be justly proud: 'These were they that in times past made all France afraid.' And he looked back to the heyday of the English longbow:

In times past the chief force of England consisted in their longbows. But now we have in manner generally given over that kind of artillery and for longbows indeed do practise to shoot compass [to send an arrow in high trajectory] for our pastime, which kind of shooting can never yield any smart stroke nor best down our enemies as our countrymen were wont to do at every time of need. Certes the Frenchmen and rutters [German troopers], deriding our new archery in respect of their corselets, will not let in open skirmish, if any leisure serve, to turn up their tails and cry 'Shoot, English!' and all because our strong shooting is decayed and laid in bed. But if some of our Englishmen now lived that served King Edward the Third in his wars with France, the breech of such a varlet should have been nailed to his bum with one arrow and another featured in his bowels before he should have turned to see who shot the first.

Shakespeare looked back too, but at the same time gave vivid expression to a number of the stock responses of the contemporary English public to France and the French: in *The Merry Wives of Windsor*, Doctor Caius, the French physician, mangles the English language in the farcical French fashion that has convulsed the Great British public to this day; Princess Katherine, in *Henry V*, fumbles over syntax and vocabulary in the winsome way that has become the stock-in-trade of beguiling female foreigners; Joan of Arc, in *Henry VI, Pt 1*, is crudely represented as a wanton or worse. *Henry V* is a thesaurus of populist features: all the French male characters save one are frisky, over-confident, class-conscious and vainglorious (the exception is the French king whose daughter Katherine, after the early death of Henry V, went on to marry Owen Tudor and so became an ancestress of Henry VII); in contrast to the foppish Dauphin, the young English king is a bluff plain-dealer, both in his relationships with his troops and in his wooing; the English succeed incredibly against overwhelming odds and, though there is a generous provision of low comedy and subversive muttering from the common soldiers, Henry V's set-piece battle speeches are accorded all the soaring rhetoric of which the youthful Shakespeare was capable. His historical tetralogy, beginning, chronologically, with *Richard II*, constitutes a national epic in which Henry V, after setting aside his youthful follies and after purging the guilt of his father's usurpation of the throne, emerges as a national hero, herald of the Tudor monarchy.

That pulsating pride in his country's past achievements and the conviction that more are possible are at the heart of Michael Drayton's splendid poem on Agincourt, written nearly two hundred years after the original event. It begins

Fair stood the wind for France
When we our sails advance,

> Nor now to prove our chance
>   Longer will tarry;
> But putting to the main
> At Kaux, the mouth of Seine,
> With all his martial train,
>   Landed King Harry.

And, recounting the king's progress in the same sprightly vein, concludes

> Upon Saint Crispin's Day
> Fought was this noble fray,
> Which fame did not delay
>   To England did carry.
> O when shall Englishmen
> With such acts fill a pen,
> Or England breed again
>   Such a King Harry!

★

Throughout the Tudor period, the prestige of French culture remained as dominant as it had been for centuries past – arguably since even before William conquered at Hastings in 1066. French became the language of the English court from the enthronement of Edward the Confessor in 1042. Though Edward had been born in England, his mother was a Norman and it was in Normandy that he lived from childhood to early manhood. His heart remained forever Norman and so were his closest companions and the highest officers of his kingdom. For centuries afterwards, French, in either its Norman or Parisian form, was to be the official language of the royal court. It became emblematic both of political power and of cultural refinement.

In his universal history, the *Polychronicon*, originally written in Latin in the middle of the fourteenth century, the Benedictine Ranulf Higden noted two reasons why, in English schools, the teaching of the native language was being neglected for French:

One is bycause that children than gon to schole lerne to speke first Englysshe and then ben compelled constrewe ther lessons in French.
Also gentilmens children ben lerned and taught from theyr yougthe to speke frenssh. And uplandish men will counterfete and liken them self to

gentilmen and are besy to speke frensshe to be more sette by. Wherefor it is sayd by a common proverbe Jack would be a gentilmen if he coude speke frensshe.

In 1521, Alexander Barclay observed in the preface to his French Grammar that in olden times: 'the French language hath ben so muche set by in England that who hath ben ignorant in the same language hath not ben reputed to be of gentyll blode. In so moche that, as the cronycles of englande recorde, in all the gramer scholes throughout englande, small scolars expounded theyr construccyons bothe in Frenche and Englysshe.'

French long remained the language most regularly used by the English when communicating with foreigners, both in conversation and in correspondence: Edward I had the papal letters he received translated from Latin into French; Edward III insisted that for military and commercial reasons, all lords, barons, knights and burgesses should ensure that their children learned French; Calvin corresponded in French with Edward VI and Protector Somerset; Henri IV wrote copious letters in French to Queen Elizabeth and her chief ministers.

Because of its obvious advantages, both commercial and cultural, French was systematically taught in England before anywhere else, France itself included. A plethora of grammar manuals and phrasebooks was produced in England from the thirteenth century onwards. At Oxford and Cambridge, a marked preference for French was shown on those rare occasions when the Fellows and students spoke a language other than Latin.

That French should have flourished for so long in England's highest places is not surprising. From the eleventh to the late fourteenth century, many kings of England were either born and educated in France or married French princesses, or both. By the end of the fourteenth century, when France was no longer the chief language of the English court, the power and prestige of French persisted. Before he became king, Henry VII lived for many years in France; his mother, the Countess of Richmond, was an accomplished French scholar; a Frenchman, Bernard André, became Historiographer Royal and Poet Laureate; and in his court at Richmond Henry sought to establish a palace as gracious as any chateau on the Loire. Henry VIII was fluent in French; more than half his seventeen surviving love letters to Anne Boleyn were written in French. For her part, Anne Boleyn was French through education and in taste. She served in France as companion to Princess Mary Tudor who, in 1513, at the age of thirteen, had pronounced in French her betrothal vows to the Prince of Castile. Queen Catharine Parr, Lady Jane Grey and Elizabeth I were all outstanding linguists, as well able to compose poetry in French as to produce an elegant translation. One of Elizabeth's first tasks had been to translate the *Miroir de l'âme pécheresse* by Marguerite de Navarre.

Against this, it should be noted that the Francophilia of the English ruling classes did not go unnoticed or, indeed, unsatirised. In 1512, Thomas More composed one of the earliest – and one of the most pointed – satires 'On an Englishman who affected to speak French':

My friend and companion, Lalus, was born in Britain and brought up in our island. Nonetheless, although a mighty sea, their languages, and their customs separate Englishmen and the inhabitants of France, Lalus is still contemptuous of all things English. All things French he admires and wants. He struts about in a little French dress; he is very fond of little French capes. He is happy with his belt, his purse, his sword – if they are French; with his hat, his beret, his cap – if they are French. He delights in French shoes, French underclothes, and, to put it briefly, in an outfit that is French from head to toe. Why, he even has one servant, and he is a Frenchman. But France herself, I think, could not, if she tried, treat him in more French a fashion: he pays the servant nothing – like a Frenchman; he clothes him in worn-out rags – in the French manner; he feeds him little, and that little poor – as the French do; he works him hard – like the French; he often strikes him – like a Frenchman; at social gatherings, and on the street, and in the market-place, and in public, he quarrels with him and abuses him – always in the French fashion. What am I saying? 'In the French fashion?' I should say rather in half-French fashion. For, unless I am mistaken, he is just about as familiar with the French language in general as a parrot is with Latin. Still, he swells with pride, and is, naturally, pleased with himself if he rattles off three French words. If there is anything he cannot say in French, then he tries to say it – granted the words aren't French – at any rate with a French accent, with open palate, a shrill set of sound, effeminate, like women's chatter, but lisping prettily you may be sure, as though his mouth were full of beans, and pronouncing with emphasis the letters which the foolish French avoid as the cock avoids the fox or the sailor the cliffs. And so it is with this kind of French accent that he speaks Latin, English, Italian, Spanish, German, and every language except only French; for French is the one language he speaks with an English accent.

In his *Description of England* (1577) William Harrison, with character-istic truculence, deplored the traditional dominance of French and looked forward to a new era of cultural and linguistic liberation:

> After the Saxon tongue came the Norman, or French, language over into our country, and therein were our laws written for a long time. Our children also were by an especial decree taught first to speak the same, and thereunto enforced to learn their constructions in the French whensoever they were set to the grammar school. In like sort, few bishops, abbots, or other clergymen were admitted unto any ecclesiastical function here among us but such as came out of religious houses from beyond the seas, to the end they should not use the English tongue in their sermons to the people. In the court also it grew into such contempt that most men thought it no small dishonour to speak any English there. Which bravery took his hold at the last likewise in the country with every plowman, that even the very carters began to wax weary of their mother tongue and labored to speak French, which as then was counted no small token of gentility. And no marvel, for every French rascal when he came once hither was taken for a gentleman only because he was proud and could use his own language, and all this (I say) to exile the English and British speeches quite out of the country.
>
> But in vain, for in the time of King Edward the First, to wit, toward the latter end of his reign, the French itself ceased to be spoken generally, but most of all and by law in the midst of Edward the Third, and then began the English to recover and grow in more estimation than before, notwithstand-ing that among our artificers the most part of their implements, tools, and words of art retain still their French dominations even to these our days, as the language itself is used likewise in Sunday courts, books of record, and matters of law.

He waxed even more indignant on the subject of would-be modish Englishmen imitating French styles of dress and personal adornment:

> Some lusty courtiers also and gentlemen of courage do wear either rings of gold, stones, or pearl in their ears, whereby they imagine the workmanship of God not to be a little amended. But herein they rather disgrace than adorn their persons, as by their niceness in apparel, for which I say most nations, do, not unjustly, deride us, as also for that we do seem to imitate all nations about us, wherein we be like to the *polypus* [octopus] or chameleon; and thereunto bestow most cost upon our arses, and much more than upon all the rest of our bodies, as women do likewise upon their heads and shoulders.
>
> [It was never] merrier with England than when an Englishman was known abroad by his own cloth and contented himself at home with his

fiine kersey hosen and a mean slop, his coat, gown, and cloak of brown-blue or puke, with some pretty furniture of velvet or fur, and a doublet of sad tawny or black velvet or other comely silk, without such cuts and garish colors as are worn in these days and never brought in but by the consent of the French, who think themselves the gayest of men when they have most diversities of jags and change of colors about them.

Shakespeare, himself an accomplished Francophone (to judge by Act III, Scene 4 of *Henry V*, which consists of a dialogue in French between Princess Katherine and her attendant Alice), mocked excessive adulation of French fashions in several of his plays. In *Hamlet*, for example, as Laertes prepares to leave for Paris, Polonius advises him on how he should dress:

> Costly thy habit as thy purse can buy,
> But not express'd in fancy, rich, not gaudy,
> For the apparel oft proclaims the man,
> And they in France of the best rank and station
> Are most select and generous, chief in that.

While in *Henry VIII*, the Lord Chamberlain expresses bewilderment at the young courtiers' addiction to French fashions:

> Is't possible the spells of France should juggle
> Men into such strange mysteries?

In travelling to Paris, presumably to complete his education, Laertes was following what, in the course of the sixteenth century, became the fashionable trend. Because the French language enjoyed such prestige, both for diplomatic and for cultural reasons, and because Paris enjoyed a high reputation for education, for printing and for social glitter, periods of residence in France became *de rigueur* for young members of the English nobility and gentry. Henry VIII sent his natural son, the Duke of Richmond, to the French court under the care of the poet the Earl of Surrey, Commander of Boulogne, who was condemned and executed at the age of thirty charged with quartering the royal arms and advising his sister to become the king's mistress. Queen Elizabeth proved more circumspect about allowing her subjects to travel into Europe. Either for political reasons or because of her Protestant fears of popery, she did not as freely as her royal predecessors allow every student 'leave to resort beyond the seas for his better increase in learning and his knowledge of foreign languages'. When young English noblemen did travel to France, it was most regularly to the French court in the entourage of an ambassador or with a private tutor. Francis Bacon visited Paris in early youth in the train of Queen Elizabeth's ambassador, Sir Amias Poulet, not the last diplomat to complain of the linguistic incompetence of his fellow countrymen abroad. In 1613, Ben Jonson visited Paris as tutor to the son of Sir Walter Raleigh and became better known there as a reveller than as a poet and dramatist. Thomas Hobbes travelled to France as the tutor to several young noblemen in turn, including William Cavendish, second Earl of Devonshire; it was while a travelling tutor that Hobbes met Galileo, Gassendi and Descartes.

Another reason for crossing the Channel was to escape the consequences of religious persecution following England's break with the Roman Catholic Church in 1534. Within each country thereafter, there was a significant religious minority, Catholic in England, Protestant in France, and periodically, members of these minorities felt compelled to cross the Channel to escape persecution. The principal centre for English Catholics became Douai where a college for laymen was established in 1568, with a seminary added in 1572; each year, a hundred or so young English Catholics arrived there to study. At the end of the sixteenth century, the largest house for English Jesuits was founded at St Omer, and this too recruited some hundred pupils each year. The English Benedictines settled near Nancy, at Dienlouard, while English convents were established at St Omer, Dunkirk, Boulogne and Paris. All these English religious houses were shut down in 1793, during the Terror, when the majority of the inmates took refuge in Britain.

In the course of the seventeenth century, travelling abroad for educational and cultural improvement became more common, though it remained largely confined to the better-off. Its benefits were not perceived as self-evident to everybody, however. In 1622, for instance, Sir Arthur Capell wrote a pamphlet, 'Reasons against the travellinge of my grandchilde Arthur Capell into the parts beyond the sea', in which he drew an alarming picture of the dangers of popery and sought to demonstrate that a young English person's time would be more profitably spent studying at home. John Evelyn perceived darker dangers when he wrote in his Diary in 1642:

There is scarce a Prince in Europ, but what have been scholars in the French Academys and which by consequence has leaven'd them all, with the mode as well as language of France, and disposed them to an undervaluing of their own Countrys with infinite prejudice to the rest of Europ: the French, naturally active, insinuating and bold having with their trifles and new modes almost debaucht all the sobriety of former times, continualy aspiring to enlarge their Tyranny, by all the arts of dissimulation; and tretchery: Tho it cannot be deneyed: that there are many worthy persons of probity, and greate learning among them, who are weary of the intollerable yoake under which they groane.

Theirs were by no means the only voices to be heard in a debate that was to be enjoined at intervals in England over the next two centuries. They were, however, to be outnumbered and, most fair-minded critics would agree, outpointed by the significantly larger number of voices arguing the opposite, adopting the premiss that foreign travel is a good in itself. Most noteworthy amongst these are Robert Dallington's *View of France* (1604), Francis Bacon's essay *Of Travel* (1625) and James Howell's *Instructions for Forreine Travel* (1642). There were also, however, many others who, in informal letters and diaries as well as didactic manuals, provided advice on the best routes to follow, the places and people to see and the pitfalls best avoided.

The most celebrated of these seventeenth-century travellers was the philosopher John Locke, who spent three-and-a-half years in France, journeying twice round the country, from Paris to the Mediterranean and back. The account of his experiences is not the most colourful in the annals of travel literature but it provides an array of useful firsthand observations of life in France at the high-point of Louis XIV's reign.

★

After the influx of Normans following the Conquest – principally officials to serve the king, the Church and the barons whose support for William I was rewarded with great estates – visitors from France to England over the following centuries were decidedly fewer in number than visitors from England to France. The most noteworthy of those early French visitors were almost invariably connected with the English Court, whether they came involuntarily, like Charles d'Orléans, who, taken prisoner at Agincourt, was kept hostage in Dover Castle for twenty-six years, or seeking patronage like Froissart, who came to

England in 1361 and obtained the protection of Queen Philippa. Other important French writers, when young, found positions at the French royal court and came to Britain as part of diplomatic missions: Charles VII sent Alain Chartier to Scotland, Charles VIII sent Robert Gaguin to England, while at various times later, other missions included Ronsard, Du Bartas, Brantôme and Saint-Amant.

Throughout the Middle Ages and the Renaissance, most French travellers of rank preferred the Italian courts. England was felt to be a savage and barbarous country, and since all well-bred Englishmen could be presumed to speak French, there was little incentive for the French to learn English. The Frenchman's grasp of English spelling and grammar remained tenuous for centuries; William Harrison tartly observed in 1577: 'It falleth out that few forren nations can rightlie pronounce our language . . . especiallie the French.' French knowledge of English literature also remained skeletal: typically, when Eustache Deschamps addressed a complimentary *ballade* to Chaucer at the end of the fifteenth century he omitted to mention *The Canterbury Tales*, and in a study of world drama published as late as 1645, Shakespeare did not merit a mention.

In the course of the sixteenth century there came the first modest growth of French travel to England and a mere handful of guides appeared in France to cater for the equally modest demand for information. The most significant of these, *Description des royaulmes d'Angleterre et d'Ecosse* (1558), by the Anglophobic priest Estienne Perlin leaves something to be desired: his account of the English constitution is intermingled with cookery recipes and generously spiced with gory stories of the deaths of kings and courtiers. The spelling is characteristically whimsical: 'Suphor' for Suffolk, 'Notumbellant' for Northumberland, 'Grek' for Grey. He introduces a theme that was to feature regularly in French travellers' impressions of England: the aggressive xenophobia of the residents.

– The people of this nation have a moral hatred of the French as their ancient enemies and they always call us *France chenesve* [knave], *France dogue*, which means 'thieving Frenchmen, French dogs' and they also call us *or son*, dirty sone of whores.

– You can say of the English that they aren't as strong in war and they aren't trustworthy in peace. As the Spanish say, 'England: good country, bad people'.

– This powerful and seditious people, with a bad conscience, never true to their word as experience has shown. These rascals hate all sorts of foreigners, even though they themselves live in a good, rich country. As I have declared before, they are always wicked and they are fickle in their loyalty. Today they may love a Prince, come a change in the wind and they will want to kill and crucify him . . . I'm annoyed that when they are in their own country they spit in our faces but when they're in France, they are honoured and revered like little gods. In this the French demonstrate the goodness of their hearts and the nobility of their minds.

Half a century later, another French visitor reached the same conclusion. Maximilien de Béthune, Duc de Sully, who came to England in 1603 as an official negotiator for the French crown, noted in his *Memoires* (1638): 'It is certain that the English hate us, and with a hate so strong and so general, that one would be tempted to list it as one of the natural dispositions of this people.'

Nevertheless, in the second half of the sixteenth century, French people began to cross the Channel in growing numbers. Just as Protestant repression in England forced English Catholics to seek refuge in France, so Catholic repression in France drove French Protestants to England. In 1550, Edward VI assigned the Augustinian Church (built in 1253) to French Protestants in London. After the Massacre of St Bartholomew in 1572, there was a great influx of French Protestant refugees, men of rank as well as many skilled craftsmen. This established England's reputation as a safe haven for religious – and, subsequently, political – refugees from across the Channel, which was to enrich the quality of life for the *émigrés* and the host country over the centuries to come.

*

With the death of Elizabeth in 1603, after a reign of forty-five years, and the accession to the English throne of James VI of Scotland, son of Mary, Queen of Scots, French hopes rose that England might return to the Catholic fold. Such hopes were soon dashed with the uncovering of the Catholic-inspired Gunpowder Plot in 1605 and James's refusal, for the duration of his reign, to allow Catholics to hold services of their own and his insistence that all his subjects should attend a Church of England service every Sunday.

French Catholic hopes were rekindled with the marriage of England's Charles I to the fifteen-year-old Henrietta-Maria, sister of Louis XIII, so devout a Catholic that she refused to attend a Protestant wedding ceremony. Her stay in England was far from happy. The king was dominated by the capricious George Villiers, first Duke of Buckingham, who had no difficulty in stirring up anti-Catholic and anti-French feelings at court and in Parliament. He argued that the presence of thirty Catholic priests in the Queen's entourage was clear evidence of a Papist conspiracy and had them sent back to France. Cardinal Richelieu thereupon claimed that 'the whole French nation is quivering with sorrow and indignation'. It quivered no less indignantly when in June 1627 Buckingham arrived with a force of ninety ships and 10,000 men off the Huguenot port of La Rochelle, then under Catholic siege. When he was forced to beat an ignominious retreat, a number of poems were composed to celebrate the French victory and gloat over the humiliation of the English. Buckingham was described in one anonymous poem as 'a lascivious goat from arrogant Albion', and in another by Marc Lescarbot, he was accused of rekindling age-old English longings to regain lost French provinces. At one point Lescarbot has him say:

> Since time immemorial, France has been our magnificent heritage. In days of yore, we had a generous share of it. Our rights still survive. Treaties between princes and nations are of no account. It's the sword which makes the law. Ponthieu, Touraine, Normandy, Poitou, Guyenne, Anjou and Maine are all part of our ancient kingdom, the true possession of our kings by legal rights of inheritance. It is high time we regained possession. The mighty town of La Rochelle holds out its arms in welcome. Once we've captured it, the whole of Guyenne lies before us and there we can quaff our fill of all those wines of Gascony which give such a fine complexion to dedicated drinkers.

Buckingham was to be portrayed more sympathetically in Alexandre Dumas's rousing novel *The Three Musketeers* (1844–5), in which he is a chivalrous lover prepared to lay down his life for the Queen of France; the true villains are the scheming Cardinal Richelieu and Milady de Winter, who, like so many English aristocratic ladies in French fiction, manages to be both cold and passionate.

On 29 October 1628, La Rochelle finally surrendered. A peace treaty was signed the following October and Henrietta-Maria was very much happier at the English court. When the poet Saint-Amant visited England in 1631, he predicted years of happiness for the royal couple:

> O blessèd pair, shining adornment of the present age, in whom all the virtues are united, may the hand of Fate who rules over human affairs with a sceptre beneath which Hell itself trembles, keep *your* sceptre in *your* royal hand for another hundred years.

Fate was not quite so kind. August 1642 brought the outbreak of the English Civil War, and in 1644 Queen Henrietta, after giving birth to a daughter, Henrietta-Anne, in Exeter, undertook the hazardous crossing from Falmouth to Brest. On 28 January 1649, Charles I was tried in a depleted House of Commons before which he refused to plead, found guilty of high treason by a majority of twenty-six votes to twenty, and executed two days later on a specially constructed scaffold outside his Palace of Whitehall.

French public opinion was outraged. A typical Anglophobe deplored the execution thus: 'After so tragic an end, we just have to accept that Polar bears or the wildest beasts in Africa are more humane than English *milords*.' In another Anglophobic outburst, Dame Rumour declares: 'You treacherous people, today is not the first occasion when, because of your rabid cruelty, you have brought your kings low and done them to death. We all know that in various parts of your country, forty-one of your princes have been cruelly murdered by your own actions or by the blade of your executioners.' She goes on to explain: 'I'll tell you how it's come about that these ape-like buggers, these raving madmen, these treacherous dogs have hacked off the head of their supreme lord. It's because they don't want to be ruled by a king.'

In the mid seventeenth century, however, Anglophobia was not omnipresent in France. The two periods of civil war in England, between the King and his Parliament (1642–46 and 1648–51), were matched by the *Frondes*, two periods of civil war in France, aristocratic rebellions against the absolutism of the Crown (1648–49 and 1651–53). That Parliament won in England while the King emerged victorious in France did not impede the signing of an Anglo–French treaty in November 1655, the arrival at the French court of Colonel Lockhart as Cromwell's official ambassador, or the dispatch of English mercenaries to reinforce the French armies then at war with Spain. French Catholics were not best pleased and in 1656 Boileau, aged eighteen, composed an ode of protest.

> Can such things be? A nation blind to the consequences of its crime, taking its king as sacrificial victim and making of his throne a horrendous spectacle – can it really believe that the heavens which witnessed so dreadful a deed has not reserved for it thunderbolt or fire?
>
> Already its fleet, with sails full billowing, seeks to brave the winds and the stars, has set forth to conquer the whole universe and firmly believes that Europe, abashed, is about to surrender the empire of the seas to its fanatical audacity!
>
> To arms, France, to arms! Seize the thunderbolt! It is your duty to reduce to ashes these bloodthirsty breakers of all the laws. Set out in quest of the victory which awaits you and take vengeance on this rebellious race for its crimes against its kings.
>
> O, may the oceans of the old world and the new soon see the bodies of the dead left to the will of the waves. Even as I speak, Neptune is full of joy as he sees the whales of the North swimming in vast numbers towards the rich feast they will soon enjoy!

There was indeed a victory to celebrate not long after Boileau's poem appeared, but by no means the one he anticipated. On 14 June 1658, the port of Dunkirk, then part of the Spanish Netherlands, was captured by a joint Anglo–French force led by Louis XIV's brilliant Marshal Turenne. In conformity with a prior agreement made by his Prime Minister, Cardinal Mazarin, it was promptly handed over to the English. This gives some indication of how complex European foreign affairs had become and needs some explanation.

The sixteenth century witnessed not only the Reformation but also the start of global exploration and the founding of what were to grow into vast overseas empires. All European countries with a western seaboard became involved: Spain in South America, Portugal in East and West Africa, Holland in the East Indies, France and England in the eastern districts of North America. The pickings were rich, the rivalry intense and the wars that inevitably resulted sometimes took little account of religious affinities. The two leading Catholic powers, France and Spain, fought over the Netherlands; the two major Protestant powers, England and Holland, fought a series of mainly maritime wars between 1652 and 1674. The link between trade and power was readily perceived. At the time of the first Navigation Act in 1651, an English commentator observed: 'What nation soever can attaine to and continue the greatest trade and number of shipping will get and keepe the Sovereignty of the Seas, and consequently the greatest Dominion of the World.' On being asked what reason should be announced for declaring war on the Dutch, England's General Monck allegedly retorted: 'What matters this or that reason? What we want is more of the trade the Dutch now have.'

Smuggling was rife, as was piracy, the most notorious bases being in the West Indies and the North African coast. Dunkirk had become the principal base for freebooters in the North Sea, so England was able to help all the maritime powers when it took over the port. England helped itself further when in October 1662 it sold Dunkirk back to France for the sum of five million *louis d'or*.

This was an auspicious period of Anglo–French relations. In 1660, Charles II had been restored to the English throne, having spent his time of exile in France and become a particularly enthusiastic Francophile. At his father's court, French influence had been particularly prominent; Charles I's wife, Henrietta-Maria, was the daughter of Henri IV and Marie de' Médicis. As at the court of Edward the Confessor, the ability to speak fluent French was a prerequisite for royal preferment. Companies of French actors came to London to perform before English audiences. The first troupe, acting at Blackfriars in 1629, was 'hissed, hooted and pipinpelted' because their play, which included female performers, was adjudged 'lascivious and unchaste'. The Puritan pamphleteer William Prynne wrote a diatribe against such stage plays and, because this was construed as an attack on the Queen, was sentenced to life imprisonment after having had both his ears removed and been placed in the pillory.

With the outbreak of the Civil War, the English royal court, together with an impressive entourage of highly born writers, took itself off to Paris. Even Puritan families willingly sent their children to be educated in France. After the Restoration in 1660, Francomania reached new heights in England. The Queen's Almoner, Cardinal d'Aubigny, was French, as was Louis de Duras, commander of the Regiment of Guards, Nicolas Lefèvre, who supervised the royal laboratory, and Blondeau, who engraved the royal coinage. French chefs ran the royal kitchen, troupes of French actors regularly played at the royal court. Ever ready to emulate their royal masters, the English nobility and the gentry in their turn expressed, often extravagantly, admiration for all things French. The most fashionable young English bloods interlarded their talk with French words and phrases and were themselves translated into *beaux* and *English Monsieurs*. To vie with them, their female counterparts wore the latest Paris dress-designs and made a fetish of French trinkets and toiletries. Katherine Philips, the 'Matchless Orinda', instituted a French-style literary salon for discussing poetry and religion. No group could be considered truly *à la mode* without its French chef or French dancing-master.

Samuel Pepys noted the latest trend in fashion in two diary entries in 1664:

> 26 August.   This day my wife tells me Mr Pen, Sir William's son, is come back from France and came to visit her – a most modish person, grown, she says, a fine gentleman.

> 30 August.   After dinner comes Mr Pen to visit me, and stayd an hour talking with me. I perceive something of learning he hath got, but a great deal, if not too much, of the vanity of the French garbe and affected manner of speech and gait – I fear all real profit he hath made of his travel will signify little.

The following year, the lay brother and reputedly Catholic priest Richard Flecknoe observed in his *Characters*:

> The French have gained so much influence over the English Fops that they furnish them with their French puppy dogs for *Valets de Chambre* . . .
>   Your French tailor is the King of Fashions and Emperor of the Mode, not onely in France, but most of its Neighbouring Nations, and his Laws are received where the King of France's will not pass.

A spirited resistance movement against this threat of sartorial imperialism was mounted by most of England's contemporary dramatists: Wycherley in *The Gentleman Dancing-Master* (1673), Dryden in *Marriage A-la-Mode* (1673), Etherege in *The Man of Mode* (1676), and Shadwell in *The Virtuoso* (1676). Each portrays the fashion-conscious English characters as gullible fools while the French are depicted as either calculating confidence-tricksters or as hot-tempered popinjays ever ready to fight a duel. In the Prologue Dryden wrote to celebrate the opening on 26 March 1674 of the new Theatre Royal, designed by

Wren, Dryden complained that the French by now controlled not only English modes of dress but contemporary stage practice too:

> 'Twere Folly now a stately Pile to raise,
> To build a Play-House while You throw down Plays.
> Whilst Scenes, Machines, and empty *Opera*'s reign,
> And for the Pencil You the Pen disdain.
> While Troops of famisht Frenchmen hither drive,
> And laugh at those upon whose Alms they live:
> Old English Authors vanish, and give place
> To these new Conqu'rors of the Norman Race;
> More tamely than your Fathers you submit,
> You'r now grown Vassals to 'em in your wit:
> Mark, when they Play, how our fine Fops advance
> The mighty Merits of these Men of France,
> Keep Time, cry *Ben* and humour the Cadence:
> Well please your selves, but sure 'tis understood,
> That *French* Machines have ne'r done *England* good.

The Restoration satirists seem to have loosed off their barbs in vain. For all their eloquence and wit, and in spite of such pungent diatribes as Samuel Butler's onslaught 'Upon our Ridiculous Imitation of the French', the smart set in England were still modelling themselves on their counterparts across the Channel half a century after the Restoration. In 1698, Henry Misson de Valberg, on a visit from France, was struck by the number of dandies in London:

In English, these characters are called *fops* and *beaux*. The theatres, the chocolate houses and the walk-ways in the parks swarm with them. Their life is spent hunting after all the latest fashions: their wigs and their coats are as thick with powder as a miller's clothes are with flour. Their faces are besmeared with snuff; they have an affected appearance – They are exactly like Molière's Marquesses, though they in fact lack the title of marquis. A *Beau* is so much the more remarkable in England because, generally speaking, Englishmen dress in a plain uniform manner.

In 1703, the anonymous author of *The Ladies' Catechism* observed:

Nothing will go down with the town now but French fashions, French dancing, French songs, French servants, French wines, French kickshaws [a corruption of *quelques choses*, light unsubstantial dishes] and now and then

French sawce [sauce] come in among them, and so no doubt but French doctors may be in esteem too.

While in 1711, writing in *The Spectator*, in whose pages was later to appear that doughty defender of all things English, Sir Roger de Coverley, Joseph Addison declared, 'I could heartily wish that there was an Act of Parliament for Prohibiting the Importation of *French* fopperies.' A year later, he roundly denounced France as 'a Country which has infected all the Nations of Europe with its Levity'.

In 1711, France was still ruled by Louis XIV whose life was as long as his ambitions were grandiose. In the last half of the seventeenth century, English patriots came to resent his countrymen not so much for the tyranny they exercised over fashion as for their military intentions. Clear evidence that age-old animosities survived on either side of the Channel is apparent from reactions to the Great Fire of London in 1666. Samuel Pepys noted in his Diary that the French were felt to have been somehow involved:

5 September.   But Lord, what a sad sight it was by moonlight to see the whole City almost on fire – that you might see it plain at Woolwich, as if you were by it. There when I come, I find the gates shut, but no guard kept at all; which troubled me, because of discourses now begun that there is plot in it and that the French had done it.

7 September.   Up by five a-clock and, blessed be God, find all well, and by water to Paul's wharfe. Walked thence and saw all the town burned, and a miserable sight of Pauls church, with all the roofs fallen and the body of the Quire fallen into St Fayths [in the crypt under the choir of old St Paul's] – Paul's school also – Ludgate – Fleet street – my father's house, and the church, and a good part of the Temple the like. So to Creeds lodging near the New Exchange, and there find him laid down upon a bed – the house all unfurnished, there being fears of the fire's coming to them. There borrowed a shirt of him – and washed. To Sir W. Coventry at St James's, who lay without Curtains, having removed all his goods – as the King at Whitehall and everybody had done and was doing. He hopes we shall have no public distractions upon this fire, which is what everybody fears – because of the talk of the French having a hand in it.

John Evelyn reported similar suspicions in his Diary:

7 September.   . . . in the middst of all this Calamity and confusion, there was (I know not how) an *Alarme* begun, that the *French* and *Dutch* (with

whom we were now in hostility) were not onely landed, but even entering the Citty; there being in truth, greate suspicion some days before, of those two nations joyning, & even now, that they had ben the occasion of firing the Towne: This report did so terrifie, that on a suddaine there was such an uprore & tumult, that they ran from their goods, & taking what weapons they could come at, they could not be stop'd from falling on some of those nations whom they casualy met, without sense or reason, the clamor & perill growing so excessive, as made the whole Court amazd at it, and they did with infinite paines, & greate difficulty reduce and appease the people sending Guards & troops of souldiers, to cause them to retire into the fields againe where they watched all this night when I left them pretty quiet, & came home to my house, sufficiently weary and broken.

To French commentators, the Great Fire was a sure sign of Divine disapproval. The court poet Isaac de Benserade declared: 'In similar fashion, long ago, famous Troy burnt down, and it had insulted neither its kings nor its gods. London is consumed with flames from end to end and suffers Troy's fate which it more richly deserves.'

Another French commentator observed: 'I rather prefer to believe – and there can be no dispute about this – that it is the hand of God, the King of Kings, which has armed itself with flame to punish the injustice and the arrogance of the English who, on so many occasions, have provoked his wrath.'

Since the Reformation, the chronic grievance of French Anglophobes of this persuasion was England's apostasy. However, Charles II's accession to power gave them grounds for hoping that he might soon lead his country back to Mother Church. Charles II was only too willing to play his part, but he had to contend with the newly won power of Parliament and the Francophobia of the English people. The Marquis de Révigny, French Ambassador at the Court of St James's between 1667 and 1678, reported to Louis XIV that while the English king was in favour of much closer union with France 'there were few in England to share his sentiments and, above all, Parliament and the majority of the Council were very averse to the interests of the French king, being fearful of his power'.

Later, on 8 March 1668, he reported: 'It is a fact, Sire, that a foolish idea is widespread that Your Majesty designs to conquer England as well as the Low Countries. This panic fills them with mistrust . . . they regard you as a rival. For that reason, there is already talk of War.'

English apprehension about France at this time was not unjustified.

From the death of Cardinal Mazarin in 1661, when Louis XIV assumed full power, until Louis XIV's death in 1715, France was by some way the dominant power in European politics. This was founded on Louis' own charismatic personality and the inherent strength of France itself. It was self-sufficient in natural resources, had the largest population in Europe, the highest tax-yield, the most efficient diplomatic corps and quite the best organised army the century had seen. At the dazzling Versailles court of *le roi soleil* the arts were lavishly patronized and potentially dangerous nobles were mollified with honorary offices. Louis could be duplicitous. In 1667, he suggested to his Ambassador in London: 'If the English would be content to be the greatest merchants of Europe and let me have for my share whatever I could conquer in a just war, it would be easy as anything for us to get on together.' Yet three years later, his great Finance Minister, Colbert, was to write to him: '[Your Majesty] has undertaken a war of money against all the states of Europe and some others, in which he has caused great misery and want, and by despoiling them he has enriched himself. Only Holland is left.' No less sinister, in the view of many Englishmen, was Louis' insistence on imposing Catholic uniformity throughout his realm and the fear that he plotted to pursue this policy elsewhere. Such fear seemed more than justified when, inspired by his Jesuit confessor and the devout Madame de Maintenon, the last of his many mistresses, whom he secretly married in 1684, Louis intensified his persecution of the Huguenots. The inevitable outcome occurred in 1685 when he revoked Henri IV's magnanimous Edict of Nantes and expelled all Protestants from France. Most of these came to England.

In the course of the seventeenth century, the French had begun to show more interest in things English. Various sixteenth-century Latin histories of England were reprinted. England began to feature in French novels and plays such as La Calprenède's *Edouard* (1639), the subject of which is Edward III's love for the Countess of Salisbury, or Tristan L'Hermite's *Le Page disgrâcié* (1643), an autobiographical novel based on the author's experiences in England. More and more French guide-books and travellers' tales began to appear, some less reliable than others; in *Les Voyages de M. Payen* (1666), the would-be French traveller is advised that the principal English coins are the 'Crhon, Alue Crhon, Toupens, Alue Pens and Farden'. Some French diplomats seemed no better informed: Louis XIV's English Ambassador called one of

London's thoroughfares 'rue Rose Street' (Rose Street Street), and some decades later the Comte de Broglie reported that he had attended a curious ceremony called a *drerum* (by which he meant a 'drawing room'). Fortunately for French visitors to England, other Francophone guides were better informed. The most outstanding of these was Samuel Sorbière, a traveller and scientist, who came to England in 1663; he met Descartes, associated with Hobbes and translated More's *Utopia*.

Like Perlin before him, he was struck — almost literally! — by the hostility shown by the English populace that greeted his arrival in Dover. He noted in his *Relation d'un voyage en Angleterre* (1667):

> The high regard I brought with me to England for a people whose pleasant appearance won for them a name which, from the etymological point of view, has bestowed on them much advantage, inhibited me from at first being scandalised at the difference I noted between the thoughtful concern with which the English are welcomed at Calais and the insults with which, most of the time, the French are greeted at Dover. Although these two towns do business together every day, you would think Frenchmen had never appeared in Dover before. The children run after them when they arrive. The 'A Mounser, Mounser!', which is to say 'Un Monsieur', which they shout out repeatedly at the tops of their voices, is the first insult they utter. But gradually, as they warm to the task, whether it's because they want to drive them away or shut them up, they move on to French dogs! *French dogs! French dogs* which means *chien de Français* which is the honourable epithet they bestow on us in England.
>
> But to tell the truth, amongst ourselves, there is some justification for their use of these terms in order to make fun of the din we make as we arrive in their country, and to criticise a certain impatience which they construe as indiscretion, in which we indeed seem to them quite ridiculous. Because it contrasts so much with the gravity and with the coldness of their manner, and with the patience with which they allow everyone to make his point, that I was myself surprised in the past, having stayed for some years in the northern countries. As far as I myself was concerned, I experienced nothing which caused me to despair but I saw others who were very much put out: as soon as they appeared on the quayside, the noise they made in dealing with their valets attracted a horde of rabble who escorted them to their lodgings with many a strange cry. Offence was taken at this, the dogs joined in as well, stones were thrown, the cascade of which had to be stopped by the middle-class townsfolk.

Other equally even-handed foreign observers of the late-seventeenth-century English scene include Maximilien Misson, a minor Protestant official of the Paris *parlement*, who came to England after the Revocation of the Edict of Nantes and became tutor to a young English nobleman, and Beat-Louis de Muralt, a Swiss Protestant moralist, whose impressions of England, recorded during a visit in 1694, were not published until 1725 and contributed significantly to the wave of Anglomania which engulfed fashionable France in the eighteenth century.

In the course of the seventeenth century, a number of distinguished refugees came to England from France for political reasons: the French Queen Mother, Marie de' Médicis, fled to London in 1630 because of the excessive power and influence of Richelieu; Hortense Mancini, forced by her uncle, Mazarin, into an unhappy marriage and unable to divorce, fled with friends to London in 1666 and soon set up a distinguished salon there; five years earlier, the displeasure of Mazarin had also driven into exile the most distinguished of all seventeenth-century *émigrés*. This was Saint-Evremond, a courageous free-thinker who publicly criticised Mazarin's treaty with Spain and took a spirited stand against religious intolerance in all its forms. He spent the remaining forty years of his life in England, at the courts of Charles II, James II and William III, and was buried in Westminster Abbey.

After the Revocation of the Edict of Nantes, what had been a mere trickle of French visitors to England became a flood. By 1700, there were sixty-five French pastors and twenty-six Huguenot churches in London. Skilled craftsmen crossed the channel in their thousands from Normandy, Picardy and Touraine. They settled principally in London, in Spitalfields, Soho and St Giles, as well as in Canterbury and Exeter. They effectively created the silk industry in England and made major contributions also to the manufacture of glass, paper, clocks, gold and silver ware, tapestries and hats. Before long, French surnames began to be anglicised: 'Lemaître' became 'Masters', 'Leroy' became 'King', 'Lenoir' became 'Black'. By the second or third generation, they were no longer refugees or visitors. As they became fully integrated British citizens, so the need for Huguenot churches diminished. By 1850, only two remained.

★

During the last quarter of the seventeenth century, and not for the only time during their lengthy relationship, England and France produced mirror images of each other. The English Parliament was so anxious to preserve its Protestant heritage that in 1673 it passed the Test Act which decreed that only members of the Church of England could hold any government posts, including commissions in the army and navy. In 1678, the sinister figure of Titus Oates emerged from obscurity and described to the highest Council of the Kingdom a plot allegedly hatched by the Pope, Louis XIV and England's leading Catholics to murder King Charles, massacre the citizens of London in their beds and force everyone to turn Catholic. It subsequently emerged that this was pure fabrication but in the meantime the supposed chief plotter, one Father Coleman, had been hanged, drawn and quartered, and large numbers of Catholics arrested on all manner of charges.

Confronted with paranoia on this scale and possibly mindful of Froissart's observation made three centuries previously that 'the Kings of England have to obey their people and do their will', Charles II had to negotiate clandestinely with Louis XIV, and the treaties which resulted – in 1670, 1676, 1677 and 1678 – were all signed in secret. These treaties all involved Anglo–French co-operation in campaigns against the Dutch, as did yet another secret treaty, concluded in September 1688 between Louis XIV and Charles's successor, James II. James was himself a Catholic, and was anxious to give English Catholics, and, for that matter, Quakers, the right to worship as they pleased. It is both ironic and somehow fitting, therefore, that he should have given up his throne without a fight, a few weeks later, to the most prominent Protestant campaigner in Europe at that time, William, the Stadtholder of Holland.

In France, the exiled Stuart royal family were given generous support by Louis XIV and accorded a warm welcome by Catholic sympathisers. Madame de Sévigné wrote to her daughter: 'I really do believe that the King and Queen of England are much better off here in their palace at Saint-Germain than in their own perfidious kingdom.' Bossuet interrupted his First Sermon on the Circumcision to sigh 'England! ah! perfidious England!' French satirical poets fulminated against the Prince of Orange, accusing him of being 'blinded with ambition, a perfidious usurper, a slippery heretic, a monarch whose word can't be trusted'. Another declared: 'The fateful title you've taken of Protector of England will ensure that all your plans will come crashing to the ground.

How happy the English will be when they see you with your face like some bird of prey, kneeling up there, twenty feet in the air, on the scaffold.'

This was not how events turned out. Having been invited to take the English throne by Parliament, William and his wife Mary were crowned in February 1689 and in May of that year, war was declared on France, the first major military confrontation between the two countries in the whole of the century. Much was at stake: Louis XIV threatened the Low Countries and England's interests there; he seemed poised to take over Spain's vast empire; he provided a comfortable haven and recruiting base for the Stuart Pretenders. There were major ideological differences in their conceptions of Europe: while William saw it as a concert of independent powers and championed national sovereignty, Louis saw it as Christendom dismembered, which needed to be reunited under the Catholic leadership of France. Because what was inevitably at stake was who should rule over England, the eight-year war has been known ever since as 'The War of the English Succession'.

There were no truly decisive victories on either side: in June 1690, the English and Dutch fleets lost to the French at the Battle of Beachy Head; in 1692, the English won the naval battle of La Hogue and thereby terminated the threat of invasion. In 1694, William himself, declaring that 'the only way of treating with France is with our swords in our hands', commanded the army that recaptured Namur. In 1697, with England all-powerful at sea and France invincible on land, the war of attrition was concluded with the Peace of Ryswick. The most crucial clauses in the treaty were those in which Louis recognised the monarchy of William and formally conceded that Protestantism was England's State religion. Thereafter, although Catholic hopes were to be intermittently rekindled with the hopes of the two Stuart Pretenders, religion ceased to be a *casus belli* between England and France.

The fact that their country was at war with France did not inhibit the English fops and *beaux* from aping the fashions and phrases of their Gallic betters. These Gallophiles, however, constituted a privileged minority then as, arguably, they always have done. The prevailing need of the majority was forcibly expressed in the anonymous *Satyr Against the French* published in London in 1691. It begins with the familiar mockery of the compulsively fashion-conscious English but then proceeds into an all-embracing indictment of French failings, moral, political and hygienic:

> Their levity of Mind is such, that none,
> Came even near 'em in comparison,
> Frisking they gaze on every Face they meet,
> And dance a Galliard when they walk the Street.
> If any serious thinking seize their Mind,
> A Violin will chase away the Fiend.
> For Persons bit by the *Tarantula*,
> Cannot be half so frolicksom as they.
> They never yet could time for thinking find,
> They never look before, nor yet behind:
> If but this moment they with Ease and blest,
> Let over-ruling Fate secure the rest.
>   Such Slaves they are to Arbitrary Power
> (Which like a sweeping Plague does all devour)
> That let their Prince command their whole Estate,
> Their Persons, Lands, Wives, Children, and what not,
> They tamely passive, quietly submit,
> And part with what by Nature was their Right.
> They'd rather live in Want and Slavery,
> Then make one bold Attempt for Liberty.
> Like *Hebrew* Servants when their Ears were bor'd,
> They then for ever were to serve their Lord.
>   Oh *France*! how feebly happy is thy State?
> What daily Blessings on thy Country wait?
> Thy King with all those noble Vertues blest,
> Which ever yet adorn'd a Tyrants Breast:
> One, who against all the World has drawn his Sword,
> And thinks it Childish for to keep his Word:
> That treats his Subjects worse than they their Dogs;
> He, like to *Aesop*'s Stork, and they the Frogs.
> The Bully of Mankind, all *Europe*'s Rod;
> The worst of Tyrants, and the Scourge of God:
> Thy Nobles beggar'd both in Mind and Purse,
> Thy Clergy Blockheads, and thy Laymen worse:
> Thy Country ruin'd, destitute of Treasure,
> And all to please a haughty Tyrant's Pleasure.
> Who but his Will, no other Law does know;
> *It shall be thus, because he'll have it so.*
>
> If from small things to greater we ascend,
> When did we ever find of *France* a Friend?

When we our ancient Histories turn o'er,
And ask our Fathers what was done before;
They'll tell us of their cursed Breach of Leagues,
State Artifice and Politick Intrigues.
But if to nearer Times we make approach,
When in our late Engagements with the *Dutch*;
Their promis'd Friendship greedily we sought,
And they their Squadrons on the Ocean brought,
When *Dutch* and *English* were engag'd in view,
They tack'd about and modestly withdrew,
Standing at distance to observe the Fight,
And not advance to help us when they might,
It was by their Advice the War begun,
And when engag'd, 'twas they who set us on,
And cry'd Halloo – much pleas'd to think how far
Their Interest gain'd by that Unnat'ral War.

There follows a catalogue of venereal diseases which are invariably and inevitably to be associated with the French because, in the anonymous poet's view, they are as promiscuous in love as they are unreliable in war. Available in just two learned libraries in Britain, the poem deserves to be better known. The merit of its bouncy couplets may be limited, but it constitutes a repository of most of the vices with which dyed-in-the-wool English xenophobes have charged the French to this day.

3 : *Cosmopolitanism and Xenophobia in the Eighteenth Century*

In France, we think too well and too ill of the English.

L'Abbé le Blanc, *Letters on the English and French Nations* (1745)

The eighteenth century began, as it ended, with England at war with France. The roots of conflict were so many and so convoluted that the period between William of Orange's accession and the final defeat of Napoleon has sometimes been called the Second Hundred Years War. Yet this was also the Age of the Enlightenment: writers and thinkers visited each other's country in increasing numbers and, for the most part, reported back enthusiastically. At the same time, the theatre of war spread out from the mainland of Europe to the continents of India and North America; and, in the last decade of the century, fighting was no longer confined to the relatively small military classes but, in the case of France, to a whole nation in arms. A period that had seemed to some to hold out the prospect of unlimited progress for mankind can be seen, in retrospect, to have presaged our own era of global war.

The first of the series in the Second Hundred Years War was, like those in the First, fought over dynastic issues. In a period when a judicious royal marriage could still secure vast tracts of territory more emphatically than victory on the battlefield, the countries readily went to war to ensure the preferment of their chosen party. The so-called War of the Spanish Succession was fought mainly to determine whether or not Louis XIV's grandson should become King of Spain but also because, after the death of James II in 1701, Louis recognised his son, another James, the Old Pretender, as the lawful King of England. The Anglo–Dutch coalition against Louis was commanded by Marlborough whose war-aims were to expel the Bourbons and their allies from the German Empire, Italy and the Netherlands; to turn the Mediterranean into a British lake; and to smash French power for good and all. Reinforced by large bodies of Dutch troops and with armies raised by the Emperor and commanded by Prince Eugène of Savoy, Marlborough won dazzling victories at Blenheim in 1704, Ramilles in 1706 and Oudenarde in 1708. His victory at Blenheim was rewarded with the great palace of that name at Woodstock, and celebrated by Addison in 'The Campaign', a poem in heroic couplets that portrayed Marlborough as divinely inspired:

> Calm and serene he drives the furious blast;
> And, pleased the Almighty's orders to perform,
> Rides in the whirlwind, and directs the storm . . .
>
> Fiction may deck the truth with spurious rays,
> And round the hero cast a borrowed blaze.
> Marlborough's exploits appear divinely bright,
> And proudly shine in their own native light;
> Raised of themselves, their genuine charms they boast,
> And those who paint them truest praise them most.

He was immortalised in the French folk-song 'Malbrough s'en va-t-en guerre'. Although less than a century later the speakers in Southey's decidedly jaundiced poem on Blenheim cannot remember the reason for the battle or the names of the participants, his distant ancestor Winston Churchill, writing in the 1930s, had no doubts at all of what Marlborough achieved for his country:

> By his invincible genius in war and his scarcely less admirable qualities of wisdom and management he had completed that glorious process that carried England from her dependency upon France . . . to ten years' leadership of Europe. Although this proud task was for a space cast aside by faction . . . the greatness of Britain and her claims to empire were established upon foundations that have lasted to this day. He had proved himself the 'good Englishman' he aspired to be, and History may declare

that if he had had more power his country would have had more strength and happiness, and Europe a surer progress.

For all his towering achievements, Marlborough, like Winston Churchill in his turn, was removed from office before he felt the time was opportune. The difficulty either side found in achieving a decisive victory was exemplified in the 'very murdering battle of Malplaquet' in 1709, when the victorious Allied losses, mainly Dutch, exceeded those of the purportedly defeated French. War-weariness set in on either side; British taxpayers resented paying out ever-increasing subsidies to foreign mercenaries for no discernible return. The Tories came to power in 1710 determined to bring down Marlborough, which they duly did. Negotiations dragged on for months before a formal peace treaty was signed at Utrecht in 1713. Gibraltar and Minorca were ceded to Britain and, in North America, Louis XIV was obliged to hand over Hudson Bay, Nova Scotia, Newfoundland and the West Indian island of St Kitts. French diplomats were able to make capital of this; Britain was made to seem acquisitive, aggressive, all too ready to abuse the near-monopoly of her sea-power and, since the negotiations for peace had been conducted in secret and ended with Britain deserting her allies, incorrigibly perfidious as always. Their reputation for inconstancy and unreliability was succinctly expressed in this extract from André Boureau-Deslandes' poetic account of his *Nouveau voyage d'Angleterre* (1717): 'Just like flighty Proteus, their thoughts, their tastes, their beliefs and their moods change a hundred times over, and sometimes, in the course of a single day, they can be merry, sad and wistful.' Forty years later, in his *Préservatif contre l'Anglomanie*, J. L. Fougeret de Montbron was to declare more pungently: 'Before the English learn that there is a God to be worshipped, they learn that there are Frenchmen to be detested.' He argued that Frenchmen should return this detestation with interest and that the only good things to be said about the English were that they bred excellent horses and dogs and that they had freed their country from the menace of wolves and monks.

*

While in the seventeenth century the English manifested a growing fondness for travel, in the course of the eighteenth, this fondness became a veritable passion. Italy remained the ultimate destination for most of these travellers, as it had been since the Renaissance; but it became fashionable to linger in France on the way to or from Italy as French literature and manners came to set the standard for the rest of Europe. Educated Englishmen often returned home bearing the works of French authors, either in translation or in the original language, and increasing numbers of them came to share Lord Chesterfield's view that the lessons of truly civilised and gracious living were best learned in Paris. He dispatched both his natural son and his godson there and, almost daily, sent them a letter advising them on questions of behaviour and good breeding. These letters epitomise an exceptionally civilised and cosmopolitan age as much as the fact that English enthusiasm for things French and regular and protracted visits to France continued unabated even while the two countries were at war.

Throughout the century, the English crossed the Channel in impressive numbers, among them some of the most colourful characters and liveliest writers of the age. They included Lady Montagu, wife of the ambassador to Constantinople in 1716, whence she wrote some delightful 'Turkish Letters' and introduced into England the practice of inoculation against smallpox. In 1739, the poet Thomas Gray reported from England 'that one sees but little of the French themselves'. He noted the tendency of these visitors to herd together, such standoffish-ness being regarded as arrogance by the French, amongst whom the phrase *riche comme un Anglais* became something of a cliché. In fact, by no means all English visitors to France in the eighteenth century were inordinately rich: they included clerics such as the Reverend William Cole, antiquarian and Rector of Bletchley, who produced a lively and picturesque journal of his journey to Paris in 1765; medical men such as Dr John Moore, who published two thick volumes of his impressions of France, Germany and Switzerland in 1779; and the unsuccessful farmer but notable agricultural theorist, Arthur Young, who became secretary to the Board of Agriculture in 1793 after producing a series of sharply detailed reports on the condition of France immediately before and after the Revolution.

English satirists were not slow to mock their fellow-countrymen's obsession with France. One of the more notable was Samuel Foote, unacted today, but hailed by his contemporaries as the English Aristophanes. Two of his lively farces, *The Englishman in Paris* (1753) and *The Englishman Returned from Paris* (1756), mock his compatriots for their excessive adulation of the French. There was little change either in the form or substance of these plays since the Restoration wits satirised the Francomania of Charles II's court; their criticisms were re-echoed with the complaint of Hannah Glass, author of *The Art of Cookery Made Plain and Easy* (1747), that 'such is the blind Folly of this Age that [the English upper classes] would rather be imposed on by a French Booby than give Encouragement to a good English cook'.

The reputation of the French for high fashion and inveterate frivolity, already commonplace in Shakespeare's day, was just as widespread in the eighteenth century. Alexander Pope observed in 1728 that

> Others import yet nobler arts from France,
> Teach kings to fiddle, and make senates dance

> (*The Dunciad*)

and James Thomson dismissed France coldly in 1730 as

> The faithless vain disturber of mankind,
> Insulting Gaul

> (*The Seasons*)

though he conceded four years later that it was 'the land where social pleasure loves to dwell' (*Liberty*). For Dr Johnson, ever the voice of blunt common sense, the French were 'a very silly People'; while his good friend Mrs Hester Thrale observed in 1777, 'The French are foppish, and will be foppish, no Philosophy can cure them.'

As well as the crowds of travellers, a significant number of eighteenth-century Englishmen, by choice or from necessity, came to settle in France. Some were political exiles. After James II and his family fled from England in 1688, they were lodged in some splendour at the *château* of St Germain-en-Laye by their cousin Louis XIV. While they awaited the call back to England, they were invited by Louis to participate in the lavish activities at Fontainebleau, Marly and Versailles, paid due respect over matters of royal precedence and awarded a pension of 600,000 *livres* a year. At St Germain, they established their own court, provided musical and theatrical entertainments, received courtiers, conferred honours and awarded pensions in their turn. They were followed into exile by large numbers of Jacobite supporters who founded substantial British colonies at Boulogne, Lyons and Montpellier. The first Viscount Bolingbroke, one of Voltaire's patrons, served for a time as James the Pretender's Secretary of State and eventually retired permanently to Chanteloup in Touraine where he wrote, among other works, his treatise on *The Idea of a Patriot King*, urging that the ideal monarch should espouse no political party, should aim to eliminate ideological faction and govern like the common father to all his people.

Some, such as Horace Walpole and Edward Gibbon, stayed for lengthy periods in Paris as part of their *éducation sentimentale*. Others served a turn in the diplomatic service; David Hume was secretary to the British Embassy in Paris between 1763 and 1765, where he was well received by the court and by literary society. Others still, such as David Garrick for his acting and Laurence Sterne for his writing, were lionised in Paris because of their artistic pre-eminence, or were welcomed in France for their technological expertise.

In keeping with the cosmopolitan spirit of the age in 1740, some 49 per cent of the Fellows of the Royal Society were foreigners. The French were quick to exploit British industrial know-how: the Jacobite John Holker became an *inspecteur* in the French textile industry and, in an attempt to modernise it, not only recruited English and Irish workers in large numbers but also smuggled over their machines; John Kay and his sons made flying shuttles in France; Matthew Boulton of Birmingham erected Watt's fire-pumps for use with the Paris water-supply; William Wilkinson advised on foundries and blast furnaces at Nantes and Le Creusot. So appreciative did the rest of Europe become of British engineering ability in the eighteenth century it has been suggested that the trek of continental visitors to view our collieries, ironworks, mills and foundries more than vied with the procession of the English gentry travelling in the opposite direction.

Amongst those who returned from France with much increased respect for it was Edmund Burke. Though he is now best known as an outspoken critic of the French Revolution, there was a time when he was happy to concede that 'England is a moon shone upon by France. France has all things within herself; and she possesses the power of recovering from the severest blows. England is an artificial country: take away her commerce and what has she?' Burke, however, was decidedly in the minority and was, in any case, Irish. The generality of native-born Englishmen remained emphatically Francophobic throughout the century. France was regarded with a mixture of envy because of its manifest cultural superiority and fear because of its economic and military might. Due to its natural resources and a population three times as large as England's, France was inherently much more powerful, and it maintained, as it had done since the time of Sir Thomas More, a large standing army. Paris was indisputably the cultural capital of Europe; French was the language of international diplomacy and of all civilised Europeans. Beside all this French polish, the English were bound to appear rough-hewn. English responses to this varied from the snide to the truculent. The *Craftsman*, an Opposition journal that regularly praised the purity of the French government as a way of attacking the corruption of Walpole's administration, dismissed France as 'the perfect mistress of all that is polite and all that is silly'. English official almanacs and other works of reference continued to list among George II's titles 'King of France'. And in this context, the national stereotypes the English fashioned of themselves are not without significance. For all the dazzling victories of Marlborough on the battlefield, the characters they felt best represented them were not latter-day versions of the Black Prince or Henry V but the country squire Sir Roger de Coverley and bluff and bucolic John Bull.

Each was of sound stock: Addison's Sir Roger de Coverley, up from his rural seat and being rowed across the Thames by a hero wounded in the Battle of La Hogue,

> made several reflections on the greatness of the *British* nation: as, that one *Englishman* could beat three *Frenchmen*; that we could never be in danger of Popery so long as we took care of our fleet; that the *Thames* was the noblest river in Europe, that London Bridge was a greater piece of work than any of the seven wonders of the world; with many other honest prejudices which naturally cleave to the heart of a true *Englishman*.

John Bull was the creation of John Arbuthnot and first appeared in 1712 as a character in a set of satirical pamphlets depicting the lawsuit he brings with Nicholas Frog (Holland) against Philip Baboon (the Duke of Anjou) who has bespoken his liveries at the shop of Lewis Baboon (Louis Bourbon, the French king). John Bull is described as an

honest plain-dealing fellow, choleric, bold and of a very inconstant temper
. . . very apt to quarrel with his best friends, especially if they pretend to
govern him . . . John's temper depended very much upon the air; his spirits
rose and fell with the weather-glass. John was quick and understood his
business very well . . . a boon companion, loving his bottle and his
diversion.

He has remained the archetype of a certain Englishman, though his
appearance and character have changed over the years. He was first
represented in graphic form by the political cartoonist James Gillray,
who portrayed him as an innocent rustic, often crude in his utterances
and his gestures, with a brutish head and sometimes a foolish leer, more
like a bumpkin than his original incarnation as a country squire. In 1803,
in the play *John Bull* by George Colman the younger (1762–1836), he
appeared in the guise of Job Thornberry, an honest tradesman, generous
and kind-hearted most of the time, but irascible when confronted by
injustice. In the nineteenth century, the cartoonists John Leech and Sir
John Tenniel made him more dignified, much tidier in appearance and
somewhat shrewder. In one of Tenniel's drawings, on the occasion of
Anglo–French tension of 1859, Napoleon III is shown closing down his
fireworks factory out of consideration for his neighbour, a confident-
looking John Bull standing in front of his residence, Roast Beef House.
One feature remained constant over the years, whatever the sartorial or
sociological changes: John Bull retained a lively distrust, if not
contempt, for the French.

It has been persuasively argued that for all the pride he took in his
comfortable home, his rich cornfields, the fresh complexion of his
womenfolk and the liberties he enjoyed in comparison with his
downtrodden neighbours, John Bull was nagged by fears throughout
the eighteenth century: fear of the pox, of Jacobites, of mobs, of aliens,
of Scotsmen, of the mounting National Debt, of the exciseman and,
from time to time, of armed invasion. In 1748, an anonymous
pamphleteer admitted: 'I am sorry to say it but true it is, that no people in
Europe are more easily wrought into Prejudice than our Countrymen
nor any get out of it with more Difficulty.'

The year before, a French observer, l'Abbé le Blanc, noted in his
Letters on the English and French Nations:

– The bulk of the English nation bear an inveterate hatred of the French, which they do not always take the pains to conceal from us . . .

– By their continual uneasiness, they seem to believe that we are in regard to them what the Persians were to the Athenians; that the king of France is the great King: hence this invincible aversion to the people who obey him, whom they suppose that they alone prevent from giving laws to the rest of Europe . . . They fear and despise us: we are the nation that they pay the greatest civilities to, and yet love the least: they condemn, and yet imitate us; they adopt our manners by taste, and blame them through policy . . .

– The English are a rational and trading people who seek only to enrich themselves and have not that powerful motive which the Romans had – to make them act for the public good preferably to their own.

Other Frenchmen expressed their antipathy more virulently. In his tract eloquently entitled *Jusques où la démocratie peut être admise dans le gouvernement monarchique*, Louis XV's Foreign Minister, the Marquis d'Argenson, declared that the English system of government was corrupt because 'with them, everything is a matter of money: people there think of nothing else'.

This charge was not unjustified. When Britain became involved in the War of the Austrian Succession (1740–48), it was ostensibly to safeguard her interests in Hanover and avert the threat of French hegemony in Europe. The continental land war proved inconclusive: in June 1743, George II in person took command of an army of German mercenaries, financed by the British taxpayer, and won a surprise victory over the French at Dettingen, near Frankfurt; in the spring of 1744, a French plan to invade England was aborted when a storm dispersed the French fleet; in 1745, at Fontenoy, near Tournai, an Anglo–Dutch force led by the Duke of Cumberland was defeated by a French army led by the Maréchal de Saxe who is reputed to have preceded the battle by a polite request for the English to fire first. More serious and more significant, however, was the fighting overseas, which continued unabated after the Treaty of Aix-la-Chapelle ended hostilities in Europe in 1748. At stake was control of the St Lawrence seaway on the eastern seaboard of Canada and the immensely lucrative islands in the West Indies which, in the mid eighteenth century, accounted for 20 per cent of all France's external trade.

As has already been noted, the need to preserve trade links had been a major consideration both in the Hundred Years War and in the French campaigns of Henry VIII. Writing at the end of the seventeenth century, the English writer Charles Davenant had observed: 'Nowadays the whole art of war is reduced to money: and nowadays, that prince who can best find money to feed, cloath and pay his army, not he that has the most valiant troops, is surest of success and conquest.'

A few years later, Montesquieu noted in his *Journal* the vital role of money in modern statecraft:

> A great maxim for France is to oblige England always to maintain a standing army. This will make her spend a great deal of money, increase the embarrassment it always feels over the existence of that army and correspondingly reduce the money available for her navy.
>
> It is scarcely possible for England to ignore the world's affairs. Queen Elizabeth took a keen interest in them. We all know about the aid she provided to the Dutch and the French and the influence she wielded in various parts of Europe. Neither James I because of incompetence, nor Charles I because of impotence, nor Charles II because of indolence, nor James II because of bigotry, ever got involved. Those four reigns were not glorious and England lost all the influence she had acquired under Elizabeth. In order to carry out her maritime business, it is not sufficient to go in search of merchandise; in addition, it is essential for her to keep the land and the rivers free to transport it.

For their part, some British merchants went even further. They wanted more than naval protection for their ships, they wanted war with France and Spain to continue because it was good for their profits. One of them stated in 1745: 'It is more in the true interest of these kingdoms in general that we should continue in a state of war with them, so that war is carried on only by sea, than in a state of peace . . . our commerce in general will flourish more under a vigorous and well-managed naval war, than under any peace which should allow an open intercourse with those two nations.' And a contemporary writer urged the English government 'so to distress the commerce and navigation of our ever-restless enemy, as to disable them in future times from maintaining that lucrative competition with us in trade, they have too long done'.

★

In the eighteenth century, however, by no means all Frenchmen were so hostile to England. Many – indeed most – of France's leading writers crossed the Channel in the course of the century and, from the 1750s onwards, French high society was copying English manners and fashions ever bit as slavishly as Charles II's court had adulated all things French. Though Voltaire is often given the credit for inaugurating and sustaining this wave of enthusiasm, he was not, in fact, the first of France's eighteenth-century Anglophiles. More than twenty years before the appearence of the *Lettres philosophiques*, French scholars and Academicians had revealed a considerable interest in the English literary scene with their close questioning of the poet Matthew Prior when he was in Paris conducting the secret negotiations that led to the peace treaty of Utrecht (1713). From 1717 on, literary journals began to appear, such as *Le Journal littéraire*, exclusively given over to reviewing English books, or *La Bibliothèque anglaise*, the remit of which was sometimes wider. An editorial proclaimed characteristically in 1722: 'Let us proclaim as loudly as we can how fortunate a place is England for all studious seekers after Truth: no Inquisition anywhere, no dragoons, no prison cells, and no gallows except for bringing to justice disturbers of the civil peace.'

In 1727, two plays were successfully staged in Paris, *Le Français à Londres* by Louis de Boissy and *L'Ile de Raison* by Marivaux. Each contrasted French wit and grace with English gravity and thoughtfulness and it was a sign of the times that the English did not invariably come off second best.

Amongst eighteenth- and indeed nineteenth-century French Anglophiles, Voltaire could be described as something of a role model. He first came to England in 1726 as a refugee from French justice, and he employed praise of things English as a means of criticising what he thought were French shortcomings. Paradoxically, one of the closest of the English friends he made was Lord Bolingbroke, who left England after championing the Old Pretender, settled in France, married a French lady and did not recross the Channel till after ten years in exile. Voltaire, who soon acquired a good grasp of English, met Pope, Swift, Congreve, Berkeley, Gay, Thomson and Young; was present at the funeral of Newton in Westminster Abbey; and attended meetings of the Royal Society, which made him an Honorary Fellow.

From the very outset of his association with England, Voltaire found much to admire. Writing to his friend Thieriot, in August 1726, he declared: 'This is a country where all the arts are honoured and rewarded, where there are differences of rank, but only those based on merit. This is a country where one thinks freely and nobly without being held back by a servile fear. If I were to follow my inclination, I would stay right here, for the sole purpose of learning to think.' To the same correspondent, he wrote two years later: 'England is a nation fond of its liberty, learned, witty, despising life and death, a nation of philosophers.' And in 1728, in the preface to his *Essai sur la poésie épique*, he declared: 'Let others give an exact description of St Paul's, Westminster, etc., I consider England from a different perspective; I look at it as the country that has produced a Newton, a Locke, a Tillotson, a Milton, a Boyle . . . Who glories in the profession of arms, politics and literature deserves to extend beyond the borders of that island.' His distinguished contemporaries shared his enthusiasm: Montesquieu praised the English constitution; Diderot hailed England as 'the country of philosophers, systematisers and men of inquiring mind'; while Buffon saluted it as 'this sensible and profoundly thoughtful nation'.

Voltaire returned to France in 1729. The detailed account of his stay in England first appeared in an English version in 1733. The French edition was published the following year and *parlement* promptly ordered it to be burnt as scandalous and subversive: Lanson was later to describe it as 'the first bomb thrown at the *ancien régime*'. Voltaire, threatened with imprisonment in the Bastille for a third time, fled from Paris and took refuge at Cirey, near the Lorraine frontier, in the house of the erudite and independent-minded Madame du Châtelet, who provided affection and support for many years. Till the end of his long literary career, he took pride in his enthusiastic advocacy of the English. In so doing, he did not always allow enough credit to other Anglophiles whose efforts to inform their fellow countrymen about their cross-Channel neighbours were no less wholehearted and no less successful.

Foremost amongst these was l'Abbé Prévost. Like Voltaire, Prévost, who first crossed the Channel in 1728, travelled to England as a refugee from France, though in his case it was religious authority that posed the threat. He found employment as secretary-cum-tutor in the house of an English peer. He remained there till 1731 when a love affair obliged him to leave for France. He returned again to England via Holland in 1733, in the company of a different young lady. Prévost became the most thoroughly anglicised of all eighteenth-century Frenchmen, acquiring a thorough knowledge of the language while he earned his living as a translator of English books. He took a lively interest in English customs, manners and culture, all of which feature prominently in his *Mémoires d'un homme de qualité,* largely written at the same time as Voltaire was writing his *Lettres philosophiques.* In his novels and particularly in the literary periodical *Le Pour et Contre,* founded in 1734, he worked diligently to remove 'certain childish prejudices, common to most men, but especially to the French, which lead them to arrogate to themselves a superiority over every other nation in the world'. Like Voltaire, he was very favourably impressed by the much greater freedom the English enjoyed compared to the French: while class divisions remained inflexible in France, Prévost believed that, in contrast, representatives of all classes in England sat together in their coffee houses, chatting together, calmly smoking their pipes, on matters of public interest. 'The coffee houses,' he once declared, 'are, as it were, the secret of English liberty.'

The spectacle of English liberty also made a vivid impression on Montesquieu who first came to England in November 1729 at the age of forty. As befitted a member of the French nobility, who was in addition a magistrate and a landowner, Montesquieu's background and passage from France to England was much more sedate than either Voltaire's or Prévost's. He was sponsored by that most cosmopolitan of eighteenth-century English statesmen, Lord Chesterfield, and the purpose of his visit was to collect material for *De l'Esprit des Lois,* his monumental treatise on the general principles and historical origins of law. While he could read and understand English well enough to follow proceedings in both Houses of Parliament and the Royal Society (which elected him to an Honorary Fellowship), he spent little time socialising. After a close study of English institutions, he advocated a monarchy with limited powers, a freely elected legislature and an independent judiciary. His ideas were, predictably, ignored by the French *ancien régime*; but they were much admired by the makers of the American Constitution and by Mirabeau, who was to become one of the great Revolutionary statesmen and orators.

Mirabeau's visit to England in August 1784 contrasted sharply with those of Voltaire and Montesquieu. Though Voltaire had incurred the displeasure of the French government, the French Foreign Secretary had furnished him with official introductions to the Duke of Newcastle and other leading ministers; Voltaire was already a literary celebrity, and the most prominent personages and hostesses of fashionable London vied with each other for the privilege of fêting him. Montesquieu travelled to England as part of his belated Grand Tour and crossed the North Sea from The Hague aboard Lord Chesterfield's yacht in the company of Lord Waldegrave who personally introduced him to George II. Mirabeau, who had served more than one jail sentence in the course of his riotous youth, came to England as a victim of the French government's displeasure, bearing no introductions to the good or the great. It seems somehow typical that during the journey from Lewes to London, his coach should have been attacked by highwaymen. Mirabeau was as pleased to learn that these were called 'gentlemen of the road' as he later was in London when he was told that he looked just like Jacques Rosbif. Mirabeau received a measure of support from the Whig magnate, Gilbert Elliott, who later became Lord Minto and Governor General of India. He met Bentham and Romilly, the leading English law reformers of the day, and he visited Edmund Burke in Beaconsfield, an eloquent advocate of limited monarchy. This appealed very much to Mirabeau, more than once the victim of *lettres de cachet*, letters sealed with the king's privy seal that ordered the imprisonment without trial of the person named in them. After his return to France in 1785, he launched a periodical, *Analysis of English Papers*, which was devoted to reprinting items from English newspapers. It came out twice-weekly between November 1787 and November 1789 and proved extremely popular. After the French Revolution had broken out, Mirabeau continued to argue passionately for a constitutional government on the English model, which would fully recognise the rights of the people but retain the king at its head. When he died on 2 April 1791, as the direct consequence of his excessive devotion both to his work and his pleasures, he was given a state funeral.

Mirabeau was not the only important personality of the French Revolution to visit and be impressed by England. Jean-Paul Marat was a doctor by profession, who studied for a while in Edinburgh and St Andrews and published an important paper on gleets. During a stay in England in 1774–75, he published *The Chains of Slavery . . . to which is Prefixed an Address to the Electors of Britain*. In it, he praised the principles of the British constitution, condemned patronage and advised the English electors to choose mature and independent men as their leaders. His manner later became considerably more vehement and the articles he wrote in 1792 for his own journal *L'Ami du Peuple* are sometimes said to have inspired the mob violence of the September massacres.

Another distinguished visitor was Rousseau, who was invited to England in 1766 by David Hume after a meeting at the British Embassy in Paris where Hume was secretary. The British Government awarded him a pension of £100 and he was fêted in London where *La Nouvelle Héloïse* and *Emile* were widely read. Garrick gave a dinner in his honour at his home in the Adelphi. None of this was to Rousseau's taste and neither was the practical joke played on him by Horace Walpole, who composed a letter, purportedly by Frederick the Great, inviting him to Berlin. Rousseau was furious, assumed Hume had had a hand in it and denounced him as 'the blackest and most atrocious villain in the world'. He departed for France and noted in his *Confessions*, 'I have never loved England or the English.' This is often represented as Rousseau's considered view of the matter but is best interpreted as an outburst of bad temper. In fact, he found much to admire in the English scene and this is best expressed in *La Nouvelle Héloïse* in which the friends and lovers spend an idyllic morning 'in the English fashion', contemplating and silently communing and in which the most sympathetically drawn character in the novel is Lord Edward, who has 'an air of grandeur which proceeds rather from the soul than from rank and a grave and stoical bearing beneath which he conceals with difficulty an extreme sensibility'; he wears the dress of an English *milord* without ostentation and carries himself with just a touch of swagger. One must remember, however, that this portrait was composed ten years before Rousseau set foot in England, and it should perhaps be seen as a mixture of wish-fulfilment and of fashionable Anglomania.

In the eighteenth century, England attracted the French for a variety of reasons. To economists such as Morellet or Gournay, co-founder of the physiocratic school, England provided a challenging alternative to a French system urgently in need of radical reform. To *philosophes* such as Delisle, Helvétius and Suard, England was the home of Bacon and Locke. To French natural scientists, England meant Newton, the Royal Society and the forefront of fresh exploration: Buffon, author of the forty-four-volume *Histoire naturelle*, Broussonet, who first introduced merino sheep and Angora goats into France, Bernard de Jussieu, the naturalist who is reputed to have planted the great cedar of Lebanon in the *Jardin des Plantes* with a seedling presented to him by Oxford's first Professor of Botany, and the two scientists Maupertius and La Condamine, who each independently measured a degree of the meridian and thereby helped confirm Newton's description of the shape of the earth, all were visitors no less distinguished in their fields than their more famous literary counterparts. The diversity of their reasons for crossing the Channel confirms the impression that in the course of the eighteenth century, England came to represent all things to all Frenchmen.

★

There was another major reason why England preoccupied eighteenth-century French observers: it had developed efficient agriculture and prosperous trade on a world-wide scale. Louis XV may have sought to counter his subjects' infatuation with England and the English; Louis XVI, at the instigation of his finance minister, Jacques Necker, positively encouraged it. As the century wore on, costumes, clubs and upper-class leisure pursuits were more and more copied from English models. By 1786, a neutral observer such as the distinguished German critic Frederick Grimm could report that horses, carriages, furniture, jewellery and all manner of woven materials were being sent over from England; in imitation of the London original, Vauxhalls were built in Paris; there was a Coliseum, a Ranelagh and even an Astley's circus, which attracted crowds as vast and enthusiastic as that other importation from England, horse racing. The spectacle of all this produced the inevitable reaction.

Eighteenth-century French satirists proved as ready to mock their compatriots' adulation of imports from across the Channel as their English predecessors had done in the previous century at the time of the Stuart Restoration. The virtues that the Anglomaniacs singled out for praise could all too readily be depicted as vices by the Anglophobes. While the former hailed the Glorious Revolution of 1688, the latter recalled the regularity with which the freedom-loving English cut off the head of their kings. Where Voltaire admired the strength and good sense of the English middle class, Boissy discerned Jacques Rosbif, stolid, philistine, full of his own importance; the Marquis d'Argenson, Louis XV's Minister of Foreign Affairs, a passionate believer in free trade, could still say of the English 'with them, everything is a matter of money: people there think of nothing else'. The great English philosophers of the seventeenth century might compel grudging admiration but the eighteenth-century Frenchmen seeking to emulate them were all too easy a target for the Anglophobe's irony. In his *Préservatif contre l'anglomanie*, J. L. Fougeret de Montbron depicts one type of French Anglomaniac, 'bundled up in a hideous great cloak', splashed with mud up to his shoulders, with a comb under his hat, setting up for a philosopher, quoting Addison and Pope, and seeming to say 'Now am I a *thinker.*' L'Abbé le Blanc, a shrewd observer of the mid-eighteenth-century French scene, records meeting another type of Anglophile, dressed in green, without a crease in his clothing or any trace of powder in his hair, who declared, 'Well! What do you think of me? Don't I look thoroughly *English?*'

The contrasting attitudes of the French towards the English are well expressed in a number of eighteenth-century French plays. One that proved particularly popular was *L'Anglais à Bordeaux*, written by Charles-Simon Favart, the son of a Paris pastry cook who became director of the Opéra-Comique. It was specially composed as part of the ceremonies celebrating the Peace of Paris in 1763 and its principal theme is the superiority of French national character over that of the English. A melancholic, haughty English *milord* and his beautiful daughter are being held prisoner by a French gentleman who captured them at sea during the Seven Years War. The host's widowed sister, a charming marquise, displaying the special French virtues of sociability and courtoisie, finally melts *milord's* icy heart while the chivalrous French host, who, all along, has been secretly paying his prisoner's debts, end by marrying the daughter: France may have lost its overseas empire but it can still teach the English the secrets of *savoir-vivre*. The author's message was not, however, primarily Anglophobic. His play included the lines 'Courage and honour knit nations together, and two peoples equal in virtue and intelligence throw down the barriers their decrees have raised, that they may be forever friends.' At the première, these words provoked tumultuous applause; Favart was dragged, protesting, on to the stage and given a standing ovation.

Two years later, Pierre Belloy's play *Le Siège de Calais* won even greater acclaim. Once again, the theme is the moral superiority of the French. The setting is Calais besieged by England's King Edward III. The six burgher hostages are released through the machinations of a devious French nobleman but on discovering they owe their freedom to a subterfuge, they voluntarily return to custody. In the end, King Edward spares their lives not, as tradition has it, because of the intercession of his consort, Queen Philippa, but because of his admiration for the prisoners' noble conduct: Edward may have won the war, but the French patriots win all the honours. Underlying the play are the twin ideas of a subject's obligation to be loyal to his king and the sacredness of the national tie that binds all the subjects of one country together in times of common danger. Contemporary critics, such as Voltaire's friend La Harpe, claimed that the success of this play exceeded everything in the previous history of French dramatic art; the Comédie-Française company gave free performances for the people of Paris and they attended in droves shouting *Vive le roi*! On 1 April 1765, Baron Grimm commented in a letter: 'This play has really been a state event . . . Those who have dared, I do not say to find fault with it, but to speak of it coldly and without admiration, have been regarded as bad citizens, or, what is worse, as *philosophers*; for the philosophers have the reputation of not being convinced of the sublimity of the piece.' Revivals in later years proved equally successful, and the English traveller Dr John Moore reported in the 1770s: 'You cannot conceive what pressing and crowding there is every night to see this favorite piece.'

Another French play marking the impact of Anglomania was Bernard Saurin's one-act comedy *L'Anglomane* (1772), which wittily mocked the excessive adulation of things English in the same way as the English Restoration wits had satirised exaggerated Francophilia a century before. Eraste, the Anglomaniac, makes his first entrance dressed 'in the English fashion, with an English coat and a little round wig'. He apologises for having kept his guests waiting with the words: 'I've been supervising the workmen in my garden where I've been transforming things in ways that may surprise you. I've gone for an English theme. This morning, I've had a great flowerbed turned into a little *boulingrin*. I want the whole works: valleys, hills, meadows, a plain, woods, a mosque, a Chinese bridge, a river, some ruins.' When his guest comments, 'You must have a vast estate, sir', he retorts, 'Me? Not at all.

Just three acres or so which was once landscaped by Le Nôtre. People heap praises on him but I prefer the English style . . .'

Three years later, Horace Walpole, one of several highly literate eighteenth-century Englishmen who spent many years in France, wrote to the Reverend William Mason that 'English gardening gains ground here prodigiously'. However, on the eve of the French Revolution, the great agricultural expert Arthur Young speculated how 'English' these fashionable enterprises really were. Of the garden at Mortefontaine he reported that it 'had been mentioned as decorated in the English style . . . with winding walks, and ornamented with a profusion of temples, benches, grottos, columns, ruins and I know not what. I hope the French who have not been in England do not consider this as the English taste.'

Yet another French play to demonstrate the extent of contemporary Anglomania was Jean-Baptiste Desforges's five-act verse comedy *Tom Jones à Londres*, first staged in October 1782 and proving successful enough to inspire a sequel, *Tom Jones et Fellamar*, which had its première in April 1787. The treatment of Fielding's novel was as cavalier as Desforges's spelling of the eponymous hero's name. The opening couplet in the first play is

> En vérité, monsieur, votre récit m'étonne!
> Quoi, monsieur Alworthy père de Monsieur Jone!

while the cast list of the second play includes Milord Fellamar (First Lord of the Admiralty), Sir Alworthy, Sir Western, Betti (*sic*), an English lady's maid, and Commodore Tom Jones of the Royal Navy.

Tom Jones had been immensely popular in France ever since it was translated in 1750. In the first half of the century, Addison's tragedy *Cato* (first produced in 1713) was the English work most esteemed by the leading French critics. In his periodical, *Le Pour et Contre*, founded in 1733 with the express purpose of publicising works of English literature, L'Abbé Prévost described him at various times as 'the wise Addison', 'the incomparable Addison', 'the illustrious Addison', and hailed *Cato* as one of the most beautiful plays in the English language. Voltaire was no less adulatory: in his *Lettres philosophiques* he described Addison as the only Englishman ever to have composed a play written with perfect elegance from first to last and hailed Cato as the finest character to have appeared in any play in any literature. Subsequently, Samuel Richardson became the divinity French writers were all too ready to worship. Rousseau declared that there was no novel in any language to vie with *Clarissa*, while Diderot vowed, in 1742, that should financial hardship compel him to sell his books in order to feed his children, he would never part with his Richardson: 'O Richardson! Richardson! as a man, you are, in my judgement, unique . . . I shall sell all my other books but I'll never part with you. You will stay there, on the shelf, with Moses, Homer, Euripides and Sophocles, and I shall read each of you in turn.'

Such praise was not confined to France's leading writers. High Society ladies translated, discussed and studied English writers and thinkers: L'Abbé le Blanc noted in a letter to Buffon that on their dressing-room tables the works of Newton had replaced such classic romances as *Le Grande Cyrus*. On an increasing scale, books were ordered from London without too much attention being paid either to the title or the subject matter: as long as they seemed authentically English, they were displayed with great delight. There was a vogue for the poetry of graveyards and the transience of human life: Thomson's poem 'The Seasons' (new edition, 1746), Young's 'Night Thoughts on Life, Death and Immortality' (1742–5) and Gray's 'Elegy in a Country Churchyard' (1751) anticipated the preoccupation with death brought about by the French Revolution and sounded the note of melancholy that became so dominant in the Romantic movement that followed.

Somewhat belatedly, and out of virtual obscurity, Shakespeare finally became fashionable: Madame de Pompadour had a set of his works in translation; her replacement as Louis XV's mistress, Madame du Barry, went one better and had his works in English; Louis XVI translated Horace Walpole's essay on *Richard III*. No small measure of the French enthusiasm for Shakespeare was generated by the performances given to Paris audiences by David Garrick in 1751, 1763 and 1765, which were wildly acclaimed by writers, actors and the theatre public alike. Inevitably, Shakespeare was the favourite author of Saurin's Anglomaniac Eraste, who insisted that the name was pronounced *Shakespéar*. No admirer was more passionate than Jean-François Ducis who made the translation and adaptation of Shakespeare's plays his life's work. He knew no English whatsoever and worked from the earlier French translations of Laplace (1745–8) and Letourneur (1776–83). To inspire him, he had portraits of Shakespeare and of Garrick on his desk and every year he would celebrate the feast of St William by draping a vast wreath of boxwood around a bust of the Bard.

No less remarkable was the violent antipathy Shakespeare aroused amongst other Frenchmen and that by far the most vituperative of these should be Voltaire, that most eloquent of Anglophiles, who had done more than anyone to introduce Shakespeare to the French in the first place. From the start, he had expressed reservations about Shakespeare's breaches with theatrical orthodoxy. Over the years, these grew more intemperate, culminating in the impassioned attack on Shakespeare and his French idolators, read on his behalf before the French Academy in August 1776. A further attack was mounted a year later. Impressive though his rhetoric undoubtedly was, the Anglophiles would seem to have had the last word. After his death in 1770, his place on the French Academy was awarded to Ducis.

★

Although waves of Anglomania continued to sweep fashionable eighteenth-century France and sons of the well-to-do English still crossed the Channel to acquire a modicum of French polish, the two countries nonetheless found it imperative to go to war with one another. The issue was no longer the substitution of one royal line for another or the imposition of this or that version of the Christian faith but straightforward commercial profit. The acquisition of overseas markets together with the weakening of French competition became the principal British objective in the so-called Seven Years War (1756–63) in which there were two quite distinct battle zones. Fighting on the European mainland principally involved Prussia, Austria and Russia, with Prussia, under Frederick the Great, emerging as the leading power in Europe. At the same time, another war, on and across the sea, was fought between England and France. This produced a rich store of incidents and personalities all once familiar to every English schoolchild: the court martial of Admiral Byng in 1756 and his death by firing squad allegedly for failing to engage the French fleet off Minorca (his execution being ordered, in Voltaire's immortal phrase, '*pour encourager les autres*'); the Black Hole of Calcutta, the small prison cell where, in that same year, 146 Britons were incarcerated by France's ally the Surajah Dowlah, Nawab of Bengal, and whence only twenty-two emerged alive; the crushing victory against heavy odds at Plassey in 1759 by Robert Clive; the capture of Quebec that same year by General Wolfe, who was mortally wounded after storming the Heights of Abraham. But the most outstanding personality of the war was William Pitt the Elder, subsequently Earl of Chatham. In November 1756, he assumed the leadership of the Commons and sole direction of the war, declaring boldly, 'I am sure that I can save the country and nobody else can.' From the outset, he declared, 'His Majesty's Ministers must never forget the basic principles of foreign policy: to see the French become a maritime, commercial and colonial power is the only thing England has to fear here below.'

Like Marlborough before him and Winston Churchill after, he was dismissed from office before the war was finally won. When, through the Treaty of Paris of 1763, France was given back the lucrative sugar islands of Guadaloupe and Martinique, together with Dakar and its rich gum trade and fishing rights off Newfoundland, Pitt and his City friends were outraged. In a three-hour harangue in the Commons, Pitt declared: 'France is chiefly, if not solely, to be dreaded by us in the light of a maritime and commercial power: and therefore, by restoring to her all the valuable West Indian islands, and by our concessions in the Newfoundland fishery, we have given her the means of recovering her prodigious losses and of becoming once more formidable to us at sea.'

For all that, England had won a spectacular victory. A few campaigns, fought at a fraction of the cost of the great but indecisive battles in Germany, were enough to give her a vast colonial empire.

Not surprisingly, the mood of the French was bellicose and vengeful. One expression of this was the popular impact of the vast painting commissioned by the monks of the Abbey at Caen: it depicted their founder, William the Conqueror, at the moment of his triumphant landing in England and proved so popular when it was shown in Paris in 1765 that it had to be kept on display well beyond its allotted time. Another manifestation was the equally popular success in Paris of Pierre Bellay's play *The Siege of Calais*, which hurled contemptuous defiance at the English. Distinctly more threatening was the policy pursued by the Duc de Choiseul, Louis XV's Foreign Minister. He set out to rebuild the shattered naval and colonial power of France and to build up a system of alliances to undermine British influence in Europe. He never abandoned his plan of one day invading England, if necessary, in time of peace. His agents sent back over one hundred sets of plans, describing the southern counties of England in some detail. His project to land 60,000 troops at Barnstaple reached an advanced stage. Another French nobleman outlined plans for a simultaneous invasion of England and Ireland, with the comment, 'The determination to abase the power of England must surely be the guiding passion of every true Frenchman.' It was no coincidence, therefore, that in 1763 there appeared the first of many popular English novels depicting England being invaded by the French. Set in the future, its title was *The Reign of George VI: 1900–1925*. Full of old-style infantry charges and great sea battles, it portrayed King George ranging triumphantly across Europe, being crowned King of France and achieving his greatest victory before the gates of Vienna in May 1918.

The opportunity to 'abase the power of England' was not long in coming with the outbreak of the American War of Independence in 1775. At the outset, Louis XV was reluctant to back the rebels: if they succeeded, it would encourage subversion against kingship everywhere and in Spain's American colonies in particular. France was, for a time, prepared to support the British if they handed back Canada but once it became clear that this was not going to happen, it sympathised more overtly with the American colonists. After Burgoyne surrendered to them with all his army at Saratoga in 1777, France formally declared war and, while its navy under Admiral de Grasse secured control of the Atlantic, a large force of French troops was dispatched to help the rebel cause under the young Marquis de Lafayette (1757–1834). Out-and-out French Anglophobes, such as François (or Olivier) Métra, exulted. In his poem 'Aux Insurgents, Salut!' (1778) he declared:

> Bravo, you brave insurgents! Victors in a just war, with your beliefs, you've created a new nation on this earth. You're steadfast, brave, patient, endowed with proud sincerity but, above all, you're *free*! Well, my friends, after such dazzling exploits, to carry on the good work, you must send your children to dance on the ruins of England. Let all other nations know that there's at least one which despises those pale, fair-haired tyrants who breathe in the coal-smoke and the fog on the Thames. The time must come when, with a grand gesture, you overthrow the representatives of these merchants, these so-called statesmen, these minuscule consuls in their House of Commons.

Other Frenchmen were more ambivalent. They wanted the

American rebels to win because this would be an exemplary victory for Liberty but they appreciated that the fountain-head of that same Liberty was England itself. In 1777, L'Abbé Morellet wrote to Lord Shelburne: 'I am very happy to tell you that not everyone is so anti-British, that I wish you great prosperity at the same time as I desire the Americans to win their freedom and I have to say that all we Philosophes are much of this opinion.' The following year, Gudin de la Brunellerie wrote to his friend Beaumarchais:

> The whole world looks to France for deliverance, the one nation well able to beat the English. Dedicate yourself wholeheartedly to these noble schemes. Set the oceans free for all the peoples of this world. Should you end on the winning side, show respect for England. Its liberties, its laws, its talents are not oppressed there beneath absurd despots. It is a model for every state. Europe looks upon it with admiration. The Universe needs it as a model for us all. So give it due praise. At the same time, force its over-weening citizens to give up America and surrender the sceptre of the seas.

Between the outbreak of the war and the early 1780s, England was obliged to 'surrender the sceptre of the seas'. It was mainly because the French navy enjoyed complete mastery of the American eastern sea-board that Cornwallis was forced to surrender at Yorktown in 1781. Thereafter, Britain's fortunes began to revive: Admiral Rodney's fleet shattered the French naval squadron in the Caribbean on All Saints Day, 1782, and so regained control of the Atlantic; Gibraltar continued to withstand the siege mounted by Spain since it entered the war in 1778 because of the Bourbon Family Compact; while in India the rebellion of Hayder Ali of Mysore mounted to re-establish French influence was crushed at Seringapatan. Nonetheless, England's cause in America was irretrievably lost and in the Treaty of Versailles, signed in 1783, the thirteen rebellious states were formally granted their independence.

In Europe, on both the diplomatic and commercial levels, relations between France and England seemed dramatically to improve. In his *Wealth of Nations* (1776), Adam Smith surveyed the bitter economic rivalry between the two countries and recalled that Colbert, Louis XIV's great finance minister, had imposed high duties on imported foreign goods; the practice had been continued into the 1760s: 'the French and English began mutually to oppress each other's industry by the like duties and prohibitions, of which the French, however, seem to have set the first example. The spirit of hostility which has subsisted between the two nations ever since has hitherto hindered them from being moderated on either side . . . These mutual restraints have put an end to almost all fair commerce between the two nations, and smugglers are now the principal importers, either of British goods into France, or of French goods into Great Britain.'

In 1785, it was reckoned that the quantity of claret being legally imported into the whole country was less than half the amount actually being drunk in London alone. The quantity of brandy legally imported barely amounted to a ninth part of total consumption. French cambrics were supposed officially to be subject to prohibitive import duty yet, as Pitt the Younger pointed out in one of his commercial speeches in Parliament, they were openly being worn by 'every gentleman in the House'.

As an admirer of *The Wealth of Nations* Pitt was resolved to put Adam Smith's free-trade theories into practice. He hoped to stimulate English industry by securing for it the richest market in Europe and he planned at the same time to end the contraband dealings which defrauded the Exchequer of vast revenues. His counterpart in France, Foreign Minister Vergennes, believed that freer trade would enrich French farmers. The Commercial Treaty was finally signed in 1786. The leading negotiators were Sir William Eden, later Lord Auckland, and Gérard de Rayneval, who had acted as France's representative during the American negotiations of 1783. The terms of the treaty established reciprocal freedom in trade and navigation: French wines were to be admitted to the United Kingdom on the same terms as those of Portugal and duties on French cambrics were to be no higher than those on imports from Flanders and Holland; a 12 per cent duty was to be levied on all cottons, woollens and porcelain and 10 per cent on iron, steel and copper goods. In the event, England did very much better than France. England's factories were better supplied with machinery, coal and iron and English sheep provided superior wool. France was flooded with English cottons and woollens and a major crisis resulted in France's cotton, earthenware and hardware trades. The regions that suffered most severely were Champagne, Picardy, Flanders and Normandy. In 1786, the Normandy Chamber of Commerce circulated a bitter pamphlet in protest:

There is not an article of habitual consumption with which England has not filled all the magazines of France, and particularly those of this province, and in the greatest number of these articles the English have a victorious preponderance. It is afflicting to see the manufacturers who suffer by this rivalship already diminishing successively the number of their workmen, and important fabrics yielding in another manner to the same scourge, by · English goods being substituted in the sale for French ones; receiving a preparation agreeable to the consumption, named, marked, and sold as French, to the infinite prejudice of the national industry. The Chamber is apprehensive of the immediate effect of the introduction of English cottons, whereof the perfection of the preparation, the merit of the spinning, united with their cheapness, has already procured an immense sale. Our potteries cannot escape a notable prejudice; the low price of coals in England enables the English to undersell us in these articles 25 per cent; considerable cargos have already arrived at Rouen. The 36,000 dozen pairs of stockings and caps of cotton, made in the *généralité*, are the produce of 1,200 looms. Within three months, it is calculated that, at Rouen alone, more than 100 have stopped. The merchants have made provision of English goods for more than 30,000 dozen pairs of stockings and caps have already been imported. Manchester is the Rouen of England, the immense fabrication of cotton stuffs, the industry of the manufacturers, their activity, the resource of their mechanical inventions, enable them to undersell us from 10 to 15 per cent. We cannot too often recur to the advantages which the English possess over all the woollens of France. The high price of our wool, and its inferiority in quality to that of England is such that this inequality alone ought to have induced the rejection of the Treaty of Commerce on the terms upon which it has passed. The opinion we develop upon this Treaty is general, and founded on a simple reflection; that France furnishes 24 millions of consumers against 8 millions which England offers in return.

In October, the following year, while travelling extensively through France, Arthur Young found that bitterness over the defects of the Treaty had inflamed public opinion to an alarming degree: 'The cry here for a war with England amazed me . . . It is easy enough to discover that the origin of all this violence is the commercial treaty . . . they would involve four and twenty million of people in the certain miseries of a war, rather than see the interest of those who consume fabrics preferred to the interest of those who make them.'

This was by no means the only portent. While the Commercial Treaty was being negotiated, Vergennes proceeded to build up French influence in Egypt, gaining access to the Red Sea with the long-term objective of recovering France's military and political ascendancy in

India. Of more immediate concern, in 1785, France concluded a formal defensive treaty with Holland. This posed the age-old threat to England's trade-routes, which, centuries before, had so concerned the Plantagenets and the Tudors. It was tantamount to the throwing down of a gauntlet and even had the excesses of the Revolutionaries not brought the countries into open conflict, it constituted a challenge that England could not afford to ignore.

And yet, Anglomania survived in France, even after the outbreak of the Revolution. In the new Assembly, Mirabeau, early on, made a valiant attempt to demonstrate the relevance of the English constitution to the situation in France. He was shouted down. One deputy cried out: 'We want nothing that is English. We've no need to imitate *anybody*.' Inevitably, however, with the declaration of war against England in 1793 and the accession to power of Napoleon five years later, the Anglophobes had the last word: age-old prejudices were revived and belief in the perfidy of Albion became both an article of faith and state policy.

4 : *The French Revolution*

England is our model – and our rival, our light – and our enemy.

J. P. L. de Luchet, *Les Contemporains de 1789 à 1790* (1790)

Well before the Bastille was stormed on 14 July 1789, premonitions of a forthcoming cataclysm may be found, like the flickering of a seismograph needle, in the writings of English observers. In a letter to his son in 1753, Lord Chesterfield advised him to inform himself

> minutely of, and attend particularly to, the affairs of France; they grow serious, and, in my opinion, will grow more and more so every day. The King is despised, and I do not wonder at it; but he has brought it about to be hated at the same time, which seldom happens to the same man. His Ministers are known to be as disunited as incapable; he hesitates between the Church and the Parliaments, like the ass in the fable, that starved between two hampers of hay; too much in love with his mistress to part with her, and too much afraid for his soul to enjoy her; jealous of the Parliaments who would support his authority; and a devoted bigot to the Church that would destroy it.
>
> The people are poor, consequently discontented; those who have religion are divided in their notions of it; which is saying that they hate one another. The Clergy never do forgive; much less will they forgive the Parliament; the Parliament never will forgive them. The Army must, without doubt, take, in their own minds at least, different parts in all these disputes, which, upon occasion, would break out. Armies, though always the supporters and tools of absolute power for the time being, are always the destroyers of it too; by frequently changing the hands in which they think proper to lodge it . . . The French nation reasons freely, which they never did before, upon matters of religion and government, and begin to be *spregiudicati*; the offers do so too; in short, all the symptoms which I have

ever met with in history, previous to great changes and revolutions in Government, now exist, and daily increase in France. I am glad of it; the rest of Europe will be the quieter, and have time to recover.

Twelve years later, in the journal of his journey to Paris in 1765, the Reverend William Cole observed: 'The present situation of France has much the appearance of being soon the theatre of civil war.' On 2 September 1788, John Charles Villiers, later Earl of Clarendon, described in a letter the all-too-evident signs of mounting popular French discontent:

> So much perturbation and heat will not easily subside: and it will be found a matter extremely difficult, if practicable, to reduce their minds, as before, to the yoke of subjection. In fact, the whole kingdom seems ripe for a *Revolution*; every rank is dissatisfied; they despise their King; they detest their Queen; the public walks are now filled in every corner with sets of politicians, and every one seems eager to have some share in the business; in private companies the chief topic is now politics, and they are as much interested, and as much agitated, as in the most troublesome times in England. That fear, which once tied their tongues, and that reverence which restrained their thoughts, is now no more; and there they are not afraid of spies, they can condemn their government, and abuse their King, with as much freedom and as little ceremony as Englishmen; though with fifty times the reason. They begin now to see that so large and rich a territory was never made for the service and the pleasure of one man; and they learn from their increased acquaintance with our country, how much the happiness, the prosperity, and the refinement of a people depend upon well-regulated laws.
>
> If the assembly of the States General takes place, according to the promise of the King, in the ensuing spring, there is little doubt but that some revolution in the government will be effected. A constitution, probably somewhat similar to that of England, will be adopted, and limitations affixed to the power of the Crown.

A fortnight later, on 17 September 1788, Arthur Young noted in his journal:

> Dined today with a party whose conversation was entirely political . . . One opinion pervaded the whole company, that they are on the eve of some great revolution in the government: that everything points to it; the confusion in the finances great; with a *deficit* impossible to provide for without the states-general of the kingdom, yet no ideas formed of what would be the consequence of their meeting: no minister existing, or to be

looked to in or out of power, with such decisive talents as to promise any
other remedy than palliative ones: a prince on the throne, with excellent
dispositions, but without the resources of a mind that could govern in such a
moment without ministers: a court buried in pleasure and dissipation; and
adding to the distress instead of endeavouring to be placed in a more
independent situation: a great ferment amongst all ranks of men, who are
eager for some change, without knowing what to look to or to hope for:
and a strong leaven of liberty, increasing every hour since the American
revolution, altogether form a combination of circumstances that promise
e'er long to ferment into motion if some master hand of very superior
talents and inflexible courage is not found at the helm to guide events,
instead of being driven by them. It is very remarkable that such
conversation never occurs but a bankruptcy is a topic: the curious question
on which is, *would a bankruptcy occasion a civil war and a total overthrow of the
government?* The answers that I have received to this question appear to be
just: such a measure conducted by a man of abilities, vigour, and firmness
would certainly not occasion either one or the other. But the same measure,
attempted by a man of a different character, might possibly do both. All
agree that the states of the kingdom cannot assemble without more liberty
being the consequence; but I meet with so few men that have any just ideas
of freedom that I question much the species of this new liberty that is to
arise. They know not how to value the privileges of THE PEOPLE: as to
the nobility and the clergy, if a revolution added anything to their scale I
think it would do more mischief than good.

At the outset, very few English voices expressed misgivings after the
storming of the Bastille. One such was that of George Selwyn who
commented in a letter written in August 1789:

> France is still in a most lawless and abominable confusion . . . It is such a
> conflagration, that the very sparks which arise from it may chance to light
> upon our own heads . . . To begin a reform, and a new constitution, by a
> *renversement de l'Etat*, is what I do not conceive, or approve . . . We are I am
> sure at the beginning only of this *roman*, instead of seeing the new
> constitution so quietly established by the first of September, as I have been
> confidently assured that it will be.

He was very much in the minority. The generality of English
observers were both enthusiastic and optimistic. The mightiest king in
the most absolute of all European monarchies had been humbled by his
subjects; the privileges of the aristocracy were denounced; the Church
was placed under secular control; a Representative Assembly was
charged with drawing up a new Constitution and the Rights of Man

were proclaimed. At the beginning of the century, the Huguenot publicist I. de Larrey had hailed the overthrow of the Stuarts, and wondered: 'Is not this auspicious revolution in England a prelude to our own, a portent to give us hope and a pathway to give us guidance?' As the century moved towards its end, democratic forces seemed everywhere on the move: there had been successful revolution in America; there was agitation for political reform in England; unrest in Ireland; an anti-Orangist rebellion in the United Provinces; and it did not seem without significance to demagogues in both London and Paris that 1788 marked the centenary of that Glorious Revolution in England itself.

Not surprisingly, among the most eloquent of England's pro-revolutionary proponents were its poets. Coleridge's 'Ode on the Destruction of the Bastille' declared that the event provided an inspiring model for others to follow:

> Shall France alone a Despot spurn?
>   Shall she alone, O Freedom, boast they care?
> Lo, round thy standard Belgia's heroes burn.
>   Tho' Power's blood-stained streamers fire the air;
>   And wider yet thy influence spread,
>   Nor e'er recline thy weary head,
>   Till every land from pole to pole
>   Shall boast one independent soul!
> And still, as erst, let favour'd Britain be
> First ever of the first and freest of the free!

William Blake flaunted his Republican allegiance by wearing the red cap of the Jacobins as he walked through the streets of London but the poems he wrote about contemporary events seem now rather less memorable: a long, windy portentous work called *The French Revolution*, peopled with allegorical figures plunged in sepulchral gloom; and the somewhat sprightlier piece beginning:

> 'Let the brothels of Paris be opened,
> With many an alluring dance,
> To awaken the physicians through the city,'
> Said the beautiful Queen of France.

Robert Southey, later to become Poet Laureate, recalled: 'Few persons but those who have lived through it can conceive or comprehend what the memory of the French Revolution was, nor what a visionary world seemed to open upon those who were just entering it. Old things seemed passing away, and nothing was dreamt of but the regeneration of the human race.'

Nowhere is that mood of high excitement more beautifully caught than in Wordsworth's great poem *The Prelude*; looking back to that time in his youth when, exactly a year after the fall of the Bastille, he set out with his university friend Robert Jones on a long trip through France, motivated both by radical enthusiasm and by a young man's appetitie for adventure:

> . . . 'twas a time when Europe was rejoiced,
> France standing on the top of golden hours,
> And human nature seeming born again.
> Bound, as I said, to the Alps, it was our lot
> To land at Calais on the very eve
> Of that great federal Day; and there we saw,
> In a mean City, and among a few,
> How bright a face is worn when joy of one
> Is joy of tens of millions. Southward thence
> We took our way direct through Hamlets, Towns,
> Gaudy with reliques of that Festival,
> Flowers left to wither on triumphal Arcs,
> And window-Garlands . . .
>
> . . . The Supper done,
> With flowing cups elate and happy thoughts,
> We rose at signal given, and formed a ring,
> And hand in hand danced round and round the Board;
> All hearts were open, every tongue was loud
> With amity and glee. We bore a name
> Honoured in France, the name of Englishmen . . .

(from Book VI)

In England, it was not merely the idealistic young who saw 'human nature seeming born again'. The leading radicals of the day were confident that what had happened in France in the summer of 1789 was the prelude to much-needed electoral reform in England. They were all members of the Revolution Society, which had been founded in 1788 to celebrate the centenary of England's own Glorious – but in their view incomplete – Revolution. The most prominent of them were religious Dissenters, who had been denied the access to high office enjoyed by Anglicans. These included Dr Joseph Priestley, distinguished for his experiments with electricity and the chemical properties of gases, who ran an Academy in Hackney, where one of his pupils was William Hazlitt, himself the son of a Unitarian Minister; and William Godwin, educated at another dissenting Academy in Hoxton, who married Mary Wollstonecraft, the author of *A Vindication of the Rights of Women* (1792).

On 4 November 1789, the Revolution Society was due to meet for dinner at the London Tavern. The pre-prandial sermon was preached by the leading Unitarian Dr Richard Price, a friend of John Adams and Thomas Jefferson. Taking as his text Verses 6 and 7 of the 122nd Psalm, Price delivered 'A Discourse on the Love of our Country'. He argued that freedom of conscience was the prerogative of all Englishmen, that Englishmen had the right to resist abuse of power and that they also had the right to choose their own rulers. He concluded with a ringing peroration:

What an eventful period is this! I am thankful that I have lived to it; and I could almost say, *Lord now lettest thou thy servant depart in peace, for mine eyes have seen thy salvation.* I have lived to see a diffusion of knowledge, which has undermined superstition and error – I have lived to see the rights of men better understood than ever; and nations panting for liberty, which seemed to have lost the idea of it. – I have lived to see THIRTY MILLIONS of people, indignant and resolute, spurning at slavery, and demanding liberty with an irresistible voice; their king led in triumph, and an arbitrary monarch surrendering himself to his subjects. – After sharing in the benefits of one Revolution, I have been spared to be a witness to two other Revolutions, both glorious. – And now methinks, I see the ardour for liberty catching and spreading; a general amendment beginning in human affairs; the dominion of kings changed for the dominion of laws, and the dominion of priests giving way to the dominion of reason and conscience.

Be encouraged all ye friends of freedom, and writers in its defence! The times are auspicious. Your labours have not been in vain Behold kingdoms, admonished by you, starting from sleep, breaking their fetters, and claiming justice from their oppressors! Behold, the light you have struck out, after setting AMERICA free, reflected to FRANCE, and there kindled into a blaze that lays despotism in ashes, and warms and illuminates EUROPE!

Tremble all ye oppressors of the world! Take warning all ye supporters of slavish governments, and slavish hierarchies! Call no more (absurdly and

wickedly) REFORMATION, innovation. You cannot now hold the
world in darkness. Struggle no longer against increasing light and liberality.
Restore to mankind their rights; and consent to the correction of abuses,
before they and you are destroyed together.

At the end of the sermon, the Revolution Society adjourned to the
London Tavern as planned. A number of toasts were proposed, one, by
Dr Price, to 'The Parliament of Britain – may it become a National
Assembly'. He later requested that a congratulatory Address be sent to
the National Assembly in Paris, welcoming the Revolution and 'the
prospect it gives, to the two first Kingdoms in the World, of a common
participation in the blessings of Civil and Religious Liberty'. On 25
November 1789, this Address was read out in the French National
Assembly by Louis-Alexandre, Duc de la Roche-Guyon et de la
Rochefoucauld, the leading liberal French aristocrat, born in 1743 and
murdered at Gisors in 1792. The effect of his recital was described in his
letter of appreciation to the Revolution Society, which was read out at
its dinner in London on 16 December: 'Your message was greatly
appreciated. It inspired a series of Anglo–Gallic constitutional toasts
which seem to announce that sooner or later, perfect harmony will
reign between our two nations. In anticipation of that happy moment,
the seed was soaked in champagne, Burgundy and floods of claret.'

Not all observers from England were quite so starry-eyed. By far the
most eloquent and influential of these was the outstanding orator
among the Whigs, Edmund Burke. He had been an outspoken
defender of the Americans in their War of Independence and might
have been expected to have championed the French Revolutionary
cause. However, on reading a copy of Price's sermon, which would
seem to have been in January 1790, he at once set about writing his
Reflections on the Revolution in France, which has been described by
Professor Alfred Cobban as 'the greatest and most influential political
pamphlet ever written and a classical contribution to the political theory
of western civilisation'. One explanation advanced for Burke's volte-
face has been that he had little or no direct contact with the French scene
and that his principal informants were close friends from the Auxerre
region, ill-informed about events in Paris, who fled from France in 1789
and ever afterwards campaigned tirelessly for the return of the *ancien
régime* and all its works. It is alleged that they fed Burke with exaggerated
stories of atrocities well before these had even been committed, at a time

when, on the evidence of Arthur Young and others, the French royal family was free to walk under guard in the Tuileries gardens, and while, for many months still, English people were allowed to circulate throughout France without let or hindrance. Another explanation is that Burke was conscious that his own political fortunes were on the wane, that he was eager to seize back the intellectual domination of the Whig party from such rivals as Charles James Fox and Sheridan and that his primary concern was not so much the danger of upheaval in France as the threat of radical changes in England.

Be that as it may, his *Reflections*, having begun as an attack on the subversive pronouncements of Price, developed into an intellectual critique of the Revolution and an impassioned defence of the traditional British social and political system. For Burke, Jacobinism was both naïvely optimistic in setting out to eradicate all prejudices from the human mind, and distinctly sinister in entrusting authority to a small group of men who claimed the insight and the need to enlighten the people. He argued that this, of necessity, meant destroying the bonds and conventions that, in its wisdom, society had gradually evolved for the protection of the individual. He condemned the concept of inherent natural rights as a pernicious illusion. The *real* rights of the people, he argued, were specific entitlements to particular advantages related to the individual's social positon (not all members of the community have equal rights to the same things) and these rights, inherited from the past, are embodied in constitutional precedent. To destroy the fabric of society and refashion it anew was, in his view, to invite chaos and disaster. Burke wrote with both head and heart, deploying all the rhetorical skills of an accomplished orator. The technique is seen to particular advantage in the celebrated evocation of Marie-Antoinette:

It is now 16 or 17 years since I saw the Queen of France, then the Dauphine at Versailles; and surely never lighted on this orb, which she hardly seemed to touch, a more delightful vision. I saw her just above the horizon, decorating and cheering the elevated sphere she just began to move in, glittering like the morning star, full of life and splendour and joy. Oh! What a revolution! And what a heart I must have to contemplate without emotion that elevation and that fall! Little did I dream that, when she added the titles of veneration to those of enthusiastic and respectful love, she would ever be obliged to carry the sharp antidote against disgrace concealed in that bosom. Little did I dream that I should live to see such disasters fallen upon her in a nation of gallant men, a nation of men of honour and cavaliers. I thought ten thousand swords would have leapt from their scabbards to avenge even a look which threatened her with insult. But the age of chivalry is gone. That of sophisters, economists and calculators has succeeded, and the glory of Europe is extinguished for ever.

In just such plangent tones, Ronsard had called upon his young fellow-countrymen to ride to the rescue of the hapless Mary, Queen of Scots – and with the same lack of success.

Yet while Burke's *Reflections* caused little blood to flow, they did generate the liveliest discussion throughout Europe. They were rapidly translated into French and German and amongst English readers provoked impassioned ideological debate. Horace Walpole wrote to his friend Jermingham on 10 November 1790: 'It is the wisest book I ever read in my life and after that the wittiest. It ought to be translated into all languages and commented and preached in all churches in portions'; while on 20 December 1790, he declared to Mary Berry: 'It is one of the finest compositions in print. There is reason, logic, wit, truth, eloquence and enthusiasm in the brightest colours.' Edward Gibbon wrote in a letter shortly after: 'Burke's book is the most admirable medicine against the French disease. I admire his eloquence and his politics, I adore his chivalry, and I can forgive his superstition.'

Predictably, the most strident opposition to Burke came from members of the Revolution Society, whose grandiloquent support of the new order in France had provoked the *Reflections* in the first place. 'Citizen' Stanhope, the third Earl of that name, who had erased the armorial bearings from his carriages as so much 'damned aristocratical nonsense', wrote to him soon after the book was published:

All warrantable political Power is derived, either mediately, or immedi-ately, from the *People*. All political Authority is a TRUST; and every wilful act of abuse of that Authority, is a *Breach of Trust*. The natural RIGHTS of the PEOPLE are sacred and *inalienable*. – *Rights*, of which Despotism may *rob* them for a time, but, which it is not in the Power of Tyranny to *annihilate*. We, therefore, commemorate with rapture, the glorious Aera, when the *Army of England* nobly refused to overturn our *free* Constitution and had the virtue to join the Standard of King William. And we exult (with Mr Fox) that the *Army of France*, last year, followed that glorious example, by refusing to become the Instruments of the servitude of their Fellow Citizens . . .

The Revolution in France is one of the most striking and memorable

The Bayeux Tapestry: An eleventh- or twelfth-century depiction of
the death of Harold at Hastings. Traditionally, Harold has been identified
as the figure with an arrow piercing his eye.

The Battle of Agincourt:
A mid fifteenth-century illustration stressing the English victory.

Calais Gate by William Hogarth, March 1748. While sketching in Calais
in 1748, Hogarth was arrested as a spy; this is how he retaliated.
The large sirloin of English roast beef arouses the envy
of the French onlookers, whose diet is more meagre.

THE CONTRAST
1793
BRITISH LIBERTY
FRENCH LIBERTY

RELIGION, MORALITY, LOYALTY, OBEDIENCE to the LAWS, INDEPENDANCE, PERSONAL SECURITY JUSTICE, INHERITANC. PROTECTION of PROPERTY INDUSTRY, NATIONAL PROSPERITY HAPPINESS.	ATHEISM, PERJURY REBELLION, TREASON, ANARCHY, MURDER EQUALITY, MADNESS, CRUELTY, INJUSTICE, TREACHERY, INGRATITUDE, IDLENESS, FAMINE, NATIONAL & PRIVATE RUIN, MISERY.

WHICH IS BEST?

Price 3 Plain Col....

Rowlandson

The Contrast – Which is Best?: poster by Thomas Rowlandson, 1793

The English Government by Jacques-Louis David, 1793–4:
Commissioned by the Committee of Public Safety.
The English government is represented by a flayed devil,
whose posterior, in the form of George III,
discharges taxes over terrified citizens.

The Contrast, or Things as they Are by James Gillray,
November 1796: France pays the price for
ignoring the lessons of Roman history.

*Promised Horrors of the French Invasion, or Forcible Reasons
for Negotiating a Regicide Peace* by James Gillray, October 1796:
Whigs cheer the arrival of the French Republican army from the balcony
of Brooks's. Across St James's Tories are harried out of their gaming-club,
White's. In the foreground Charles James Fox whips William Pitt.

Fear of Invasion, 1803: The French divert the English forces by air
and sea while advancing in secret through their Channel tunnel.

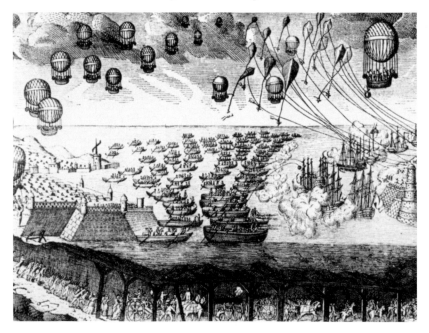

The First Kiss this Ten Years! by James Gillray, January 1803: Citizen François embraces Britannia after the Peace of Amiens.

The Plumb-pudding in Danger by James Gillray, February 1805: Following Napoleon's peace overture to George III on 2 January 1805, Pitt and Napoleon are shown carving out their respective spheres of influence.

Voilà les Anglais! Quelles Drolles [sic], July 1825: The plain clothes of the English visitors give rise to incredulity among elaborately dressed Parisians.

Les Anglais en Bourgogne by François Janet, 1814: Nineteenth-century English lager louts in Burgundy unable to hold their drink.

A *Duel to the Death* by John Tenniel, July 1870: France, in the person of Napoleon III, is portrayed as the aggressor in the Franco-Prusian war, intent on fighting out what the original caption terms 'an old family quarrel'.

A *French Lesson* by John Tenniel, April 1871: Britannia asks a French Communard, 'Is *that* the sort of thing you want, you little idiot?'

A Victorian view of French culture: The works of Zola were the chief target of the Anti-Naturalist crusaders.

SANCTA SIMPLICITAS!

Mamma. "DON'T STAND IDLING THERE, TOMMY! WHY DON'T YOU READ *FRENCH* SOMETIMES! LOOK AT DEAR PAPA, HE HASN'T MUCH TIME FOR READING; BUT WHENEVER HE'S GOT A SPARE MOMENT OR TWO, HE TAKES A FRENCH BOOK OUT OF HIS POCKET AND READS IT—*JUST TO KEEP UP HIS FRENCH, YOU KNOW!*" [*Dear Papa is much tickled, but keeps his amusement to himself.*

An American View of the Channel Tunnel Scare by Graetz,
in *Puck*, 1886: General Wolseley and the terrified British lion flee
from the ferocious French cock emerging from the Tunnel.

Vanqueur . . . Enfin! by
Caran d'Ache: a French
right-wing comment
from *Le Rire* on the
end of the Boer War.

Britannia by Jean Vebrun,
with Edward VII
as her rump.

pages in History; and no political event was, perhaps, ever more pregnant with good consequences to future ages. That great and glorious Revolution will, in time, disseminate throughout Europe, liberality of sentiment, and a just regard for Political, Civil and Religious Liberty. It will, in all probability, make the World, for Centuries, prosperous, free, and happy, when the Author of the *Sublime and Beautiful* shall be no more, and the WHIG Principles from St Omers be forgotten.

Another Radical supporter, Sir Brooke Boothby, also wrote to him:

In your view of France you seem to have been so awestruck with the magnificence of the court, and so enamoured of the rising beauties of the dauphiness, that you had no attention left to bestow upon the people. If at your return from Versailles you had looked into the Morgue, where the bodies of those unfortunate wretches whose miseries had drawn them to seek the last refuge from despair were daily exposed in frightful numbers; if you had followed the peasant or the artisan to his scanty meal on a morsel of black unsavoury bread, such spectacles would not have been lost upon a heart like yours. They would surely have abated something of your partial regard for the destructive splendour of a court, or the redundant and invidious wealth of a lazy and luxurious priesthood.

On 28 May 1791, the Constitutional Society proposed and adopted the following resolution:

The Society for Constitutional Information, vigilant to prevent the dangerous Influence of Publications detrimental to Civil and Religious Liberty, think it may be useful to the Public to express their disapprobation of the indecent virulence with which Mr Edmund Burke has, with deplorable inconsistency to his former professions, censured the illustrious Patriots of a neighbouring Kingdom, for delivering more than twenty-five millions of their Fellow Creatures from a state of abject oppression, and civil bondage.

But the most famous of all the critics of the *Reflections*, as redoubtable and as eloquent in his own fashion as Burke, was Tom Paine. Son of a Quaker staymaker, he went to America on the advice of Benjamin Franklin where, between 1776 and 1783, he published a series of pamphlets encouraging American independence and resistance to England; he also wrote against slavery and for the emancipation of women. In 1791, he published the first part of *The Rights of Man* in which he mounted a spirited counter-attack on Burke's dismissal of the

French Revolution and sought to demolish his argument, point by point:

Not one glance of compassion, not one commiserating reflection, that I can find throughout his book, has he bestowed on those who lingered out the most wretched of lives, a life without hope, in the most miserable of prisons. It is painful to behold a man employing his talents to corrupt himself. Nature has been kinder to Mr Burke than he is to her. He is not affected by the reality of distress touching upon his heart, but by the showy resemblance of it striking his imagination. He pities the plumage, but forgets the dying bird. Accustomed to kiss the aristocratical hand that hath purloined him from himself, he degenerates into a composition of art, and the genuine soul of nature forsakes him. His hero or his heroine must be a tragedy-victim expiring in show, and not the real prisoner of misery, sliding into death in the silence of a dungeon . . .

Among the incivilities by which nations or individuals provoke and irritate each other, Mr Burke's pamphlet on the French Revolution is an extraordinary instance. Neither the people of France, nor the National Assembly, were troubling themselves about the affairs of England, or the English Parliament; and that Mr Burke should commence an unprovoked attack upon them, both in parliament and in public, is a conduct that cannot be pardoned on the score of manners, nor justified on that of policy.

There is scarcely an epithet of abuse to be found in the English language, with which Mr Burke has not loaded the French nation and the National Assembly. Everything which rancour, prejudice, ignorance or knowledge could suggest, is poured forth in the copious fury of near four hundred pages. In the strain and on the plan Mr Burke was writing, he might have written on to as many thousands. When the tongue or the pen is let loose in a phrenzy of passion, it is the man, and not the subject, that becomes exhausted.

Hitherto Mr Burke has been mistaken and disappointed in the opinions he had formed of the affairs of France; but such is the ingenuity of his hope, or the malignancy of his despair, that it furnishes him with new pretences to go on. There was a time when it was impossible to make Mr Burke believe there would be any Revolution in France. His opinion then was, that the French had neither spirit to undertake it nor fortitude to support it; and now that there is one, he seeks an escape by condemning it . . .

The enemies of the French revolution are, at present, in dismay – for the King has signed the constitution, and they begin seriously to fear that the liberties of France will be firmly established – Their great hope, however, is in the confederacy of 'the kings of the earth' against it, particularly that of the Northern powers; which, if they do unite, will be the first instance, in the annals of mankind, of an union of tyrants to crush a people who profess to have no other object than to obtain, for themselves, that liberty which is the undoubted birth-right of all mankind – I do not, my friend, fear that all 'these tyrannous breathings of the North' will destroy the lovely tree that has thus taken vigorous root in the finest country of the world, though it may awhile check its growth, and blight its produce; but I lament, that in despite of the pacific intentions of the French towards their neighbours, its root must be manured with blood – I lament still more, the disposition which too many Englishmen shew to join in this unjust and infamous *crusade* against the holy standard of freedom; and I blush for my country!

In the year that followed the storming of the Bastille, while English commentators on the event loosed off their shafts at one another, diplomatic relations between France and England remained amicable. On 25 August 1790, in a report to the Diplomatic committee on France's foreign treaties, Mirabeau stated:

We do not consider any people as our enemy – and certainly not the country which an insidious policy has up till now represented it as our rival. Though it's a country in whose tracks we have followed, which has provided the great examples which inspired us to win our liberty and which is so close to us for all sorts of reasons. A new spirit of competition, the need to vie with it in passing good laws, will replace the old rivalry which was inspired by politics and ambition. No, do not believe that a free and enlightened people wishes to take advantage of our temporary difficulties to ignobly renew the evils of war, to attack our newfound liberty, to stifle the happy development of the principles with which it inspired us. It would be sacrilege for them to try. It would be sacrilege for us to believe them capable of trying. Doesn't the same political philosophy today unite France and Great Britain? Don't we both consider despotism and its allies as our common enemy? Won't the English not be more likely to remain free if they have the free French as their allies? However, as we pay homage to the philosophy of these people, our elder brother in liberty, let us nonetheless listen to the voice of prudence.

In similar spirit, Pitt told the House of Commons also in 1790:

The present convulsions of France must sooner or later terminate in general harmony and regular order ... Whenever the situation of France shall become restored, it will prove freedom rightly understood, freedom resulted from good order and good government; and thus circumstanced, France will stand forward as one of the most brilliant Powers in Europe; she will enjoy just that kind of liberty which I venerate, and the valuable existence of which it is my duty, as an Englishman, peculiarly to cherish; nor can I, under this predicament, regard with envious eyes, an approximation in neighbouring States to those sentiments which are the characteristic features of the British people.

Pitt's euphoric vision did not take long to fade. On 1 February 1791, in a speech to the Commons, he declared: 'France has trampled under foot all laws, human and divine. She has at last avowed the most insatiable ambition and greatest contempt for the law of nations, which all independent States have hitherto professed most religiously to observe; and unless she is stopped in her career, all Europe must soon learn their ideas of justice, law of nations, models of government, and principles of government from the mouth of the French cannon.' This expressed the age-old English fear of French militarism rather than revulsion at the Revolutionaries' excesses. These were to come slightly later. Between 21 and 24 June that year, the *biens nationaux*, lands belonging to Crown, Church and *émigrés*, were confiscated by the State. At the same time, with the repudiation of the Concordat of 1516, the Church was freed from Papal control and subordinated to the government. On 21 June, Louis XVI and Marie-Antoinette, attempting to flee the country, were arrested at Varennes, in the Argonne, and brought back to Paris. The following day, the *Assemblée* passed a decree suspending the King from his functions. On 15 July, the *Assemblée* refused the Republicans, still in the minority, to put the King on trial, and used armed force to stamp out opposition.

Meanwhile, in England, conflict had bitterly intensified between those who believed, with Paine, that the proclamation of Liberty, Equality and Fraternity heralded an age of reason, prosperity and peace for all, and those who believed, with Burke, that the Revolution would inevitably mean social anarchy in which no man's life or property would be secure. Ironically, the worst manifestations of social disorder came from Burke's supporters. In July 1791, a 'Church and King' mob in Birmingham destroyed the house of Dr Priestley after he had announced his intention of celebrating the second anniversary of the attack on the Bastille.

While suspicion and resentment continued to intensify between governments, private English individuals were still free to go unmolested about their business in France till the end of 1791. On 1 December, the wife of Henry Swinburne, who had served as a page to Marie-Antoinette, wrote in a letter:

When I had obtained my passports for myself and maid, I asked to take leave of the queen, and the interview was granted, which is a great favour, for she sees no one. She received me graciously, even kindly, and the manner in which she spoke of my son was calculated to set my heart at ease concerning him. She wished me every happiness. '*Vous allez dans votre heureuse famille,*' said she, '*dans un pays tranquille, où la calomnie et la cruauté ne vous poursuivront pas! Je dois vous porter envie.*' I ventured a few words of consolation, hinting that times were now improving, and that her popularity and happiness would be restored. She shook her head. We were alone. I know not how I was worked up to it, or had courage to make the proposal; but I did so – that if she thought herself in danger, my services were at her command, and that she could come with me to England in the disguise of my maid, whom I could easily dispose of, by sending her under some pretext to her friends at St Germain. She thanked me, and smiled faintly, but said nothing would induce her to leave her family. She added that she had refused other offers of the same sort. 'Besides,' and she looked round, '*si je voulais, cela ne se pourroit pas; il y a trop d'espions.*' I took leave of her with regret and affection.

On 15 December 1791, William Beckford, the author of *Vathek* (1786), wrote to Sir W. Hamilton:

A thick cloud hangs over Paris at this moment, fraught with some confounded crackers. I expect an eruption every minute. The assembly know not which way to turn themselves, and publick credit is at the lowest ebb . . . Notwithstanding the confusion of the moment, all my baggage, plate, books, horses, carriages, etc. have been admitted duty free, and I must own nothing can exceed the civilities I meet with from the nation; but there is no living in comfort with a sword suspended over one's head by a thread. I take the dear nation itself to be in that disagreeable predicament . . . I have a short stumpy pen, and write more from the fist than the fingers, and make sad blots; no wonder! Two or three Deputies are chattering at one end of my room, and swilling tea, and observing that, since the introduction of this English beverage, *on ne pense plus librement*, etc., etc., a deel of French stuff.

In the spring of 1792, William Cobbett was equally well received but, like Beckford, he was all too aware of the gathering storm:

I arrived in France in March 1792, and continued there till the beginning of September following, the six happiest months of my life. I should be the most ungrateful monster that ever existed, were I to speak ill of the French people in general. I went to that country full of all those prejudices that Englishmen suck in with their mother's milk against the French, and against their religion: a few weeks convinced me that I had been deceived with respect to both. I met everywhere with civility, and even hospitality, in a degree that I had never been accustomed to. I found the people among whom I lived, excepting those who were already blasted with the principles of the accursed revolution, honest, pious, and kind to excess. People may say what they please about the misery of the French peasantry under the old government: I have conversed with thousands of them, not ten among whom did not regret the change . . . I did intend to stay in France till the spring of 1793, as well to perfect myself in the language, as to pass the winter at Paris. But I perceived the storm gathering; I saw that a war with England was inevitable; and it was not difficult to see what would be the fate of Englishmen in that country, where the rulers had laid aside even the appearance of justice and mercy.

On the larger European stage, events rumbled inexorably towards disaster. Marie-Antoinette's brother, King Leopold of Austria, and Frederick William II of Prussia declared their readiness to send in an army to rescue the French royal family. On 20 April, the *Assemblée législative* anticipated attack by declaring war on Austria. Some of the dwindling band of English Radicals still remained loyal to the Revolutionary cause. Samuel Romilly, for example, wrote to a French friend on 15 May 1792:

My opinion, however, is not in the least altered with respect to your Revolution. Even the conduct of the present Assembly has not been able to shake my conviction that it is the most glorious event, and the happiest for mankind, that has ever taken place since human affairs have been recorded; and though I lament sincerely the miseries which have happened, and which still are to happen, I console myself with thinking that the evils of the revolution are transitory, and all the good of it is permanent.

He was right to anticipate that further miseries were still to happen. With pressure massing from the foreign armies and the *émigré* forces led by French royal princes, the *Assemblée* declared '*la patrie en danger*', a decree that the King refused to sanction. On 10 August, the monarchy fell and the citizens' defence army attacked and took the royal palace of the Tuileries. Prominent in its ranks was a detachment of *fédérés*, who had marched from Marseilles singing the anthem composed for them on 25 April 1792 by the minor poet, Claude-Joseph Rouget de Lisle. His marching song became the battle hymn of the French republic and remains the French national anthem. Inspiring though it has always sounded, the Revolutionary armies went on suffering defeats, at the time attributed to Royalist treason. Between 2 and 5 September, the Paris mob, inflamed by Marat's rhetoric, invaded the prisons and slaughtered over 1,200 prisoners.

English public opinion was outraged. Horace Walpole spoke for the majority of his countrymen when he wrote, on 18 August 1792, to Lady Ossory: 'There is neither substantive nor epithet that can express the horror they have excited! Brutal insolence, bloody ferocity, savage barbarity, malicious injustice, can no longer be used but of some civilized country, where there is still some appearance of government . . . I have lived too long! I confess I did not conceive how abominable human nature could be on so extensive a scale as from Paris to Versailles.'

To the same correspondent, he wrote a month later of the September massacres: 'A whole nation of monsters is burst forth. This *second* massacre of Paris has exhibited horrors that even surpass the former.'

Even so, there were still Englishmen prepared to stand up and express their whole-hearted support for the Republican cause. The most conspicuous of these was Tom Paine. After the appearance earlier in 1792 of the second part of *The Rights of Man*, he was warned by William Blake that the English authorities were about to arrest him. He promptly crossed the Channel, where he was adopted by the National Assembly as a Citizen of France and was elected as a member of the National Convention, which on 21 September 1792 succeeded the *Assemblée*. On 25 September, Paine addressed an Open Letter to the People of France:

FELLOW CITIZENS!

I receive, with affectionate gratitude, the honour which the late National Assembly has conferred on me, by adopting me a Citizen of France, and the additional honour of being elected by my fellow citizens a Member of the National Convention. Happily impressed, as I am, by those testimonies of respect shown towards me as an individual, I feel my felicity increased by seeing the barrier broken down that divided patriotism by spots of earth, and limited citizenship to the soil, like vegetation.

I came not to enjoy repose. Convinced that the cause of France is the cause of all mankind, and that liberty cannot be purchased by a wish, I gladly share with you the dangers and honours necessary to success.

I am well aware that the moment of any great change, such as that accomplished on the 10th August, is unavoidably the moment of terror and confusion . . . But let us now look calmly and confidentially forward, and success is certain. It is no longer the paltry cause of Kings, or of this or of that individual, that calls France and her armies into action. It is the great cause of all. It is the establishment of a new era, that shall blot despotism from the earth, and fix, on the lasting principles of peace and citizenship, the great Republic of Man . . .

The scene that now opens itself to France extends far beyond the boundaries of her own dominions. Every nation is becoming her colleague, and every court is become her enemy. It is now the cause of all nations, against the cause of all courts . . .

In entering on this great scene, greater than any nation has yet been called to act in, let us say to the agitated mind, be calm. Let us punish by instructing, rather than by revenge. Let us begin the new era by a greatness of friendship, and hail the approach of union and success.

Paine's hopes of lasting peace were shortly to be dashed. On 20 September, the Revolutionary Army of the north inflicted a crushing defeat on the Prussian and *émigré* armies at Valmy, in the Argonne, and, fired by this success, the more extreme of the Revolutionaries threatened to export their doctrines beyond France's boundaries by force of arms. Danton declared in a speech to the French Convention: 'Let us conquer Holland. Let us revive the republican party in England. Let us set France on the march and we will go gloriously to posterity.'

On 19 November 1792, the Convention passed its Edict of Fraternity, offering the protection of France to any people that rose against its government. On 15 December, it passed a further decree to the effect that wherever the French armies should come, the existing regime would be abolished, the property of the government and its adherents would be confiscated and a new government instated on the French model. England had remained resolutely neutral all this while but once France invaded the Netherlands in November 1792 and took command of the mouth of the Scheldt, England's all-important gateway to its European markets, the outbreak of war could not be for long delayed. On 31 December 1792, anticipating military intervention by England, Gaspard Monge issued the following decree:

The King and his Parliament mean to make war against us! Will the English republicans suffer it? Already these free men show their discontent and the repugnance which they have to bear arms against their brothers, the French. Well! we will fly to their succour; we will make a descent on the island; we will lodge their fifty thousand caps of liberty; we will plant there the sacred tree, and we will stretch out our arms to our republican brethren; *the tyranny of their government will soon be destroyed.*

Inevitably, over the preceding months, public opinion in England had, in its turn, hardened dramatically. November 1792 saw the inauguration of the Association for the Preservation of Liberty and Property against Republicans and Levellers. In late 1792 and early 1793, effigies of Tom Paine were publicly burned in dozens of English towns. The xenophobia of the populace was inflamed by all manner of cheap tracts, a typical example being 'One Pennyworth More' (1792) in which the author, one William Jones, described how the French:

> picked two famous Englishmen, *Thomas Paine* and the *Birmingham Doctor* [Priestley] to assist them in the work of teaching *John Bull* to eat *Revolutionary Soup*, dished up with human flesh and French Pot-Herbs. I love liberty *with Law* such as we have in England, as well as anybody does: but Liberty without Law, which makes men eat one another, can only come from the devil who would eat us all.

In another tract, *The Life and Adventures of Job Nott, Bucklemaker of Birmingham*, issued on 1 January 1793, the author, Theodore Price, affecting to speak for the English working-man, declared: 'I refuse to learn French. I want nothing to do with such a nation while ruled by such blood minded barbarians, why they are worse than the Antipoads that kill'd and chop'd our brave sailor Captain Cook to pieces.'

In Paris, events moved inexorably to a bloody climax. On 21 January 1793, after a trial that had begun on 11 December 1792, Louis XVI was executed. To his credit, Tom Paine spoke out against this action. He was imprisoned for a year and narrowly escaped being guillotined himself. Ten days after the execution of the King, Danton declared to the French convention: 'Let us fling down to the Kings the head of a King as a gage of battle.' The challenge would not go unanswered for long. On 31 January 1793, Pitt made what was effectively the first of his war speeches to the House of Commons: 'England will never consent that France shall arrogate the power of annulling at her pleasure, and under the pretence of a natural right of which she makes herself the only judge, the political system of Europe, established by solemn treaties and guaranteed by the consent of all the Powers.'

The next day, England formally declared war on France.

★

In claiming that England was fighting to defend the rule of international law, Pitt was reasserting the basic principle that governed English foreign policy for centuries: no single mainland power should be allowed to establish hegemony over the continent of Europe. Some of his contemporaries found additional reasons for fighting. For Horace Walpole, the epitome of civilised living, the French were barbarous monsters and had to be put down like mad dogs. Writing to Hannah More on 9 February 1793, he declared: 'I have no words that can reach the criminality of such *inferno-human* beings – but must compose a term that aims at conveying my idea of them – for the future it will be sufficient to call them *the French*.' And to the same correspondent, on 10 September 1793, he insisted, 'Unless the earth is purged of such monsters, peace and morality will never return. This is not a war of nation and nation: it is the cause of everything dear and sacred to civilized men, against the unbounded licentiousness of assassins.'

Hannah More was one of the leading lights of the Blue Stocking Circle, a group of cultured and articulate ladies who met regularly to converse in London in the second half of the eighteenth century. Her personal stock-in-trade became tracts aimed to improve the conditions of the poor and, once war had formally been declared against France, she found no difficulty in transforming these into propaganda leaflets for the English cause. Typical of the genre is her 'Village Politics' (1793). Purportedly written by 'Will Chip, a Country Carpenter', it was addressed to 'all the Mechanics, Journeymen and Day Labourers in Great Britain', and it took the form of 'a Dialogue between Jack Anvil the Blacksmith and Tom Hod, the Mason'. Observing that Tom is looking dismal, Jack asks him what the matter is:

TOM: Matter? Why I want liberty.
JACK: Liberty! What has anyone fetched a warrant for thee? Come man, cheer up, I'll be bound for thee. – Thou art an honest fellow in the main, tho' dost tipple and prate a little too much at the Rose and Crown.
TOM: No, no, I want a new constitution.
JACK: Indeed! Why I thought thou hadst been a desperate healthy fellow. Send for the doctor then.
TOM: I'm not sick: I want Liberty and Equality, and the Rights of Man.

JACK: O now I understand thee. What thou art a leveller and a republican I warrant.

TOM: I'm a friend to the people. I want a reform.

JACK: Then the shortest way is to mend thyself.

TOM: But I want a general reform.

JACK: Then let every one mend one.

TOM: Pooh! I want freedom and happiness, the same as they have got in France.

JACK: What, Tom, we imitate *them*? We follow the French! Why they only begun all this mischief at first, in order to be just what we are already . . . But bear one thing in mind: the more we riot, the more we shall have to pay. Mind another thing too, that in France the poor paid all the taxes, as I have heard 'em say, and the quality paid nothing . . .

TOM: I know we shall be undone, if we don't get a new constitution – that's all . . .

JACK: . . . Tom! I have got the use of my limbs, of my liberty, of the laws, and of my Bible. The two first, I take to be my *natural* rights; the two last my *civil* and *religious*; these, I take it, are the true Rights of Man, and all the rest is nothing but nonsense and madness and wickedness. My cottage is my castle; I sit down in it at night in peace and thankfulness, and 'no man maketh me afraid'. Instead of indulging discontent, because another is richer than I in this world, (for envy is at the bottom of your equality works) I read my bible, go to church, and think of a treasure in heaven.

TOM: Aye; but the French have got it in *this* world.

JACK: 'Tis all a lye, Tom. Sir John's butler says his master gets letters which *say* 'tis all a lye. 'Tis all murder, and nakedness, and hunger; many of the poor soldiers fight without victuals, and march without clothes. These are your *democrats*! Tom . . .

TOM: What then dost thou take French *liberty* to be?

JACK: To murder more men in one night, than ever their poor king did in his whole life.

TOM: And what dost thou take a *Democrat* to be?

JACK: One who likes to be governed by a thousand tyrants, and yet can't bear a king.

TOM: What is *Equality*?

JACK: For every man to pull down every one that is above him, till they're all as low as the lowest.

TOM: What is *the new Rights of Man*?

JACK: Battle, murder, and sudden death.

TOM: What is to be an *enlightened people*?

JACK: To put out the light of the gospel, confound right and wrong, and grope about in pitch darkness.

TOM: What is *Philosophy*, that Tim Standish talks so much about?

JACK: To believe that there's neither God, nor devil, nor heaven, nor hell. – To dig up a wicked old fellow [Voltaire]'s rotten bones, whose books, Sir

John says, have been the ruin of thousands; and to set his figure up in a church and worship him.

TOM: And what mean the other hard words that Tim talks about – *organisation* and *function*, and *civism*, and *incivism*, and *equalization*, and *inviolability* and *imperscriptible*?

JACK: Nonsense, gibberish, downright hocus-pocus. I know 'tis not English; Sir John says 'tis not Latin; and his *valet de sham* say 'tis not French neither.

What divided the English and French ways of life was set out even more starkly in a number of the *Northampton Mercury* in the early days of the war. It consisted of a series of antonyms, set out in parallel columns, headed *British Liberty* and *French Liberty*, and entitled *The Contrast*: Religion was paired with Atheism, Loyalty with Rebellion, Obedience to the Laws with Anarchy, Industry with Idleness, National Prosperity with Private Ruin and, finally, Happiness with Misery. At the foot of the balance sheet, the paper's readers were asked the simple question 'WHICH IS BEST?'

Other tracts and handbills reproduced in verbal form the crude stereotypes made popular through Gillray's cartoons: on one side, the figure of John Bull, admired by foreigners for his fat, jolly face and ample belly, whose basic diet is roast beef and pudding, and who is invariably blunt, honest and sensible; and on the other side, what passed then for the archetypical Frenchman, with 'thin jaws and lank guts', the result of his diet of 'French frogs and soup meagre', irredeemably 'saucy, envious, unreliable and deceitful'. The outlook is encapsulated in a ballad that appeared in *The Star* on 2 December 1793. It accompanied two engravings by Hogarth that ridiculed the idea of a French invasion:

> With lantern jaws and croaking gut
> See how the half-starv'd Frenchmen strut,
>   And call us English dogs;
> But soon we'll teach these bragging foes,
> That beef and beer give heavier blows,
>   Than soup and roasted frogs.
>
> The priests inflam'd with righteous hopes,
> Prepare their axes, wheels and ropes,
>   To bend the stiff-neck'd sinner;
> But should they sink in coming over,

Old Nick may fish 'twixt France and Dover,
And catch a glorious dinner.

★

Between English and French propagandists during the Revolutionary Wars, there are clear differences in both content and style. Each group proclaimed that it was fighting for civilised values and for self-survival. Inevitably, the tone of the French was more strident because they were in greater danger: beyond their borders was the menace of the massed armies of the First Coalition (Austria and Prussia now reinforced by Britain, Spain and Sardinia), while from within there was a Royalist guerrilla campaign of significant dimensions in Normandy and the Vendée. France's great orator at times of danger was the dauntless Danton. In September 1792, as the Prussian armies besieged Verdun, his counsel had been to counter-attack: '*Pour les vaincre, il nous faut de l'audace, encore de l'audace, toujours de l'audace, et la France est sauvée.*' On 10 March 1793, with news of fresh disasters coming by every post from France's frontiers, he urged the Convention to fight on, with the prospect of prizes truly glittering:

> Pitt clearly feels that since he has everything to lose he must spare nothing. If we take Holland, then Carthage is destroyed and England will have to embrace Liberty if it wants to survive. If Holland is won over to the cause of Liberty, then, the business-conscious aristocracy – which, at the moment, rules the roost in England – will rise up against the government which will be exposed as having led it into this war of despotism against a free people. It will overthrow this stupid Prime Minister who believed that the *ancien régime* had the talents to stifle the spirit of Liberty which hovers over France. Once this Minister has been overthrown by business interests, the Freedom party will come out into the open for it isn't dead. If you wake up to your duties, if your agents set out here and now, if you reach out your hand to the foreigners who are yearning for the destruction of every form of tyranny, then France will be saved and the whole world will be free.

In this brief extract there are several noteworthy features: the firm conviction that the French were fighting a crusade on behalf of oppressed peoples everywhere and the mistaken belief, doubtless based on communications from the Revolution Society and from Tom Paine, that the English Radicals commanded considerably more support than they ever actually did. Whereas English propagandists tended to cover all Frenchmen with the same blanket condemnation, their French counterparts more regularly hailed the ordinary English people as their brothers-in-arms, waiting to be liberated, and concentrated their vituperation on Pitt and the ruling classes. In so doing, their rhetoric was appreciably more elevated than the English: while English propagandists were consistently earthy, if not downright crude, their French counterparts regularly had recourse to Classical allusions and to history, both ancient and modern. When, in 1793, the William Tell Paris section issued a proclamation against Pitt, it did so in the following terms: 'Pitt, ah what an odious name! He is the destroyer of all virtue, the source of universal corruption, the enemy of liberty, the scourge of the human race: his memory will be more abhorred than Attila.'

In the same year, a French popular song was composed to fit the tune of 'La Marseillaise'. It was entitled 'Pot pourri républicain', and the first verse ran: 'This ambitious Carthage, which supports the wicked *émigrés*, has dared in its blind rage to raise up evil arms against us! Covered desolate France with crimes and acts of horrible infamy. Armed Frenchmen against Frenchmen. Raised rebellion in the desolate Vendée. To arms, citizens. Quickly, quickly, force the perfidious English to choose between peace or ruin.' On the surface of this lyric, the obvious analogy is between the barbarism of Carthage (present-day England) and Rome, the fount of civilisation (modern France). The sub-text assuredly evokes ancestral memories: the Hundred Years War, when the ruthless English devastated France with fire and with sword, and, to further its treacherous aims, set Armagnac against Burgundian.

The appeal to national history, the most regular ploy of the Anglophobic French demagogues, is once again manifest in the report on the State of the Republic, made by Bertrand Barère on 1 August 1793 to the second Committee of Public Safety:

> In his impious ambitions and his cold calculations, Pitt might have thought that he could impose a king on France which long ago saw an English king upon its throne. He would do well to remember that when, all those centuries ago, the English, aided by circumstances, by the lack of discipline among our troops, by the incompetence of our generals, by the indecisiveness of our people, succeeded in occupying three-quarters of our lands, they were nonetheless driven out – even though, because of the dazzling victories won by force of arms, they seemed to have gained an ascendancy that would never be broken . . .
>
> There is now a government in Europe which after boasting for so long of its love of liberty, has now become its cruellest oppressor. English Cabinet

Ministers and politicians you who are so proud of your royal Constitution, you commit every crime there is: arson, murder, bribery, spying, treachery. Are these your version of republicanism, the spurious fame of which has been spread by a handful of publicists and philosophers who are as venal as you are yourselves? The National Convention puts the British Government in the dock in front of the England people. France denounces it to Europe, to people everywhere. History accuses you before the whole of the human race.

What's to stop the English government, through all sorts of crimes, from stealing from us the liberty it has always detested? Why shouldn't it go on infecting us with the monarchy which it adores so fanatically? Why should the English Government not try, by its acts of cruelty, to get revenge for America's independence, by making slaves of us? It's a country whose avarice has caused so many crimes, whose politics have done so much wrong . . .

This is the government which is using its loot from India to make Europe a slave state, the profits from big business to extinguish liberty, the benefits of modern communications to corrupt fellow-men, and the taxes from its people to exterminate the French. O Kings of Europe, made vassals of English commerce by your pride and your wretchedness, so many crimes will not go unpunished. Your rule will give way to that of the Englightenment. Your power, which has now been vested in your ministers, is all too clearly vanishing away. And this appalling war you are waging against liberty is, mercifully, royalty committing suicide.

Citizens, do not be surprised that the English government should be the most committed and most cunning of your enemies. It is faithful to what it calls its principles. Where it can't conquer, it corrupts. In its own country, it has drawn up a price list of men, orators and Members of Parliament. It has tried to do the same for ordinary people. But the price list of the people has just two words on it: Liberty & Equality!

Right to the last, the leaders of the French Revolution persisted in their belief that their quarrel was not with the English people but with its government. In a speech made to the Jacobin Club on 28 January 1794, the by now all-powerful Robespierre declared.

Our aim should be to enlighten the English people and fill the hearts of the French people with bitter anger over what the English government is doing.

We didn't need to lecture the English people. All we needed to do was let them follow our discussions and they would see our republican virtues and our glory. We simply needed to let them help themselves to whatever might have suited them from our constitution. It was a bad move to brandish it at them in the way we did. This was tantamount to throwing it in their faces . . .

To win over any nation, you must appeal to its weaknesses. You must speak its language. However, you'd be wrong to assume that the morality and the intelligence of the English people can vie with yours. No, they are two centuries behind you. If they hate you, it is because they do not know you, because it has always been English government policy to twist the truth. They hate you because, for several centuries now, it has always been English government policy to arm the English against the French and because waging war has always been a way of countering political opposition within its own country.

It doesn't follow from this that the English people will not rise in revolution. They will revolt because they are oppressed and because they are ruined. It will be your agents who will cause that revolution. It will happen because the Prime Minister is corrupt. Pitt will be overthrown because he is an imbecile. Pay no heed to his reputation: it has been greatly exaggerated.

This might sound blasphemous to the ears of some Englishmen; to any reasonable person, it's the simple truth.

To prove it, I need only mention our armies, our warships, the great, indeed sublime situation in which we find ourselves, and the cries of protest against Pitt right across England. The first Minister of a lunatic king is an imbecile because unless you're an imbecile, you cannot prefer being employed as the Minister of a lunatic king to the honourable title of 'virtuous citizen'.

That same missionary zeal together with seemingly unbounded optimism sounds throughout Danton's address to the Constituent Assembly on 4 February 1794, when he urged the delegates to abolish slavery throughout the world:

We are working for generations yet unborn. Let us spread liberty into the colonies and the English will die this very day. Inject liberty into the New World and it will grow deep roots and bear rich fruit. Pitt and his cronies will try for political reasons to nip this in the bud but they will be dragged down into oblivion. And France will be rewarded with the position and the prestige which it is guaranteed by its power, its land and its people.

It was one of the last speeches he was ever to make: soon afterwards both he and Robespierre, who vaunted the powers of reason, were literally to lose their heads.

★

Both England and France had a real need of propagandists to vaunt their own virtues and to highlight the vices of the enemy because, in sober truth, the Revolutionary war was not going well for either of them. Britain had overwhelming naval superiority but the chief focus of maritime activity was the Caribbean, by then far the richest overseas possession of both the warring powers: the fighting was inconclusive while 60 per cent of all military losses were caused by malaria and yellow fever. In Europe, Britain's plans to attack French naval bases all failed: an attack on Dunkirk was repulsed in 1793; Toulon was occupied, at the invitation of the French Royalists that same year, but had to be evacuated with only partial damage to French ships and stores; plans to attack Brest in 1794 were aborted for lack of troops and because the royalists in western France, in spite of the expenditure of 'Pitt's Gold', were unable to create a major diversion. Britain was unable to mount attacks in Europe and the French overseas empire simultaneously and was obliged to provide large subsidies to its mainland allies at the expense of the British taxpayers. They remained, for much of the time, unenthusiastic about the war. Restoring the Bourbons to their throne was never a popular cause, and gifted and persuasive critics such as Charles James Fox were able to castigate Austria and Prussia as wanton aggressors and to rejoice in the triumphs of the Revolutionary armies as just punishment for wanton greed. Only when invasion seemed iminent was English popular feeling aroused, as it was, for example, in 1795 when the mood was caught, paradoxically enough, by Scotland's two leading poets: Robert Burns in his rousing

> Does haughty Gaul invasion threat?
>   Then let the loons beware, Sir,
> There's wooden walls upon our seas,
>   And volunteers on shore, Sir.

and Walter Scott, with his 'War Song of the Edinburgh Light Dragoons':

> To horse! to horse! the standard flies
>   The bugles sound the call;
> The Gallic navy stems the seas,
> The voice of battle's on the breeze –
>   Arouse ye! one and all!

The Light Dragoons may well have been aroused, at any rate temporarily, but amongst those who stopped to consider the conduct and the purpose of the war against France, the mood was more sombre. Coleridge doubtless expressed it in an article he wrote for his radical Christian paper, *The Watchman*, in March 1796. It took the form of a balance sheet, items grouped under certain dates, in which aspirations are paired with achievements. In every instance, what actually took place is the exact opposite of what was intended. So, under December 1792, the objective 'To prevent the opening of the Scheldt' results in 'its being solemnly opened'; 'to save Holland' is paired with 'its being conquered'; and 'to prevent the aggrandizement of France' with 'France conquering territories almost equal in extent to her own'. Under June 1793, the aim of achieving 'security for the future' results in 'making France an armed nation, and the greatest military power in Europe'; while earning 'gratitude from our Allies' is juxtaposed with 'most of whom have taken our money and left us in the lurch, and the others only fight with us so long as we can pay them'. The parallel columns wend their melancholy way down to the bottom of the balance sheet which ends in March 1796 when 'God knows the object of the War!' is coupled with 'God knows whether it is obtained'.

France's leaders found it rather easier to sustain their people's morale: they were fighting to make actual the grandiose dreams of the Revolution and, throughout their brief reign, for the country's survival against massive and sustained attack. Its overseas objectives proved as impossible to achieve as Britain's on the mainland of Europe. Just as the British over-estimated the degree of Royalist support available within France, so the French proved over-optimistic in their assessment of the Republican cause in Britain. Dreams of exploiting potential areas of disaffection in Scotland and Ireland came to naught and an attempted landing in Wales proved futile. In England, though the Government suspected that radical conspiracies were at various times afoot, the only noteworthy incidents were the naval mutinies in 1797 at Spithead in April and the Nore in May. No charismatic popular leader emerged in England to exploit social discontent: Dr Price died in 1791 and Dr Priestley fled to America. The forces of order were well organized in England's cities while the stolidity of the rural parishes did much to keep the nation stable.

Within France, the leaders of the Revolution continued to wage a crippling land-war on several fronts, while simultaneously seeking to restructure French society at dizzying speed: the monarchy was abolished, the First Republic established in its stead, *biens nationaux* were confiscated and redistributed, all within a period of months. To emphasise more dramatically that France was now part of a brave new world, the months of the year were reorganized and renamed by a law of 5 October 1793, while in another decree, of 18 *Floréal* of Year II (7 May 1794), God and Christianity were officially abolished and the 'Cult of the Supreme Being' inaugurated in their stead. While all this was being enacted, a power struggle of increasing ferocity was being waged between the leading Revolutionaries. As one faction after another was denounced as being either too moderate or too extreme, it was summarily eliminated. Apart from Mirabeau, who died of violent, though natural, causes in 1791, virtually all the leading Revolutionaries had been put to death by the end of July 1794.

At the beginning of June 1793, Brissot and twenty of the so-called Girondins were arrested for protesting against the violent measures being taken by Robespierre, Danton and Marat. In retaliation, Marat was assassinated in his bath on 13 July by Charlotte Corday, a descendant of Corneille's sister. On 17 September 1793, the Terror began with the passing of the *loi des suspects* ordering the arrest of anyone suspected of disloyalty to the Revolution: during the ten months while the law was in force, some 20,000 people were executed throughout France, Marie-Antoinette being one of the earliest victims, on 16 October, followed a fortnight later by the captive Girondins. 13 March 1794 witnessed the execution of Hébert, one of the most extreme of the Revolutionaries, editor of the paper *Le Père Duchesne*, whose often obscene and violent language was justly notorious. On 5 April, Danton went to the guillotine. He was accompanied by Fabre d'Eglantine, who had devised the poetic new names for the Revolutionary calendar and Camille Desmoulins, who sealed his own fate when he protested in his newspaper, *Le Vieux Cordelier*, against the bloodshed of the Terror; the closing words in the last number he produced were *Les dieux ont soif*. On 27 July, nemesis finally overtook the chief organiser of the Terror, Robespierre, the 'Seagreen Incorruptible'; he was guillotined the following day together with Saint-Just, the most fanatical of his lieutenants.

During this time, the Revolutionary armies had won victory after victory, and during the reaction that followed the downfall of Robespierre, a ferocious campaign was waged against the Royalist rebellions in the provinces. On 5 October one of the bloodiest uprisings of the whole Revolutionary period took place in protest against the continued existence of the *Convention*. It was successfully put down by forces led by the twenty-six-year-old Revolutionary General, Napoleon Bonaparte. On 26 October, the *Convention* met for the last time, decreed a general amnesty for anti-revolutionary acts and abolished capital punishment. The *Place de la République* in Paris, where so many were guillotined, was renamed the *Place de la Concorde*.

With England, however, no concord was conceivable: apart from a relatively brief respite in 1802, the war would continue for another twenty years.

There were still some English observers who professed love for and faith in the French people. Mary Wollstonecraft, for instance, wrote from Paris to her friend Ruth Barlow, in February 1793: 'All the affection I have for the French is for the whole nation, and it seems to be a little honey spread over all the bread I eat in their land'; Horace Walpole dismissed her as 'a hyena in petticoats'. She was a friend of Helen Maria Williams, an independent spirit who chose to live in Paris for most of her life from 1788 onwards. In 1795, she wrote in a letter:

> In the first days of the Revolution, when Liberty and Property went hand-in-hand together, what a moral revolution was instantly effected throughout Europe, by the sublime and immortal principles which this great change seemed about to introduce into government! But what eternal regrets must the lovers of liberty feel, that her cause should have fallen into the hands of monsters, ignorant of her charms, by whom she has been transformed into a fury, who, brandishing her snaky whips and torches, has enlarged the limits of wickedness and driven us back into regions of guilt hitherto unknown . . .
>
> Yet it is some consolation, amidst this mighty mass of evil, that France is at length beginning to learn wisdom from the things she has suffered . . . We may now approach the altar of liberty with confidence and hope; the hideous spectres that haunted it have fled for ever; and its incense in future will rise grateful to heaven, and spread fragrance over a regenerated land.

A voice as sweetly reasonable as this was, at that time, too soft to be heard above the hymns of hate intoned by the good and the great on each side of the Channel. On 20 July 1794, Bertrand Barère laid down the line that French officialdom was to follow till Waterloo, and, indeed, for long afterwards:

> So there it is, then, that nation – and we must never get tired of talking about the English – that nation which has boasted of being philosophical and free. There is that unjust and barbaric government which dared to try and deceive other nations about its secret and savage politics. We must go on exposing for all the world to see and print indelibly across the pages of History, the fearful phantom of the overlordship Britain plans to exercise over the whole of Europe of which it forms no part, of its plans to enslave the kings it claims to support, to seize control of the governments it presents to defend, to protect religion while it has no religion of its own, to prattle on about liberty even as it plots to destroy it and – about promoting business when it really means monopoly to all the new generations of free people who will follow one another on our Republican soil, we must tell the truth about this Neronian government which after extended its commercial empire across every continent in the world, is now about to cross the oceans to enslave them and, into every land where it sets its foot, to instal despotism and disease, slavery and chains, cut-throat competition, money-lending and all its attendant evils.

While the French insisted that the English were barbaric, hypocritical and venal, the English persisted in believing, with Horace Walpole and the leading political cartoonists of the day, that the French were less than human. On 13 January 1795, Lord Rupert Stephen Fitzgerald wrote to Lord Grenville:

> I may add, *par parenthèse*, that if his Revolution has been attended with misery and wretchedness to nations and millions of individuals, that it has also been productive of some good in opening the eyes of men on the real character of Frenchmen, and of exhibiting to the world in its true colours that horrid mass of infamy, perfidy, and wickedness of every description, which had been so long concealed under the veil of politeness and urbanity, to the great misfortune, at all ages, of those who mistook the appearance for the reality. Sorry am I to say that I think there are but very few exceptions to be made amongst them, but how can it be otherwise with men who are become the agents of the Devil, and who, openly disavowing God and the truth, harden their hearts against everything that has hitherto been held sacred amongst men. They are become like a second race on earth, and it may truly be said that the world is inhabited by two sets of human beings, by men and Frenchmen.

Blanket condemnations of this sort invariably need qualifying and

Lord Fitzgerald's is no exception. As well as being inaccurate it was conspicuously uncharitable in omitting any reference to the large number of refugees who fled to England because of the excesses of the Revolution: there were some 180,000 of them and many settled in London. The most noteworthy from several points of view was Chateaubriand, who returned to France from America in 1792 on hearing of the fall of the monarchy, fought with the first corps of the royalist *armée des émigrés*, was wounded during the siege of Thionville and escaped to England in 1793. Apart from a brief interlude at Bungay in Suffolk, he spent his exile in London, where he eked out a meagre existence as a translator and wrote his prose epic *Les Natchez* and his *Essai historique*, first published in London in 1797. Like many of the *émigrés*, of high and low estate, he returned to France at the turn of the century and unlike most of them, as we shall see, went on to achieve considerable fame and fortune.

A transformation, almost as dramatic, took place in the attitudes of those erstwhile radical English poets who had, at the outset, hailed the Revolution with lyrical enthusiasm. In 1795, Coleridge pronounced on 'The Example of France as a Warning to Britain':

> The annals of the French Revolution have recorded in Letters of Blood, that the Knowledge of the Few cannot counteract the Ignorance of the Many; that the Light of Philosophy, when it is confined to a small Minority, points out the Possessors as the Victims, rather than the Illuminators, of the Multitude. The Patriots of France either hastened into the dangerous and gigantic Error of making certain Evil the means of contingent Good, or were sacrificed by the Mob, with those prejudices and ferocity their unbending Virtue forbade them to assimilate. Like Sampson [*sic*], the People were strong – like Sampson, the People were blind.

The following year, he went even further. On 15 October, he wrote to Charles Lloyd to announce that he was ready to become an English patriot: 'I have snapped my squeaking baby-trumpet of sedition and have hung up its fragments in the Chamber of Penitences.' In the months that followed, his poetic peers were to emulate him.

Of all the English commentators who pronounced on the Revolution in its early stages, Burke was the one who had the least need subsequently to eat his words. In his much-maligned *Reflections* he predicted that France would fall under the control of the oligarchy of *nouveaux riches* made wealthy through the confiscation of estates, and that this would be followed by disorder and bloodshed. To rescue the nation from increasing chaos, Burke foresaw that 'some general, who understands the art of conciliating the soldiery and who possesses the true spirit of command, shall draw the eyes of all men upon himself'. Inevitably, thereafter, this new despot would proceed to exercise 'the most completely arbitrary power that ever appeared on earth'. And so indeed it came to pass. The *Directoire*, which replaced the *Convention Nationale* in October 1795, provided feeble and divisive government. Young dandies reappeared in society – the so-called *Incroyables* and *muscadins* – and, at a time when penury was still prevalent, scandalised the public with their profligate life style. National bankruptcy threatened within, military disaster without. The moment was ripe for Burke's Man of Destiny and it came on 9 November 1799 (*le 18 Brumaire, An VIII*, in the new calendar). General Napoleon Bonaparte seized command of Paris, a new mode of government was set up, over-ruled by three Consuls and of these, the First and most powerful was Bonaparte himself.

5 : *Napoleon*

England and France have held the fate of the earth and especially of
European civilisation in their hands. How much evil we have inflicted
on each other! How much good we might have done!

Napoleon, 20 April 1816

Throughout the Revolutionary and Napoleonic Wars, France
was consistently confronted by military alliances of the European Powers. There were seven such coalitions, the partners
sometimes changing as one or other was battered to defeat before, after
an interval, re-arming and re-entering the war. From first to last,
however, over a period of twenty years, Britain was a constant
antagonist. It is not surprising, therefore, that the majority of
Napoleon's many public pronouncements on the subject of England
and the English were outspokenly hostile. There were, for all that,
occasions when, for diplomatic reasons, he professed fulsome admiration for the fortitude of his opponents and for features of their
constitution, and there were details in his personal life it was preferable
to leave unpublicised. He always got his razors, with their mother-of-
pearl handles, from England, considering Birmingham steel superior to
anything that could be produced in France. In 1783, when England and
France ended six years of naval warfare with the Treaty of Versailles, he
conceived the idea of becoming a cadet at Portsmouth Naval College.
This was still an age when one could serve under a foreign flag with
honour and even with distinction: one of the greatest of France's
eighteenth-century generals, Marshal de Saxe, victor over the Duke of
Cumberland at Fontenoy in 1745, was the natural son of Augustus II,
Elector of Saxony. With some help from his local schoolmaster,

Napoleon wrote a letter of application to the English Admiralty. Whether he received a reply is not known. One can only speculate, therefore, on the course history might have taken had he become a comrade-in-arms in the same service as Horatio Nelson.

In the event, Napoleon was cast for a dramatically different role. Two years after applying to Portsmouth Naval College, he was commissioned, at the age of sixteen, as a lieutenant in a French artillery regiment. By 1795, he was already a general in one of the Revolutionary armies. After saving the Convention in Paris from attack by armed insurgents, he was put in command of the army in north Italy and on 14 January 1797 won the first of his many spectacular victories by defeating the Austrians at Rivoli, a village near Mantua. This led to the break-up of the First Coalition.

As events were to prove, however, Napoleon's interests and talents extended far beyond things military. On 26 May 1796, he wrote to Citizen Oriani, France's foremost astronomer:

Science, which dignifies the mind of men, and Art, which beautifies life, and transmits its great achievements to posterity, ought to be specially honoured by every free government. Every man of genius, every office-holder in the Republic of Letters, in whatever country he may have been born, is a citizen of France . . . The French people sets a higher value upon the acquisition of a learned mathematician, a famous painter, or the distinguished exponent of any branch of study, than upon that of the richest and most populous city in the world.

The interest of this passage is not simply the evidence it provides that the young Bonaparte took the same lofty view of France's cultural pre-eminence as Louis XIV and Robespierre had done before him. He was shortly to translate it into dramatic action. When he led his expedition to Egypt in 1798 he had two quite different aims in view: one was to cut England's vital trade route to India by taking possession of Egypt; the other was to increase knowledge of the Middle East by transporting with his troops a team of France's most eminent scholars. The latter objective proved easier to attain than the former: the academic results were successful and lasting; the military expedition was thwarted by Nelson's decisive naval victory at Aboukir Bay. This first major defeat for Napoleon established Nelson as a national hero and his achievement was fêted as enthusiastically by coalition members as by the English people. On 20 October 1798, Coleridge wrote to his wife, from Hanover, which was then still ruled by the King of England: 'At the dinner which was given in honor of Nelson's victory, 21 guns were fired by order of the Military Governor, and between each Firing the Military Band played an English Tune – I never saw such enthusiasm, or heard such tumultuous shouting, as when the Governour gave as a toast "The Great Nation" – By this name they always designate England in opposition to the same title self-assumed by France.' Nelson, for his part, stuck resolutely to the single-minded philosophy that both fashioned and finished his naval career. On 4 August 1799, he wrote to Captain Louis: 'There is no way of dealing with the Frenchman but to knock him down. To be civil to them is only to be laughed at, when they are enemies', while in his *Life of Nelson* (1813) Robert Southey reported him as saying: 'You must consider every man your enemy who speaks ill of your king . . . and you must hate a Frenchman as you hate the devil.'

Nelson's pugnacity was well matched by Napoleon's. On 18 October 1797, the day after France signed the Treaty of Campo Formio, putting an end to its war with Austria, Napoleon wrote to Talleyrand: 'The Austrians are dull and greedy: no people less intriguing and less dangerous to our interior affairs than the Austrian people. The English, on the contrary, are spirited, conniving and active. Our government must destroy the English monarchy or must expect to be destroyed by the corruption and intrigues of these active islanders.' When Napoleon returned to Paris, at the end of 1797, he was welcomed by Barras, then the most powerful member of the *Directoire*, and told that he was the conqueror designate of England. 'Go,' said Barras, 'go and capture the giant corsair that infests the seas. Go to London and punish the outrages that have been for too long unchastised.' Napoleon needed no second bidding. He promptly wrote to Talleyrand: 'Let us concentrate all our activity on our fleets and destroy England. Once that is done, all Europe is at our feet.' The Duchess d'Abrantès later recalled a conversation with Napoleon at this time when he declared: 'If my voice has any influence, England will never have an hour's respite from us. Yes, yes! War to the death with England! Always – until she is destroyed!'

Ever since the *The Reign of King George VI* first appeared in 1763, stories depicting imaginary invasions of England had remained in vogue. Soon after it became a best-seller, such dramatic advances as the Montgolfiers' balloon-ascents and Watt's invention of the steam-engine encouraged populist story-tellers to chill their readers' blood with visions of gigantic Charlières' balloons, each equipped with several decks of cannons, transporting hundreds of troops over oceans and mountains. Real life threatened to surpass melodramatic art when Napoleon was appointed 'Commander of the Army against England'. While fleets of landing-craft were assembled in the French Channel ports, Chatham and Dover Castles were heavily fortified, the Royal Military Canal was constructed as a defensive obstacle between Hythe and Appledore, and a line of forty-foot-high blockhouses was erected along the Kent coast: they were called Martello Towers, deriving their name from a tower in Mortella that had proved notoriously difficult to capture in 1794. Ironically, this original was in Napoleon's native Corsica.

On each side of the Channel, popular fiction, drama and poetry depicted either the British triumphantly repelling the invading French or the French routing the English as effectively as William and his Normans had conquered Harold at Hastings. A particularly popular drama, which played to packed houses at the Théâtre des Variétés in Paris in 1798, was *La Descente en Angleterre* by J. Coriande Mittié. The scene is Dover, and the hero, Fergusson, is a tavern-keeper, who organises a group of conspirators to seize Dover Castle and so provide the invading French Army with a secure bridgehead:

GORDON: My friends, I will not remind you of the crimes of the English Government: the long tyranny which it has exercised upon the seas; the disasters which it has carried into the Colonies; the perfidiousness which it employs to perpetuate the scourge of war. I will not talk of Pitt. You all know that cunning is his instrument, deception his element, and that his infernal policy would sacrifice all the belligerent nations to his ambition.

FERGUSSON: Yes, it is time to put a stop to the murderous plots of that destroyer of the human race.

A CONSPIRATOR: Philosophy has already devoted him to the execration of the people.

GORDON: English Patriots, you have already heard the thundering eloquence of Fox. He summons you to assert your rights.

FERGUSSON: We shall know how to defend them.

GORDON: His voice invokes liberty.

FERGUSSON: We will gain it at the expense of our lives.

GORDON: But let us not stop for idle talk; let us think of carrying out our plan. You are all decided in favour of a French descent that will shatter your chains and bring freedom to your degraded country?
CONSPIRATORS: Yes! Yes!
FERGUSSON: We swear it.
GORDON: The guarantees of victory are Fox and his friends; our courage and Buonaparte. The genius of liberty watches over the people and will soon crush their tyrants. [He unfolds a large piece of paper.] In two hours the descent will be made. The regiment in this town is commanded by the brave Houssey. We can count on him; but we have everything to fear from the Commander of the port; he is sold to Pitt and his infamous agents. We must anticipate him and strike the first blow.

On the other side of the Channel, in rather more sombre vein, Coleridge wrote his 'Fears in Solitude'. It begins as an act of contrition, pleading, in effect, that 'we are all guilty':

> What uproar and what strife may now be stirring
> This way or that way o'er these silent hills –
> Invasion, and the thunder and the shout,
> And all the crash of onset; fear and rage,
> And undetermined conflict – even now,
> Even now, perchance, and in his native isle:
> Carnage and groans beneath this blessed sun!
> We have offended, Oh! my countrymen!
> We have offended very grievously,
> And been most tyrannous. From east to west
> A groan of accusation pierces Heaven!
> The wretched plead against us; multitudes
> Countless and vehement, the sons of God,
> Our brethren! Like a cloud that travels on,
> Steamed up from Cairo's swamps of pestilence,
> Even so, my countrymen! have we gone forth
> And borne to distant tribes slavery and pangs,
> And deadlier far, our vices, whose deep taint
> With slow perdition murders the whole man,
> His body and his soul!

It ends as a nationalistic anthem:

> But, O dear Britain! O my Mother Isle!
> Needs must thou prove a name most dear and holy
> To me, a son, a brother, and a friend,
> A husband, and a father! who revere

All bonds of natural love, and find them all
Within the limits of thy rocky shores.
O native Britain! O my Mother Isle!
How shouldst thou prove aught else but dear and holy
To me, who from thy lakes and mountain-hills,
Thy clouds, thy quiet dales, thy rocks and seas,
Have drunk in all my intellectual life,
All sweet sensations, all ennobling thoughts,
All adoration of the God in nature,
All lovely and all honourable things,
Whatever makes this mortal spirit feel
The joy and greatness of its future being?
There lives nor form nor feeling in my soul
Unborrowed from my country! O divine
And beauteous island! thou hast been my sole
And most magnificent temple, in the which
I walk with awe, and sing my stately songs,
Loving the God that made me! –

In the event, English fears of invasion in 1798 proved groundless. On 23 February, Bonaparte reported to the Directory Executive that to transport his army across the Channel was, for the present, not a practical proposition:

Whatever efforts we make, it will still be many years before we achieve supremacy at sea. To carry out an invasion of England without command of the sea is as difficult and daring a project as has ever been undertaken. It could only be done by a surprise crossing – either by eluding the fleet which is blockading Brest and the Texel, or by landing in small boats, during the night, after a 7 or 8 hours' crossing, at some point in the counties of Kent or Sussex. This operation would require long nights and therefore winter-time. It can't be attempted later than April. Any such invasion by means of sloops during a calm spell in the summer is not practicable: the enemy would offer insurmountable obstacles to our embarkation and still more to our passage. Our fleet is no further advanced than it was when we mobilised the army of invasion four months ago . . . The English therefore seems to me impossible until next year; and then it will probably be prevented by fresh embarrassment on the continent. The real moment for preparing this invasion has passed, perhaps for ever . . .

We should accordingly give up any real attempt to invade England and content ourselves with the appearance of it, whilst devoting all our attention and resources to the Rhine, so as to deprive England of Hanover and Hamburg . . . Or we might well make an expedition into the Levant, and threaten the commerce of India.

If none of these operations is feasible, I see no alternative but to make peace with England. I am confident that the terms refused by Malmesbury [Pitt's chief peace-negotiator in 1796 and 1797] would be acceptable to them today.

Napoleon returned to his notion of making peace with England on Christmas Day 1799 when he made a personal appeal to George III:

Called by the will of the French people to hold the highest office in the Republic, I think it proper, upon assuming my functions, to inform Your Majesty of the fact by my own hand.

Is there to be no end to the war which, for the past eight years, has desolated every quarter of the globe? Is there no means by which we can come to an understanding? How is it that the two most enlightened nations in Europe, both stronger and more powerful than their safety and independence require, consent to sacrifice their commercial success, their internal prosperity, and the happiness of their homes, to dreams of imaginary greatness? How is it that they do not envisage peace as their greatest glory as well as their greatest need?

Such sentiments cannot be strange to Your Majesty's heart, for you rule a free nation for the sole end of making it happy . . .

If France and England abuse their power, they can, for a long time yet, stave off exhaustion; but it would be an international disaster; and I make bold to say that the fate of every civilised nation depends upon the ending of a war which is embroiling the whole world.

George III's response was to dictate a letter on 1 January 1800 at 7.00 a.m. to his Foreign Minister, Grenville, refusing to treat in person with 'a new, impious, self-created aristocrat' and ordering him to address the reply to Talleyrand. And in the House of Commons on 17 February, challenged to state in one sentence why war with France was still being waged, Pitt replied:

I know not whether I can do it in one sentence; but in one word I can tell him that it is *security*: security against a danger, the greatest danger that ever threatened the world. It is security against a danger which never existed in any past period of society. It is security against a danger which in degree and extent was never equalled; against a danger which threatened all the nations of Europe, and resisted by none with as much success as by this nation, because by none has it been resisted so uniformly and with so much energy.

And so the war went on, with England mistress of the seas and France seemingly unbeatable on land.

On 14 June 1800, Bonaparte won another overwhelming victory over the Austrians, this time at Marengo, in Piedmont. After the Austrians were routed again, at Hohenlinden in Bavaria, on 3 December 1800, they withdrew from the Second Coalition when they concluded the Treaty of Lunéville, signed on 9 February 1801. Hopes of a more general and durable peace in Europe were appreciably higher with the signing of the Peace of Amiens on 27 March 1802. Fighting ceased between France and Britain and it was agreed that English monarchs, who had continued to call themselves 'King of France' since the reign of Edward III, would renounce all claim to the title.

★

No sooner had the fighting ended than great numbers of English people, deprived of their opportunity for more than a decade, streamed across the Channel and made for Paris. Among their number was the painter Turner, making his first visit to Paris expressly to see the exhibition of pictures looted by Napoleon. A concerted effort was made to upgrade the main roads and pro-English plays were put on in Paris for their delectation: one, *Le Peintre français à Londres*, went so far as to present Nelson in a favourable light. The uniform reaction of the English visitors was delight at the warmth of their welcome and surprise at the signs of prosperity that were everywhere apparent. A typical response was that of Anne Plumptre, daughter of the President of Queens' College, Cambridge. In her *Narrative of Three Years' Residence in France . . . from the year 1802 to 1805*, she reported:

> I was as perfectly free as I am in England, I went whithersoever I was desirous of going, and was uniformly received with the same politeness and hospitality as while peace still subsisted between the two countries. I never witnessed harsh measures of the government but towards the turbulent and factious; I saw everywhere works of public utility going forward; industry, commerce, and the arts encouraged; and I could not consider the people as unhappy, or the government as odious . . . I have found speech everywhere as free in France as in England: I have heard persons deliver their sentiments on Bonaparte and his government, whether favourable or unfavourable, without the least reserve; but in the most public manner, and in the most mixed societies, in diligences, and at tables-d'hôte, where none could be previously acquainted with the character or sentiments of those with whom they were conversing, and where some one among the company might be a

spy of the police for anything that the others knew to the contrary – yet this idea was no restraint upon them.

Another witness, equally impresed, was Fanny Burney, who had frequented the Blue Stocking Circle in her youth and, in 1793, married the *émigré* General d'Arblay. In her *Diary*, she described their arrival in Calais in the spring of 1802:

We were all three too much awake by the new scene to try for any repose, and the hotel windows sufficed for our amusement till dinner; and imagine, my dearest sir, how my repast was seasoned, when I tell you that, as soon as it began, a band of music came to the window and struck up '*God save the King*'. I can never tell you what a pleased emotion was excited in my breast by this sound on a shore so lately hostile, and on which I have so many, so heartfelt motives for wishing peace and amity perpetual . . . !

Beggars we saw not – no, not one, all the time we stayed or sauntered; and for civility and gentleness, the poorest and most ordinary persons we met or passed might be compared with the best dressed and best looking walkers in the streets of our metropolis, and still to the disadvantage of the latter. I cannot say how much this surprised me, as I had conceived an horrific idea of the populace of this country, imagining them all transformed into bloody monsters.

Another astonishment I experienced equally pleasing, though not equally important to my ease; I saw innumerable pretty women and lovely children, almost all of them extremely fair. I had been taught to expect nothing but mahogany complexions and features hideous instantly on crossing the strait of Dover. When this, however, was mentioned in our party afterwards, the Highlander exclaimed, 'But Calais was in the hands of the English so many years, that the English race there is not yet extinct.'

Her diary entry for 5 May 1802 describes a reception in Paris when she had a close-up view of Napoleon himself:

At length, the two human hedges were finally formed, the door of the Audience Chamber was thrown wide open with a commanding crash, a vivacious officer-Centinel – or I know not what, nimbly descended the three steps into our Apartment, &, placing himself at the side of the door, with one hand spread as high as possible above his head, & the other extended horizontally, called out, in a loud & authoritative voice, 'Le Premier Consul!' You will easily believe nothing more was necessary to obtain attention; not a soul either spoke or stirred as he & his suite passed along; which was, so quickly, that had I not been placed so near the door, & had not all about me facilitated my standing foremost & least crowd-obstructed, I could hardly have seen him: as it was, I had a view so near, though so brief, of his face, as to be very much struck by it: it is of a deeply impressive cast, pale even to sallowness, while not only in the Eye, but in every feature, Care, Thought, Melancholy, & Meditation are strongly marked, with so much of character, nay, Genius, & so penetrating a seriousness – or rather sadness, as powerfully to sink into an observer's mind: – yet, though the Busts & Medallions I have seen are, in general, such good resemblances, that I think I should have known him untold, he has by no means the look to be expected from Bonaparte, – but rather that of a profoundly studious & contemplative man, who 'o'er Books consumes' – not only the 'midnight oil', but his own daily strength, & 'wastes the puny body to decay' by abstruse speculations, & theoretic plans, or, rather, visions, ingenious, but not practicable. But the look however, of the Commander who heads his own army, who fights his own Battles, who conquers every difficulty by personal exertion, who executes all he plans, who performs even all he suggests – whose ambition is of the most enterprizing, & whose bravery of the most daring cast – This, which is the look to be expected from his situation, & the exploits which have led to it, the spectator watches for in vain. The plainness, also, of his dress, so conspicuously contrasted by the finery of all around him, conspires forcibly with his countenance, which seems 'Sicklied o'er with the pale hue of Thought', to give him far more the air of a Student than of a Warrior.

During the period of peace, Charles James Fox, the Francophile leader of the Opposition in the Commons, visited Paris to discuss what seemed a particularly promising scheme with Napoleon. This was the project of a tunnel beneath the Channel drawn up by a French mining engineer, Albert Mathieu, who had unveiled his plans early in 1802 in the Luxembourg Palace. It was anything but modest, consisting of two sections, each eighteen miles long, paved and lit by oil-lamps for the whole of their length; there was to have been a freshly constructed artificial island in mid-Channel where the passengers would have emerged from the tunnel to admire the view and refresh themselves. Fox hailed the project as 'one of the great enterprises we can now undertake together'. When hostilities resumed again in 1803, Napoleon examined the feasibility of utilising the tunnel for his invasion of England, using the mid-Channel island to refresh the cavalry's horses. There remained the practical problem of coping with the Royal Navy. When his admirals assured him that they would by then have destroyed the British fleet, Napoleon's prompt comment was that if the Royal Navy was eliminated, there would be no need of a Channel Tunnel.

From that moment on, M. Mathieu became a mere footnote in transport history.

When the Peace of Amiens ended, in May 1803, each side accused the other of back-sliding and prevarication. On 2 May, Napoleon, who had been made Consul for life on 4 August 1802, issued the following order to General Junot, Governor of Paris: 'All Englishmen from the ages of eighteen to sixty, or holding any commission from his Britannic Majesty, who are at present in France, shall immediately be constituted Prisoners of War. This measure must be executed by seven this evening. I am resolved that tonight not an Englishman shall be visible in the obscurest theatre or restaurant of Paris.' Amongst the thousand who were arrested as a result of this order were Fanny Burney and her husband; they remained interned till 1812.

At the same time, Napoleon set out his reasons for the renewal of hostilities in *Le Moniteur universel*, a daily newspaper founded in 1789, which had now been accorded semi-official status. The content and the rhetoric had changed but little since the heyday of the Revolution:

> England's greed and ambitions are finally out in the open. The mask is off. England allows just thirty-six more hours for peace to endure. She has gambled on sudden war so that she may seize at one fell swoop, on all the high seas, all the riches that had long been stored up in warehouses which the Spanish, Portuguese and Dutch colonies were able at long last to send to their mother countries, as well as the warships of the French Republic and the commercial vessels which had only just begun to revive our trade. For the sake of indulging her malignant and all too powerful passions, England disturbs the peace of the world, wantonly violates the rights of nations, tramples underfoot the most solemn treaties, and breaks her pledged faith – that ancient, eternal faith which even hordes of savages acknowledge and religiously respect.
>
> One single obstacle stands in the way of her policies and her ambitious course – victorious, moderate, prosperous France; her vigorous and enlightened government; her illustrious and magnanimous leader. These are the targets of England's delirious envy, of her repeated assaults, of her implacable hatred, of her diplomatic intrigues, of her maritime conspiracies and of the official denunciations to her Parliament and Subjects. But Europe is watching. France is arming. History is recording. Rome destroyed Carthage!

Once again, as in 1798, Napoleon's thoughts turned to the invasion of England. His preparations were characteristically thorough. He arranged for a printed placard to be displayed in every public office throughout France bearing the inscription: *Guerre au gouvernement anglais*. Broadsheets, cartoons, engravings and popular songs were all utilised to drive home the message that the English were a nation of unprincipled merchants whose exclusive concern was the extending of their commercial empire. Preparations for the invasion went steadily forward. On 16 November 1803, he wrote from Boulogne to his fellow Consul Cambacérès:

> The Minister of Marine arrived two days ago. I have spent the last three days in the camps and the port. Everything here is beginning to fall into place and to be moving in the right direction.
>
> From the heights of Ambleteuse [on the French coast, a few miles north of Boulogne], I have seen the English coast as clearly as one can see the Cavalry from the Tuileries. One could pick out the houses, and see people moving about. The Channel is a mere ditch, and will be crossed as soon as someone has the courage to attempt it.
>
> The Seine must be very high at Paris; it has never stopped raining here. We have more than 200 vessels, between Saint-Mars and this place, either at anchor or sailing to join us. I am expecting the arrival of a division today.

On 29 November, he wrote from Paris to Citizen Chaptal, Minister for Home Affairs: 'I want you to get a song written, to go to the tune of the *Chant du Départ*, for the invasion of England. While you are about it, have a number of songs written on the same subject, to go to different tunes. Plenty of topical plays, I know, have been produced. Make a selection of them, so that they may be put on in various Paris theatres – better still, at Boulogne, Bruges, and other places where the army is encamped.'

Bonaparte had his own very firm opinions on the appropriate way to address the troops and he made these clear in a sharp memorandum he sent on 9 September to Joseph Fouché, his Minister of Police. The Barère in question was the great Revolutionary orator who survived the blood-letting of the Terror:

> I see that Barère has written a 'Letter to the Army'. I haven't read it, but I am sure that there is no need to talk to the Army: it doesn't read the idle gossip of pamphleteers; one word in the Orders of the Day would do more than a hundred volumes of Cicero and Demosthenes. One can encourage the troops against England without talking to them; and nothing could be more absurd than to write them a pamphlet. It suggests distrust and intrigue and

the army needs none of it. Tell Barère, whose rhetoric and sophistry ill accord with his great reputation, not to do any more writing of this kind. He is always thinking the mob must be roused to exitement: on the contrary, the right way is to guide them without their knowing it. In short, he is a man of little ability.

Napoleon contributed many articles of his own, often unsigned, to *Le Moniteur universel* and regularly addressed personal *bulletins* to his troops. Whether he was more adept than Barère may perhaps be judged by the fact that the expression *mentir comme un bulletin* soon achieved proverbial status.

While Napoleon's preparations for the invasion proceeded, often clearly visible from the other side of the Channel, English emotions ran as high as they had done in 1798. Distinguished writers who, in their younger days, had travelled to France to luxuriate in the dawn of the Revolution, now vied with each other in patriotic appeals to their fellow countrymen as vibrant as Shakespeare's Henry V outside the walls of Harfleur or on the field at Agincourt. In 1803 Wordsworth composed a sonnet for those most directly threatened, 'To the Men of Kent':

> Vanguard of Liberty, ye Men of Kent,
> Ye Children of a Soil that doth advance
> Its haughty brow against the coast of France,
> Now is the time to prove your hardiment!
> To France be words of invitation sent!
> They from their fields can see the countenance
> Of your fierce war, may ken the glittering lance,
> And hear you shouting forth your brave intent.
> Left single, in bold parley, Ye of yore,
> Did from the Norman win a gallant wreath;
> Confirmed the charters that were yours before; –
> No parleying now! In Britain is one breath;
> We are all with you now from Shore to Shore: –
> Ye Men of Kent, 'tis Victory or Death!

Cobbett, once an enlisted soldier who had earlier fled the country to avoid prosecution for openly accusing his officers of peculation, returned to England from America and became the most grandiloquent of patriots. In 1803 he produced a pamphlet entitled 'Considerations for the People of this Country':

Shall we submit to misery and degradation like this, rather than encounter the expenses of war; rather than meet the honorable dangers of military combat; rather than make a generous use of the means which Providence has so bounteously placed in our hands? The sun, in his whole course round the globe, shines not on a spot so blessed as this great and now united Kingdom. Gay and productive fields and gardens, lofty and extensive woods, innumerable flocks and herds, rich and inexhaustible mines, a mild and wholesome climate, giving health, activity and vigour to fourteen millions of people; and shall we, who are thus forward and endowed; shall we, who are abundantly supplied with iron and steel, powder and lead; shall we, who have a fleet superior to the maritime force of all the world, and who are able to bring two millions of fighting men into the field; shall we yield up this dear and happy land, together with all the liberties and honours, to preserve which our fathers so often dyed the land and sea with their blood; shall we thus at once dishonour their graves, and stamp disgrace and infamy on the brows of our children; and shall we, too, make this base and dastardly surrender to an enemy whom, within these twelve years, our countrymen have defeated in every quarter of the world? No; we are not so miserably fallen; we cannot, in so short a space of time, have become so detestably degenerate; we have the strength and will to repel the hostility, to chastise the insolence of the foe. Mighty, indeed, must be our efforts but mighty also is the need. Singly engaged against the tyrants of the earth, Britain now attracts the eyes and hearts of mankind; groaning nations look to her for deliverance; justice, liberty, and religion are inscribed on her banners; her success will be hailed with the shouts of the universe, while tears of admiration and gratitude will bedew the heads of her sons who fall in the glorious contest.

However, the radical in Cobbett could not be long suppressed. In 1804, he wrote an equally lively article attacking flogging in the army and was sentenced to two years' imprisonment.

For those same, long-suffering English soldiers, a handbill was specially produced in 1803, inciting them to stiffen their sinews through what was, in effect, a history lesson:

Brave Soldiers

Defenders of your COUNTRY

The road to glory is open before you. – Pursue the great career of your forefathers, and rival them in the field of honour. *A proud and usurping* TYRANT (a name ever execrated by Englishmen) dares to *threaten our shores with INVASION, and to reduce the free born Sons of Britain to SLAVERY and SERVITUDE.* Forgetting what English Soldiers are capable of, and ranking them with the hirelings of the powers who have fallen his prey on the Continent, he supposes his threat easily executed. *Give him a lesson, my brave Countrymen, that he will not easily forget, and that France may have by heart, for a Century to come!* Neither the vaunting Hero (who deserted his own Comrades and Soldiers in Egypt), nor the French Army, have ever been able to cope with British valour when fairly opposed to it. Our Ancestors declared that *ONE ENGLISHMAN was ever a match for THREE FRENCHMEN* – and that man to man was too great odds in our favour. We have but to feel their sentiments, to confirm them – you will find that their declaration was founded on experience; and that even in our day, within these three years, an army of your brave Comrades has convinced its admiring Country that the balance is still as great as ever, against the enemy. Our EDWARD, *the illustrious Black Prince, laid waste the country of France, to the Gates of Paris, and, on the Plains of Cressy, left 11 Princes and 30,000 men dead upon the Field of Battle* – *a greater number than the whole English Army boasted at the beginning of the action.* The same heroic Prince, having annihilated the Fleet of France, *entirely routed her Army at Poitiers, took her King prisoner, and brought him Captive to London, with thousands of his Nobles and People, and all this is against an Army SIX TIMES AS NUMEROUS AS THAT OF THE ENGLISH!* Did not our Harry the Fifth invade France, and at Agincourt *oppose an Army of 9,000 men, sickly, fatigued, and half starved, to that of the French, amounting to 50,000;* and did he not leave 10,000 of the enemy dead upon the field, and take 14,000 prisoners, with the loss of only 400 men?

Have we not, within this century, to boast a MARLBOROUGH, who, (besides his other victories) at Blenheim slew 12,000 of the French, and made 14,000 Prisoners, *and in less than a month conquered 300 miles of Territory from the Enemy?* Did not the gallant WOLFE, in the year 1759, gain the Heights of Abraham with a handful of British Troops, and, afterwards, *defeat the whole French Army, and gain possession of all Canada, &c.?*

And are not the glories of our ABERCROMBY *and the Gallant ARMY of EGYPT* fresh in your minds? *An Army of 14,000 Britons, who landed in the face of upwards of 20,000 troops of France,* and drove from a country, with whose strongholds they were acquainted, and whose recourses they knew how to apply, a host of Frenchmen, enured to the Climate, and Veterans in arms? *Did they not cut in pieces that vaunted Corps of Buonaparte's, whose successes against other Powers had obtained for it the appellation of INVINCIBLE* – And is not their Standard (all that is left of it) a trophy, at this moment, in our Capital?

The Briton fights for his Liberty and Rights, the Frenchman fights for *Buonaparte,* who has robbed him of both! Which, then, in the nature of events, will be most zealous, most active, and most terrible in the Field of Battle? the independent supporter of his country's cause, or the Slave who trembles lest the arms of his comrades should be turned against himself; who knows that his Leader, his General, his *Tyrant, did not hesitate, after having*

MURDERED 4,000 disarmed Turks, in cool blood, to POISON 300 of his own sick Soldiers, of men who had been fighting his battles of ambition, and been wounded in his defence — English soldiers will scarcely credit this, but it is on record, not to be doubted, never to be expunged. But more; read and blush for the depravity even of an enemy. It is not that these bloody deeds have been perpetrated from necessity, from circumstances however imperious at the moment; they were the acts of cool and deliberate determination, and his purpose, no less sanguinary, is again declared in the event of success in his enterprise against this Country. Feeling that even the slavish followers of his fortune were not to be forced to embark in this ruinous and destructive expedition, he declares to them, in a public proclamation, or decoy, that *when they have landed in this Country, in order to make the booty the richer, NO QUARTER shall be given to the BASE ENGLISH who fight for their perfidious Government — that they shall be PUT TO THE SWORD, and their Property distributed among the Soldiers of the Victorious Army!!!* Say, is this the conduct of a Hero? is this the man who is destined to break the spirit of Englishmen? *shall we suffer an ASSASSIN to enter our blessed Country, and despoil our fields of their produce — to massacre our brave Soldiers in cool blood, and hang up every man who has carried arms?* Your cry is vengeance for the insult — and Vengeance is in your own hands. It must be signal and terrible! Like the bolt from Heaven, let it strike the devoted Army of Invaders! *Every Frenchman will find his Grave where he first steps on British ground, and not a Soldier of Buonaparte's boasted Legions shall escape the fate his ambitious Tyrant has prepared for him!*

BRITONS STRIKE HOME!

Or your Fame is for ever blasted, – Your Liberties for ever lost!!!

The English soldiery was by no means the only group to be assailed by jingoistic handbills. A twopenny booklet was widely circulated in 1803 under the title 'Address to the People of the United Kingdom of Great Britain and Ireland on the threatened Invasion':

Among the inexpressibly dreadful consequences which are sure to attend the conquest of your Island by the French, there is one of so horrible a nature, as to deserve distinct notice. This barbarous, but most artful people, when first they invade a country in the conquest of which they apprehend any difficulty, in order to obtain the confidence of the people, compel their troops to observe the strictest discipline, and often put a soldier to death for stealing the most trifling article. Like spiders they artfully weave a web round their victim, before they begin to prey upon it. But when their success is complete they then let loose their troops, with resistless fury, to commit the most horrible excesses, and to pillage, burn, and desolate, without mercy, and without distinction. But the practice to which I particularly allude will make your blood freeze in your veins. These wretches are accustomed, whenever they prevail, to subject the women to the most brutal violence, which they perpetrate with an insulting ferocity, of which the wildest savages would be incapable. To gratify their furious passions is not however their chief object in these atrocities. Their principal delight is to shock the feelings of fathers and brothers, and husbands! Will you, my Countrymen, while you can draw a trigger, or handle a pike, suffer your daughters, your sisters, and wives, to fall into the power of such monsters?

Striking fear into English citizens' hearts was not the only tactic employed to counter the threat of invasion. In his preparations at Boulogne, Napoleon had stressed the importance of martial music. The direct counter to this was the patriotic popular song, and a characteristic example of this is 'The Ploughman's Ditty' (1803) which had both as subtitle and explanatory gloss 'Being an Answer to that foolish Question "What have the Poor to Lose?"'

Because I'm but poor,
And Slender my store,
That I've nothing to lose is the cry;
Let who will declare it,
I vow I can't bear it,
I give all such praters the lie.

Tho' my house is but small,
Yet to have none at all,
Would sure be a greater distress, Sir;
Shall my garden so sweet,
And my orchard so neat,
Be the pride of a foreign oppressor?

On Saturday night,
'Tis still my delight,
With my wages to run home the faster;
But if French-men rule here,
I may look far and near,
But I never shall find a *pay-master*.

I've a dear little wife,
Whom I love as my life,
To lose her I should not much like;
And 'twould make me run wild,
To see my sweet child,
With its head on the point of a pike.

I've my Church too to save,
And will go to my grave
In defence of a Church that's the best;
I've my King too, God bless him!
Let no man oppress him,
For none has he ever opprest.

British Laws for my guard,
My cottage is barr'd;
'Tis safe in the light or the dark.
If the Squire should oppress,
I get instant redress,
My orchard's as safe as his park.

My cot is my throne,
What I have is my own,
And what is my own I will keep.
Shou'd *Boni* come now,
'Tis true I may plough,
But I'm sure that I never shall reap.

Now do but reflect,
What I have to protect;
Then doubt if to fight I shall choose –
King, Church, Babes and Wife,
Laws, Liberty, Life –
Now tell me I've nothing to lose.

Then I'll beat my ploughshare
To a sword or a spear,
And rush on these desperate men!
Like a lion I'll fight;
That my spear, now so bright,
May soon turn to a ploughshare again!

Another well-rehearsed tactic, common in human conflicts before and since, has been to represent the enemy not so much as fearsome as comic and contemptible. On one memorable occasion, the *Morning Post* characterised Napoleon as 'an indefinable being, half-African, half-European, a Mediterranean mulatto' and populist cartoons represented French soldiers either as gaunt and unkempt or as subhuman and simian.

In France, Napoleon exercised draconian control over the national press. The *Directoire* had imprisoned or deported journalists suspected of supporting the return of the monarchy. Napoleon went further still and in 1800 he suppressed sixty out of seventy-three political papers then being produced in Paris. Over the thirteen remaining, a Bureau under police control maintained tight vigilance; departmental *préfets* supervised the press in the provinces. The same thoroughness was applied to the production of anti-English propaganda. Hand-picked experts were encouraged to write books and articles to denigrate England and the English, for example the Comte d'Hauterive, who in 1800 declared in his report *De l'Etat de la France à la fin de l'An VIII*:

> English vessels cover every sea: she sends soldiers, arms, gold, agents to the four quarters of the world; there is no colony so remote that her distant expeditions do not threaten it; there is no empire, however much a stranger to European intercourse, to which she does not labour to procure access and to secure exclusive establishments there. Countries Europe scarcely knows have received from England names which she regards as marks of ownership: those still unknown await English appellations; and as she extends the realm of nautical geography, she enlarges at the same time that of English maritime domination.

Another was Joseph Fiévée, who, in 1802, in his *Lettres sur l'Angleterre* reiterated the charge regularly made by Anglophobes, that the English are fundamentally barbaric:

> If you set politics aside and define civilisation as the art of making society gentle, comfortable and agreeable, then the English are the most uncivilised people in Europe. The lack of sociability you find in their nature has three main causes: one, the high regard they have for money; two, the boredom they feel in the presence of women; three, the exaggerated opinion they have of themselves, which borders on mania.
>
> The store the English set by wealth is such that when they want to express their admiration for anyone, they say he's worth a great deal of money and they even stipulate the sum. For this reason, before they form an opinion about a person, they show a great deal of curiosity about the value of his possessions.
>
> It's because they want to get down to drinking that Englishmen get the women to withdraw after dinner. Often, at eleven o'clock at night, they're still sat around the same table while the women are yawning their heads off in some upstairs drawing-room. It's not uncommon for the master of the house to which the wife has invited guests, to leave their company and go off to the tavern to drink, chat and play to his heart's content with his friends. Salon life is unbearable for your Englishman, yet, remarkably, he's more comfortable in it than men in any other country.

Yet another of Napoleon's propagandists was the Irishman Arthur O'Connor, who declared in his report on *The Present State of Great Britain* (1804) that Britain was both barbaric and aggressively imperialistic:

> Rome has given us an example of the extent to which dominion may be carried by exacting tribute from the nations she has vanquished; but it has been reserved for Great Britain to unite the passion for domination with the insatiable spirit of mercantile exaction.
>
> An island at one extremity of Europe, with a population of scarcely eleven millions, she bestrides the other three-quarters of the earth; one foot on the vast continent of America, the other upon the Indies, she consigns Africa to external barbarism and slavery, that the produce of the Antilles may swell the list of her imports; collecting annually in kind, by a mixt system of commerce, exaction, plunder and tribute to the amount of $17\frac{1}{2}$ millions from the produce of the different nations she had conquered, which she deals out to the nations of Europe at the exorbitant rate of a monopoly price; making those which are territorially free, but maritimely enslaved, feel a part of the injustice she uses to those unfortunate countries over whose liberties she exercises an uncontrolled dominion.

In spite of – or even because of – these policies and pronouncements, there still remained free spirits in France resolved to indulge their enthusiasm for all things English. One such was Louis Crozet, who wrote in January 1806 to his friend Stendhal:

> I'm swotting up English three hours every day. Once I've mastered it, then in order to make myself original and give myself a social *persona* different from myself, I want to practise anglomania. I'll have powder in my wig and my side-burns, an English jacket, wide-flared trousers, a big walking-stick, a hat with a low crown and a turned-down brim and my general demeanour will be grotesque and grave. At the same time, I'll have a cup of tea continuously beside me. In the end, I'll take my anglomania so far that I'll even put on a frock coat. Then I shall say nothing or do nothing lest people start laughing at me and calling me an Eccentric.

Stendhal, on this subject as on all others, was very much his own man, both ambivalent and ironic. In March 1806, he wrote to his sister Pauline from Marseille to express his opinions of French Anglomaniacs:

> They claim to be apostles of liberty so they've started to praise England for absolutely everything. Everybody has learned English and I've seen these

Anglomaniacs getting enthusiastic over 'The Rape of the Lock', a bad little poem of Pope's, not having read 'Le Lutrin' by Boileau which is worth a whole wigful of such locks! They prefer Shakespeare to Corneille. If these two geniuses had written in the other's language, of course they'd prefer Corneille to Shakespeare because of the same cultural prejudice. Be on your guard against such folly, my dearest. Admire English writers for the power, the imagination and the truth with which they depict nature but don't be bowled over by their flowery style or the vastness and the blackness of their imagination.

While Stendhal prized his own freedom of judgement and of movement, he also admired *énergie*. It is not, therefore, altogether surprising that in that same year he re-enlisted in Napoleon's army with the Commissariat.

In the meantime, Napoleon had continued to provide spectacular evidence not only of his unquenchable *énergie* but also of his ruthless ambition. Determined to eliminate any semblance of Royalist opposition from his progression to supreme power, in March 1804 he sent his agents into Germany, to Ettenheim, near Baden, whence they kidnapped the Duc d'Enghien. Thirty-two years old, and the last in line of the House of Condé, the Duc d'Enghien had fought in the *Armée des émigrés*. On 21 March, he was charged at Vincennes with plotting to overthrow Napoleon, taken down to the moat, where he was shot, and unceremoniously buried at midnight in a grave already waiting for him.

This event did Napoleon's reputation much harm. It prompted the resignation of Chateaubriand from the Embassy at Rome, to which Napoleon had appointed him largely because of the fame achieved by *Le Génie du Christianisme*, which appeared in 1802 at the moment when Roman Catholicism once again became the official religion of France. This bond with the Church was further strengthened on 2 December 1804 when Pope Pius VII attended the Mass in Notre Dame when Napoleon had himself crowned as Emperor.

One month later, on 2 January 1805, no longer a commoner but now a fellow monarch, Napoleon again addressed a personal letter to the King of England:

Monsieur my Brother: called to the throne of France by Providence, and by the votes of the Senate, the people, and the army, my first impulse is to pray for peace. France and England are using up their resources. They might well go on fighting each other for centuries. But are not their governments failing in the most sacred of all their duties? And will not their own consciences reproach them with so much useless and pointless bloodshed? I think it no dishonour to make the first advances. I have shown the world enough evidence, I fancy, that I shrink from nothing that war may bring, but there is no need for that to cause alarm. Peace is my heart's desire though war has never been alien to my notion of glory. I beg your Majesty not to reject the honour of being the world's first peacemaker. Do not leave this pleasant task to your children! . . . During the last ten years Your Majesty has gained in territory and in riches more than the whole area of Europe. Your nation is at the very peak of prosperity. What more do you hope from war? To form a coalition of some of the continental powers? But the continent will not move, and a coalition would merely underline the preponderance of France on the continent. To revive our internal disorders? But the times are not what they were. To ruin us financially? But a financial system based on good agriculture is indestructible. To deprive France of her colonies? But colonies are, for France, a matter of secondary importance, and does not Your Majesty already possess more than you can defend? If Your Majesty really thinks about it, you will see that the war has no aim, and offers no guarantees of a favorable outcome for you. Lord, what a sad Prospect it is, to make men fight just for the sake of fighting! The world is big enough for both our nations to live in, and commonsense is surely strong enough to let us find the way to resolve all our differences if both of us have the will to do it.

Napoleon's overtures were again rebuffed, so preparations proceeded for the long-delayed invasion of England. On 23 August 1805, he wrote to Talleyrand from his army camp at Boulogne, still aware of the considerable risks and already considering alternatives:

My fleet left Ferrol on 26 Thermidor with thirty-four sail; there was no enemy in sight. If it obeys orders, joins the Brest fleet, and sails up the Channel, there is still time; England is mine. If on the other hand, my admirals hesitate, manoeuvre badly, and fail in their task, I have no alternative but to wait for the winter to get my flotilla across. It is a risky operation . . . Things being so, I am off at full speed. I am striking camp and replacing my fighting battalions with reserves which, in any case, give me a formidable enough army at Boulogne. So there I am, on the 1st of Vendémiare, in the middle of Germany with 200,000 men and another 25,000 in the Kingdom of Naples. I march on Vienna and refuse to lay down arms until I've got Naples and Venice and have so augmented the Elector of Bavaria's territory that I have nothing more to fear from Austria.

In the event, Napoleon decided not to launch the invasion in August. Instead, he advanced into Germany, determined to smash the Third

Coalition, which in September he described in a proclamation to his troops as 'this new league which the hatred and gold of England has woven'. On 13 October, he addressed his troops on the eve of the battle of Ulm, a fortified town in Würtemberg: 'We ought today to be in London. We would have avenged six centuries of injury and restored the freedom of the seas. But remember that tomorrow you will be fighting the ally of England.'

The Austrians were yet again crushed, but French jubilation was short-lived: just one week later, the French fleet was defeated in the battle of Trafalgar. English celebrations were necessarily overshadowed by the news that Admiral Nelson, the hero of the hour, had died on the deck of HMS *Victory*, his spine shattered by a French cannon ball. A further calamity lay in store. On 9 November 1805, William Pitt, architect of the Third Coalition, made what was to prove his last public speech at the Lord Mayor's Banquet. To the assembled company, he declared: 'I return many thanks for the honour you have done me; but Europe is not to be saved by a single man. England has saved herself by her exertions and will, I trust, save Europe by her example.' A few weeks later he was dead, though he lived long enough to receive news of the devastating victory with which Napoleon rounded off the year, at Austerlitz, now in Moravia but then part of the Austrian Empire.

Before the battle against the combined armies of Austria and Russia, led by their Emperors in person, Napoleon described the opposing troops as 'the hired servants of England who are animated by so intense a hatred of our nation'. After his crushing victory, in a bulletin to his soldiers, he declared on 3 December:

> Never did a battlefield look more horrible. From the middle of the immense lake, the screams of thousands of men could be heard, but there was no way of coming to their aid. It will take three days before all the enemy wounded can be evacuated to Brünn; one's heart bleeds. May all this bloodshed, may all these miseries be avenged at last on the perfidious islands who are responsible. May the cowardly oligarchs in London be visited with punishment for so much suffering!

Clearly, England remained the principal enemy. Until it had been decisively defeated, Napoleon could not consider his cause truly won.

*

The leaders of the French Revolution not only transformed the face of society, they also radically changed the way of waging war. Throughout the eighteenth century, armies had remained relatively small. Often soldiers felt little emotional allegiance to the government for which they fought and the armies of many absolute monarchs regularly contained many mercenaries. Pitched battles, being almost as costly to the victors as to the vanquished, were, whenever possible, avoided; campaigns consisted, for the most part, of outmanoeuvring and wearing down one's opponent. In general, civilians became involved only when their area became the scene of a military campaign. Wars could still be waged in a chivalrous spirit, like some medieval joust. Before the battle of Fontenoy in 1745, the commander of the French decorously invited the English to fire first. At the height of the Seven Years War, Sterne could travel to France to recuperate from illness and be openly fêted by Parisian society. During the American War of Independence, Sir George Rodney was detained in France not because he was the leading English admiral but because he was a debtor. The French Admiral Maréchal de Biron generously paid Rodney's debts and graciously permitted him to recross the Channel and resume command of the English fleet. There were no recriminations when Rodney then proceeded to smash the French fleet off the Iles des Saintes.

The French Revolutionaries put an end to such old-world niceties, as to so much else, and Napoleon carried on where they left off. From now on, the battle-plan of army commanders was not just to outmanoeuvre but to annihilate the enemy. Nationalism increasingly became the force motivating the troops. Instead of the mercenary battalions of the absolutist kings of old, now entire peoples were called upon to fight each other. The huge armies at Napoleon's disposal and his brilliant use of them on the battlefield enabled him to place his brothers on the thrones of his immediate neighbours and to fulfil, albeit briefly, Louis XIV's dream of French hegemony over Europe. He was to say on one occasion: 'I have succeeded not to the throne of Louis XIV but to that of Charlemagne.'

As well as his tireless energy, his ability to think with total clarity and his meticulous attention to detail, Napoleon had one further great military quality: his capacity to improvise and innovate. In a bulletin to his troops in Warsaw on 22 January 1807 he showed that he had glimpsed the concept of germ-warfare:

Now that the English can no longer make the world believe that the Russians, the Tartars and the Kalmuks are about to swallow up the French army – for even in the London coffee-houses they now realise that these worthy allies of theirs just cannot withstand the sight of our bayonets – they are now making appeals to dysentery, bubonic plague and every sort of epidemic disease. If these scourges were at the disposal of the London Cabinet, there is no doubt that not only our army but even our provinces and the entire working class of the Continent would become their victims.

In October 1808, unwilling finally to relinquish his dream of invading England, he instructed his master mathematician, Gaspard Monge, to evaluate a scheme submitted by his War Ministry for transporting his Army across the Channel in a hundred gigantic Montgolfier balloons. A more effective way of striking at England, at least in theory, was to impose an economic blockade, the so-called Continental System, which was designed to exclude British goods from all the ports in Europe.

In August 1807, he described 'English vessels laden with useless wealth wandering around the high seas, where they claim to rule as sole masters, seeking in vain from the Sound to the Hellespont for a port to open and receive them'. This was the rhetoric of a wishful thinker. The Continental System could be effective only if operated over a relatively long period. In the event, it was rigorously applied only from mid 1807 till mid 1808 and from mid 1810 till mid 1812. England was hard pressed but survived at a high price. The cost was a doubling of the National Debt (up to £700 million by the end of the war), and a dramatic loss in the esteem of its European neighbours. The English could, when circumstances demanded, be as ruthless as Napoleon. Their response to the Continental System was a rigorous blockade of the ports of France and of her allies and this caused considerable resentment in the non-belligerent countries. Resentment as well as bitterness and anger also resulted from the pre-emptive strikes launched by Britain against the Dutch naval base at Helder in 1799 and, even more, by the bombardment of what was still neutral Copenhagen in 1807 (an episode Vichy propagandists were all too ready to recall when the Royal Navy attacked the French fleet at Mers-el-Kebir in 1940). A few years later, a young English nobleman and his tutor visiting the arsenal at Copenhagen found that they were obliged to pass for Frenchmen in order to avoid the insults of the Danish sailors, while, travelling at about the same time in Sweden, Henry Crabb Robinson found the anti-English feeling so general 'that I was advised to travel as a German through the country and I did so'. Such dislike of the English was not confined to Europe. In March 1810, Thomas Jefferson, a faithful Francophile, wrote to Langdon explaining why he felt unable to join the British side against Napoleon: 'Britain might take a separate peace and leave us in the lurch. Her good faith! The faith of a nation of merchants! The *Punica fides* of modern Carthage! Of the friend and Protector of Copenhagen!' The content and the terminology of this pronouncement are a direct echo of the Anglophobes of the French Revolution.

Napoleon inherited all the problems that had confronted the leaders of the First Republic: the need to implement radical reforms at home and to defeat their many enemies abroad. He carried out the former with consummate speed and kill, reconstructing local as well as national government, transforming the country's financial and legal systems. Five separate legal codes were devised, governing civil law, civil procedure, commercial law, criminal law and penal law: all were instituted between 1804 and 1810. Napoleon himself presided over the Commission that drafted the *Code Civil*, which was given the alternative title of the *Code Napoléon* in 1807. It is enshrined in three books that contain over two thousand articles, each a model of lucidity. Stendhal later told Balzac that when he was writing *La Chartreuse de Parme*, he read two pages of Napoleon's code each morning to establish his literary tone.

In 1808, to demonstrate that he ruled over a real Court, Napoleon inaugurated his own *noblesse impériale* with a hierarchy of *ducs, princes, barons, comtes* and *chevaliers*. In other key areas, where he did not innovate, he amended. So, the *Ecole normale supérieure*, first established by the *Convention* in 1794 to provide leading teachers for the State's education system, was re-established to supply staff for the *Université impériale*, which was inaugurated by Napoleon in 1808. It is still located in the rue d'Ulm in Paris, renamed after his great victory of 1805. (This was standard practice for the times. England was soon to have its Trafalgar Square with Nelson's Column in its centre. When the railways came, London acquired its Waterloo Station and Paris its Gare Austerlitz.) Similarly, the *Ecole polytechnique*, also founded by the *Convention* in 1794, to provide civilian engineers, was transformed by Napoleon into a military college, and day pupils became boarders.

Napoleon was in constant need of trained personnel because the war with England seemed unending. While the armies of the First Republic and of Napoleon's Empire regularly won spectacular victories on land, England continued to rule the seas. The dilemma was succinctly expressed by Joseph de Maistre, sometimes called 'the right-wing Voltaire', who, after refusing to swear allegiance to the French Republic, fled to Switzerland and later, in 1803, became Sardinia's envoy to Russia. On 15 February 1806, he wrote to M. le Chevalier de Rossi: 'The English are lovers of the liquid element: on dry land they rarely find firm footing.' On 17 September 1809, he wrote to Prince Koslowski: 'Are the French short of intelligence, of courage or of energy? Are they not great mathematicians and great businessmen? Yet again and again they are overwhelmed at sea. It's the same for the English on land for all their bravery and all their outstanding talent.'

While this was fair comment on the earlier phases of the Napoleonic wars, by 1809 it needed revising. By then, Napoleon's judgement and good fortune had begun to play him false. Though his Continental System brought limited dividends, for the first time in his dazzling career, one of his land campaigns was not crowded with the customary crushing victory. His soldiers battled on in Spain in the teeth of dogged nationalist resistance, and an opposing general fully able to vie with him emerged in the person of Arthur Wellesley, later to be ennobled as the Duke of Wellington. Napoleon lost the best of his troops in the ill-fated march on Moscow in 1812 and was soundly defeated at Leipzig on 16–18 October 1813 by the armies of the massive Sixth Coalition (Austria, Britain, Prussia, Russia, Spain and Sweden).

In January 1814, the Coalition armies invaded France and began their advance on Paris. Between the perennial protagonists, England and France, the mutual antagonism as well as the forms of insult were as bitter as ever. Nicolas Soult, Duke of Dalmatia and Marshal of France, sought to rally his troops with the cry: 'Does there exist upon the face of the globe a point known to the English where they have not destroyed by seditions and violence all manufactures which could rival their own?' The English counterview was grandiloquently expressed by Robert Southey who, like his close friends Coleridge and Wordsworth, had been transformed by historical events from a radical to a patriot. Back in 1795, he had been less than complimentary about one of England's great victories over the French in his poem on 'The Battle of Blenheim' in

which none of the latter-day local inhabitants could recall the winners
or the point of the conflict. Now, as Poet Laureate and the author of a
fine *Life of Nelson*, he felt obliged to voice his country's feelings in his
'Ode written during the negotiations with Buonaparte in 1814':

> O France! beneath this fierce Barbarian's sway
> Disgraced thou art to all succeeding times;
> Rapine, and blood, and fire have mark'd thy way,
> All loathsome, all unutterable crimes.
> A curse is on thee, France! from far and wide
> It hath gone up to Heaven. All lands have cried
> For vengeance upon thy detested head!
> All nations curse thee, France! for whereso'er
> In peace or war thy banner hath been spread,
> All forms of human woe have follow'd there.
> The Living and the Dead
> Cry out alike against thee! They who bear,
> Crouching beneath its weight, thine iron yoke,
> Join in the bitterness of secret prayer
> The voice of that innumerable throng,
> Whose slaughter'd spirits days and night invoke
> The Everlasting Judge of right and wrong.
> How long, O Lord! Holy and Just, how long!
>
> A merciless oppressor hast thou been,
> Thyself remorselessly oppress'd meantime;
> Greedy of war, when all that thou couldst gain
> Was but to dye thy soul with deeper crime,
> And rivet faster round thyself the chain.
> O blind to honour, and to interest blind,
> When thus in abject servitude resign'd
> To this barbarian upstart, thou couldst brave
> God's justice, and the heart of human kind!
> Madly thou thoughtest to enslave the world,
> Thyself the while a miserable slave.
> Behold the flag of vengeance is unfurl'd!
> The dreadful armies of the North advance;
> While England, Portugal, and Spain combined,
> Give their triumphant banners to the wind,
> And stand victorious in the fields of France . . .
>
> France! if thou lovest thine ancient fame,
> Revenge thy sufferings and thy shame!
> By the bones which bleach on Jaffa's beach;
> By the blood which on Domingo's shore

Hath clogg'd the carrion-birds with gore;
By the flesh which gorged the wolves of Spain,
Or stiffen'd on the snowy plain
Of frozen Moscovy;
By the bodies which lie all open to the sky,
Tracking from Elbe to Rhine the Tyrant's flight;
By the widow's and the orphan's cry;
By the childless parent's misery;
By the lives which he hath shed;
By the ruin he hath spread;
By the prayers which rise for curses on his head;
Redeem, O France! thine ancient fame,
Revenge thy sufferings and thy shame,
Open thine eyes! . . . too long hast thou been blind;
Take vengeance for thyself, and for mankind!

In the event, on this occasion it was not France that took vengeance on Napoleon but the Coalition. The Allied armies entered Paris on 31 March 1814 and Napoleon abdicated on 6 April. By the Treaty of Paris, which was signed on 30 May 1814, Louis XVIII became king while France lost her colonial gains and was reduced to the territorial boundaries of January 1792.

Napoleon was treated with reasonable leniency, and was allowed to retire to the island of Elba in the Mediterranean. In March 1815, he returned to France at the head of a mere seven hundred men. He re-entered Paris on 20 March to wild popular acclaim: his troops and the cheering populace carried him to the Tuileries in triumph, Louis XVIII having had the good sense to depart for Belgium on the previous day. It was in Belgium, by the village of Waterloo, south of Brussels, that Napoleon was finally and conclusively defeated on 18 June 1815. Though he had two massive armies arrayed against him, the United Army (British, Dutch, Hanoverian and Brunswickian troops) under the Duke of Wellington and the Prussian Army led by Blücher, victory remained in doubt almost till the last. Wellington described it as a 'damned nice thing – the nearest run thing you ever saw in your life'. His other, better known, comment, that 'the battle of Waterloo was won in the playing fields of Eton', is surely somewhat wide of the mark. The battle was finally won with the belated arrival of Blücher's main force, which took Napoleon's front-line troops in the flank as they were mounting one last desperate assault against Wellington's hard-pressed squares. The French, now facing ferocious onslaught from two sides at once, broke and were routed, except for Napoleon's crack Imperial Guard. When, at length, totally surrounded, they were called upon to surrender, their commanding officer, General Cambronne, is reported to have professed the elegant reply '*La garde meurt et ne se rend pas.*' What, in fact, he actually retorted was terser but more emphatic: '*Merde!*'

When it became clear to him that his cause was, this time, irretrievably lost, Napoleon used rather more words. On Bastille Day 1815, he wrote to England's Prince Regent, comparing himself to the illustrious Greek general Themistocles who, on being rejected by his fellow-citizens, found honourable retirement with their erstwhile arch-enemies, the Persians: 'Your Royal Highness: victimised by the factions which divide my country, and by the hostility of the European powers, I have ended my political career; and I come, as Themistocles did, to claim a seat by the hearth of the British people. I put myself under the protection which I claim from Your Royal Highness, as the strongest, the stubbornest, and the most generous of my foes.' The English, doubtless mindful of Napoleon's spectacular escape from Elba and of the charismatic influence he continued to exercise over his people, proved distinctly less generous to their distinguished enemy than the Persians had been towards Themistocles. The days had long since past when a defeated French ruler, such as Jean le Bon, could be feasted by the victorious Black Prince, could cross voluntarily into England, be hailed by the London populace and accommodated for the rest of his life in a royal palace. Napoleon was banished to the desolate island of St Helena, far out in the South Atlantic, and there, confined in his villa called Longwood, he spent quietly the remaining years of his previously noise-filled life.

An anonymous poem that was first published in the *Morning Chronicle* on 31 August 1815, and reprinted in October 1815 in No. LXXXV of the *Gentleman's Magazine*, would seem to indicate that Napoleon deserved more generous treatment. It is written in decidedly populist vein (in the 1990s, it would have appeared in a tabloid paper such as the *Sun* or the *Daily Mirror*) and the allusions are all to heroes of the boxing fraternity ('the Fancy'): Tom Cribb was a popular champion of the day, famous for his sportsmanship, while 'the Cheesemonger' was a Life Guardsman, killed in the course of a memorably savage bout:

Epistle from Tom Cribb to Big Ben
Concerning some Foul Play in a Late Transaction

What! BEN, my big hero, is *this* thy *renown*?
Is *this* the new go? – kick a man when he's down?
When the foe has knock'd under, to tread on him then –
By the fist of my father, I blush for thee, BEN!
'Foul! foul! all the Lads of the Fancy exclaim –
CHARLEY SHOCK is electrified – Belcher spits flame –
And MOLYNEUX – aye, even BLACKY cries 'Shame!'

Time was, when JOHN BULL little difference spied
Twixt the foe at his feet and the friend at his side;
When he found (such his humour in fighting and eating)
His foe, like his beef-steak, the sweeter for beating! –
But this comes, Master BEN, of your curst foreign notions,
Your trinkets, wigs, thingumbobs, gold lace and lotions;
Your Noyaus, Curaçaos, and the Devil knows what –
(One swig of *Blue Ruin* [gin] is worth the whole lot!)
Your great and small *crosses* – (my eyes, what a brood!
A cross-buttock from *me* would do some of them good:)
Which have spoilt you, till hardly a drop, my old porpoise,
Of pure English claret is left in your corpus;
And (as Jim says) the only one trick, good or bad,
Of the Fancy you're up to, is *fiibbing*, my lad!
Hence it comes – BOXIANA, disgrace to thy page! –
Having *flloor'd* by good luck, the first *swell* of the age,
Having conquer'd the prime *one*, that *mill'd* us all round,
You kick'd him, old BEN, as he gasp'd on the ground! –
Aye – just at the time to show spunk, if you'd got any –
Kick'd him and jaw'd him and lag'd him to Botany.

Oh Shade of the Cheesemonger! – you, who, alas!
Doubled up, by the dozen, those Mounseers in brass,
On that great day of milling, when blood lay in lakes,
When kings held the bottle and Europe the stakes, –
Look down upon BEN – seen him, dunghill all o'er,
Insult the fall'n foe that can harm him no more! –
Out, cowardly *spooney*! – again and again,
By the fist of my Father, I blush for thee, BEN.
To *shew the white feather* is many men's doom,
But, what of *one* feather? BEN shows a whole PLUME!

Stendhal was clearly unaware of Tom Cribb's Epistle when, in his article on Napoleon I, published in 1818, he protested over the way in which his personal and national hero had been treated:

Napoleon, who had appealed to the much-vaunted magnanimity of the English people, is confined to a rock on which, using indirect methods, and avoiding the shame of resorting to poison, he is being done to death. I won't say that the English nation is viler than another; I'll merely observe that Heaven has given it an unfortunate opportunity to demonstrate how vile it can be. What protests have there been against this great crime? Where is the outburst of generosity from the mass of the populace at the news of this infamy? Where the denunciation of this government, before all the other nations? O Saint-Helena, a rock which will henceforth be forever notorious, you are the reef on which English honour has foundered!

Three years later, writing his *Souvenirs d'Egotisme*, his attitude might seem to have softened, but he was merely replacing one Anglophobic grievance with another: 'The English, I think, are the most obtuse and the most barbaric people on earth . . . to such a degree that I can forgive them for the infamies of Saint-Helena: they weren't even aware of them! These worthy English, forever haunted by the threat of dying of hunger if they for a single instant forget to work, dismissed thoughts of Saint-Helena as they dismiss thoughts of Raphaël as a total waste of time. That's all there is to it.'

★

Napoleon, for his part, would seem to have harboured little resentment for the English. His comments, recorded by the few visitors he was occasionally allowed, are remarkably free of rancour; they suggest that at the end of his life, he regarded England as he seems to have done at the outset, with something like indulgence. Some of these comments were noted by the Comte de Las Cases who followed Napoleon to St Helena and stayed there till he was expelled from the island in November 1816. After Napoleon died, his *Mémorial de Sainte-Hélène* (1822–23) became a bestseller in France. It was the most treasured book of Julien Sorel, the youthful hero of Stendhal's novel *Le Rouge et le Noir*.

On 3 March 1816, Napoleon told Las Cases what would have happened had his army succeeded in crossing the Channel:

I had left open the possibility of a landing in England. I had the best army that ever was – the army that was to win at Austerlitz, and with that I have said all that needs to be said. Four days would have been enough to reach London. I would not have entered as a conqueror but as a liberator – a new

William of Orange, but more generous and disinterested. The discipline in my army would have been exemplary; it would have behaved in London as if it were still in Paris. No sacrifices, not even war taxes would have been exacted from the English. We would have appeared to them not as victors but as brothers who had come to restore to them their freedom and their rights. I would have told them to form an assembly and to achieve their regeneration through their own efforts. I would have told them that in political legislation they were our seniors; that we wanted nothing from them except to rejoice in their happiness and prosperity – and I would have been scrupulously faithful to my words. And thus after a few months, these two nations, these ruthless enemies, would have become united in their identical principles, their policies and their interests.

However, on 20 April, he painted a less rosy picture: 'In my scheme, England was in nature bound to become a mere appendix of France. Nature has made her one of our islands, just like Oléron or Corsica.'

Another of Napoleon's visitors was Barry O'Meara, a British naval surgeon, who recorded a conversation they had in 1817 on a remark which, then and ever since, gave considerable offence:

You were greatly offended with me for having called you a nation of shop-keepers. Had I meant by this that you were a nation of cowards, you would have had reason to be displeased, even though it were ridiculous and contrary to historical fact. But no such thing was ever intended. I meant that you were a nation of merchants and that all your great riches and your great resources arose from commerce, which is true. What else makes up the wealth of England? It is not the extent of your territory or the size of your population. It is not mines of gold, silver or diamonds. Moreover, no sensible person ought to be ashamed at being called a shop-keeper. But your Prince and your mistress appear to wish to change altogether the esprit of the English and to make you into a different nation; to make you ashamed of your shops and your trade, which have made you what you are, and to sigh after nobility, titles and decorations . . . Stick to your ships, your commerce, and your counting-houses, and leave ribbons, decorations and cavalry uniforms to the Continent, and you will prosper.

In his anxiety to be diplomatic, Napoleon was here being either disingenuous or forgetful. The phrase 'a nation of shop-keepers' would seem to derive from Adam Smith's classic *Inquiry into the Nature and Causes of the Wealth of Nations* (1776). In Book IV, Chapter 7, Smith stated: 'To found a great empire for the sole purpose of raising up a people of customers, may, at first sight, appear a project fit only for a nation of shop-keepers.' Smith's was a book that Napoleon is known to have read.

In the following year, Napoleon had a further conversation with O'Meara, in which he deplored both the English class system and the way in which the English treated their ordinary soldiers and sailors:

> There is not a population in the world, not even the Prussian, worse treated than the English. Apart from their obligation to have to serve as soldiers, the German rabble are better off than yours. You've no more regard for yours than if they were so many serfs, and that's precisely the way you treat them. On my lords and my ladies, to the aristocracy and the *gentlemen*, oh, indeed, you lavish every kind of attention and regard. Nothing can be too good for them; no treatment can be kind enough. But for your ordinary people – bah! they're so many dogs. As your contractors said when supplying provisions to the French prisoners: 'It's too good for those French dogs.' You yourself have a lot of aristocratic arrogance in your head. You appear to look down on your common people as if they were a race of inferior beings. You go on about your *freedom*! But can anything be more horrible than your pressing of seamen? You send your boats ashore to seize hold of every male they can find. If he has the bad luck to be a common person, if he can't prove that he's a gentleman, then he's rushed on board ship and must serve as a seaman in every quarter of the globe. And then you have the gall to criticise conscription in France! It wounds your pride because it falls upon *all ranks*. Oh, how shocking that a gentleman's son should be required to defend his country just as if he were one of the riffraff! And that he should be compelled to expose his body or put himself on the same level as a vile plebeian! Yet God made all man alike. Who makes up the nation? It isn't your lords or your fat prelates and churchmen, or your gentleman or your oligarchy. Oh, one day the people will take their revenge. There will be terrible scenes.

It is instructive to compare this with some comments on French officers and men made by Napoleon's arch-enemy the Duke of Wellington, recorded by Earl Stanhope in his *Notes of Conversations with the Duke of Wellington: 1831–1851*:

> I never on any occasion knew them behave otherwise than well. Their officers too were as good as possible. The French soldiers are more under control than ours. It was quite shocking what excesses ours committed when once let loose. Our soldiers could not resist wine. The French too could shift better for themselves, and always live upon the country . . .
>
> The French system of conscription brings together a fair sample of all classes; ours is composed of the scum of the earth.

Throughout his exile on St Helena, Napoleon's constant companion was the Comte de Montholon, a general who had served as his aide-de-camp during the Hundred Days. To him Napoleon dictated the *Mémoires pour servir à l'histoire de France sous Napoléon* (1823) and he it was, therefore, who noted his final comments on the fortune he foresaw for Anglo–French relations:

> The Bourbons will not last. When I am dead, there will be a universal reaction in my favour, even in England. That is a fine inheritance for my son. It is possible, that, in order to wipe out the memory of their persecutions, the English will favour the return of my son to France. But in order to live on good terms with England, it is necessary at all costs to favour her commercial interests. This necessity entails two consequences: either fight England or share the world with her. The second alternative is the only possible one in our day.

How prescient these comments turned out to be will be examined in the following chapter. For the moment, it suffices to observe that on his death-bed, England clearly continued to preoccupy Napoleon as it had done throughout his stupendous career. These remarks were dictated on 17 April 1821; he died, it was presumed of cancer of the stomach, on 5 May.

*

A character so charismatic and events so prodigious could not fail to challenge the poet, the novelist and the historian. While he lived, he became an object of execration to England's leading poets, all of whom set out with high democratic ideals and who quickly came to see Napoleon as the most ruthless of despots. The evolving attitudes of Coleridge, Wordsworth and Southey have been noted. Byron, who was shortly to become a cult-figure himself in France, and who in *Childe Harold's Pilgrimage* (1816) provides a vivid evocation of the first sounds of Waterloo reaching Brussels, admired Napoleon's larger-than-life heroic qualities but was disappointed 'that he forsooth must be a king'. Throughout his short life, Shelley remained consistently opposed to despotism in general and to Napoleon in particular: his poem 'Ozymandias' has often been seen as an ironic epitaph on what was, for him, the humiliating dénouement to Napoleon's Egyptian adventure and, for that matter, the whole of his vainglorious career.

Adequate though it may have been as a summation of Napoleon's expedition to the Levant, Shelley's desolate desert scene proved singularly inappropriate as an analogue for the aftermath to his lonely death. He remained a powerful source of inspiration for major poets and novelists. His personality is evoked with dramatic effect by Stendhal both in *Le Rouge et le Noir* and *La Chartreuse de Parme*; by Hugo in *L'Expiation*, in which his heroic presence is ironically contrasted with what was, for Hugo, the puny figure of his nephew, Napoleon III; and by Tolstoy in *War and Peace*. In English, by far the most impressive representation of him is to be found in Hardy's vast poem *The Dynasts* (1904–1908), subtitled 'an epic-drama of the War with Napoleon in Three Parts, nineteen Acts and one hundred and Thirty Scenes'. Partly in blank verse, partly in prose, it deals with every significant event in Napoleon's career from 1805 onwards, and the list of *dramatis personae* includes not only Wessex rustics and English and French soldiers but presences such as the Ancient Spirit of the Years, the Shade of the Earth; dominating everybody and everything is the Immanent Will, the all-powerful force, unconcerned with destiny of ordinary mortals, which moves 'the unintelligible world'.

Since Napoleon's death, a cast list of scholars as vast as that of *The Dynasts* has clashed over his career and achievements as fiercely as ever his armies did with those of successive Coalitions. At one extreme were sceptics such as Michelet, who in his *Tableau de la France* (1833) depicted Napoleon as a vulgar and corrupted soul who betrayed the French Revolution. Nonetheless, when it came to describing Napoleon's final defeat at Waterloo, Michelet, could not let slip the opportunity to denigrate the English – just as he did in his more celebrated account of the life and times of Joan of Arc:

> England! England! On that day it was not a one-to-one combat. You had the rest of the world on your side. How can you claim all the glory for yourself? What is the point of your Waterloo Bridge? Is there really so much cause for pride in the fact that the mutilated survivors of a hundred battles and the newest of France's recruits, a beardless battalion, straight from school, their lips still wet with their mother's farewell kiss – that these should have been broken by your army of mercenaries, all battle-hardened, held back in reserve to finish us off like a soldier in ambush stabbing his assailant?

Victor Hugo was no admirer of Napoleonic despotism but for him, too, the recent memory of Waterloo caused Anglophobic hackles to rise. Writing about his travels in *En voyage* (1837), he declared:

> I decided there was no point in visiting Lord Wellington. I find Waterloo more odious than Crécy. It represents something more than the victory of Europe over France. It represents the complete, absolute, dazzling, incontrovertible, definitive and supreme triumph of mediocrity over genius . . . I shall visit Waterloo only when a wind from France blows over that Flemish lion from which Saint Louis once removed the claws, the teeth, the tongue and the crown, and when it is replaced on a pedestal by a bird of France, whether eagle or cock is of no consequence.

To his credit, Hugo had the grace to add: 'I am well aware that anything I write here can be turned into a couple of lines of doggerel but that's all one to me. It's well known that there's this stupid, jingoist side to me.'

No such irony or self-deprecation is to be found in the writings of French historians at the opposite extreme to Michelet, dyed-in-the-wool Anglophobes such as Armand Lefebvre, Frédéric Masson, Albert Vandal and Arthur-Lévy, whose massive studies of Napoleon are so many exercises in hagiography. A couple of brief extracts convey the flavour. In his *Napoléon et Alexandre Ier*, Count Albert Vandal declared in 1890:

> Throughout the whole of his reign, Napoleon pursued one unchanging objective in his foreign policy: to secure, by a genuine peace with England, stability for his achievement, the greatness of France, and the peace of the world . . .
>
> The government of Napoleon was nothing less than a twelve-year-long battle fought all over the world against the English. His campaigns were no isolated and independent actions, at the end of which he could have hammered home the boundary stakes of his domain and put an end to the bloodshed. They formed the indissolubly connected parts of a single whole, of one and the same war, in which our nation finally fell, trampled on by Europe after having swept through it and rebuilt it – a war in which France itself was defeated but in which the French idea was victorious.

In 1902, Arthur-Lévy asserted in his *Napoléon et la Paix*:

> During the whole of his reign, Napoleon's sole aim was to arrive at a just and lasting peace which would ensure to France that status to which she is entitled . . . England's remorseless rivalry, the terror of old-established thrones confronted with the spectacle of a dynasty which has sprung up

overnight, the hope of building a dam to hold back the spread of libertarian ideas, every party's secret desires – these were the elements from which the succession of Coalitions was forged and against which Napoleon's pacific endeavours were always dashed.

Slightly simplified, those represent to this day the views of the ordinary Frenchman. Overlooking the bloody consequences of his military megalomania, he believes Napoleon more sinned against than sinning, finally defeated through typical English perfidy and then humiliated out of petty spite. The average Englishman has an even simpler view. Napoleon is not famous either for his administrative achievements or for his martial prowess but for his amorous exploits – or, more accurately, for the lack of them. If he is remembered at all, it is because, when doubtless exhausted by all those 'French tricks', he said to his importunate mistress those three imperishable words: 'Not tonight, Josephine.'

6 : *Love, Hate and Suspicion:*
1814–1914

We have no eternal allies and we have no perpetual enemies. Our interests are eternal and perpetual, and those interests it is our duty to follow.

Lord Palmerston, speech to Parliament, 1 March 1848

Of the many distinguished French writers who sought to explain England and the English to their nineteenth-century compatriots, none experienced more dramatic reversals of fortune than the Vicomte de Chateaubriand. In the 1790s, he eked out a threadbare existence as an *émigré* hack in London. After winning considerable fame as a writer in 1802, he had served briefly as one of Napoleon's diplomats, been elected to the *Académie française* and served as one of Louis XVIII's ministers at Ghent. In 1822, he returned to London as French Ambassador. Like the inveterate Romantic he always was, he made the maximum literary use of the dramatic contrast between his earlier life of penury on the streets of London and the great style in which he could now entertain the good and the great at the Court of St James; at the same time, he reflected on the transience of human life and mourned the passing of what he took to be Old England. He wrote in 1822:

As I conjure up before me England's lost centuries, watching one famous personage after another rise up then descend one by one into the abyss, I feel a sort of melancholy vertigo. Where are they now, those brilliant and tumultuous days of Shakespeare and Milton, Henry VIII and Elizabeth, Cromwell and William, Pitt and Burke? All, all are gone: the famous and the obscure, the joy and the misery, the oppressors and the oppressed, the executioners and their victims, the kings and their subjects – they all sleep in the same dust. Of what nothingness must we be made, if this is the fate of the most brilliant members of the human race, of the genius which lingers on like a ghost of times gone by in the present generation but which no longer has life of its own and which is no longer aware that it existed.

How many times in the space of a few hundred years has England been destroyed? Through how many revolutions has it not had to pass before arriving at the brink of an even greater, more radical revolution which will engulf posterity? I have seen those famous British parliaments at the peak of their power. What is to become of them now? I have seen the ages-old customs and the ages-old wealth of England: everywhere the lonely little church with its tower, Gray's country churchyard, everywhere the narrow, sanded lanes crowded with cattle, heathlands mottled with sheep, parks, castles, cities . . .

Today its valleys are hidden beneath the smoke of its forges and its factories, its lanes transformed into iron tracks; and along the roads where Shakespeare and Milton wandered, trundle steaming locomotives. Already, those nurseries of knowledge, Oxford and Cambridge, are assuming an air of desolation: their colleges and Gothic chapels, now half-abandoned, are poignant to behold, whilst in their cloisters, beside the sepulchral stones from the Middle Ages, lie neglected the marble annals of the people of Ancient Greece – ruins guarded by ruins.

The elegiac note is compelling and characteristic: it reveals both the strength of Chateaubriand's method and its limitations. As an expression of his deep personal feelings, it is exemplary. As a diagnosis of the state of England, past, present and to come, it is more notable for what it omits than what it includes. He could not reasonably be expected to have foreseen the extent of the franchise in nineteenth-century England nor the spectacular exploitation of the industries that was to make it a world power, but he makes no mention of consequence to one of the most striking phenomena of the period in and of which he was writing: the great wave of Anglomania that was sweeping France.

Back in 1814, with the restoration of the Bourbons and the banishment of Napoleon to Elba, the English crowds streamed across the Channel with the same eagerness as they did with the Peace of Amiens in 1802. Among the throng was a Quaker gentleman farmer, Morris Birkbeck, who, in his *Notes on a Journey through France, 1814*, voiced the general view that a new age of amity was dawning:

I do not believe that there is among the French a feeling of jealousy towards us, a sentiment of national rivalship such as I am sorry to see cherished on this side of the water. They have no idea of the English and French being natural foes; the animosity which has been said to prevail between the two nations they refer exclusively to the Governments. How long shall forty millions of civilized people, in the two countries, remain the dupes of that wretched and disgraceful policy, by which governments foment perpetual rivalship and war, under the hackneyed plea of supporting social order and religion!

Two years later, Edward Stanley wrote equally enthusiastically to his wife:

This is the most comical thing. Paris is no longer recognizable. Where are the French? Nowhere. Everything is English. English coaches fill the streets and you don't see a single luxury coach which isn't English. In the boxes at the theatre, in the hotels, in the restaurants, in a word, *everywhere*, John Bull has installed himself and taken possession . . . Just occasionally, around the Tuileries, or here and there about the town, a few little powdered old men, relics of Times Past, might appear, wandering around with uncertain step, dry and wrinkled as mummies, with their ribbons and crosses of Saint Louis.

The triumphalism of the latter was as ill-founded as the optimism of the former. French animosity over English victories, modern and ancient, was not so easily assuaged.

As far as the generality of French people were concerned, the restoration of the Bourbon monarchy looked less like the beginning of a prosperous new future than a return to the deprivations of the past. The English were the age-old enemies who had triumphed at Crécy, Poitiers and Agincourt, burnt Joan of Arc at the stake, thwarted the Revolution and Napoleon at every turn. While the terms of the peace treaty were being negotiated, England was seen as an Occupying Power out for plunder. The chief spokesman for French resentment against this was the populist poet Pierre-Jean Béranger, who regularly complained of English greed, cruelty and perfidiousness. In 'Complainte d'une de ces demoiselles', Béranger's punning refrain was

> Faut que lord Villain-ton ait tout pris
> On 'a plus d'argent dans c'gueux de Paris.
>
> (Lord Villain-ton must have taken everything,
> There's no money left in this down-and-out Paris.)

In August 1814, he waxed sarcastic over the very latest manifestation of French Anglomania in his poem 'Les boxeurs':

Although they wear such ugly hats, *God dam!* I like the English: they're such pleasant people! How very polite they are! Better still, how very tasteful are their pleasures! No, a thousand times no! We don't want those punches in the face which are all the rage in England.

And now we've got *boxers* in Paris. Let's rush to place our bets – if need be, in the presence of a lawyer! In boxing, it's a one-to-one contest – which makes a change for the English. No, a thousand times no! We don't want those punches in the face which are all the rage in England.

Now they're in the ring, let's admire the gracefulness of these two likely lads. Such gracefulness never fades. They look like a pair of market porters but they could be a couple of *milords*. No, a thousand times no! We don't want those punches in the face which are all the rage in England.

Well now, my ladies, what do you make of it all? It's for you to judge the blows. What's that? The scene bowls you over? The blood's beginning to flow . . . Clap your hands, then! Lord above! how human these English are! No, a thousand times no, we don't want those punches in the face which are all the rage in England.

Ah you English! We have to copy everything you do: your laws, your fashions, your tastes, even the way you wage war. We go on applauding your diplomats and your racehorses. But no, a thousand times no, we don't want those punches in the face which are all the rage in England.

Béranger's Anglophobic outbursts were echoed by a populist chansonnier, Marc-Antoine Désaquier, who sneered at the English for eating, willy-nilly, plum-pudding and beef-steak, washing these down with rum, madeira, beer and tea:

They say that *we're* ill-mannered but it's the English
who've got the habit of gritting their teeth when they sing
and of never laughing out loud in public.

L'Anglais avec son sang-froid habituel (once mistranslated as 'the Engishman with his perpetual bloody cold') had been a conventional French stereotype, and Désauquier revived it in 1816 in a cabaret song entitled 'Les Anglais et les Français':

Who's this character with the stiff and solemn manner? That's your

Englishman for you. And who's this friendly fellow, so spritely, so sparkling, so *sympathique*? That's, of course, your Frenchman.

Who is it who, after drowning twenty pots of beer, will carry on drinking and say never a word? That's your Englishman for you. And who's the one who, between sips of champagne, sings such a merry song? That's, of course, your Frenchman.

You only get groans from the dreary drama, the dismal offshoot of Shakespeare. That's your Englishman for you. The song from the little music hall trips gaily through the town. That's, of course, your Frenchman.

The fashion-conscious in nineteenth-century Restoration Paris were as impervious to the satirical attacks of their fellow-countrymen as had been their English counterparts in seventeenth-century London: in both instances, each modish group was convinced that the ideal models in *l'art de vivre* were those provided by their social peers on the other side of the Channel and was impatient to copy them. In 1816, an anonymous columnist in *Le Rôdeur français ou les moeurs du jour* asserted: 'Anglomania has made a great advance here over the last century. We've borrowed from the English, in turn, their horses, their clothes, their eccentricities and even that contempt for life which consists in having the courage to end it simply to escape from troubles which aren't likely to last for ever.' Two years later another anonymous report appeared in *L'Hermite rôdeur ou Observations sur les moeurs et usages des Anglais et des Français*: 'Honest John Bull has made great progress and his neighbours have learned from him a whole host of things such as the art of training and saddling horses, of drinking copiously or of swearing and gambling frenetically.'

English shops and taverns appeared in various parts of Paris: the Great Nelson Hotel in the rue Neuve-Saint-Augustin and the India Tea Warehouse in the Place Vendôme; the pâtisserie in the rue Neuve-du-Luxembourg became the 'Pastry Cook and Biscuit-Maker'. The height of fashion was to dine at the Taverne Katcomb, where vast quantities of beef and mutton would be consumed in total silence. Paris restaurateurs quickly made their fortunes, vast sums were won and lost at the gambling tables at Frascati's and the Cercle des Etrangers. Respectable *milords* and leading dandies married French ballerinas. English upper-class ladies opened salons and gave lavish receptions. Ambitious young Frenchmen were lured to Paris at the prospect of marrying a wealthy English heiress; Balzac more than once produced variations on this theme. An anonymous writer in *L'Hermite rôdeur* complained, 'Never,

never have the English done us more harm since these ancient enemies of ours became our allies. They've exported to us whole cargo-loads of rich and ugly heiresses who have deprived our own women of all their hopes of marriage.'

However, during those heady years after the defeat of Napoleon, not every English visitor to France was well-to-do. The English middle classes 'discovered' Paris too and their experiences there provided the basis of two comic books, somewhat dated now but immensely popular in their day. In *The Fudge Family in Paris* (1818), Thomas Moore sought to distil 'the concentrated essence of the various forms of cockneyism and nonsense of those groups of ridiculous English who were at the time swarming in all directions throughout Paris'; and in *Jorrocks's Jaunts and Jollities* (1838), Robert Surtees involved his cockney grocer, Mr Jorrocks, in a series of misadventures which prompted Dickens to do the same thing for Mr Pickwick.

Not all English travellers were bent on pleasure, though, and not all journeys ended in Paris. Calais and Boulogne served, as they had done traditionally, as havens for English folk down on their luck or seeking to escape their creditors: Nelson's Emma Hamilton died penniless in Calais in 1815; Beau Brummell also died there, insane and destitute, in 1840. For all that, these two Channel ports proved popular both with English travellers out for a good time and with English writers. They were the favourite 'watering-places' of Charles Dickens, and Thackeray wrote *The Newcomes* at the château de Brequereque, close to Boulogne. In that same town, the poet Thomas Campbell, author of such patriotic anthology-pieces as 'The Soldier's Dream' and 'Ye Mariners of England', died and was buried.

But Paris remained the most popular of destinations in the early decades of the nineteenth century, adding to its traditional tourist attractions the sites of recent Revolutionary activities: the ruins of the Bastille, the Tuileries Palace, its walls riddled with bullets when the monarchy fell on 10 August 1792; the Place de la Concorde, where Louis XVI was guillotined on 21 January 1792; the Louvre Palace, filled with Napoleon's plunder. The spectacle of the victorious English gaping in such crowds at the evidence of France's recent humiliations did nothing to turn back the tide of French Anglomania. It remained a conspicuous feature of the Paris scene throughout the 1820s and for much of the following decade. In the course of his account in *Choses vues* of the coronation of Charles X at Rheims in 1825, Victor Hugo observed: 'At this time, the English enjoyed in France all the popularity that it's possible to enjoy outside the ordinary people. Some salons admired them because of Waterloo, which was still not far distant in time, and in ultra-Royalist circles, it was the done thing to anglicise the French language.' In 1830, in her book of reminiscences *La France en 1829 et 1830,* the prolific popular novelist Lady Morgan declared:

> English ways are all the rage with the upper classes and with little hostesses. English literature is championed by a great many writers in the same way as the English arisocracy is by French high society. Every sportsman, whether he stalks bears or shoots sparrows in the Paris suburbs, adopts English equipment for the hunt . . .
> I have to tell you that everything English is now held in great esteem in Paris and held to be romantic. So we have Romantic tailors, ladies' fashion-shops, pastry cooks and even Romantic doctors and apothecaries.

And an anonymous columnist, writing in the January/March 1830 number of *La Mode*, noted that the English fondness for suicide seemed in danger of becoming fashionable:

> In an age obsessed by pleasure, the man who's grown *blasé* will sharpen his appetite for life by putting it at risk. This is the only way to explain why he chooses to pursue peril without glory in the form of steeple-chasing. This will no doubt remain the thing to do till it becomes fashionable to let oneself die of consumption. It's with very real regret that we report the manifestation of the symptoms of such a fatal malady which threatens to strike at the very heart of our French nation. Despair can prove contagious and it's difficult to estimate how far the ravages of self-disgust have affected our country, which was once so gay. Young men of high and low estate have fallen victim. *La Mode* wishes to draw attention to the fast-spreading decadence into which we're all being plunged by our unhealthy imitation of the present practices and long-established traditions of Great Britain.

There seemed to be no lengths beyond which the Anglomanic French were not prepared to go. In the city that had once set the fashion for literary *salons* presided over by *femmes savantes*, clubs exclusively for gentlemen were now established: what was to become the most exclusive of these, the Jockey Club, was founded in 1833 by Lord Seymour, with the avowed aim of maintaining the high quality of French racehorses. It became fashionable to import these from England, together with carriages (Tilburys, landaus and jaunting-cars), furniture, keepsakes and clothes. There was a 'fashionable' way of tying one's tie, of carrying one's cane and of mounting one's horse as the English were supposed to do. A French journalist, Albert Cler, observed: 'Things have reached the point where some of our dandies are having their teeth discoloured so as to make themselves look like authentic Englishmen.'

While the more extrovert of French Anglomaniacs frequented race tracks and hobnobbed with jockeys and boxers, the more literate would invite friends to a *râout* (the gallicised form of 'rout' – now an archaic term for an evening reception), where they would find, casually displayed, copies of those classic English 'Gothic' stories *The Castle of Otranto* (1764) by Horace Walpole, *The Mysteries of Udolpho* (1794) by Ann Radcliffe, *The Monk* (1796) by Matthew Lewis and *Melmoth the Wanderer* (1820) by Charles Robert Maturin. Balzac, Hugo, Gautier and Nodier each sought to emulate them with horror stories of their own; the English originals were still very much in vogue in France under the Second Empire. But the true cult figures were Scott and Byron. The wild enthusiasm for them is conveyed in this – partly tongue-in-cheek – anonymous article, which appeared in 1821 in the journal *L'Abeille* (formerly *La Minerve littéraire*):

> Walter Scott! Walter Scott! Hurry along there, Gentlemen, and you too, Ladies, even more! It's marvellous! It's NEW! Hurry along there! The first edition's been sold out! The whole of the second's already been spoken for! The third will be snapped up as soon as it comes off the press. Run, don't walk! And buy, buy, buy. Good, bad or indifferent, what does it matter? Sir Walter Scott's given his name to it, so that's good enough! And long live England and the English! Dear children of the Thames! Everything's going their way right now . . . On the one side, there's Milord Byron, with his vampires who've given nightmares to all our poetic scribblers. On the other side, there's Sir Scott, Sir Southey, Sir Somebody Else, and a misty retinue of Misses, Mistresses and Miladies, have captured all the outlets of our booktrade. There isn't a salon where you don't hear the question 'Have you read the latest masterpiece by Lord Byron?' You can't give the merest glance at the window-display in a single one of our bookshops without spotting a novel from the other side of the Channel. The result is that all our poets can do is imitate and as for our novelists – Good God, our novelists will soon be reduced simply to *translating*.

When Scott visited Paris in 1826, he was fêted on a scale that used once to be accorded to martial heroes and is now reserved for members of the entertainment industry. He noted in his journal:

> November 5.   I believe I must give up my Journal till I leave Paris. The French are literally outrageous in their civilities – bounce in at all hours and drive one half mad with compliments. I am ungracious not to be so entirely thankful as I ought to this kind and merry people . . . they have a natural good-humour and gaiety which inclines them to be pleased with themselves and everything about them . . .

> November 6.   Cooper came to breakfast but we were *obsédés partout*. Such a number of Frenchmen bounced in successively and exploded, I mean discharged, their compliments, that I could hardly find an opportunity to speak a word or entertain Mr Cooper at all . . .

> November 10.   Ere I leave *la belle France*, however, it is fit I should express my gratitude for the unwontedly kind reception which I met with at all hands. It would be an unworthy piece of affectation did I not allow that I have been pleased – highly pleased – to find a species of literature intended only for my own country has met such an extensive and favourable reception in a foreign land when there was so much *a priori* to oppose its progress.

Even greater homage was to be paid to him. All the most talented and ambitious French writers of the day – Balzac, Vigny, Hugo, Alexandre Dumas *père* and Mérimée – responded, each in turn, to the challenge of writing a historical novel to vie with their Scottish master.

As for Byron, it was the man himself rather than his poetry that generated the most enthusiasm in Parisian high society. Claire-Elisabeth, la Comtesse de Rémusat, lady-in-waiting to the Empress Josephine, voiced the aspirations of a whole generation of women when she announced, 'I've read Lord Byron. He entrances me. I would like to be young and beautiful and unattached. Then I think I'd go in search of him and try to tempt him back to the ways of happiness and virtue.' Her husband Charles declared, 'Byron is the Napoleon of poetry!' The greatest of French nineteenth-century historians, Jules Michelet, looked back from old age to his youth and admitted, 'I *devoured* Byron. To have reacted any differently was quite impossible. I was like one of those people who become addicted to strong liquor. After that, every other drink seemed insipid.'

But perhaps the clearest measure of the onward march of French

Anglomania was the transformation of the critical fortune of Shakespeare. One M. Penley, together with his wife and daughter, had the temerity to stage *Othello* in a Paris theatre in 1822, a year after the lonely death of Napoleon. The Bonapartists turned the occasion into an Anglophobic carnival: potatoes, fruit and bad eggs were thrown, the actors' voices were drowned by catcalls or jeering laughter, and there were loud cries of '*A bas Shakespear! C'est le lieutenant de Wellington!*'

Thereafter, the pendulum swung dramatically. In 1823 and 1825, Stendhal produced a pair of powerfully argued pamphlets, under the collective title 'Racine et Shakespeare'. He was an Anglophile and Anglophobe both at once: he detested the English bourgeoisie because of its obsessive dedication to the work ethic but his admiration for Shakespeare knew no bounds. He placed him higher than the great French master-dramatist because, unfettered by the classical stage conventions, he could not only depict passions but portray some of the great events in history. He could also combine tragic and comic elements within a single play, a feature that the young Victor Hugo acclaimed in the provocative preface he wrote in 1827 for his play *Cromwell*, the choice of subject being one more demonstration of French preoccupation with things English. In that same year, another Shakespeare touring company visited Paris. It included the leading stars of the day, Macready, Kemble and Kean. The extracts of the plays they performed met with triumphant acclaim and the young composer Hector Berlioz, who could not speak or understand a word of English, fell in love with the company's leading actress, Harriet Smithson, and married her. They would seem to have lived unhappily ever after.

There was also a French cult, albeit a minority one, for English political thinking. In the eighteenth century, when they sought to discredit the absolute monarchy of the *ancien régime*, Voltaire and Montesquieu had cited England's parliamentary democracy as the ideal model. After the excesses of the Revolution and the calamitous campaigning of Napoleon, the political stability and civic freedoms enjoyed by England seemed particularly desirable. Writing in 1818, Benjamin Constant declared, 'I am quite satisfied that the constitution of England should be extolled. I have always thought that the English owed the qualities which have for long earned them the esteem of Europe largely to this constitution . . . England, the freest country in the world, is worthy of serving as our model.' In a country that remained in political ferment throughout the century, Constant's was a minority view. It was echoed in 1856 by the Comte de Montalembert, born in London of an *émigré* father and a Scottish mother: he praised English institutions 'which created, maintained and twenty times saved their national character, which it would have been even better for us to imitate than to admire'; and again, in 1865, by the Comte de Rémusat, who declared, 'For me, I willingly confess that the dream of my life has been the English system of government in French society.' The facts of political life decreed that his dream could never be realised in his life-time: whatever freedoms the English people may supposedly have enjoyed, effective power was still wielded by the wealthy and there was no way in which this could be reconciled with democracy. The attitude of French politicians to England accordingly remained ambivalent. As Balzac once observed, 'England is either Machiavellian Albion or the model country we're all supposed to copy. It's Machiavellian Albion whenever French interests are thwarted or if Napoleon is ever involved. It's the model country whenever Opposition politicians need to taunt the Government.' Over the age-old question of hegemony in Europe and the emerging problem of who was to be the dominant power in North Africa and the Levant, England was to display the same ambivalence towards France, oscillating between the same extremes of adulation and antipathy.

*

While Anglomaniacs continued to dominate Paris high society, British statesmen observed France with a somewhat beadier eye. After recent events, France spelled trouble: it had made a major contribution to England's defeat in the American War of Independence and anxieties about the evolving state of English society were greatly intensified by fears that the French Revolutionary virus might prove contagious. In February 1817, a report of a secret committee of the House of Commons on the disturbed state of the country described a plot to seize power by radical societies in London: the intended insurrection assumed the symbols of the French Revolution; a Committee of Public Safety, of twenty-four members, was agreed upon, a tri-colour flag and cockades were actually prepared; the flag was openly carried and displayed at the first meeting.

Wellington was convinced that the Revolution of July 1830 could be linked with the movement for electoral reform in Britain and hardened his reactionary views. Cobbett, no less characteristically, warmly welcomed the news and on 16 August, presided over a grand dinner in London in honour of the French nation. In his view, the 1830 Revolution had been carried through not by the aristocracy, not by military gentlemen, not by gentlemen with whiskers or long spurs, not by gentlemen of any description in fact, not even by the middle classes, but by the working people alone; by men who quitted their shops, who laid down their needles, their awls, their saws, and, rushing out into the streets of Paris, said, 'If there be no alternative but slavery, let us put an end to the tyrants.'

On a visit to England in 1817, Stendhal had observed the preparations for a political rally due to be addressed by Cobbett. He described what he saw in *Rome, Naples et Florence* (1817): 'When I was in England, I saw some working-class people preparing to go to a *meeting* [English in the original] where Cobbett was due to speak. They didn't have the nerve to sit down in the carts that had brought merchandise to market. An English shoemaker said with profound respect: "Those places are reserved for *Gentlemen* [English in the original]".'

It was his awareness of these rigid class-differences that encouraged Hugo to believe, like the Revolutionary leaders in the 1790s, that French egalitarian ideas were eminently exportable. Writing in September 1830 of the July Revolution, he declared:

It is a mistake to think that European equilibrium will not be upset by our revolution. It cannot fail to be. What makes us strong is that we can unleash the people of any country against any king who orders his army to attack us. There will be a revolution on our behalf wherever we want one. England on its own is formidable for a thousand reasons. The English Prime Minister is being nice to us at present because we've aroused in the English people an enthusiasm which is putting pressure on their government. All the same, Wellington knows just how to get back at us: when the time is right, he'll get at us through Algeria or through Belgium. What, therefore, we need to do to keep their Prime Minister respectful is to forge an ever closer alliance with the English people. To bring that about, we should choose a popular ambassador to send to England, Benjamin Constant, for example. they'd unhitch his coach at Dover and twelve hundred Englishmen would pull it to London. At a stroke, our ambassador would become the most popular fiigure in England, and you can imagine the marvellous reaction there'd be in London, in Manchester and in Birmingham, if England were to declare war on France! To plant the idea of France in English soil, what a great political stroke that would be.

Three years later, in his magisterial *Histoire de France*, Michelet, not for the first or last time, expressed his antipathy towards England and, like Hugo, looked forward with some relish to the time when its people would rise up against its leaders:

When confronted with Europe, with Dunkirk, with Antwerp in ruins, this odious country of England seems to me truly mighty. All the other countries – Russia, Austria, Italy, Spain, France – have their capitals in the west and look towards the setting sun. The great ship of Europe seems to float there, its sails distended by the wind blowing out of Asia. England alone has its prow in the east, as though it is preparing to confront the world, *unum contra omnia*. This furthest territory of the ancient continent is the land of heroes, the last refuge of exiles and of men of energy. All those who have ever fled from servitude, Druids being hounded by Rome, Gallo-Romans pursued by the Barbarians, Saxons banished by Charlemagne, starving Danes, hungry Normans, persecuted Flemish businessmen, defeated Calvinists – all of these crossed the sea and made the great island their home . . . In this fashion, England grew fat on hardship and was built up from ruins. But when all these refugees, all gathered together within this tight little island, began to look at each other, and as they began to notice the differences of race and of faith which divided them, as they identified themselves as Welsh, Gaels, Saxons, Danes and Normans, then hatred and conflict began to grow. It was like those bizarre combats which once entertained Rome, combats between animals astonished to find themselves herded together: lions and hippopotamuses, tigers and crocodiles. And when, in their circus hemmed in by the ocean, these amphibious creatures had had enough of nipping each other to pieces and gnawing lumps out of one another, they took to the seas and started biting France. But make no mistake about it, their internal war isn't over yet. It's all very well for the victorious beast, crouching there on its sea-girt throne, to give itself airs and graces before the rest of us. In its sneering smile there's also an angry clenching of teeth, either because it's wearing itself out turning the cruel and screeching wheels of Manchester, or because the Irish bull, which it has pinioned to the ground, has turned round and started bellowing.

While the well-to-do in Paris and London delighted in each other's company, and Romantics like Hugo dreamed occasionally of the ordinary people in both countries joining in a common democratic cause, there were always voices or occasions to ensure that the two countries remained well apart. In February 1831, for example, Louis-Philippe's son, the Duc de Nemours, was elected 'King of the Belgians'. Belgium and the Low Countries were an area in which for centuries past, since the palmy days of its wool-trade, England had always shown particular interest. Palmerston truculently accused the French of unwarrantable interference. The ever-wily Talleyrand warned that for Nemours to accede to the Belgian throne would inevitably mean war. The French popular opposition newspaper *Le Constitutionnel* trumpeted *Aux armes! Aux armes!* Louis-Philippe exercised commendable tact: Nemours withdrew and was replaced by Prince Leopold of Saxe-Coburg, who was to prove Queen Victoria's most influential relative. In a letter of 31 May 1831, a gratified Palmerston first coined a version of the phrase '*l'entente cordiale*' when he declared, 'We feel sincerely how much a good and cordial understanding, a firm friendship between England and France must contribute to the maintenance of freedom and the happiness of nations.' The fragility of that 'cordial understanding' was made manifest a few weeks later when a French army was sent into Belgium to repel the Dutch invasion and Lord Londonderry declared to the House, 'I can see France lording it over all of us; I dread the thought of her exercising in Europe that preponderance which has hitherto been reserved to the wisdom and genius of England.'

It was not only the English who remained sceptical over the prospect of any meaningful *entente*. On 1 March 1832, in *Le National*, which was the official paper of the French Republican cause, an unsigned writer declared:

> There can be no possibility of an alliance between the France of July 1830 and aristocratic England.
>
> For our part, we believe that England resents us for a Revolution that keeps it on tenterhooks, leaves its credit suspended, stirs up its working classes and reopens the whole question of the 1815 treaties, its master stroke. When we express our opposition to the English alliance, it's not out of disrespect for its great people. It's because we have taken stock of the situation of its aristocracy and we don't believe that their greatness can co-exist with ours.

In 1833, when that tireless campaigner for *rapprochement* Richard Cobden argued eloquently that Free Trade would ensure a truly effective *entente cordiale*, a broadsheet circulating in France proclaimed: 'England is marching with giant strides towards a universal monopoly.

She is attacking us once more on our soil not, as in the old days, with arms in hand to enslave us, but by bringing ruin and misery to our countryside and to our working-classes.'

The mutual antagonism was not confined to demagogues on either side, then as now all too well aware how to gain plaudits and votes by the blatant appeal to xenophobia. It is also apparent in the parentheses or seemingly casual asides to be found in the work of major historians. Here, for example, is Michelet, in 1833, writing what purports to be a History of France:

> The great English people has very many good and solid qualities but it also has one vice which spoils them all. That immense, deep-rooted vice is pride. It is a cruel affliction but, for all that, it determines the way they live, it explains all their contradictions and is the hidden motive of all their actions. As far as they are concerned, pride is almost always at the root of both their good and bad deeds. It can also lead them to cover themselves in ridicule. This pride of theirs is tremendously sensitive and painful. They suffer terribly because of it and it's a matter of even greater pride for them to conceal their suffering. Nonetheless, that suffering has to reveal itself and the English language has made all its own two terms which express it particularly well: *disappointment* and *mortification*. Self-adoration, the creature's secret worship of itself, is the sin which caused Satan's fall, the supreme act of sacrilege. This is why, in spite of its human virtues, its seriousness, its outward probity, its Biblical cast of mind, no other nation is as far removed from grace. They are the one race who could never claim to have written *The Imitation of Christ*: a Frenchman could have written that book, a German or an Italian, but never an Englishman. From Shakespeare to Milton, from Milton to Byron, their great and sombre literature is sceptical, Judaic, Satanic, in a word, anti-Christian. The American Indians, who can sometimes be so penetrating and so original, used to say in their own distinctive fashion: 'Christ was a Frenchman the English crucified in London: Pontius Pilate was an officer in the pay of Great Britain.'

And here, in 1837, is Carlyle, writing in Book 1, Chapter 7 of his great history of *The French Revolution*, about what was for him one of the most fearsome phenomena of those momentous times, the Paris mob:

> If Voltaire once, in splenetic humour, asked his countrymen: 'But you, Gualches, what have you invented?' they can now answer: 'The Art of Insurrection.' It was an art needed in these last singular times: an art for which the French nature, so full of vehemence, so free from depth, was perhaps of all others the fittest.

Accordingly, to what a height, one may well say of perfection, has this branch of human industry been carried by France, within the last half-century! Insurrection, which Lafayette thought might be 'the most sacred of duties', ranks now, for the French people, among the duties which they can perform. Other mobs are dull masses; which roll onwards with a dull fierce heat, but emit no light-flashes of genius as they go. The French mob, again, is among the liveliest phenomena of our world. So rapid, audacious; so clear-sighted, inventive, prompt to seize the moment; instinct with life to its finger-ends! That talent, were there no other, of spontaneously standing in queue, distinguishes, as we said, the French people from all Peoples, ancient and modern.

Carlyle's depiction of the Paris mob in all its raging fury was to prove richly influential on the most popular of English novels about the French Revolution: in Dickens's *A Tale of Two Cities* (1859), in Baroness Orczy's *The Scarlet Pimpernel* (1905) and in the Roger Brook tales by Dennis Wheatley, the Paris mob looms menacingly large but is eventually outwitted or circumvented by a dashing English hero. In the most important French novels about the Revolution, the writers' plots and preoccupations are dramatically different. In *Les Chouans* (1829) by Balzac, *Le Chevalier des Touches* (1864) by Barbey d'Aurevilly and *Quatre-vingt-treize* (1873) by Hugo, all of which deal with Royalist insurrection in Britanny, and in *Les Dieux ont soif* (1912) by Anatole France, which portrays the Terror in Paris, the novelists concentrate almost exclusively on the manifold ways in which rival groups of Frenchmen set out to destroy each other: the English feature neither as heroes nor as villains.

At the end of the 1830s, however, French memories, modern and ancient, were still sufficiently bitter for observers to remain pessimistic about the chances of lasting peace. In his *Paris Sketch Book*, Thackeray observed in 1839:

Don't let us endeavour to disguise it, [the French] hate us. Not all the protestations of friendship, not all the wisdom of Lord Palmerston, not all the diplomacy of our distinguished plenipotentiary, Mr Henry Lytton Bulwer – and let us add, not all the benefit which both countries would derive from the alliance – can make it, in our times at least, permanent and cordial. They hate us. The Carlist organs revile us with a querulous fury that never sleeps; the moderate party, if they admit the utility of our alliance, are continually pointing out our treachery, our insolence, and our monstrous infractions of it; and for the republicans, as sure as the morning comes, the columns of their journals thunder out volleys of fierce denunciations against our unfortunate country. They live by feeding the natural hatred against England, by keeping old wounds open, by recurring ceaselessly to the history of old quarrels; and as in these we, by God's help, by land and by sea, in old times and late, have had the uppermost, they perpetuate the shame and mortification of the losing party, the bitterness of past defeats, and the eager desire to avenge them. A party which knows how to *exploitter* this hatred will always be popular to a certain extent.

In the middle decades of the nineteenth century, opportunites to *exploitter* xenophobic hatred on either side were not infrequent: they could all too readily be provoked in either country. A case in point was a direct confrontation in the Middle East, a focus for Anglo–French rivalry for generations. In July 1840, Palmerston informed a friend in a private letter:

> Guizot said that the French Government would now feel it necessary to be in force, in great force, in the Levant. Be it so. We shall not be daunted . . . We shall go to work quietly in our own way, in presence of a superior force . . . just as undisturbed as if it were laid up in ordinary at Toulon. France knows full well that if that superior force should dare to meddle with ours, it is *war*, and she would be made to pay dearly for war so brought on.

In October 1840, the English made a pre-emptive strike by capturing Beirut, while the Royal Navy began to blockade the Syrian and Egyptian coasts. The French public reacted as though Normandy had been invaded. Strains of the *Marseillaise* echoed through the streets of Paris accompanied by cries of *Guerre aux Anglais!* Palmerston kept his nerve. On 29 October 1840, he wrote to Earl Granville:

> I can assure you that you would be most usefully supporting the interests of peace by holding a firm and stout language to the French Government and to Frenchmen . . . It is quite right to be courteous in words, but the only possible way of keepng such persons in check is to make them clearly understand that one is not going to yield an inch, and that one is quite strong enough to repel force by force . . .
>
> My opinion is that we shall not have war now, but that we ought to make up our minds to have war with France before many years have passed. Now we are allied with and backed by all Europe, and France is not mad enough to break her head against such a coalition. But I have for some time seen a spirit of bitter hostility towards England growing up among Frenchmen of all classes and of all parties; and sooner or later this must lead to conflict

between the two nations. Broglie and Guizot pass for being Anglomanes, but be assured that neither of them are friendly to us in their hearts.

All Frenchmen want to encroach and extend their territorial possessions at the expense of other nations, and they all feel what the *National* has often said, that an alliance with England is a bar to such projects. I am not in the least surprised that the *doctrinaires* in Thiers' Government should have been the most warlike. I should rather have expected it to be so. I do not blame the French for disliking us. Their vanity prompts them to be the first nation in the world; and yet at every turn they find that we outstrip them in everything. It is a misfortune to Europe that the national character of a great and powerful people, placed in the centre of Europe, and capable of doing their neighbours much harm should be such as it is; but it is the business of other nations not to shut their eyes to the truth, and to shape their conduct by prudent precautions so as to prevent this nation from breaking loose as long as possible.

While the leading politicians and the rabble rousers on either side were busily flexing their muscles, the young Queen Victoria, actively encouraged by Leopold of the Belgians, was seeking a *rapprochement* with Louis-Philippe. The bellicose Palmerston was less than encouraging but when, in 1841, his ministry was replaced by that of Peel, hopes of a closer union rose significantly. Lord Aberdeen, the new Foreign Secretary, admired France, while his opposite number, François Guizot, was an enthusiastic Anglophile. Between them, they arranged for Louis-Philippe to receive Victoria and Albert in his château at Eu, near Dieppe, the first meeting of a French and English sovereign on French soil since the Field of the Cloth of Gold. In 1844, Louis-Philippe came to Windsor, the first French king to set foot on English soil since Jean II arrived as a state hostage after the battle of Poitiers in 1356. Genuinely warm though the monarchs' personal feelings would seem to have been, their subjects were not over-impressed. After the 1844 visitation, a cartoon depicted the royal pair in a torrid embrace, surrounded by the remains of a picnic. Beside them is a sketch for a monument meant to commemorate the occasion: it is to consist of a plinth bearing a British bulldog and a French cock who are staring nonplussed at one another over a bare-looking bone. The caption reads: 'To be erected in mid-channel – when they find a good foundation for it'.

Subsequent events demonstrated that such cynicism was well justified. In that same year, an over-zealous English missionary called Pritchard had the temerity to set foot on the heathen soil of Tahiti and to claim it for his Protestant God, Queen and Country. Since Tahiti happened, at the time, to be a French protectorate, he was unceremoniously expelled. The jingoist press in each country had a field day: the British papers waxed indignant at the insult, the French fulminated when their Government formally apologised. As a direct consequence, the Delavigne brothers wrote the libretto of Halévy's opera *Charles VI* in which the most popular refrain was

> *Guerre à l'Anglais! Jamais, jamais en France*
> *Jamais l'Anglais ne règnera!*

On 5 September 1844, Hugo commented loftily in *Choses vues*:

> This row between France and England over Tahiti and Pritchard makes me think of some café brawl between two second lieutenants because one gave the other a funny look. And it ends up with a duel to the death. But two great nations ought not to behave like two musketeers. And in a duel to the death between two nations such as England and France, it would be civilisation that would be killed.

However, in July 1846, Hugo was as aggressive as any Anglophobe might have desired: during a debate in the French Upper House on minor works required in some western seaports threatened by erosion from the sea, he made a typically grandiloquent speech demanding that the seaboard be fortified to counter the threat of English invasion. One can only assume that what he beheld in his mind's eye was the phantom fleet described by Casimir Delavigne in his poem 'Le Retour'. The occasion was Delavigne's return visit to his native Le Havre:

> It's out there! It's still out there! The great storm of waters sweeping our coast is not the only despot. Out there still, before me, I can see those hostile sails, spewed out from the Thames to block the way to our ocean.
> I love all the martial paraphernalia of the port where I was born. I loved the black cannons that guarded these shores. I loved the mighty voice that those ancient bronze guns sent reverberating along the coast, making the earth shake. As a child, I loved France. And, at that time, to love France meant that you hated England.
> What was it our sailors used to say, whenever they sought vengeance for England's eternal tyranny and brandished their clenched fists at the horizon? And what was the message I heard in the wind about England? Implacable enemy! Faithless friend! People would talk about England's

vows and her promises so quickly broken, commercial treasures seized even in times of peace and her Punic cruelty. The proof of this is those prisoners, buried away for twenty years, twenty years wasting away in floating hulks – all thanks to British liberty!

In 1846, Hugo was not the only prominent personage to speak out on the subject of national defence. In September of that year, the Duke of Wellington wrote from Walmer Castle to Lord Mahon to demonstrate both how and why meaningful friendship with France was so slow in coming:

> There is no individual more convinced than I am of the necessity for peace, and indeed good understanding, possibly even *entente cordiale*, with France, in the existing state of the politics of the world. But the relation should be no other than patent; we ought to preserve our own independent existence, views and national interests; and, above all, we ought to be in such a state of national defence, as that we could at any time speak out upon a case of national interest or national honour.

What constituted 'national interest or national honour' was at that time open to a wider variety of interpretations than today. In 1846, they seemed inextricably involved with one of those royal dynastic issues that so regularly over the centuries had led the countries into war. The issue on this occasion was: who was to provide a husband for young Queen Isabella of Spain? The House of Coburg, allied to England, or the House of Orléans, connected to France? In the event, the French cause triumphed, a result Queen Victoria denounced as 'infamous'. Palmerston summed up the British view when he wrote in January 1847: 'In so far as concerns our good friends and neighbours, the French, you can't trust them from one week to another, or even from one day to the next. Even when they have no fixed intention to deceive, their inconsistency, their vanity and their love of shuffling make them the most untrustworthy of allies.'

Not for the first time, it was left to Richard Cobden to express a more enlightened – but, at the time, minority – view. On 18 September 1847, he wrote to the formidable anti-Corn Law orator, John Bright, who was, like Cobden himself, a member of the manufacturing class that rose to prominence in England after the 1832 Reform Bill:

> My object in writing again is to speak upon the Marriage question. I have

seen with humiliation that the daily newspaper press of England has been lashing the public mind into an excitement (or at least trying to do so) upon the alliance of the Duke of Montpensier with the Infanta. I saw this boy and girl married, and as I looked at them I could not help exclaiming to myself, 'What a couple to excite the animosity of the people of England and France!' Have we not outgrown the days when sixty millions of people could be set at loggerheads by family intrigue? Yes, we have probably grown wiser than to repeat the War of Succession, but I see almost as great an evil as actual hostilities in the tone of the press and the intrigues of the diplomatists of England and France. They keep the two nations in a state of distrust and alienation, they familiarize us with the notion that war is still a possible event, and worse still, they furnish the pretext for continually augmenting our standing armaments, and thus oppressing and degrading the people with taxation, interrupting the progress of fiscal reforms, and keeping us in a hostile attitude ready for war.

I have always had an instinctive monomania against this system of foreign interference, protocolling, diplomatizing, etc., and I should be glad if you and our other Free Trade friends, who have beaten the daily broad-sheets into common sense upon another question, would oppose yourselves to the Palmerston system, and try to prevent the Foreign Office from undoing the good which the Board of Trade has done to the people. But you must not disguise from yourself that the evil has its roots in the pugnacious, energetic, self-sufficient, foreigner-despizing and pitying character of that noble insular creature, John Bull. Read Washington Irving's description of him fumbling for his cudgel on the earth, and bristling up with anger at the very idea of any other people daring to have a quarrel without first asking his consent or inviting him to take a part in it.

In that same year, 1847, Thackeray drew a devastating picture of John Bull disporting himself abroad in *The Book of Snobs*:

We are accustomed to laugh at the French for their braggadocio propensities, and intolerable vanity about 'la France, la gloire, l'Empereur' and the life; and yet I think in my heart that the British Snob, for conceit and self-sufficiency and braggartism in his way, is without parallel. There is always something uneasy in a Frenchman's conceit. He brags with so much fury, shrieking, and gesticulation – yells out so loudly that the Français is at the head of civilisation, the centre of thought, &c. – that one can't but see the poor fellow has a lurking doubt in his own mind that he is not the wonder he professes to be.

About the British Snob, on the contrary, there is commonly no noise, no bluster, but the calmness of profound conviction. We are better than all the world: we don't question the opinion at all: it's an axiom. And when a Frenchman bellows out, 'la France, Monsieur, la France est à la tête du monde civilisé!' we laugh good-naturedly at the frantic poor devil. *We* are the first-chop of the world; we know the fact so well in our secret hearts, that a claim set up elsewhere is simply ludicrous. My dear brother reader, say, as a man of honour, if you are not of this opinion. Do you think a Frenchman your equal? You don't – you gallant British Snob – you know you don't: no more, perhaps, does the Snob your humble servant, brother.

And I am inclined to think it is this conviction, and the consequent hearing of the Englishman towards the foreigner whom he condescends to visit, – this confidence of superiority which holds up the head of the owner of every English hat-box from Sicily to St Petersburg, that makes us so magnificently hated throughout Europe as we are; this – more than all our little victories, and of which many Frenchmen and Spaniards have never heard – this amazing and indomitable insular pride, which animates my Lord in his travelling-carriage as well as John in the rumble.

At the opposite pole from the loud-mouthed English jingoist portrayed by Cobden and Thackeray stands the English intellectual whose principal article of faith is Sterne's dictum that 'they order things better in France'. In the past, it had been regular practice to praise the French for their pre-eminence in the arts. Dryden had felt obliged to claim as much for Louis XIV: 'Setting prejudice and partiality aside, though he is our enemy, the stamp of a Louis, the patron of all arts, is not much inferior to the medal of an Augustus Caesar.' Lord Chesterfield had echoed this in a letter to his son: 'It must be owned that the Graces do not seem to be natives of Great Britain . . . Since barbarism drove them out of Greece and Rome, they seem to have taken refuge in France.' And over the excellence of French cooking there had never been much dispute. Arthur Young had roundly declared: 'Of their cookery there is but one opinion . . . that it is far beyond our own, I have no doubt in asserting'; and in 1849, Thackeray, whose generous shape suggested that he put his money where his mouth was, proclaimed in *Punch*: 'A man who comes to Paris without directing his mind to dinners, is like a fellow who travels to Athens without caring to inspect ruins.' Now, in March 1848, English Francophiles found another subject for adulation: the French working class.

The occasion was the *Révolution du 24 février* when, after the French Government had refused to permit a patriotic banquet to be held in Paris, crowds took to the streets, and King Louis-Philippe abdicated in favour of his ten-year-old grandson, the Comte de Paris. The revolutionaries would have none of this. They invaded the Chamber of

Deputies and demanded a provisional government. This was set up on 25 February, headed by the Romantic poet Lamartine, whose lyrical speeches made him, for a brief while, an idol of the populace. Louis-Philippe fled to England and spent the last two years of his life at Claremont, in Surrey, as the Comte de Nevilly. The most powerful of his ministers, the Anglophile François Guizot, followed him and spent a year of exile in England.

The setting up of the Second Republic was hailed by George Eliot in March 1848 in a letter she wrote to John Sibree: 'Our working classes are eminently inferior to the mass of the French people. In France the *mind* of the people is highly electrified – they are full of ideas on social subjects – they really desire social *reform* – not merely an acting out of Sancho Panza's favourite proverb: "Yesterday for you, today for me".' Writing to his sister, on 10 March 1848, Matthew Arnold expressed both enthusiasm and apprehension:

> What agitates me is this, if the new state of things succeeds in France, social changes are *inevitable* here and elsewhere, for no one looks on seeing his neighbour mending without asking himself if he cannot mend in the same way; but, without waiting for the result, the spectacle of France is likely to breed great agitation here, and such is the state of our masses that their movement now *can* only be brutal plundering and destroying. And if they wait, there is no one, as far as one sees, to train them to conquer, by their attitude and superior conviction; the deep ignorance of the upper and middle classes, and their feebleness of vision becoming, if possible, daily more apparent. You must by this time begin to see what people mean by placing France *politically* in the van of Europe; it is the *intelligence* of their *idea-moved masses* of England which makes them, politically, as far superior to the *insensible masses* of England as to the Russian serfs, and at the same time they do not threaten the educated world with the intolerable *laideur* of the well-fed American masses, so deeply antipathetic to continental Europe.

Queen Victoria expressed real alarm in a letter to Viscount Melbourne on 15 March 1848: 'Lord Melbourne will agree with the Queen that the last three weeks have brought back the times of the last century, and we are in the midst of troubles abroad. The Revolution in France is a sad and alarming thing . . . The state of Paris is very gloomy; the rabble armed – keeping the Government in awe – failures in all directions, and nothing but ruin and misery.'

The Duke of Wellington, still Commander-in-Chief of Britain's armed forces, was convinced that the great Revolution of the 1790s was about to repeat itself and took extensive precautions against a possible Chartist uprising. He believed that young Ireland wished to relieve the Queen of her crown and to establish a republic.

In the event, there was indeed something of a revolution in Paris but on a much less dramatic scale than fifty years previously. The leaders of the Second Republic were soon as divided amongst themselves as those of the First. The more cautious wanted merely to improve existing conditions, the more extreme advocated the creation of a new social order. The Provisional Government demonstrated its humanitarian idealism and its lack of practicality by setting up a system of *ateliers nationaux*, which set unemployed men to work on such pointless projects as levelling the Champ-de-Mars. When, in June 1848, the *ateliers* were scrapped by Assembly decree, the Paris crowds took to the streets. The fact that their number included Baudelaire (wielding a rifle and proclaiming his determination to shoot his stepfather General Aupick) later established him as a hero in the eyes of Sartre, for whom street agitations in the name of public issues were to become a way of life. By the same token, he roundly condemned Flaubert for remaining aloof from the events. Flaubert, however, could be said to have had the last word: he was later to provide the most authentic account of the years leading up to the 1848 Revolution as a backcloth to the drama of his hero's emotional relationships in *L'Education Sentimentale* (1869).

The savage street fighting went on for just four days before being bloodily repressed by troops under the personal command of General Cavaignac. On 29 June 1848, speaking in the French Assembly, Hugo expressed his sense of outrage:

> What increases my inexpressible grief is that others take delight in and profit from our calamities. While Paris writhes about in agony, which our enemies believe to be our very death throes (but how wrong they are!), London is ecstatic. London rejoices. Its business has tripled. Luxury, industry, wealth have all taken refuge there . . . Yes, indeed, at the present time, England has taken its seat on the edge of the abyss into which France has fallen.

He was even more outraged when, on 2 December 1851, Louis-Napoleon seized power in a *coup d'état* not unworthy of his uncle, Napoleon I himself. Exactly one year later, he was proclaimed Emperor

Napoleon III. Hugo, a peer of France since 1846, left Paris disguised as a workman. After a few months in Brussels, he remained in flamboyant exile in the Channel Islands until the Second Empire collapsed in ignominy in 1870.

He was not the only distinguished political exile. Louis Blanc, who had been a member of the 1848 provisional government that set up the *ateliers nationaux*, took refuge in London for twenty years and contributed a series of articles on English political life to *Le Temps*. Alexandre Ledru-Rollin, an associate of Blanc's, was an equally prominent politician, who championed universal suffrage and stood as a candidate for the French Presidency in 1848 against Louis-Napoleon. Soon after he went into exile in London, he produced his study *De la décadence en Angleterre* (1850), a translation with commentary of official reports on the evils of the English social system.

An equally penetrating and more prolific critic of the English scene was Alphonse Esquiros, a member of the Legislative Assembly after the 1848 Revolution, who went into exile after Louis-Napoleon's *coup d'état* of 1851. His regular articles for *La Revue des Deux Mondes*, subsequently republished in five volumes, cover a remarkably wide range: the origins of the British race, English gypsies, the Kent hop-fields, London's street musicians, the production of salt in Cheshire, the 'ragged-schools' of London, England's military academies, London's clubland, the romance of horse-racing, fox-hunting, the mysteries of cricket – including a match played by teams without arms or legs, which must have made the game seem even more impenetrable to reporter and readers alike.

★

The reaction of some Englishmen to Louis-Napoleon's *coup* was alarm that a French invasion was imminent and that insufficient concern was being shown by the government. Tennyson, shortly to be made Poet Laureate, voiced the mood of many in a number of bellicose poems. One of these, entitled 'The Penny-Wise', appeared in the *Morning Chronicle* on 24 January 1852, and begins:

> O where is he, the simple fool,
> Who says that wars are over?
> What bloody portent flashes there

Across the straits of Dover?
Four hundred thousand slaves in arms
May seek to bring us under:
Are we ready, Britons all,
To answer them with thunder?
　　　Arm, arm, arm!

It continues in similar vein for another three stanzas before arriving at
the resonant peroration:

O gather, gather, volunteers
In every British village!
Or have the tigers of Algiers,
　　Your licence here to pillage?
O babbling Peace Societies
Where Bright or Cobden trifles!
Is this a time to cry for peace
When we should shriek for rifles?
　　　Arm, arm, arm!

O big-limbed yeomen, leave awhile
　　That fattening of your cattle;
And if indeed ye long for peace,
　　Make ready to do battle –
To fight the battle of the world,
　　Of progress and humanity,
Spite of his eight million lies
And bastard Christianity,
　　　Arm, arm, arm!

He followed this with three similar poems in quick succession: one with
the resounding refrain 'Britons Guard Your Own!'; the next, published
in the *Examiner* and signed 'Merlin'; and the third, under his own name,
praising 'Merlin' for his patriotism.

Not all of his fellow-countrymen were persuaded by Tennyson's
rodomontade. Crowds of English visitors were attracted to Paris in the
1850s as Baron Haussmann's bold rebuilding programme was put into
effect. The picturesque gabled houses and dark narrow streets of the old
city were swept away as he drove his two great highways from south to
north and from east to west. The *Exposition Universelle* of 1855 heralded
the age of mass excursions to Paris organised by the first of the modern-
style travel organisers, Thomas Cook.

Among the other public works that were so prominent a feature of Napoleon III's Empire was the spectacular expansion of the French railway network for the construction of which thousands of British navvies were recruited. Travel became more comfortable, safer and cheaper, ceasing to be the prerogative of the upper and cultured classes. In October 1855, the *Quarterly Review* tartly observed: 'Cheap excursion trains, as our readers will remember, in 1849–50–51, brought hundreds of Parisian National Guardsmen to our shores and safely delivered thousands of English excursionists in Paris whom we could well spare in exchange.' The package tourist of the modern era was already in the process of replacing the solitary wanderer of old.

If this was one modern development inaugurated in the middle of the nineteenth century so also was the English adoption of the Côte d'Azur. As early as November 1789, Horace Walpole had noted that 'there were above sixty English families at Nice'. However, in the course of the nineteenth century, the most striking of the modern English 'settlements' in France was Cannes. The prime mover was Lord Brougham, in his time Lord Chancellor and one of the founders of the *Edinburgh Review,* who had a house built there for his invalid daughter when an outbreak of cholera dissuaded them from travelling on to Nice. He had a residence constructed there in 1838, named Château Eléonore-Louise after his daughter. Another founder of the Cannes 'settlement' was T. R. Woolfield, who settled in the Villa Victoria where he laid out a croquet lawn, planted gooseberry bushes and sowed eucalyptus trees with seed from the Royal Botanic Gardens in Sydney. In 1855, he obtained permission from the French Government to build an English Church at his own expense. The cemetery is full of touching details of the many English settlers who went to Cannes to live – and to die.

*

When Louis-Napoleon became Emperor of France, the prospects of a real *rapprochement* with England grew significantly brighter. Napoleon III was genuinely fond of England, having lived there during several long periods of exile. He appreciated the comparative freedom of the English way of life; and he had even served as a special constable in London during the Chartist riots of 1848. His long-standing mistress, Miss Howard, was English; and at the very first State ball of the Second

Empire, he chose an Englishwoman, Lady Cowley, to partner him in the opening *quadrille d'honneur*. By March 1854, English and French troops were on their way together to wage war against the Russian army in the Crimea. To Queen Victoria, this was altogether incredible. What would her grandfather George III have said? He used to stump about the terrace of Windsor Castle, demanding of Eton schoolboys, 'I hope you hate the French? What?' And one of her serving generals, demonstrating that, like the Bourbons, he had learned nothing or forgotten nothing, regularly referred to the enemy in the Crimea as 'the French'. In spite of, or even because of that, Napoleon III made it his special business to charm the surprisingly susceptible English queen, and he succeeded spectacularly.

In the course of his State visit to London in April 1855, he declared that he had been captivated by his first sight of her at the opening of Parliament in 1837 and he told her that he once paid £40 for a box simply to see her on a State visit to the theatre. Queen Victoria promptly expressed her fascinated admiration in a memorandum and it was decided to arrange a return visit with the minimum of delay. From his self-imposed exile in Guernsey, writing on 8 April 1855, Hugo declared his disgust: 'The land of Thomas More, of Hampden, of Bradshaw, of Shakespeare, of Milton, of Newton, of Watt, of Byron . . . that England, which has no bridle round its neck . . . has no need of some ragamuffin from the mud of Montmartre . . . In a single year of their alliance, Napoleon III has done more harm to England than Napoleon I was able to do in fifteen years of war.'

Queen Victoria, for her part, was shrewd enough to see both the advantages that could accrue from a closer relationship with Napoleon III and the need for caution. On 2 May 1855, she wrote at the end of a lengthy memorandum:

The great *advantage* to be derived for the permanent alliance of England and France, which is of such vital importance to both countries, by the Emperor's recent visit, I take to be this: that, with his peculiar character and views, which are very personal, a kind, unaffected, and hearty reception by *us personally* in our own family will make a lasting impression upon his mind; he will see that he can rely upon our friendship and honesty towards him and his country so long as he remains faithful towards us; naturally frank, he will see the advantage of the former dynasty, he will see that it arose *chiefly* from a *breach* of pledges . . . and will be sure, if I be not very much mistaken in his character, to *avoid* such a course. It must likewise not be overlooked that this kindly feeling towards us, and consequently towards England (the interests of which are *inseparable* from us), must be increased when it is remembered that we are almost the only people in *his* own position with whom he has been able to be on any terms of intimacy, consequently almost the only ones to whom he could talk easily and unreservedly, which he cannot do naturally with his inferiors. He and the Empress are in a most isolated position, unable to trust the only relations who are near them in France, and surrounded by courtiers and servants, who from fear or interest do not tell them the truth. It is, therefore, natural to believe that he will not willingly separate from those who, like us, do not scruple to put him in possession of the real facts, and whose conduct is guided by justice and honesty, and this the more readily as he is supposed to have always been a searcher after truth. I would go still further, and think that it is in our power to keep him in the right course, and to protect him against the extreme flightiness, changeableness, and to a certain extent want of honesty of his own servants and nation. We should never lose the opportunity of checking in the bud any attempt on the part of his agents or ministers to play us false, frankly informing him of the facts, and encouraging him to bring forward in an equally frank manner whatever he has to complain of. This is the course which we have hitherto pursued, and as he is France in his own sole person, it becomes of the utmost importance to encourage by every means in our power that very open intercourse which I must say has existed between him and Lord Cowley for the last year and a half, and now our personal acquaintance, between ourselves.

That personal acquaintance was renewed in August 1855, when Queen Victoria visited Paris with her family. She was entranced by the cheering crowds and the glitter of the imperial entertainments, and not a little nonplussed to find herself standing in the Invalides, paying her respects to Napoleon I: 'There I stood at the arm of Napoleon III, his nephew, before the coffin of England's bitterest foe; I the grand-daughter of that king who hated him most, and who most vigorously opposed him, and this very nephew, who bears his name, being my nearest and dearest ally!' She was not the only member of the English royal house to be entranced. Her eleven-year-old son Bertie, later Edward VII, was delighted by the wild cheers of the crowd as he appeared in his little kilt; and when he stood with Napoleon III on the terrace of the Tuileries he is reported to have said, 'You have a nice country. I would like to be your son.' Queen Victoria returned to England from Paris convinced that an Anglo–French alliance had been definitively established. She wrote to Leopold of Belgium: 'The *complete* Union of two countries is stamped and sealed in the most satisfactory

and solid manner, for it is not *only* a Union of the two Governments –
the two sovereigns – it is that of the two *Nations*!'

The moment seemed opportune to reconsider the project for a
Channel Tunnel. The latest designer was again a Frenchman, Thomé
Aimé de Gramond, a forty-eight-year-old hydrographer who produced an array of options including a steel tube on the sea bottom, a
twin-track rail-tunnel, and bridges linked to an artificial island built up
from the Varne Bank, ten miles east of Folkestone, which would be just
fifteen feet below the surface at low tide. The latter scheme was
enthusiastically supported by the famous bridge-builders Robert
Stephenson and Isambard Kingdom Brunel, as well as by Prince Albert.
Queen Victoria, who suffered from seasickness, was also enthusiastic
when the project was discussed in London in 1858. She assured de
Gramond that if this tunnel was built, she would bless him on behalf of
all the women in England. Unfortunately and characteristically, Lord
Palmerston took a different view. He questioned the feasibility of
expending public money on a scheme that would have the effect of
reducing the distance between the two countries that was already too
small, and he observed, with due deference, that Prince Albert would
see matters differently if he had been born on the island of Britain.
Thereafter relations between Britain and France deteriorated for other
reasons.

In January 1858, there was an assassination attempt on Napoleon: the
chief terrorist was an Italian, Felix Orsini, but the plot was hatched in
London and the bombs were made in Birmingham. A group of French
colonels bitterly denounced the British Government for having given
asylum to the Emperor's enemies; writing in the official *Moniteur*, they
begged for orders to seize London 'and destroy for ever the infamous
haunt in which such infernal machinations were planned'. Anti-French
sentiment was as readily roused in England a year later when Napoleon
mounted his Italian campaign and annexed Savoie. Palmerston
suspected it was all part of a plot to avenge Waterloo. An array of
concrete redoubts was erected around Portsmouth and Plymouth,
which came to be known as Palmerston's Follies. At the populist level in
England, anti-French feelings ran strong. By the summer of 1860, over
130,000 men had enrolled in the Volunteer Movement and, in August
of that year, 20,000 of these paraded before Queen Victoria in Hyde

Park. She expressed the hope that this display of patriotic enthusiasm would check the sinister designs of our turbulent neighbour.

There were, nonetheless, Englishmen Francophile and courageous enough to speak out in Napoleon III's defence, even when, in 1859, he had led a foolhardy expedition into his uncle's most propitious battle zone of north Italy. One such was Matthew Arnold, who made a spirited plea on Napoleon's behalf in his essay 'England and the Italian Question':

> [There is] a positive element in his character which makes him unapt to be out of sympathy with the masses of his people. It is an element which he has repeatedly manifested in his writings, his speeches, and his actions. It is the most interesting feature of his character. It is his great advantage over the kings and aristocracies of Europe. It is that he possesses, largely and deeply interwoven in his constitution, the popular fibre . . .
>
> The intimate alliance of the English with the French is no doubt ardently to be wished for, but is it possible? It is my profound conviction that at present it is not, and that the obstacles to it, the incurable want of sympathy, exist no more on the side of the French nation than on ours. There remains the alliance between the two governments. And here let me render justice to the Emperor Louis-Napoleon. I believe that he is unfeignedly, disinterestedly, and deeply inclined to the English alliance. I believe that he knows and values the English nation almost as well as the truest friends of England, M. Guizot or the lamented M. de Tocqueville. I believe that, in many respects, and putting out of question his strong natural leaning to ideas, which is not English, the English character is more sympathetic to him than the French. But he must not be expected to remain firm to the English alliance to the detriment of his position in France. He remains firm to it as long as he can, but the moment fatally arrives, when his perseverance brings him into collision with the sympathies and wishes of the French people; then he releases his hold on it, sorrowfully, hesitatingly but inevitably.

Another witness for Napoleon III's defence was Captain Rees Howell Gronow, a long-time English resident in France. His delightful *Reminiscences and Reflections* (1862) deserves to be better known, if only because in the Second World War it was one of Churchill's favourite bedside books:

> I have lived long enough to find hundreds of my countrymen participating in a real knowledge of the French, and believing with me that they are a brave, intelligent, and generous nation. Nearly half a century of experience

amongst them has taught me that there is much to learn and much that is worthy of imitation in France. The social habits of the French, and their easy mode of communication, always gain the admiration, and often invite the attachment of foreigners. They are less prejudiced than we islanders, and are much more citizens of the world than ourselves. I have received an immense amount of courtesy in France; and if there be less of solid friendship – which, however, in England is based too often on a similarity of birth, position, and wealth – in France, you have, at least, a greater chance than in England of making a friend of a man who neither looks to your ancestors nor your amount of riches before he proffers you the most sincere intimacy, and, if necessary, disinterested aid, purely on the ground of your own merit and character.

The great man who now wields the destinies of France possesses many of the remarkable qualities of the founder of his dynasty: his energetic will, his extensive and varied knowledge, his aptitude for government, his undaunted bravery, and that peculiar tact that leads him to say the right thing at the right time. To those rare gifts he joins the most princely generosity, and a kind and gentle heart: he has never been known to forsake a friend, or leave unrewarded any proofs of devotion shewn to him in his days of exile. He is adored by the vast majority of the French nation, and even his political opponents, if accidentally brought under the influence of his particularly winning and gracious manner, are, in spite of themselves, charmed and softened. There can be no doubt that Napoleon III enjoys a well-merited popularity, and that there is throughout all classes a deep and earnest confidence that the honour and glory of France are safe in his hands.

It is just this mighty power, founded on the love and trust of his people, which is the surest pledge that peace will be maintained between our country and France. Napoleon III does not require to court popularity by pandering to the anti-English prejudices still retained by a small minority of his subjects; and, unlike the representatives of less popular dynasties, he can afford to shew that he is not only the beloved and mighty ruler of the French nation, but also the firm ally and faithful friend of England.

More practical grounds for optimism were provided by Richard Cobden who, over the years, had worked tirelessly in the cause of free trade. Like the younger Pitt in the 1780s, he believed that the surest way of avoiding war between England and France would be to conclude a mutually advantageous trade treaty. Writing to Michel Chevalier in September 1859, he declared:

I should be glad to see a removal of the impediments which our foolish legislation interposes to the intercourse between the two countries. I see no other hope but in such a policy for any permanent improvements in the *political* relations of France and England . . . The people of the two nations must be brought into mutual dependence by the supply of each other's wants. There is no other way of counteracting the antagonism of language and race. It is God's own method of producing an *entente cordiale*.

At the outset, the Commercial Treaty seemed to have fulfilled all the high hopes of its progenitors. A whole new class of English visitors made their appearance on the French scene, representatives of all manner of English business interests. In his study *Modern France: its Journalism*, published in 1863, A. V. Kirwan observed:

> The treaty of commerce and the abolishing of passports have put the commercial, manufacturing and shop-keeping classes throughout our realm in motion; and there is hardly a mercantile or manufacturing house of any eminence in any of our great cities or towns, that does not send its junior partners or *commis voyageurs* to Paris, Lyons or Bordeaux or Marseilles. This crowd of active, vigorous and pushing men are all great readers of newspapers, and it is not unimportant to consider, in a political and moral sense, how their minds may be affected by French journalism. French journals, too, though still far from circulating largely amongst us, now in their decadence circulate more largely in clubs, coffee-houses, reading-rooms and hotels than at any former period, and have no inconsiderable effect on the writings and tone of thought of a portion, we mean the cheap portion, of our own metropolitan and provincial press.

Of as much interest as the barbed comment here on the vulgar taste of the English lower orders is the easy assumption that France and decadence are virtually synonymous. The English have attributed moral laxity to the French for as long as the French have associated perfidy with the English and, as will be seen, protests on that particular score were to join in strident chorus before the end of the century. In the meantime, events were to determine that in the 1860s, at the level of Heads of State, the *entente* was to become less than *cordiale*.

After the sudden death of Prince Albert in November 1861, London was plunged by royal decree into deepest mourning for several years. Paris, in contrast, seemed to be permanently *en fête*, Napoleon III having declared, 'One of the first duties of a sovereign is to amuse his subjects of all ranks in the social scale. He has no more right to have a dull court than he has to have a weak army or a poor navy.' Accordingly, life at the Tuileries was an endless round of entertainment. There were parties, receptions and balls without number and the Imperial Court was reckoned to be the most dissolute in Europe. The twenty-year-old Prince of Wales found it so irresistible that his mother had to insist that he spend as little time there as possible. Parisian 'high life', for its part, was as enthusiastically Anglophile under the Second Empire as it had been at the Restoration and under Louis-Philippe. English nannies were much in demand; the Prince Impérial was brought up by a Miss Shaw. Dress-design was dictated by Charles Frederick Worth. Born in Lincolnshire in 1826, the son of a solicitor who had gambled away the family's money, Worth left school at the age of eleven, and travelled to Paris before he was twenty. His fortune was assured when the Empress Eugènie bought her first Worth dress in 1859. His designing sessions were theatrical occasions. A contemporary observer noted: 'When this truly great man is composing, he reclines on a sofa, and one of the young ladies of the establishment plays Verdi to him. He composes chiefly in the evenings and says that the rays of the setting sun gild his compositions.'

In 1864, Henry de Pène, writing in *Paris Amoureux* under his pseudonym 'Mané', declared:

We are *Englishing* ourselves more and more. Women are beginning to wear leather belts *à l'anglaise*, with steel trimmings: they have leather-coloured dresses, and dresses trimmed with leather. They have an Englishman, the famous Worth, as their *couturier;* they buy plaids and tweeds. In the meanwhile, men are not being cured of their whiskers *à l'anglaise*, their suits *à l'anglaise*, their bearing and jargon *à l'anglaise*. Those purveyors of Parisian elegance who are not called Worth are called 'John's' or 'Peter's'.

In his account of *Court and Social Life in France under Napoleon III* (1867), the *Daily Telegraph's* regular correspondent, Felix M. White-hurst, reported on the Paris scene on the eve of the 1867 Exhibition: 'Among other curious indications of the coming season is a slight eruption of Anglomania. English signs begin to appear, and curious announcements . . . "Coffee and beer always ready, roast beef and plum pudding all day, and *stakes* from London every day and night" . . . One restaurant startles us with this horrible advertisement: "Real *live* turtle soup".'

The following year, writing in his diary, Joseph Primoli, nephew of the Princess Mathilde, noted that the cultural reign of Worth was as powerful as ever:

> I have been with mother to Worth's. He is the great couturier in fashion. He charges sixteen hundred francs for a simple little costume. Ladies arrange to meet at Worth's, and they talk politics as they sip tea. At Worth's, the faubourg Saint-Germain sits between two kept women, and the world of officialdom meets the faubourg Saint-Germain. Perhaps M. Worth does not even realise what he is doing, but . . . he is reconciling all political parties, and mingling all social classes. An artistically rumpled bit of fabric has achieved what wit had been unable to contrive.
>
> And so M. Worth gives delightful matinées. I don't only mean on his first floor in the rue de la Paix, where all the young men look like embassy attachés with their English accents, curled hair, pearl tie-pins and turquoise rings . . . I don't only mean the apartment which exhales some atmosphere of degraded aristocracy, some heady fragrance of elegance, wealth and forbidden fruit . . . Besides this apartment, I may add, M. Worth has a country house at Suresnes, and the noble faubourg aspires to the honour of being received there. This villa, it appears, is full of marvels of every kind. People go there in *séries*, as they do to Compiègne.

French Anglomania under the Second Empire was not confined to the world of high fashion. While the novels of Charles Dickens were not so richly influential on French literature as those of Scott, translations of them did, nonetheless, command a considerable popular following. When he visited Paris in 1855, he was fêted as extravagantly as Scott had been thirty years before. On 24 October, he wrote to W. H. Wills:

> You cannot think how pleasant it is to me to find myself generally known and liked here. If I go into a shop to buy anything and give my card, the officiating priest or priestess brightens up, and says: '*Ah! c'est l'écrivain célèbre! Monsieur porte un nom très distingué. Mais! je suis honoré et interessé de voir Monsieur Dick-in. Je lis un des livres de Monsieur tous les jours*' (in the *Moniteur*). And a man who brought some little cases home last night said: '*On connaît bien en France que Monsieur Dick-in prend sa position sur la dignité de la littérature. Ah! c'est grande chose! Et ses caractères* (this was to Georgina, while she unpacked) *sont si spirituellement tournées* (sic)! *Cette Madame Tojare* (Todgers), *ah! qu'elle est drôle et précisément comme une dame que je connais à Calais.*

On 12 December, he wrote to Wilkie Collins:

Le petit Chaperon rouge by Bruno, in *L'Intransigeant*, 1904: Britannia, with a banner bearing the names of English infamies, embraces Marianne (Little Red Riding Hood), while her boots are licked by the French Foreign Minister Delcassé. The caption reads: 'Comme vous avez de grandes dents quand vous êtes aimable!' ('O what big teeth you have when you smile!')

Punch, in the guise of Jack Tar, prepares to drink a toast poured by Marianne.

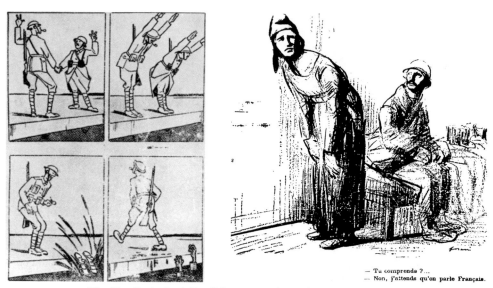

— Tu comprends ?...
— Non, j'attends qu'on parle Français.

The Bloodbath: Anti-English cartoon from the First World War
on the theme 'the English will fight to the last Frenchman'.
It was circulated by the Germans as a propaganda leaflet in 1939.
Versailles Peace Conference of 1919 by Forain: Poilu asks Marianne
if she can understand what is going on. She replies
that she's waiting till they start speaking in French.

PLUS NOUS SERONS ENSEMBLE, ENSEMBLE, ENSEMBLE,
PLUS NOUS SERONS ENSEMBLE, PLUS NOUS SERONS HEUREUX!

M.DOUMERGUE

ENTENTE CORDIAL

Vive L'Entente Cordiale! by Sidney Strube, May 1927: An English view of
the Entente cordiale from the *Daily Express*. The words are a literal translation
of the popular song 'The More We Are Together, the Happier We'll Be'.

Sir W. C. by Clivanel, July 1940: 'Messieurs les Anglais, tirez les premiers!'
– a mocking echo of the Maréchal de Saxe's words before the battle of Fontenoy in
1745.
Les assassins reviennent toujours sur les lieux de leur crime: Anti-English poster
of 1943. Joan of Arc rises above the pyre of Rouen following an allied air raid.

The Peace-seeker's Progress by David Low, August 1940:
On Pétain's suspected dealings with the Germans.

L'Europe – C'est Moi! by David Low, November 1948: De Gaulle elaborates on his world view to Truman and Attlee.

Herr de Gaulle is no Nationalist by Vicky, September 1958: Based on a remark by the then West German Chancellor, Dr Adenauer.

Macmillan attempts in vain to join the Common Market.
Above, Michael Cummings in the *Sunday Express*,
September 1962; *below*, Vicky in the *New Statesman*,
August 1962; de Gaulle and Adenauer on the tractor.

A decade later, the Common Market is again the focus of attention for cartoonists. *Above*, Bernie in *Aux Ecoutes*, 1971: Pompidou reassures the British lion: 'Who me? . . . No! . . . I am not like de Gaulle!'. *Below*, *Shotgun Wedding* by Arthur Horner in the *New Statesman*, May 1971: Edward Heath, dressed as John Bull, forces a reluctant Britannia into a union with the Common Market; Pompidou looks on.

SHOTGUN WEDDING

The Channel Tunnel. *Above*, Paul in *Punch*, September 1986:
Familiar imagery conveys age-old anxieties.
Below, JAK in the *Evening Standard*, June 1990:
'Will passengers from the French high-speed train arriving
from Paris transfer to the number 11 tram for King's Cross!'

Anglo-French relations. *Above*, Giles in the *Daily Express*,
January 1986, on the announcement of the Channel Tunnel
go-ahead: 'It'll be much more fun knowing your wife could
hop over in three hours!' *Below*, Nicholas Garland's parody
of the Bayeux Tapestry in the *Daily Telegraph*, October 1984:
Mitterrand and Thatcher in a tentative move towards European unity.

Every Frenchman who can write a begging letter writes one, and leaves it for this apartment. He first of all buys any literary composition printed in quarto on tea paper with a limp cover, srawls upon it '*Hommage à Charles Dickens, l'illustre Romancier*', encloses the whole in a dirty envelope, reeking with tobacco-smoke, and prowls, assassin-like, for days, in a big cloak and an enormous cache-nez like a counterpane, about the scraper of the outer door.

It was by no means merely the novel-reading Parisians who enthused over English writers. An entry in the Goncourts' *Journal* for 1863 describes a conversation between Hippolyte Taine and Sainte-Beuve. In that same year, Taine, the most distinguished *anglicisant* of the day, published his monumental three-volume *Histoire de la littérature anglaise*.

14 March. . . . A propos of a fresh eulogy of England by Taine, I heard Sainte-Beuve confide in him his disgust over being a Frenchman: 'I know that people say that to be a Parisian is not to be a Frenchman; but one is, nevertheless, a Frenchman, which is to say that one is nothing, that one counts for nothing. A country full of policemen. I should like to be an Englishman: at least an Englishman is somebody. As a matter of fact, I have some English blood. I was born in Boulogne, you know. My grandmother was English.'

Saint-Beuve was by now the *doyen* of French literary critics and had occupied the most prominent place in Matthew Arnold's private pantheon of literary idols since he first discovered him while still an undergraduate at Balliol. Another of his French idols was Ernest Renan whom he first met on a visit to Paris in 1859 and with whom, on the subject of morality and intelligence, he found himself 'singularly at one'. His sense of kinship with such distinguished thinkers, just as much as what he observed in the French schools he visited in 1859 as one of Queen Victoria's Inspectors of Education, must surely have been what inspired him to express his admiration for French intellectual pre-eminence. In 1861, in his *Report on the Popular Education of France*, he declared: 'From Messina to Archangel, and from Calais to Moscow, there reigns a universal striving after Parisian civilisation; the ideas which move the masses (I do not speak of aristocratic and learned coteries) are, when ideas reach them at all, French ideas. Cross the Straits and you are in another world: in a world where French ideas have not a breath of influence.' In November 1864, in *The Function of Criticism at the Present Time*, he heaped praise not on Paris alone but on the whole of the French populace:

> That a whole nation should have been penetrated with an enthusiasm for pure reason, and with an ardent zeal for making its prescriptions triumph, is a very remarkable thing, when we consider how little of mind, or anything so worthy and quickening of mind, comes into the motives which alone, in general, impel great masses of men . . . As no sincere passion for the things of the mind, even though it turn out in many respects an unfortunate passion, is ever quite thrown away and quite barren of good, France has reaped from hers one fruit – the natural and legitimate fruit, though not precisely the grand fruit she expected: she is the country in Europe where *the people* is most alive.

In that same year, one's impression that the leading writers of each country had joined in a Mutual Admiration Society is enhanced by the fact that it saw the publication of Victor Hugo's massive book *William Shakespeare*. It was written to accompany the translation by his younger son, Jean-François Victor, of the complete plays, following his translation of the *Sonnets* in 1857. The translations of both poems and plays are of a high order, by common critical consent the best of several attempted in France in the nineteenth century. Hugo *père*'s book is a bizarre performance; lengthy stretches of windy rhetoric interspersed with lists of the world's great men and critical insights of acute perception. Of Shakespeare's greatness, he was totally convinced: in Hugo's view he was one of the greatest men who had ever lived:

> Shakespeare is England's greatest glory. In politics, England has Cromwell: in philosophy, Bacon; in science, Newton. Three towering geniuses. But there is a streak of cruelty in Cromwell and a certain meanness in spirit in Bacon. As for Newton, his edifice is now starting to crumble. Shakespeare is pure, which Cromwell and Bacon are emphatically not, and quite unshakeable, which Newton is not. More than that, he is the loftier genius. Above Newton, there are Copernicus and Galileo. Above Bacon, there are Descartes and Kant. Above Cromwell, there are Danton and Bonaparte. Above Shakespeare? There is no one. Shakespeare has his equals but there is no one superior to him . . . His place is amongst that elite of absolute geniuses, the ranks of which, just occasionally, are increased by an illustrious newcomer, which crown civilisation and bathe the whole human race in their rays. Shakespeare is legion. On his own, he counter-balances the whole of our beautiful seventeenth century and most of the eighteenth as well.

But towards the end of this dithyrambic peroration, the Anglophobe ever-present in Hugo cannot resist the chance of scoring one final point: 'When you arrive in England, the first thing you look for is its statue to Shakespeare. You find a statue to Wellington.'

There follows a list of the statues the English establishment has erected to its Good and its Great:

> Statues for three or four Georges, one of whom was an idiot . . . For having drilled the Infantry, a statue. For having commanded the Horse Guards on manoeuvres, a statue. For having defended the Old Order, for having squandered England's riches on propping up a Coalition of Kings against 1789, against Democracy, against the Enlightenment, against the upward movement of the human spirit – set up a pedestal, quickly, a statue for Mr Pitt. To find the nation's tribute to England's greatest genius, you have to penetrate deep into the dark recesses of Westminster Abbey, and there, over-shadowed by four or five enormous monuments where, in marble or bronze, unknown royal personages stand in splendour, you are shown, on a tiny pedestal, a little figurine: beneath this figurine you read the name: WILLIAM SHAKESPEARE.

Hugo was by no means the only French commentator through whose imagination stalked the figures of his country's ancient enemies. Writing one of his *Lettres sur l'Angleterre* in 1866, the socialist historian Louis Blanc, like Hugo an exile from the Second Empire, claimed that the English people still needed to exorcise the centuries-old ghosts of invaders from across the Channel:

> It is curious to see the juvenile ardour with which this serious-minded people plays at soldiers in the midst of peace. Lawyers, doctors, shop-keepers, errand boys, and the Lord knows what else, stand ready to rush to war and want to learn the best way of killing . . . The English, though they won't admit it even to themselves, are tormented by a spectre named Invasion. They might almost like us if they did not believe us to be infected, as if with an incurable disease, by a passion for expansion. Why is it that France and England should be separated more effectively by suspicion than by the Channel?

English suspicions about French expansionism seemed justified by events four years later when Napoleon III went to war. Even though it was Prussia rather than Britain that was attacked, hardened English Francophobes gave full tongue to their animosity and the faith of the most ardent of Francophiles was tested beyond its breaking-point.

★

Once again, the ostensible pretext for war was a contested royal succession. In the summer of 1870, the Spanish throne fell vacant, and the Prussian Prince Leopold of Hohenzollern-Sigmaringen declared himself as a candidate. The French foresaw a real possibility of their being hemmed in, from the south and east, by Prussian power and protested vehemently. The Prince withdrew but the King of Prussia refused to accede to French demands that he oppose his son's candidature should he choose to renew it. While it has been persuasively argued that Bismarck engineered matters from the start, it was Napoleon who made the declaration of war, and in so doing was made to appear a wanton aggressor, like his uncle before him. Queen Victoria wrote to her daughter, the Crown Princess of Prussia on 16 July 1870: 'We must be neutral as long as we can, but no one here conceals their opinion as to the extreme *iniquity* of the war, and the unjustifiable conduct of the French! Still, *more, publicly*, we cannot say; but the feeling of the people and the country is *all* with you . . . My whole heart and my fervent prayers are with beloved Germany!'

The eminent historian John Richard Green emphatically shared her views. On 1 August 1870, he wrote to his close friend and fellow professor, E. A. Freeman, to report how keen ordinary Germans were to take part in the war: 'The head of a large lunatic asylum in Hanover writes – "Nine of my keepers are gone to the war and I am in great straits how to manage the patients; but my chief sorrow is that I cannot go to the war *myself*." I hope when the war is over they will just lock up all France – turn it into a gigantic National Asylum and keep every man of 'em in a strait-jacket.'

By August 1870, the French military forces were faced with disaster. One part of the army, under General MacMahon, had withdrawn to Châlons, where it was joined by Napoleon III. He had relinquished his position as Commander-in-Chief of the main army now commanded by General Bazaine, which was trapped in Metz. Patriotic feelings, which were running just as high in Paris as they were in the Hanover lunatic asylum, compelled the Emperor to march to the relief of Metz instead of taking the more sensible course of falling back on Paris. The German High Command promptly diverted two of its advancing armies to encircle the Emperor's forces. On 22 August, Queen Victoria wrote once more to her daughter, and revealed that her feelings towards the French had softened:

> The position of the French seems to get hourly worse! Such a complete tumbling to pieces of their empire and its far famed army has really never been seen. It does seem like a judgement from heaven! Everything seems to fail! Odiously impertinent, insulting and boastful as the French have always been, one cannot help feeling for them; for to see a great – or at least a powerful – nation so utterly crushed is a fearful and sad thing! And how awful is this loss of life! And for what? One shudders! Most unhappy Emperor to have this sin, and these thousands of innocent lives on his head!

On 31 August, Professor Green again wrote to Freeman not to exult over the success of Germany but to express his love for their personal image of France:

> I am German to the core, but like Joan of Arc I have pity for that *bel royaume de France*. How strange it seems now to remember the night when you and I looked from the Quai Voltaire over Seine on the Tuileries and chaunted a psalm about a green bay tree. But L.N.B. is gone, and France remains, vain, ignorant, insufferable if you will, but still with an infinite attraction in her, at least to me. There is a spring, an elasticity about her, a 'light heart' that has its good as well as its bad side, a gaiety, a power of enjoyment, which Europe can't afford to miss. I'm a little like Heine, I think: with an infinite respect for Berlin, I should prefer *living* at Paris.

On the following day, 1 September, the two German armies encircled MacMahon's army at Sedan. The French cavalry made repeated efforts to break out (described vividly in Zola's novel *La Débâcle*) but their heroism was in vain. At five o'clock in the afternoon, Napoleon ordered the white flag to be raised. The Germans insisted on unconditional surrender and the Emperor and his large army were marched off, the next day, into captivity.

English Francophobes exulted. Edward Fitzgerald, best known for his translation of *The Rubáiyát of Omar Khayyám* (1859), wrote to W. F. Pollock on 1 November 1870:

> I must say that my savageness against France goes no further than wishing that the new and gay part of Paris were battered down; not the poor working part, no, nor any of the People destroyed. But I wish ornamental

Paris down, because then I think the French would be kept quiet till they had rebuilt it . . . I believe it would be a good thing if the rest of Europe would take possession of France itself, and rule it for better or worse, leaving the French themselves to amuse and enlighten the world by their Books, Plays, Songs, Bon Mots, and all the Arts and Sciences which they are so ingenious in. They can do all things but manage themselves and live at peace with others: and they should themselves be glad to have their volatile Spirits kept in order by the Good Sense and Honesty which other Nations certainly abound in more than themselves.

Carlyle, who in 1851 had given advance notice of his feelings by entitling a travel book *Excursion (futile enough) to Paris*, revealed he was even more curmudgeonly in his old age. In conversation with his German translator, Friedrich Althaus, he declared:

I wish the Germans well from the bottom of my heart. They are a peace-loving, brave, industrious, firm and noble race, and surely they have endured long enough the arrogance and interference of the French. Oh, for more than three hundred years they have tortured and exasperated. Francis I began the game, and then came the insufferable, meddling Louis XIV and Napoleon after him, and so on till now at last these French broke loose upon them exactly as the highwaymen on Bagshot Heath used to hold their guns to their neighbours' faces, crying – 'Your money or your life!' Never was there a more innocent war. Never were victories more richly deserved than these German victories.

George Meredith, who had agonised over the war from its outbreak, was at once more sensitive and more prescient. He had spent two years at school in Germany and loved German poetry but, in the conflict, his sympathies went out to France. In December 1870, he composed a heartfelt 'Ode to France', which began:

> We look for her that sunlike stood
> Upon the forehead of our day,
> An orb of nations, radiating food
> For body and for mind alway.
> Where is the shape of glad array;
> The nervous hands, the front of steel,
> The clarion tongue? Where is the bold, proud face?
> We see a vacant place;
> We hear an iron heel . . .

For him, the explanation of Napoleon's spectacular defeat after just six weeks of war was France's military adventuring earlier in the nineteenth century. For Queen Victoria, there was a different explanation: it was divine retribution for French immorality. On 17 September 1870, she wrote to her daughter:

> All was after all not so entirely unexpected in France!! The system of corruption, immorality and *gaspillage* was dreadful. Nothing annoyed dear Papa more than the abject court paid to the Emperor and the way in which we were forced to flatter and humour him, which was shortsighted policy and spoilt him . . . Your elder brothers unfortunately were carried away by that horrid Paris (beautiful though you may think it) and that frivolous and immoral court did frightful harm to English society (that Papa knew and saw) and was very bad for Bertie and Affie. The fearful extravagance and luxury, the utter want of seriousness and principle in everything – the many crimes in France all show a rottenness which was sure to crumble and fall, but certainly not so soon or so suddenly when it did come.

Her views on Paris were not dissimilar to those of Carlyle, who said of it in his old age: 'I think there never was a more corrupt abominable city, nothing but a brothel and a gambling Hell!'

Napoleon III's humiliating surrender at Sedan contributed to a marked change in the attitudes of Matthew Arnold. He had spent much of his long professional career eloquently praising France's litarary and intellectual virtues and her superior educational system. In 1859, impressed by Haussmann's rebuilding of Paris and by the glittering displays of pageantry regularly mounted by Napoleon, he had predicted that the French army, which he took to be equally well organised, would see off the forces of Prussia and Austria combined. How, then, could he account for the catastrophe of 1870? He wrote to his mother on 31 January 1871:

> Immense as are her advantages and resources, it does not seem as if France *could* recover herself now as she did in 1815, or indeed could recover herself within our time at all. Whatever may be said of the harshness of such a sentence, it is yet true that her fall is mainly due to that want of a serious conception of righteousness and the need of it, the consequences of which so often show themselves in the world's history, and in regard to the Graeco-Latin nations more particularly. The fall of Greece, the fall of Rome, the fall of the brilliant Italy of the fifteenth century, and now the fall of France, are all examples . . . The qualities of the French genius, their directness of intellect, and social charm, must always make themselves felt,

as the far higher qualities of the Greeks did and do. But it is quite a question whether the practical military and political career of France may not now be ending not again to revive, as that of Greece did after the Macedonian conquest.

Arnold expressed both disillusionment and alarm over the turn of events in Paris in the spring of 1871. After the collapse of the Second Empire, a new republic was proclaimed in Paris and a Government of National Defence inaugurated. It was composed of the deputies of the department of the Seine, all of whom were moderates. The Germans proceeded to besiege Paris, whose citizens suffered extreme hardship throughout the winter. While a peace treaty was being negotiated in February 1871, a new National Assembly was elected and it proposed to conduct its business from Versailles. It was markedly royalist in make-up and this, together with the news that the Germans were going to be permitted to occupy Paris unopposed, provoked mass popular uprising. The insurrectionists seized power in March 1871 and proclaimed a Conseil Communal or Commune. Paris was again besieged, this time by regular French troops commanded by MacMahon. After ferocious street fighting, the Commune was suppressed to be followed by severe reprisals. On 20 March 1871, Arnold wrote to his mother:

> What news from Paris! One hardly knows what to wish, except that the present generation of Frenchmen may pass clean away as soon as possible and be replaced by a better one. I am not sorry that the English sightseers who, with the national vulgarity, have begun to flock over to the show of fallen Paris and France, should be put to a little fright and inconvenience. One thing is certain, that miserable as it is for herself, there is no way by which France can make the rest of Europe so alarmed and uneasy as by a socialist and red republic. It is a perpetual flag to the proletaire class everywhere – the class which makes all governments uneasy.

Lord Salisbury, who had supported the French cause from the beginning of the Franco–Prussian War, believed that France was still infected with the virus of the French Revolution, 'the great modern exemplar and source of her evils'. During the siege of Paris, he wrote, 'Whatever else Bismarck does, I do hope he will burn down the Faubourg St Antoine and crush out the Paris mob. Their freaks and madnesses have been a curse to Europe for the last eighty years.'

In the course of these traumatic months, Britain maintained its reputation as a safe-haven for French political refugees of every class and persuasion. After Napoleon III surrendered at Sedan, the Empress Eugénie escaped to Hastings, via Deauville and the Isle of Wight, before setting up home at Camden Place, Chislehurst. Other refugees from the Franco–Prussian War included the painter Camille Pissarro, whose house at Louveciennes was looted and all his pictures destroyed. He joined Claude Monet in London, where their technique of landscape painting was strongly influenced by the work of Constable and Turner. After his release from captivity, Napoleon III crossed the Channel and was cheered and pelted with flowers by a vast welcoming crowd at Dover; when he died three years later, he was buried at Chislehurst. The left-wing activist Jules Vallès, who had been imprisoned for his revolutionary activities in 1853 and was subsequently exiled and condemned to death *in absentia* for his involvement in the Commune, spent nine years in London. He was based, like many French refugees of his generation, in Soho, and contributed regularly to *L'Evénement*. These articles, published in book form in 1884 as *La Rue à Londres*, provide particularly graphic descriptions of London working-class life, of the dramatically contrasting life-styles of England's rich and poor and, like Mérimée and others before him, a warmly appreciative picture of the British Museum.

Soho swarmed with refugees from the Commune. They congregated in various centres: the Café de la Sablonnière, the Duke of York pub in Gray's Inn Road, or restaurants such as Victor's in Old Compton Street (*Déjeuner* one shilling and sixpence, *vin ordinaire* a shilling) or the Hotel de la Seine in King Street. For their more serious activities, the Communards met at the Cercle d'Etudes Sociales in Francis Street, or attended lectures in a room above the Hibernia Stores on the corner of Old Compton Street or at the Spread Eagle, founded by earlier refugees after the 1851 *coup*. Karl Marx's home in Hampstead was a 'refuge of Justice' and he willingly dispensed advice and aid to any French refugees who cared to call. However, the prime progenitor was Eugène Vermersch, a militant revolutionary who had been condemned to death by one of the post-Commune tribunals and to whom the *Daily Telegraph* had devoted a front-page article, demanding his immediate expulsion as soon as he landed in England. He was allowed not only to stay but to set up a printing works for the production of left-wing journals. That he was not without a sense of humour and that the

English authorities had been wise to let him and his co-revolutionaries stay is evident from a letter he wrote to a friend on 12 August 1872:

> They've founded clubs, reunions, lodges, circles . . . study-circles, circles for proletarians, for Communards, for revolutionaries (this last is a secret society – apart from the whole of London, nobody knows about it), a Lodge of the Federation, a Lodge of the Revolution, etc. Naturally, this one excludes that one, who fulminates against the next one, who calls the fourth a spy, who denounces the fifth as a traitor, who orders the sixth to produce the accounts. This last, who has made off with the kitty, is eating, drinking and living it up and doesn't give a toss for the five others.

England's 'open house' attitude towards French political escapees continued till the end of the century, at no time more dramatically than when England provided a haven both for Emile Zola, who was sentenced for publishing his open letter, *J'accuse*, protesting against the wrongful imprisonment of Captain Dreyfus, and for the real villain of the affair, Commandant le Comte Walsin-Esterhazy. The latter died in England in 1924 and is buried in St Nicholas churchyard, Harpenden, in Hertfordshire.

★

Matthew Arnold's unease at the possible spread of proletarian revolution marked the beginning of his increasing disillusionment with the French scene. His objections to the way he thought France was degenerating were not so much political as moral, and in the eighteen years left to him after the collapse of the Second Empire, he disavowed, one by one, the principal features of his Francophilia. The first of these was Paris, once the City of Light. In 1874, Arnold declared in his essay 'Literature and Dogma':

> It is not enough perceived what it is which gives to France her attractiveness for everybody, and her success, and her repeated disasters. France is *l'homme sensuel moyen*, the average sensual man: Paris is the city of *l'homme sensuel moyen*. This has an attraction for all of us. We all have in us this *homme sensuel*, the man of the 'wishes of the flesh and of the current thoughts' but we develop him under checks and doubts, and unsystematically and often grossly. France, on the other hand, develops him confidently and harmoniously. She makes the most of him, because she knows what she is about and keeps in a mean, as her climate is in a mean, and her situation. She

does not develop him with madness, into a monstrosity, as the Italy of the Renaissance did; she develops him equally and systematically. And hence she does not shock people with him but attracts them; she names herself the France of tact and measure, good sense, logic . . . This explains the great attraction France exercises upon the world. All of us feel, at some time or other in our lives, a hankering after the French ideal, or disposition to try it. More particularly is this true of the Latin nations; and therefore every-where, among those nations, you see the old indigenous type of city disappearing, and the type of modern Paris, the city of *l'homme sensuel moyen*, replacing it. *La Bohème*, the ideal, free, pleasurable life of Paris, is a kind of Paradise of Ishmaels. And all this assent from every quarter, and the clearness and apparent reasonableness of their ideal besides, fill the French with a kind of ecstatic faith in it, a zeal almost fanatical for propagating what they call French civilisation everywhere, for establishing its predominance, and their own predominance along with it, as of the people entrusted with an oracle so showy and taking.

Compared to Carlyle's, this is the voice of sweet reason itself but the moral message is not dissimilar: Paris is a city of sin.

In 1864, Arnold had hymned the praises of France's educational system in his essay 'A French Eton'. By 1882 he had reversed his position. In an article in the *Fortnightly Review* he described how far France had fallen: 'a modern French schoolboy, Voltairean and emancipated, reading *La Fille Elisa* and *Nana*, making it his pastime to play tricks on his chaplain, to mock and flout him and his teaching – the production of a race of lucid schoolboys of this kind is a dangerous privilege'. The two novels he names, by the Goncourt brothers and Zola, both have a prostitute as their central character, and they were indicative of a growing trend in French literature that Arnold deplored. The Romantic writers, whom he had admired and come to know personally, were by now dead. The Naturalist writers, who now seemed dominant, together with the author's of *risqué* French plays playing to packed houses in London, were all dismissed as worshippers 'of the great goddess Lubricity'.

In that same decade, a number of influential English writers and magazine editors seem to have shared Arnold's moral views. In 1881, the historian J. A. Froude described his reactions to *Le Père Goriot*, which he read for the first time in the course of a cruise off the Norwegian coast:

I tried a dozen novels after the other without success; at last, perhaps the morning we left Elversdale, I found on the library shelves 'Le Père Goriot'. I had read a certain quantity of 'Balzac' at other times, in deference to the high opinion entertained of him. N——, a fellow of Oriel and once member for Oxford, I remembered insisting to me that there was more knowledge of human nature in 'Balzac' than in Shakespeare. I had myself observed in the famous novelist a knowledge of a certain kind of human nature which Shakespeare let alone – nature in which healthy vigour had been corrupted into a caricature by highly seasoned artificial civilisation. Hothouse plants, in which the flowers had lost their grace of form and natural beauty, and had gained instead a poison-loaded and perfumed luxuriance, did not exist in Shakespeare's time, and if they had, they would probably not have interested him. However, I had not read 'Le Père Goriot', and as I had been assured that it was the finest of Balzac's works, I sat down to it and deliberately read it through. My first impulse after it was over was to plunge into the sea to wash myself. As we were going ten knots, there were objections to this method of ablution, but I felt that I had been in abominable company. The book seemed to be the very worst ever written by a clever man.

In his study of Swinburne, Sir Edmund Gosse describes what happened when the young Swinburne was caught reading a Balzac novel while staying with the Trevelyan family. His host, Sir Walter Trevelyan, snatched the book – and flung it straight into the fire.

Tennyson, who had once sought to rally the nation against the French invaders who never came, felt it was his patriotic duty, in 1886, to warn the populace of the true character of Naturalism. In 'Locksley Hall, Sixty Years After', he proclaimed:

Tumble nature heel o'er head, and yelling with the yelling street,
Set the feet above the brain and swear the brain is in the feet.
Bring the old dark ages back without the faith, without the hope,
Break the State, the Church, the Throne, and roll their ruins down the
    slope.
Authors – essayist, atheist, novelist, realist, rhymester – play your part,
Paint the mortal shame of nature with the living hues of art.
Rip your brother's vices open, strip your foul passions bare;
Down with Reticence, down with Reverence – forward, naked, let them
    stare.
Feed the budding rose of boyhood with the drainage of your sewer;
Send the drain into the fountain, lest the stream should issue pure.
Set the maiden fancies wallowing in the troughs of Zolaism –
Forward, forward, aye, and backward, downward too into the abysm.

In 1887, Andrew Lang said in an article in the *Contemporary Review*: 'If I were to draw an indictment I might add that some of the Naturalists have an almost unholy knowledge of the nature of women . . . Such analysis makes one feel uncomfortable in the reading, makes one feel intrusive and unmanly.'

And on 22 September 1887, George Meredith wrote in a letter to his friend, Maxse: 'Oh! what a nocturient, cacaturient crew has issued of the lens of the sun of the mind on the lower facts of life! – on sheer Realism, breeder at best of the dung-fly!'

The power and influence of French fiction became a public issue, giving credence to the comment made by Wilkie Collins to Dickens that 'The morality of England is firmly based on the immorality of France.' A National Vigilance Association was established and launched a crusade for the protection of England's young against the 'pernicious literature' of Flaubert, Zola and Maupassant. One of the Association's members, Mr Smith MP, submitted the following motion to the House of Commons: '*Resolved*, that this house deplores the rapid spread of demoralising literature, and is of opinion that the law against obscene publications and indecent pictures should be vigorously enforced and, if necessary, strengthened.' Mr Smith's motion was passed unanimously and it was not long before a campaign was mounted to make an example of Henry Vizetelly, the publisher of Zola's work in English translation. On 21 April 1888, an anonymous reviewer in *Society* launched the following attack:

Realism according to latter-day French lights means nothing short of sheer beastliness; it means not only the insinuation of petty intrigue, but the laying bare of social sores in their most loathsome forms; it means the alternation of the brutal directness of the drunken operative of today with the flabby sensuality of Corinth in the past. In a word it is dirt and horror pure and simple; and the good-natured Englishman who might smilingly criticize the French novel for being 'rather thick' will be disgusted and tired with the inartistic garbage which is to be found in Zola's *La Terre*. Yet Messers Vizetelly, of Catherine Street, Strand, are allowed with impunity to publish an almost word for word translation of Zola's bestial *chef d'oeuvre*. In the French original its sins are glaring enough in all conscience, but the English version needs but a chapter's perusal to make one sigh for something to take the nasty taste away.

Vizetelly, by now seventy years old, was brought to trial at the

Central Criminal Court and fined £100. He carried on publishing and was summoned to appear again. On this occasion, advised by his lawyer to throw himself on the mercy of the court, he received a three-month prison sentence. Some 125 prominent statesmen, scientists and writers then signed a petition to secure his release. Among the signatories were: Thomas Hardy, George Moore, H. Rider Haggard, Hall Caine, George du Maurier, Mrs Frances Hodgson Burnett, Olive Schreiner, Havelock Ellis and Edmund Gosse. The war went on, regardless.

In January 1889, Emily Crawford wrote in an essay on Zola in the *Fortnightly Review*:

> Zola is not necessarily a vicious man, he merely has an immoderate taste for the crude and salacious . . . What Byron saw and enjoyed of Italian dissipation was presumably seen and enjoyed by a long line of Zolas who were citizens of Venice . . . Nevertheless, he stands on a higher plane than the brothers Goncourt or Guy de Maupassant . . . The underlings of the naturalist school are like dogs battening upon carrion offal. They imitate the master when he is offensive and go beyond him in reeking foulness . . . How can we expect the young to escape from spring blights if that beautiful and natural guard against them, the sense which calls the mantling blush to the cheek, is broken down by literature that is wantonly purulent.

That same year, an anonymous contributor to the *Sentinel* reported that he had seen a copy of one of Zola's novels in translation opened so that passers-by might read a certain episode: 'The matter was of such a leprous nature that it would be impossible for any young man who had not learned the Divine secret of self-control to have read it without committing some form of outward sin within twenty-four hours after.'

In April 1890, the writer of an article on 'The Modern French Novel' published in the *Quarterly Review* announced: 'Naturalism is the conquering anarch of our time . . . holding the mirror up to Nature, Gallic nature, which, we should do well to bear in mind, is human – with a difference.'

On 29 December 1891, Henry Adams, the American man of letters, said in a letter to Elizabeth Cameron: 'At every interval of years I come back here with a wider experience of men and knowledge of races, and always the impression becomes stronger that, of all people in the world, the French are the most gratuitously wicked. They almost do me good. I feel it a gain to have an object of dislike.'

And in 1892, the anonymous author of an article on 'The French

Decadence', which appeared in the *Quarterly Review*, said of Maupassant:

> in crude but quite unimpassioned language and sometimes with amusement, he throws down his lively sketches of a depravity which has long since passed the bounds of permissible human speech.
>
> In *Notre Coeur* there is a kind of murderous enchantment which takes prisoner soul and sense, though certainly not those of an Englishman, who despises what to his Gallic neighbours might seem luxuries of feeling . . . M. Guy de Maupassant is a gentleman by birth and education, but he does not write like one.

Thereafter, the voices raised in moral outrage over French immorality would seem to have grown fainter and more sporadic – temporarily, at any rate. However, the conviction that the French are preoccupied with sexuality appears to be so deeply imprinted onto the English consciousness as to be quite indelible. Whatever form it may have assumed over the centuries – *amour courtois* in the lyric poetry of the medieval troubadours or of Chrétien de Troyes, the *escadron volant* of the court of Catharine de' Médicis, the gallants and predatory dancing-masters of the English Restoration, promiscuous *petits-maîtres* and cynical seducers such as Valmont in the eighteenth century – all bear testimony to the claim made by Sterne that 'the French have the reputation for knowing more about love and of making it better than any other race on earth'. In one of their occasional fits of public morality, the English waxed indignant on the subject in the 1880s.

By 1908, when Arnold Bennett published his novel *The Old Wives' Tale*, he could treat the subject with characteristic ambivalence, a mixture of envy and contempt. In this passage, Sophia is on honeymoon in Paris with her husband, Gerald:

> She was obliged to walk slowly because Gerald walked slowly. A beautiful woman, or any woman not positively hag-like or venerable, who walks slowly in the streets of Paris becomes at once the cause of inconvenient desires, as representing the main objective on earth, always transcending in importance politics and affairs. Just as a true patriotic Englishman cannot be too busy to run after a fox, so a Frenchman is always ready to forsake all in order to follow a woman whom he has never before set eyes on. Many men thought twice about her, with her romantic Saxon mystery of temperament, and her Parisian clothes; but all refrained from affronting her, not in the least out of respect for the gloom in her face, but from an expert

conviction that those rapt eyes were fixed immovably on another male. She walked unscathed amid the frothing hounds as though protected by a spell.

Loyalty to this romantic belief was to become one of the principal articles of faith of many a twentieth-century Francophile, both male and female – a far cry, indeed, from the shattered vision of Matthew Arnold.

★

For all this moral outrage, France continued to exert its perennial appeal to English people of artistic and epicurean disposition. Earlier in the century, there had been those, such as Lord Macaulay or John Stuart Mill, who, like Horace Walpole and Edward Gibbon before them, spent many months in France as part of their liberal education; Thackeray chose to live in Paris between 1836 and 1837 to improve his drawing; Robert and Elisabeth Barrett Browning lived for lengthy periods in France in the middle years of the century because they believed it to be the fountainhead of contemporary culture. Others came on account of their parents. It was because his father was put in charge of the Indian Section of Arts and Manufactures at the Paris Exhibition in 1878, that the schoolboy Rudyard Kipling came to France for the first of many visits; and it was because he had actually been born in France that Hilaire Belloc, at the age of twenty-one, enlisted for obligatory military service with the Tenth Battery of the Eighth Regiment of Artillery at Toul. He was discharged after a year and ever afterwards spoke French, literally, like a French trooper.

The traffic was by no means in one direction only. England and the English presented an abiding challenge to French historians and political scientists. They were intrigued by the crucial differences between France and England, both in how each country was organised and in how their citizens lived their private lives. Alexis de Tocqueville in the 1830s, Hippolyte Taine in the 1860s and Paul Bourget in the 1880s were among the most perceptive and articulate of the many French observers who addressed themselves to these questions, demonstrating their national propensity to generalise and theorise: for them, England was an intellectual conundrum demanding to be solved.

To other Frenchmen in the nineteenth century, as in the eighteenth, England proved attractive for a variety of reasons. For poets and artists, England held out the promise of fresh inspiration: Gautier and Verlaine recorded their impressions in prose and verse; Claudel's record of his visit to the Isle of Wight was the first of his writings ever to be published; Paul Valéry gave up writing poetry and came to work briefly in London for the British South Africa Company. He was later to confess that 'On London Bridge I found myself guilty of the crime of poetry.' To others, England came to represent love and/or marriage: after he married Lydia Bunbury, Alfred de Vigny was obliged to spend months in London, fighting a Jarndyce v. Jarndyce-style legal action to recover monies withheld by in-laws who disapproved of him; Mallarmé spent the first two years of his married life in London; Verlaine and Rimbaud lived together in Camden Town, advertising their services as two Parisian gentlemen teachers in the *Daily Telegraph*; Villiers de l'Isle-Adam came to London dressed in a fur-trimmed overcoat and equipped with a fresh set of false teeth, hoping to meet a complaisant English heiress with a rich dowry; Apollinaire came to Landor Road, Clapham, vainly hoping to persuade his beloved Annie Playden to return to France with him. For other young Frenchmen, a short or long stay in England was adjudged by their parents to be vital for their professional advancement: so, in the summer of 1905, Alain-Fournier was sent to work as a clerk with Sanderson's the wallpaper-makers in Chiswick and, in 1908, the young Paul Morand was sent for what was to prove an idyllic academic year at the University of Oxford.

And yet for most French people England remained both an enigma and a challenge. Augustine Favre de Coulevain, who wrote under the pseudonym of Pierre de Coulevain, published her account of life in modern England in the form of a novel. It appeared in 1904, and after more than two centuries of distinguished French writing about England and the English she still felt it appropriate to entitle her book *L'Ile inconnue*.

*

For many French people at the end of the nineteenth century, England was not so much *inconnue* as what it had always been: *l'Albion perfide*. Though the royal widows, Victoria and ex-Empress Eugénie, remained close personal friends, there was serious tension at both diplomatic and populist levels. While France's young men were drilled for *La Revanche* (the crusade against Germany that would retrieve the nation's honour by regaining the lost provinces of Alsace and Lorraine), the not-so-young and the less well-educated would seem to have gone on believing in a more traditional enemy. In 1888, when General Boulanger was about to capitalise on the mounting national desire for a war of vengeance against Germany, Maupassant published one of his most outstanding short stories, 'Le Rosier de Madame Husson'. In it, his narrator declares at one point: 'I am a Norman, a true Norman. I tell you, I may feel bitter about the Germans and I may want my revenge, but I don't detest them. I don't have the instinctive loathing for them that I feel for the English. They're the true enemy, the hereditary enemy, the Normans' natural enemy. That's because the English swept across this land of my ancestors, pillaged it, ravished it twenty times over. Hatred for those treacherous people was passed on to me by my father when he conceived me.'

In Proust's *Sodome et Gomorrhe*, not published till 1923 but portraying the same period in French history as Maupassant, a butcher-woman remains firmly convinced that the English fought alongside the Prussians in the débâcle of 1870: 'As my sister was just explaining, since that war that the English fought against us in '70, we're being ruined by these commercial treaties. After we've beaten them, we won't let a single Englishman come into France any more unless they pay three hundred francs entrance-fee – just as we've got to pay now to go to England.'

In the French general elections of 1893, Clemenceau was suspected of being the personal protégé of Queen Victoria. His campaign speeches were punctuated with derisive cries of 'Aoh yes!' and, for all his persuasive personality, such was the power of public Anglophobia at that time that he lost the election. The root-cause of such powerful animosity in the last decade of the nineteenth century was the same as it had intermittently been in the second-half of the eighteenth and in the 1840s: imperial rivalry. On this occasion, the issue was who was to be the dominant European power in Egypt. Britain won the opening rounds in the contest: France was ousted from Egypt and, in 1898, was obliged to withdraw Colonel Marchand's token force from the town of Fashoda, on the Upper Nile. Predictably, the French right-wing press were vituperative, and the French openly championed the Boers against the British in their war at the turn of the century.

A number of studies were published in Paris in the closing years of the nineteenth century seeking to raise shattered French morale. Some followed a truculent line such as 'Aristide's' diatribe *Les crimes de John Bull: les Anglais sont-ils une nation grande? Non!* (1890). Others were more reflective, such as E. Desmolins's *A quoi tient la supériorité des Anglo-Saxons?* As an odd echo to Matthew Arnold's earlier study, *A French Eton*, Desmolins found the answer in England's public-school system with its stress on character development, team games and love of country: to follow those lines would make France equally strong again. There was also the military option. In 1900, at the request of Foreign Minister Delcassé, the *Conseil Supérieur de la Guerre* drew up a number of contingency plans in the event of a war with Britain. These included the invasion of Egypt or even of England itself.

There were those in England who still considered this a real possibility. Novels about the war to come against France remained popular in the second half of the nineteenth century and their titles are an accurate indication of the subject-matter: *A History of the Sudden and Terrible Invasion of England by the French in the month of May, 1852* (1851), *How John Bull Lost London* (1882) and *The Sack of London in the Great French War of 1901* (1894). The likelihood of real life overtaking fiction threatened to come appreciably closer in 1882 when serious discussions again took place on the feasibility of a Channel Tunnel. The *Nineteenth Century*, a periodical of repute, organised the following petition:

> The undersigned, having had their attention called to certain proposals made by commercial companies for joining England to the Continent of Europe by a Railroad under the Channel, and feeling convinced that (notwithstanding any precautions against risk suggested by the projectors) such a Railroad would involve this country in military dangers and liabilities from which, as an island, it has hitherto been happily free – hereby record their emphatic protest against the sanction or execution of any such work.

The signatories included Browning, Tennyson, T. H. Huxley, Herbert Spencer, the Archbishop of Canterbury, five dukes, ten earls, twenty-six MPs, seventeen admirals, fifty-nine generals, two hundred clergymen and six hundred other VIPs. At the same time, the following ditty was widely sung:

> By the Great Ruler of the Earth and Heaven
> This Island was from a Continent riven;

> Where mountains could not shield from spoil and slaughter
> He – for a national Bulwark – gave THE WATER!

And the Adjutant-General of the British Army submitted a memorandum listing his arguments against the enterprise: 'A couple of thousand armed men might easily come through the tunnel in a train at night, avoiding all suspicion by being dressed as ordinary passengers, or passing at express speed through the tunnel with the blinds down, in their uniform and fully armed.' He estimated that a force of five thousand men could easily seize the tunnel installations. He added: 'Half that number, ably led by a daring, dashing young commander, might, I feel, some dark night easily make themselves masters of the works at our end of the tunnel – and then England would be at the mercy of the invader.'

However, for all these paranoid prognostications and the xenophobic rabble-rousing that proceeded apace on either side of the Channel, momentous changes were in train. A significant pointer was to be found in yet another tale of a future war. In the view of many critics, it remains the best of its kind. Written by Erskine Childers, then a clerk in the House of Commons, its title is *The Riddle of the Sands*. With its appearance, in 1903, the nationality of England's most menacing enemy ceased dramatically and significantly to be French and instead became German. Not surprisingly, for geographical and recent historical reasons, the French were even more alert to the increasing menace of Germany. They needed all the allies they could muster. Once again, a *rapprochement* between Britain and France appeared on each country's agenda. The auguries were favourable. Edward VII, who had been a fervent Francophile ever since his first childhood visit to Paris, succeeded to the throne in 1901. On 1 May 1903, he made a speech at the British Chamber of Commerce in Paris. It won him and his country many French friends because, unusually for a royal personage making a public declaration, he revealed his private feelings:

> It is scarcely necessary to tell you with what sincere pleasure I find myself once more in Paris, to which, as you know, I have paid very frequent visits with ever-increasing pleasure, and for which I feel an attachment fortified by so many happy and ineffaceable memories. The days of hostility between the two countries are, I am certain, happily at an end. I know of no two countries whose prosperity is more interdependent. There may have been misunderstandings and causes of dissension in the past; but that is all happily over and forgotten. The friendship of the two countries is my

constant preoccupation, and I count on you all, who enjoy French hospitality in their magnificent city, to aid me to reach this goal.

Three months later, President Loubet returned the visit. He stayed at St James's Palace, as befitted the first French Head of State to have crossed the Channel on an official visit since Napoleon III. And again, King Edward VII expressed his genuine Francophilia:

> I hope that the welcome you have received today has convinced you of the true friendship, indeed I will say the affection, which my country feels for France. I shall never forget the reception that was recently given to me, and the sentiments I now express are those which I have always entertained. I hope our countries will always retain the most intimate relations and the deepest friendship.

Patient negotiations proceeded between the Foreign Ministers and their advisers and, on 8 April 1904, yet another *Entente Cordiale* was formally signed. The effect of the principal clauses was to allow Britain a free hand in Egypt and the Nile Valley, while France was allowed to safeguard its special interests in Morocco. Additional documents settled long-standing difficulties over fishing rights off Newfoundland and ended legal disputes over land-titles and commercial rights in Siam, Madagascar and the New Hebrides.

Though news of the *Entente* was generally welcomed on each side of the Channel, not everybody rejoiced. Théophile Delcassé, France's Foreign Minister and its principal negotiator in the matter, was pilloried by the traditionally Anglophobic French right for conceding too much. The English press was divided. On 9 April, the Liberal *Daily News* rejoiced:

> We report today with unqualified satisfaction the news of the signature of the colonial treaty between France and Great Britain . . . It is hard to believe that only the other day we were shouting for war with France for the possession of an African swamp . . . We see in the treaty a guarantee of the reduction of armaments as well as a crushing blow to the anti-foreign party in this country, who have been preaching the noxious doctrine that national success is only to be won at the expense of the foreigner.

Two days later, the Tory *Morning Post* argued, with some vehemence, that the *Entente* was cause for censure rather than euphoria:

Amazement is the only word which expresses the feelings with which we have read the account . . . of the Agreement between the British and French Governments signed yesterday . . . Never in our recollection has Great Britain given away so much for nothing.

If the idea is that France will be hereafter grateful for the advantages she has reaped by the Agreement, we can only say that gratitude between nation and nation is not a political asset, and that if that is the calculation it condemns the Agreement. For if the Agreement were a good Agreement, gratitude would be equally due from Great Britain to France.

With the advantages of hindsight, one can now see that scoring points over the detail of the *Entente* treaty now seems as petty and as poignant as passengers criticising the seating-plan for the captain's table shortly before the *Titanic* struck the iceberg. After 1904, the march of events and the alignment of forces were set inexorably in train towards the catastrophe of the First World War in which the *Entente* was to be tested to breaking-point and from which both France and Britain were to emerge traumatically diminished.

7 : *Uneasy Entente in the Two World Wars*

> It is not at all in the interests of France to form an offensive and defensive alliance with England. The help of France is prompt; but that of England is subject to the delay and uncertainty attendant on deliberations. It is true that France is more exposed than England, and thus has more often need of help.
>
> Montesquieu, *Pensées*

Right up to the outbreak of the First World War on 4 August 1914, the French were uncertain about the lengths the British would go to to support them. They could not have been encouraged in June 1911 when the Kaiser had sent the cruiser *Panther* to Agadir in Morocco to demonstrate that Germany did not acknowledge France's colonial rights there. On that occasion, the French Ambassador in London had reported back to Paris, 'If the Germans occupy Agadir, Sir Edward Grey reserves the right of consulting his colleagues in the Cabinet.' The British Admiralty was strongly in favour of a 'blue water strategy', confident that the Navy on its own was well able to defend the United Kingdom's vital interests.

In the opening decade of the twentieth century, novels, depicting imaginary wars remained immensely popular in Britain; with the significant change that the invading armies were now German. *The Invasion of 1910*, by far the most successful of such novels, appeared in 1905. Written by William Le Queux, Queen Alexandra's favourite novelist, who had established his earlier reputation with romances such as *Stolen Sweets* and *Indiscretions of a Lady's Maid*, it sold over a million copies throughout the world and was translated into twenty-seven languages including Arabic, Chinese and Japanese. In Britain, it was serialised in the *Daily Mail* and marketed with considerable flair. Sandwichboard men, dressed in German uniforms, paraded through London, to remind the public that the progress of the great invasion was being reported only in the *Daily Mail*; many provincial newspapers printed detailed local maps pinpointing the district the German armies were due to invade next morning. The virtues of the novel were enthusiastically endorsed by Lord Roberts, whose message to the nation, like that of Tennyson sixty years previously, was 'Arm! Arm! Arm!'

For all that, neither the English populace nor the journalists who wrote for them adopted a particularly warlike posture when, on 28 June 1914, Franz Ferdinand, heir to the Crown of Austro-Hungary, and his wife were assassinated at Sarajevo by Austrian citizens of Serb descent. For one thing, the events involved a region, and personalities, of which most Britons knew nothing. For another, there seemed to be a more menacing situation much closer to hand with Ulster threatening to take up arms rather than become part of an Ireland that looked likely soon to achieve independence. As both Germany and Russia adopted ever more threatening postures towards each other on behalf of their central European allies, public opinion in Britain remained divided. So, on 24 July, the *Daily Mail* observed: 'The situation which has arisen between Austria-Hungary and Servia out of the crime of Sarajevo is admittedly disquieting. But it is necessary to steer a straight course between excessive alarm and undue optimism.' On 27 July, the *Morning Post* declared that England's honour was at stake: 'The question of peace or war for England, as for the other powers, cannot be dismissed on the ground that England has no vital interests in Servia . . . Her vital interest is in the reign of equality and right in Europe and in the maintenance of her own character.' On 30 July, the *Manchester Guardian* had pleaded no less eloquently for English neutrality:

> Let us for a moment drop solicitude for Europe and think of ourselves . . . We care as little for Belgrade as Belgrade cares for Manchester. But though our neutrality ought to be assured, it is not. Sir Edward Grey walks deliberately past opportunities of saying that we will be neutral in the quarrels of Europe . . . If Russia makes a general war out of a local war, it will be a crime against Europe. If we, who might remain neutral, rush into

the war or let our attitude remain doubtful, it will be both a crime and an act of supreme and gratuitous folly.

And on the same day, the *Daily News* likewise proclaimed: 'The free peoples of France, England and Italy should refuse to be drawn into this dynastic struggle. We must not have our Western civilisation submerged in the sea of blood in order to wash out a Servian conspiracy.'

On 31 July, the *Morning Post* took a radically different line, repeating that the country's honour was in the balance: 'The nation is not bellicose; it has no desire for war. It has no enmity to gratify. Its watchword in the hour of crisis is duty. The national instinct we believe to be that England must stand by France . . . The Government would be supported in any action aiming at peace which was seen to be consistent with the settled purpose of whole-hearted support for France if she did have to go to war.'

To most British readers, all of this must still have seemed largely academic as long as the roots of contention were in the remote Balkans. So they spent August Bank Holiday Monday (then at the beginning of the month) blithely unconcerned. By the night of 3 August, after Germany and Russia had proclaimed general mobilisation and German armies had driven deep into neutral Belgium, it was clear that war was by now inevitable. On 4 August, the *Morning Post* enthusiastically endorsed Sir Edward Grey's declaration that Britain had to take up arms in a just cause: 'England is now a united nation about to fight in a cause for which she has stood before, of the independence of the nations of Europe, the cause of freedom.' And the *Daily Mail*, even more emphatically, invoked the special relationship between Britain and France:

> The story of our relations with France was set forth by Sir Edward with warm sympathy for our friend. He closed this part of his statement with the great appeal: 'How far our friendship entails obligations let every man look into his heart and judge for himself.' There can be only one answer. The British Navy, as he showed, is bound in honour and duty to protect the coast of France from attack by Germany. That coast has been bared of French ships in reliance upon us. The British people is not prepared basely to desert its friend in this hour when the German armies, marching through neutral territory and treacherously violating the integrity of the small States, are already menacing France with their assault. A felon blow is being struck. We cannot look on.

The French, for their part, were by no means convinced that the English would rally to their cause. In this respect, Alain-Fournier was not untypical. Like all young Frenchmen of his generation, he had had to endure two harsh years of compulsory Army service in anticipation of *La Revanche*. Fournier had been something of an Anglophile all his young life, but on his way to the battlefields of the Marne, where he was shortly to meet his death, he could nevertheless write to his mistress on 5 August 1914 complaining of English prevarication: 'Why this shady policy of the English? Are they going to repeat their role of 1870 and confine their interest just to the Channel coast? Are they, just for once, going to rise to the occasion and perform an action which is neither selfish nor hypocritical? I've never had much confidence in them. In any case, we'll put up a good fight without those close-shaved faces, without those roastbeefs!'

In the event, the overwhelming majority of the British people acclaimed the outbreak of war, as did the French and Germans. Sceptical voices were either unheard or ignored. Arnold Bennett noted in his journal on 6 August 1914:

> Russia is the real enemy, and not Germany . . . a *rapprochement* between England and Germany is a certainty . . . I think that the belligerency of England is a mistake for England . . . Sir Edward Grey's astounding mistake in his big speech was the assertion that the making of the war would not much increase our suffering. It will enormously increase it. The hope for us is the honesty and efficiency of our administration. The fear of France springs from the fact that the majority of French politicians are notoriously rascals, out for plunder. The corruption of Russian administration is probably even worse . . . If Germany is smashed in this war, the man most imperilled will be the German Emperor. If she is not smashed the man most imperilled may be the Tsar.

Bertrand Russell wrote to the *Nation* on 15 August:

> Against the vast majority of my countrymen, even at this moment, in the name of humanity and civilisation, I protest against our share in the destruction of Germany.
>
> A month ago Europe was a peaceful comity of nations; if an Englishman killed a German, he was hanged. Now, if an Englishman kills a German, or if a German kills an Englishman, he is a patriot, who has deserved well of his country . . . Those who saw the London crowds, during the nights leading up to the Declaration of War, saw a whole population, hitherto peaceable

and humane, precipitated in a few days down the steep slope to primitive barbarism, letting loose, in a moment, the instincts of hatred and blood lust against which the whole fabric of society has been raised . . . Behind the diplomatists, dimly heard in the official documents, stand vast forces of national greed and national hatred – atavistic instincts, harmful to mankind at its present level, but transmitted from savage and half-animal ancestors, concentrated and directed by Governments and the Press, fostered by the upper class as a distraction from social discontent, artificially nourished by the sinister influence of the makers of armaments, encouraged by a whole foul literature of 'glory', and by every text-book of history with which the minds of children are polluted.

For adhering to those views throughout the war, Russell was deprived of his Fellowship at Trinity College, Cambridge, and eventually imprisoned. In comparison, the attitude of Lytton Strachey, another member of the Bloomsbury set, seems frivolous. On 27 September 1914, he wrote to his brother:

I think one must resist, if it comes to a push. But I admit it's a difficult question. One solution is to go and live in the United States of America. As to our personal position, it seems to me quite sound and coherent. We're all far too weak physically to be of any use at all. If we weren't we'd still be too intelligent to be thrown away in some really not essential expedition, and our proper place would be the National Reserve. I suppose God has put us on an island, and Winston has given us a navy, and it would be absurd to neglect the advantages – which I consider exactly to apply to able-bodied intellectuals.

   On the whole I don't care much about England's being victorious (apart from personal questions) – but I should object to France being crushed. Mightn't it be a good plan to become a Frenchman?

Dissident voices such as these were very much in the minority in England. The mood of the peer group of Russell and Strachey was more accurately caught by the Prime Minister Herbert Asquith when he declared to the House of Commons on 5 August: 'No nation has ever entered into a great struggle – and this is one of the greatest in history – with a clearer conscience and a stronger conviction that it is fighting not for aggression or the advancement of its own interests, but for principles whose maintenance is vital to the civilised world.' And these views were reiterated, more truculently, by Horatio Bottomley, writing in the widely read popular paper *John Bull* ten days later: 'We are fighting not for shadowy political advantages, not for the lust of power, not for the hegemony of Europe, but for our very existence as an independent nation . . . we say quite simply that the German Fleet must be swept from the face of the seas.' J. B. Priestley enlisted in the belief that war offered 'movement, colour, adventure and drama'. Julian Grenfell exulted in his luck 'to have been born so as to be just the right age and just in the right place – not too high up to be worried – and to enjoy it to the most!' Rupert Brooke rejoiced more lyrically:

> Now, God be thanked Who has matched us with His hour
> And caught our youth, and wakened us from sleeping,
> With hand made sure, clear eye, and sharpened power,
> To turn, as swimmers into cleanness leaping.

Edward Thomas, writing after Grenfell and Brooke were dead, and not long before he too was killed in action, could still declare:

> Now all roads lead to France
> And heavy is the tread
> Of the living; but the dead
> Returning lightly dance . . .

In the event, British troops did not immediately take the road to France in significant numbers. While France decreed general mobilisation and put ninety-four divisions into the field, the British Government, meeting on 6 August 1914, agreed to send just four divisions. Conscription was not introduced in England until 27 January 1916. Till the end of 1914, therefore, Wilfred Owen, then twenty-one, was quite free to continue his job as a teacher of English in Bordeaux; he did not enlist until October 1915. And in 1915, before enlisting, like Owen, in the Artists' Rifles, Edward Thomas was able to complete a book on the life of Marlborough, in which he noted that the great Duke's soldiers had fought over the same Flanders terrain where the English and German armies were currently embroiled.

Relatively small though the British Expeditionary Force was at the outset, it fought valiantly at Mons and on the Aisne in the campaigns of 1914 and sustained heavy casualties in the major battles for St Quentin and Loos in 1915. Even when not involved in those abortive thrusts at the German line that were mounted at intervals throughout the war, the British sustained heavy casualties day by day through shelling, sniping and skirmishing both in the dangerously exposed Ypres Salient in Flanders and in the Somme sector in Picardy. Even so, relations between the French and British generals remained for the most part strained. Until 1917, there was no unified command, and communication between the so-called allies left much to be desired. The French officer class was traditionally Anglophobic and there were occasions when this was made manifest. The daring but doomed Gallipoli campaign of 1915 was a case in point. The French were so preoccupied with the war on the Western Front that they agreed to the English plan of attack on the Dardanelles without bothering to ask how and why it was meant to be achieved. They soon came to suspect that it was really a cloak for England's traditional imperialist designs on this area. England's Ambassador, Lord Bertie, wrote that the French believed that

> the proposal was started by Mr Churchill without proper consideration by the Military Authorities; that he obtained the concurrence of the French Ministry of Marine by flattery . . . The French also feel that the French and British military press sent to the Dardanelles might, more usefully to France, have been directed to the fighting lines in Flanders. The Dardanelles Expedition is regarded by ordinary Frenchmen as undertaken in the interests of Russia materially, and of England politically, to secure her position in India and Egypt.

French resentment was intensified when the Dardanelles campaign was finally aborted in November 1915: 252,000 British and French troops were killed, wounded or missing, while the German front-line across France seemed as impregnable as ever.

1916 saw two determined attempts to break the deadlock. In February, the battle for Verdun began. The Germans attacked remorselessly, knowing that the French would go on resisting whatever the cost. When the fighting ended after ten months, the French had suffered 315,000 casualties, the Germans 281,000. With the dual objective of relieving the French and smashing through the German lines, the British launched their own offensive on the Somme on 1 July. They lost 57,470 men on the first day alone and 400,000 by the time the action was called off in November. There was still no unified Allied command and the effects of this are all too apparent in the private diary of British Commander-in-Chief, Sir Douglas Haig; it is also evident that he had a low opinion of his French allies:

25 April 1915.   [After the Germans, attacking the French at Ypres, had used poison gas for the first time] This surprise of the French should never have happened. It seems to have been a distinctly bad performance, and the possibility of its happening was never realized by Foch and Co. These French leaders are a queer mixture of fair ability (not more than fair) and ignorance of the practical side of war. They are not built for it by nature. They are too excitable, and they never seem to think of what the enemy may do. And they will not see a nasty situation as it really is, and take steps to meet it. However, the enemy in this case is probably as much surprised at the magnitude of his success as are the French, and he does not seem to have sufficient troops on the spot to follow up his first success – luckily for the Allies!

16 January 1916.   I think the French man-power situation is serious as they are not likely to stand another winter's war.

Matters should in theory have improved from 27 February 1917 onwards, when the Allied armies in north and northeast France were placed under the supreme command of France's Marshal Nivelle till the end of the war. Haig was not best pleased. They disagreed over strategy: he planned to drive north and liberate the Belgian coastline whereas Nivelle wanted the British to immobilise the Germans in the Arras-Bapaume sector while he led a spectacular attack along the Chemin des Dames. More seriously, Haig had lost all confidence in the French troops' will or ability to fight. In conference with Lloyd George in January 1917, he recounted his experiences with the French in the field over the previous two-and-a-half years: 'The general opinion amongst the British Army is that the French Army lacks discipline and thoroughness. On a number of occasions we know they did not attack though ordered to do so'; and he added that his two French liaison officers had both reported 'the French infantry is no longer in existence (*n'existe plus*).' This was something of an exaggeration in January 1917 but there were significantly fewer French infantrymen by the end of April, when Nivelle's foolhardy offensive had to be abandoned after two days with 187,000 casualties. Nivelle, already ill with consumption and with just a year more to live, was relieved of his command and replaced by the much more cautious Marshal Pétain, the saviour of Verdun. The attempt to work under a unified command was given up. On 1 June 1917, Haig noted in his diary:

The 'Major-General' of the French Army arrived about 6.30 p.m. and stayed to dinner. His name is General Debeney. He brought a letter from General Pétain saying that he had commissioned him to put the whole situation of the French Army before me and conceal nothing. The French Army is in a bad state of discipline. Debeney then stated that the French soldiers were dissatisfied because leave had been so long suspended. Leave must consequently be opened at once. This would prevent Pétain carrying out his promise to attack on June 10th!

And on 9 November 1917:

Gemeau said that the state of the French Army is now very good but at the end of May there were 30,000 'rebels' who had to be dealt with. A whole Brigade of Infantry had marched on Paris with their rifles after looting a supply column. Another lot seized a motor convoy. Some others occupied a village and a Brigade of Cavalry had to be employed to round them up. This was not done without opening fire on the village. This shows how really bad the condition of the French Army was after Nivelle's failure, and Pétain had a very difficult job to get things in order.

In 1917, disquiet against the continuation of the war was not confined to mutinous French soldiers. There were strikes in various German cities; revolution in Russia; and the Allies outlined to President Wilson of the still-neutral United States a set of peace plans which were not significantly different from those finally implemented in the Treaty of Versailles. The most conspicuous act of protest in England came early in 1917 with a personal proclamation issued by Siegfried Sassoon, whose individual deeds of derring-do on the Western Front had earned him the nickname of 'Mad Jack'. Sickened by the senseless slaughter, he drafted a letter to his commanding officer in France and arranged for Bertrand Russell to deliver a copy to Parliament. In it, he alleged that the war was being deliberately prolonged by those who had the power to end it. He went on, 'I believe that this War, upon which I entered as a war of defence and liberation, has now become a war of aggression and conquest.' He expected – indeed wanted – to be court-martialled. In the event, he was incarcerated in a mental institution, treated by the famed psychologist W. H. R. Rivers and subsequently returned to combat duties in France, where he once again distinguished himself in action.

An equally eloquent protest was made in November 1917 by Lord Lansdowne, principal British architect of the *Entente Cordiale* of 1904. It took the form of an open letter in the *Daily Telegraph* almost identical to

a secret memorandum he had placed before the Cabinet a year earlier.
His principal argument was:

> We are not going to lose this war but its prolongation will spell ruin for the
> civilised world, and an infinite addition to the load of human suffering
> which already weighs upon it. Security will be invaluable to a world which
> has the vitality to profit by it, but what will be the value of the blessings of
> peace to nations so exhausted that they can scarcely stretch out a hand with
> which to grasp them.

Though the letter was warmly received by the English provincial press,
it was ferociously attacked in *The Times* and the Rothermere and
Hulton Presses. It had a mixed reception in France: *Le Figaro* ignored it
altogether; some reproduced the vituperative comments in *The Times*;
L'Intransigeant, the most widely read of the evening papers, positively
welcomed it; others felt it was a further demonstration of traditional
English duplicity.

French belief in the perfidiousness of the English seemed to them
justified in 1917 when they were shown a memorandum from the Chief
of the Imperial General Staff on Britain's war objectives. It included the
following comments:

> For centuries past – though unfortunately by no means continuously – our
> policy has been to help to maintain the balance between the Continental
> Powers which have always been divided by their interests and sympathies
> into opposing groups. At one time the centre of gravity has been in Madrid,
> at another in Vienna, at another in Paris and at another in St Petersburg. We
> have thwarted, or helped to thwart, each and every Power in turn which
> has aspired to Continental predominance; and concurrently as a conse-
> quence we have enlarged our own sphere of Imperial ascendancy. As part of
> this policy we have arrived at maintaining British maritime supremacy and
> at keeping a weak Power in possession of the Low Countries. In more
> recent years a new preponderance has been allowed to grow up, of which
> the centre of gravity has been in Berlin, and the result of it is the present war.
>   . . . The basis of the peace negotiations must be the three principles for
> which we have so often fought in the past, namely:
>
> (a) The maintenance of the balance of power in Europe.
> (b) The maintenance of British maritime supremacy.
> (c) The maintenance of a weak Power in the Low Countries.
>
>   . . . If the balance of power in Europe is to be maintained, it follows that

the existence of a strong Central European Power is essential and that such a State must be Teutonic.

. . . On the other hand, as Germany is the chief European competitor with us on the sea, it would be advantageous to make such terms of peace as would check the development of her Navy and of her mercantile marine. In other words, it would be to the interests of the British Empire to leave Germany reasonably strong on land but to weaken her at sea.

Copies of this memorandum were widely used in France in 1917 for pacifist and anti-English propaganda.

In the meantime, British commitment to the fighting was undiminished. Between 21 July and 10 November of that same year, Haig mounted his Passchendaele offensive, and 400,000 Britons were killed, wounded or lost in the mud to gain 500 yards of swampy earth.

On 21 March 1918, aware of the threat posed by the arrival in Europe of massive American reinforcements, Ludendorff launched a massive offensive against the British and French armies. Almost overwhelmed by the ferocity of the assault, the Allied armies were placed under the Supreme Command of Marshal Foch on 26 March. Emerging from the meeting at which this had been agreed, Clemenceau remarked to one of his French generals on the new-found atmosphere of cordiality belatedly apparent between the French and British high commands. He declared, 'That's almost worth a victory over the Germans.' His General replied, 'It certainly was a victory – but over *the English*!'

Not all French serving officers were so Anglophobic, or confirmed the gloomy prediction of Viscount Esher, who forecast in the spring of 1918, 'If one thing is sure about this war, it is that the English and French will be thoroughly sick of each other.' André Maurois, one of the most enthusiastic of twentieth-century admirers of all things British, became a lifelong Anglophile as a result of his experiences as a French liaison officer with the Highland Division, whom he first saw in action at the Battle of Loos:

The spectacle of the troops on their way to take up combat posts with heads bent before the passage of shells like wheat bowed down by the wind, the fresh shell holes smelling of earth and powder, awoke in me a keen longing that I had not felt for a long time – the desire to write. The contrast between the calm of the khaki-clad soldiers, who stood at the cross-roads directing traffic with calm gestures of policemen in Piccadilly Circus, and the danger of their position seemed to me beautiful and worthy of being recorded;

sadder, but less beautiful, was the contrast later on between the appearance of the General on the morning of battle, very courteous and dignified, in a uniform resplendent with red and gold, and the return that same evening of his corpse stained with blood and mire.

His admiration shines through the affectionately satirical portraits of the British officer stereotypes who are paraded in *Les Silences du Colonel Bramble*, which won considerable acclaim when it appeared in 1918.

Before the Armistice ended the war in Western Europe on 11 November 1918, bitter rivalry between England and France surfaced over the carving up of the Middle Eastern Empire of the defeated Turks. France wanted Syria and most of the Levant; Britain was anxious to safeguard Arab interests, to meet both Zionist aspirations in Palestine and to ensure that Palestine remained in friendly hands so as to ensure the safety of the major trade-route of the Suez Canal. Over who was to command the Allied Fleet in the Eastern Mediterranean, Lloyd George was quite peremptory. Writing to Clemenceau on 15 October 1918, he declared:

> We have taken by far the larger part of the burden of war against Turkey in the Dardanelles and in Gallipoli, in Egypt, in Mesopotamia and in Palestine . . . I do not see how I could possibly justify to the people of the British Empire that at the moment when the final attack upon Turkey was to be delivered, the command of Naval Forces which are overwhelmingly British, in a theatre of war associated with some of the most desperate and heroic fighting by troops from nearly every part of the British Empire, should be handed over to a French admiral.

Writing privately to a colleague, he was even more outspoken: 'The French Government were great at promises . . . They sent assistance right enough. A handful of niggers were sent to see that we didn't steal the Holy Sepulchre! That was all the assistance we got!' The Levant remained a contentious area between Britain and France throughout the 1920s and '30s and during the Second World War.

Relations grew more embittered with the problems of making the peace once the Armistice was declared.

*

From the moment Germany requested an armistice, there were sharp differences between France and Britain over what the peace terms should be. The conflict continued right up to the presentation of the revised terms of the Versailles treaty in June 1919 and the repercussions were felt until the outbreak of the Second World War. Clemenceau repeated regularly the story of his saying to Lloyd George, 'Within an hour after the Armistice, I had the impression that you had become once again the enemies of France', and of Lloyd George's replying, 'Has not that always been the traditional policy of my country?'

Clemenceau's over-riding concern was for the security of France, so he insisted on swingeing reparations, a permanent diminution in Germany's military strength and secure land frontiers. Lloyd George gave the highest priority to Britain's national and commercial interests, which meant maintaining over-lordship of the world's seaways and avoiding military involvement in continental affairs. The Peace Conference seemed foredoomed not only because the problems it was supposed to solve were intractable but because of the mutual suspicions and linguistic incompetence of the principal participants. Clemenceau alone could speak and understand English and French; Lloyd George and Wilson spoke only English; the Italian representative, Vittorio Orlando, spoke only French. Often, after a speech, Lloyd George would cross the hearthrug to reinforce his case by some *ad hominem* argument in private conversation. There was general upheaval and disorder, as the President's advisers and British experts milled around, all of which reinforced French suspicions that the Anglo-Saxons were arranging a deal without their full knowledge. J. M. Keynes, who attended the Conference, recalled Clemenceau standing silent and aloof on the outskirts; 'dry in soul and empty of hope . . . Clemenceau had one illusion – France; and one disillusion – mankind, including Frenchmen and his colleagues not least.'

Profound suspiciousness was not confined to the French. On 26 January 1919, Sir Douglas Haig wrote in his diary: 'The rascally French intrigue and steal away as many of the plums as they can lay hands on, while Balfour talks on the moral obligations of Nations to one another. He is too much of a gentleman to be able to withstand this crowd of harpies who are at the Conference.' When Sir George Riddell observed that 'the French were entitled to every possible protection' because 'it would be one of the most terrible calamities in history if the French civilisation were wiped out', Lloyd George commented, 'I can see you have fallen victim to the fascination of French women!' General Smuts of South Africa was appalled by what he described as 'France's insensate spirit of revenge' and accused her of shortsightedness for not appeasing Germany in order to provide a bulwark against the on-coming Bolshevism of eastern Europe, an argument that was to be repeated in France with increasing stridency from the mid 1930s onwards. On 1 May 1919 Harold Nicolson noted in the diary he kept on the peace-making process, 'the French cannot see beyond their noses', though he went on to insist, 'one must *force* oneself to see the French point of view . . . It is not militarism in the least'. The most empathetic commentator of all, however, was George Bernard Shaw, who in 1919 wrote in his essay 'Peace-Conference Hints: Enter History, Exit Romance': 'It is easy enough to sit down behind the British fleet, or at the other side of the Atlantic, and ask the inhabitants of Picardy and Belgium to feel safe in a new moral world within range of Long [*sic*] Bertha, and within a few minutes' flight of aeroplanes that drop earthquake bombs on sleeping cities.'

By the late spring of 1919, the British consensus was critical of France and inclined to be sympathetic towards Germany. Balfour dismissed as hysterical the French scenario of Germany's considerably larger population, her inevitable economic recovery, the impotence of the League of Nations, another German invasion and a likely French defeat. An unsigned and undated 'Memorandum on the Foreign Policy of His Majesty's Government', which must have been written about this period, observed, 'We have got all that we want – perhaps more. Our sole object is to keep what we have and live in peace . . . We keep our hands free in order to throw our weight on to the scale on behalf of peace.'

It did not seem to British observers that the scale should be weighted in France's favour when, on 6 April 1920, the French sent a military force across the border to occupy Frankfurt. That same day Sir Maurice Hankey, secretary to the British Cabinet, conjured up in his diary 'the danger of being dragged at the heels of the French, who are a very provocative people, into a new war'. What particularly provoked public opinion in Britain was that the French occupying forces included a detachment of black African troops. The British Left expressed outrage. The *Daily Herald* of 9 April bore the headline: 'FRANKFURT RUNS WITH BLOOD: FRENCH BLACK TROOPS USE MACHINE GUNS ON

CIVILIANS'. The following day, the *Herald* carried a front-page article by E. D. Morel, a distinguished left-wing intellectual whose associates included Bertrand Russell, Norman Angell, Ramsay Macdonald and Clement Attlee. He was founder of the Congo Reform Association and of the Union of Democratic Control, and had condemned the Versailles treaty as vindictive and economically suicidal. In his article, which appeared under the headline 'BLACK SCOURGE IN EUROPE, SEXUAL HORROR LET LOOSE BY FRANCE ON RHINE. DISAPPEARANCE OF YOUNG GERMAN GIRLS', Morel wrote that 'France is thrusting her black savages . . . into the heart of Germany . . . primitive black barbarians, carriers of syphilis, have become a terror and a horror to the Palatinate countryside.' He alleged that the 'barely restrainable beastiality [*sic*] of the black troops, the most developed sexually of any race' had led to many rapes, 'some of them of an atrocious character', and he denounced the whole enterprise 'aimed to ruin, enslave, degrade, dismember and reduce to the lowest depths of despair and humiliation a whole people' as a cynical scheme devised by a 'ruthless and militaristic French government'.

The article was extravagantly praised. Mrs Philip Snowden called on God to bless the *Daily Herald* for its courage in printing it. The *Herald* proclaimed: 'Women of England arise. Will not British women make their voice heard on the sexual horror involved in the setting up of brothels for savage soldiers brought from Africa by the French government and used in Germany.' The British Association of Women's International League for Peace and Freedom held an emotional rally at Central Hall, Westminster. Liberal journals such as the *Contemporary Review* complained of the 'admitted sexual excesses of these Africans . . . and the setting up of filthy French brothels in tranquil and clean little towns'. Bernard Shaw speculated that since black troops had been marched into the homeland of Goethe, they might, before long, be quartered in Stratford-upon-Avon. Norman Angell evoked the prospect of 'cannibals from the African Forests' making war on the Workers' Republic. Fifty thousand Swedish women signed a petition protesting against this outrage 'upon womankind the world over'.

After a fact-finding trip to Germany in the summer of 1920, Morel expanded his article into a pamphlet entitled 'The Horror on the Rhine' in which he alleged that French militarists had forced German officials to evict law-abiding citizens from their homes and turned them into brothels for black and white French soldiers; what was more, the German authorities were obliged to pay for such establishments as part of the costs of occupation. The pamphlet was a spectacular success: each delegate to the Trades Union Congress of September 1920 was presented with a free copy, and by April 1921 eight editions had been sold out. By the summer of 1921, the furore had abated in England but in *Mein Kampf* Adolf Hitler fulminated at the thought that '7,000,000 people languish under alien rule and the main artery of the German people flows through the playground of Black African hordes'. And in 1928, he was still ranting about 'the de-Germanisation, Negrification and Judaisation of our people'. In 1930, the Nazi ideologue Alfred Rosenberg denounced France for 'contributing to the dehumanisation of Europe by means of the blacks, just as it had by introducing Jewish emancipation 150 years before'.

While the British Left never espoused the cause of anti-Semitism, they were certainly anti-French and pro-German over the terms and the implementation of the Versailles treaty. E. D. Morel declared that the object of French policy was 'to tear the lungs and heart out of the living body of Germany'. Another left-wing intellectual, H. N. Brailsford, argued that

> The relative military power of France is now vastly greater than that of Germany ever was . . . The disparity will be permanent . . . France has recovered the military predominance which she enjoyed under the first Napoleon. Her partial eclipse during the last fifty years that followed Sedan has obliterated our recollections of the persistent military tradition of this most nationalist of peoples . . . A nation of small peasant owners and small investors will never be Liberal in the British sense of the word.

For some English observers, by no means all on the left of the political spectrum, the French posed a potential threat to Britain as well as to Germany. When the notion of building a tunnel beneath the Channel was mooted in November 1919, the secretary of the Cabinet, Sir Maurice Hankey, mobilised Balfour and the majority of the Cabinet against it. He noted in his diary: 'What power lies in the draughtsman's hands. As matters stand, I may be able to block the whole thing . . . I will stop at nothing to prevent what I believe to be a danger to this country . . . France may become hostile . . . How should we like the Channel tunnel then?'

A Foreign Office memorandum of 1 May 1920 noted that it was 'almost certain that we shall have conflicts with France in the future as we have had in the past . . . Nothing can alter the fundamental fact that we are not liked in France, and never will be, except for the advantages which the French people may be able to extract from us.'

The Royal Air Force was concerned over the threat of French air power; in a draft paper for the British Cabinet, Sir Hugh Trenchard estimated that this was more predominant than ever was her military strength under Napoleon or Louis XIV. However, H. G. Wells, reporting on a conference held in Washington in 1920, on the limitation of world armaments, foresaw danger in quite another area. Declaring himself to be baffled by Briand's insistence on France's need to rearm, he could think only of a sinister explanation:

> The plain fact of the case is that France is maintaining a vast army in the face of a disarmed world and she is preparing energetically for fresh warlike operations in Europe and for war under sea against Great Britain . . . M. Briand excused France for wanting submarines in quantity because, he said, she was liable to attack on these coasts but . . . France is in about as much danger of an attack on her three coasts as the United States of America is upon her Canadian frontier. Her ships are as safe upon the sea as a wayfarer on Fifth Avenue. If she builds submarines now, she builds them to attack British commerce and for no other reason whatsoever.

Three years later, in an article entitled 'A Year of Prophesying', he foresaw a 'French millennium' with 'nothing left upon the continent of Europe but a victorious France and her smashed and broken antagonists and her servile and uncertain allied peasant states'.

France's insistence on security and the case for reparations exasperated even English Francophiles. Harold Laski wrote to Mr Justice Holmes on 30 April 1922: 'If only the French would cease to occupy themselves with politics, they would be the most attractive people in the world.' In July 1924, Ramsay Macdonald, never the most diplomatic of statesmen, declaimed against 'the whole crew of French politicians – underhand, grasping, dishonourable'; and that same year, surrounded by the political good and the great one summer day at Versailles, he bluntly asked Madame Herriot: 'Can you tell me if there's an honest man here, besides your husband?' To which she had the wit to reply, 'Yes, I think there are two.'

How far Macdonald's dislike of the French derived from innate prejudice and how far from inadequate briefing, one cannot be sure. In the 1920s, where France was concerned, the British press tended towards sensationalism or bewilderment, and the reports of Britain's ambassadors revealed just how ignorant they were of the French economy, the professions and the world of letters. Writing to Hankey as early as 7 April 1919, Viscount Esher declared that Lloyd George and other British politicians were the victims of inadequate briefing:

> He chose deliberately to take his impressions from official sources, that is to say from men who, owing to habits and customs of diplomacy, take their opinions from a comparatively small knot of official persons and from a limited section of French society with which they come into contact. Over and over again throughout my life I have found that English officials, with the solitary exception of Lord Lytton, know nothing of France.

If, in their attitudes to France, Britain's politicians were the victims of prejudice and misinformation, her foreign policy-makers were, no less, the prisoners of tradition. On 25 March 1925, the British Foreign Secretary, Sir Austen Chamberlain, declared:

> All our greatest wars have been waged to prevent one Great Power from dominating Europe and, more particularly, from being in sole occupation of the Channel coast and the ports of the Low Country.
>
> That is the reason why our forefathers fought Spain at the height of her power, our grandfathers fought Napoleon and we ourselves have just been to war with Germany.
>
> It is a question of our own security.

It was because of this ingrained attitude that the British Right opposed all France's aims and policies during the Locarno Conference in October 1925, which was meant to ensure peace and security in Europe. Britain refused to coerce Germany into paying France reparations, refused to pledge military assistance to France should German aggression recur, was unsympathetic to France's case for building up its own armaments, and indifferent to the defensive alliances France signed with Poland, Czechoslovakia, Yugoslavia and Romania. The British Left continued to view France as vindictive, nationalistic and militaristic.

★

In the 1920s, there were few English voices raised in justification of France's attitude and policies. One such was Rudyard Kipling's. Though he continued to grieve for the loss of his only son on the Western Front in September 1915, he could still write to his friend and fellow writer Rider Haggard in April 1925, 'Just think what we'd do if we'd had the guts trampled out of a section of England, thirty by 250 miles. Would *we* pay our debts or put our defences in order first?'

For the soldiers who, unlike John Kipling, survived the war, France and the French meant memories and associations they would prefer to have forgotten: the Front Line signified constant exposure to shot, shell, mud, rats and lice, and images of death and mutilation; the brief periods of respite away from the Front left images no more consoling of dearly bought pleasure in bar and brothel, or the disquieting experience of returning briefly to England and finding something like pre-war normality within earshot of the not-far-distant guns. For men of sensitive disposition, as the war poets inevitably were, their impressions of northern France proved traumatic and indelible. The most sensitive of all, such as Ivor Gurney, cracked under the strain and never recovered; those who lived on remained haunted for the rest of their lives.

The most famous of the English war poets wrote relatively few poems specifically about the French. The best of these convey their horror at the spectacle of futile slaughter, the incompetence of the High Command and the jingoism or blithe indifference of armchair warriors safe across the Channel in England: they are too familiar to need quoting here. For their reactions to the country in which they were obliged to fight, one has to turn to their letters and memoirs. Edmund Blunden, a gentle and idealistic nature lover, was outraged at the wanton devastation of the French countryside. In his poem 'Report on Experience', he observed

> I have seen a green country, useful to the race,
> Knocked silly with guns and mines, its villages vanished,
> Even the last rat and last kestrel banished –
> God bless us all, this was peculiar grace . . .

His beautifully written account of his service at the Front, *Undertones of War*, concludes with him about to return home on sick leave, ironically unaware that the slumberous landscape he calmly surveys will shortly be devastated by Ludendorff's spring offensive. Shortly before his death in 1975, after a distinguished literary and academic career, he wrote: 'My experiences in the First World War have haunted me all my life and for many days, I have, it seemed, lived in that world rather than this.'

While they were actively engaged on the Western Front, the poets registered their reactions in verse; they seem to have required at least a decade to set down their more complex experiences in prose. *Undertones of War* was published in 1928. The following year brought the war memoirs of Robert Graves, *Goodbye to All That*. He describes how, while trying to study at Oxford in 1919, memories of trench warfare still haunted him:

Edmund Blunden . . . was taking the same course. The war still continued for both of us, and we translated everything into trench-warfare terms. In the middle of a lecture I would have a sudden very clear experience of men on the march up the Béthune–La Bassée road; the men would be singing, while French children ran along beside us, calling out: 'Tommee, Tommee, give me bullee beef!' and I would smell the stench of the knacker's yard just outside the town. Or it would be in Laventie High Street, passing a company billet; an N.C.O. would roar: 'Party, 'shun!' and the Second Battalion men in shorts, with brown knees, and brown expressionless faces, would spring to their feet from the broken steps where they were sitting. Or, I would be in a barn with my first platoon of the Welsh Regiment, watching them play nap by the light of dirty candle stumps. Or in a deep dug-out at Cambrin, talking to a signaller; I would look up the shaft and see somebody's muddy legs coming down the steps; then there would be a sudden crash and the tobacco smoke in the dug-out would shake with the concussion and twist about in patterns like marbling on books. These day-dreams persisted like an alternate life and did not leave me until well into 1928. The scenes were nearly always recollections of my first four months in France; the emotion-recording apparatus seemed to have failed after Loos [in 1915].

The eighteenth century owed its unpopularity largely to its Frenchness. Anti-French feeling among most ex-soldiers amounted almost to an obsession. Edmund, shaking with nerves, used to say at this time: 'No more wars for me at any price! Except against the French. If ever there's a war with them, I'll go like a shot.' Pro-German feeling had been increasing. With the war over and the German armies beaten, we could give the German soldier credit for being the most efficient fighting-man in Europe. I often heard it said that only the blockade had beaten the Fritzes; that in Haig's last push they never really broke, and that their machine-gun sections held us up long enough to cover the withdrawal of the main forces.

Some undergraduates even insisted that we had been fighting on the wrong side: our natural enemies were the French.

Similar sentiments are expressed by Christopher Tietjens, the hero of Ford Madox Ford's superb trilogy *Parade's End*, published between 1924 and 1928. Tietjens, a Tory landowner and high-ranking Civil Servant before the outbreak of the First World War, is seriously wounded on the Western Front. He admires the French 'for their tremendous efficiency, for their frugality of life, for the logic of their minds, for their admirable achievements in the arts, for their neglect of the industrial system, for their devotion, above all, to the eighteenth century'. Nonetheless, he assures his wife that the next war England will have to fight will be against France:

> We're the natural enemies of the French. We have to make our bread either by robbing them or making cat's-paws of them . . . It's the condition of our existence. We're a practically bankrupt, over-populated, northern country: they're rich southerners with a falling population. Towards 1930 we shall have to do what Prussia did in 1914. Our conditions will be exactly those of Prussia then.

By the time this period was reached in reality, the dominant mood of the English populace, like that of the French, was pacifistic. The last years of the 1920s, which brought a spate of war memoirs, also saw the première of the most successful English play inspired by the First World War, R. C. Sherriff's *Journey's End*, which set Laurence Olivier on the road to stardom. Like the Cenotaph in Whitehall, and the more modest memorials in every town and village, it established a seemingly adamantine link between France and death and loss.

For a growing number of Englishmen, however, many of whom, for one reason or another, missed the war, France had quite different associations. For members of the Bloomsbury set, France was all that England was not: appreciative of the arts while England was philistine, pre-eminently cultured and civilised while England was irredeemably barbarous. Lytton Strachey, who once claimed that *he* was the Civilisation for which the war was being fought, and whose personal contribution was to knit mufflers 'for the soldier and sailor lads', maintained, as did his fellow aesthete Clive Bell, that French civilisation was in full flower in the eighteenth century. In his essay on Marie, the

Marquise du Deffand, who was hostess of one of the most glittering of all French eighteenth-century *salons*, Strachey declared:

> Never, certainly, before or since, have any set of persons lived so absolutely and unreservedly with and for their friends as these high ladies and gentlemen of the middle years of the eighteenth century. The circle of one's friends was, in those days, the framework of one's whole being; within which was to be found all that life had to offer, and outside of which no interest, however fruitful, no passion, however profound, no art, however soaring, was of the slightest account . . . Each individual was expected to practise, and did in fact practise to a consummate degree, those difficult arts of tact and temper, of frankness and sympathy, of delicate compliment and exquisite self-abnegation – with the result that a condition of living was produced which, in all its superficial and obvious qualities, was one of unparalleled amenity.

Not every Francophile in the inter-war years singled out eighteenth-century France for particular praise as did Tietjens or the Bloomsbury Group. For others, and certainly for the majority of England's leading writers, their greatest enthusiasm was reserved for Proust's great novel, *A la recherche du temps perdu*, unwinding in successive instalments at intervals in the 1920s, though read by most in the less than immaculate translation of Scott-Moncrieff. While it was in the process of being published, one of the most celebrated twentieth-century English Francophiles was serving his literary apprenticeship. This was Charles Morgan. After being interned in Holland for the greater part of the war, he joined the editorial staff of *The Times* in 1921, and between 1926 and 1939 was its principal drama critic. He wrote a number of novels in the 1930s that were well received: *The Fountain* (1933) won the Hawthornden Prize, and for this and *Sparkenbroke* (1938) he was awarded the *Légion d'Honneur*. This is indicative of a fast-developing trend: at the height of his considerable fame, it is no exaggeration to say that Morgan received as much adulation in France as ever Proust did in England.

In the early 1920s, Paris became something of a Mecca for literary expatriates mostly, though by no means exclusively, American. Ezra Pound, Gertrude Stein, Ernest Hemingway all lived and wrote there as did Ford Madox Ford, who took up residence there in 1922, and published their work in Ford's *Transatlantic Review*. Younger writers, still to establish their reputations, served their apprenticeships in a variety of occupations. In *Down and Out in Paris and London* (1933), George Orwell described how, living in 'fairly severe poverty', he carried out the most menial of tasks in the kitchens of insalubrious hotels. In *A Cab at the Door* (1968), the first of two volumes of autobiography, V. S. Pritchett describes the rather more colourful succession of jobs he took during seven years of self-imposed exile; working in a photographer's shop, selling glue and shellac for a photographer's business, then ostrich feathers and theatre tickets. His love for France and the French emerged enhanced.

Other writers found delight in France away from Paris. George Bernard Shaw and Rudyard Kipling were particularly fond of Biarritz. Dornford Yates, whose novels were extremely popular during the inter-war years, lived at Pau in the Pyrenees, an area much loved by Hilaire Belloc. Other writers were more attracted by the warmer sun and the readily available food and drink of the Riviera. In the early 1920s, Katherine Mansfield, doomed soon to die of consumption, found temporary relief and much literary inspiration at Bandol and Menton. The stricken D. H. Lawrence also stayed at Bandol, in 1929, then moved inland to Vence where, in the following year, he died and was buried. By the late 1920s, Beaulieu had its avenue Edith Cavell, Nice had a Scotch Tea Shop and Monte Carlo had tea-shops with names such as Bide-a-Wee, where customers could read the *Illustrated London News*. James Barrie and Michael Arlen had homes in Cannes, Frank Harris in Nice, H. G. Wells in Grasse and Edith Wharton in Hyères.

The most durable of all modern English ex-patriots, however, proved to be Somerset Maugham, who acquired his Villa Mauresque in Cap Ferrat in 1926 and who lived there, apart from the five years of exile enforced by the Second World War, till his death in 1965. That he settled there so effortlessly doubtless had much to do with his early French background. He was born in 1874 in the British Embassy in Paris, his parents having gone there to ensure that he would be counted as a British citizen: had he been born anywhere else in France, he would have been treated as a French national and become liable for military service. His mother had been raised in France from infancy and Maugham's first ten years of life were spent in Paris, where she got him to recite La Fontaine to guests at her tea parties. In the First World War, he served as an interpreter on the Western Front with the Red Cross. In the opening months of the Second World War, still one of the most commercially successful authors of his day, he was commissioned to write a book on the French war effort by the British Ministry of Information. Under the title *France at War*, it was published in March 1940 just a few weeks before the invading German panzer units swept across the frontier and demonstrated how over-optimistic his prognosis had been.

If the most significant factor in that overwhelming defeat was the superior might and strategy of the German High Command, another was the conflicts between the French themselves, which had grown increasingly bitter during the 1930s. The contrast between French Anglophiles and Anglophobes is symptomatic. In the inter-war years, some of France's distinguished writers were enthusiastically Anglophile: these included the diplomats Paul Claudel and Paul Morand, as well as André Maurois, who followed his best-selling trio of books involving Colonel Bramble with a series of well-received biographies of Shelley, Disraeli, Byron and Edward VII. But their cultured voices were less audible than those of the extreme and sometimes rabid polemicists on the far right of the French political spectrum. Unlike English Francophobes, whose attacks on things French in populist tabloid newspapers rarely rise above the puerile, French Anglophobes have regularly been writers of high intelligence and considerable literary ability. They have all been practitioners of the political pamphlet, a distinct sub-genre that has no real equivalent in modern English life: essays in the English quality press are seldom if ever published, like French pamphlets, as independent entities. Whether their enemies were located within France itself or abroad, these French pamphleteers were ferocious haters. They despised moderation and eschewed compromise. They preferred emotional to rational arguments. While they could destroy an opponent's reputation with the cold precision of a hired killer, they regularly sought to bludgeon their enemies' arguments with invective rather than analysis. They were all too ready to subscribe to great conspiracy theories and, at the heart of every conspiracy, they nearly always discerned the lurking presence of England.

The most venerable of them was Charles Maurras (b. 1868), a formidable classical scholar, founder and editor of *L'Action française*, the newspaper of the monarchist movement of that name whose younger members, who took to the streets in the 1930s, called themselves *les camelots du roi* (the king's newspaper-boys). So ingrained was his Anglophobia that he once insisted on deleting the name of Shakespeare from an article he was editing for his literary journal on the grounds that it already featured on another page of that particular issue: to print the hated name *twice* was more than Shakespeare deserved. A more typical example of the Anglophobic conspiracy theorist is Robert Boucard, whose study *Les Dessous de l'espionnage anglais* was published in 1929. Dedicated to the 'shades of the great Cromwell, inventor of the Secret Service and past master of espionage', it purports to be an in-depth study of the workings of British Intelligence:

> It is emphatically not in any spirit of vengeance or of base vindictiveness quite unworthy of a true Frenchman and totally alien to our magnanimous and chivalrous character, that we propose to unveil to the reader this vast and powerful spy-system, the mysterious network of which extends throughout the entire world and the purpose of which is to impose in every domain – military, diplomatic and social – the greatness of the British Empire and its supremacy over all the nations of the Universe.

He outlines its history, from Tudor times to the present, describing the training provided in the Spy School at an unidentified location in Devon. Among the diverse activities of the Service, he lists spying on the French Air Force, the assassination of Lord Kitchener, drowned in 1916 with the sinking of HMS *Hampshire* (a coup for which, he claims, the Germans never claimed the credit), and the supplying of vast quantities of coal, oil and copper throughout the First World War to Scandinavia, in the full and certain knowledge that these would be re-exported to a beleaguered Germany, at huge profit to British Big Business.

While Boucard's charges were lurid, his language was relatively restrained. This cannot be said of Henri Béraud's fifty-page pamphlet, 'Faut-il réduire l'Angleterre en esclavage?' Published in 1935 it was the most strident and sustained piece of anti-English polemic to appear between the two world wars. Béraud's fury was unleashed by the spectacle of 144 ships of the British Mediterranean Fleet appearing off the Italian coast. The tactic was meant to pressurise Italy into ending its war against Abyssinia. Because Italy had entered the First World War in

1915 on the Allied side, Béraud argued that Mussolini should have been rewarded by England's support for what he perceived to be its legitimate colonial cause. He ascribed England's hostility to imperialist designs of its own and saw it as the latest demonstration of Albion's perfidiousness, which he proceeded to catalogue and then to castigate:

> From time immemorial, our hardworking and combative race have continued to believe that England's policy has always been to weaken us and diminish us. We recall that in the ancient chronicles, our ancestors thought that the English were like some divine curse, comparable in every way to famine or the Black Death. Everything goes to show that for the French people, this is an ingrained belief that nothing can dispel. Absolutely nothing. All the same, there are those who try to argue the contrary. People will say, for instance, that John Bull did Jacques Frenchman a good turn when, in 1914, he came and fought by his side in the Flanders trenches. Jacques Frenchman wouldn't disagree. He accepts that the English fought alongside us. But he can't be certain that they fought *for* us. And stubborn Jacques Frenchman goes on to say that England would have done France and the whole world a much better turn if King George had replied without delay to a certain letter that President Poincaré had sent from Paris to London during the small hours of 31 July/1 August 1914 . . . Jacques Frenchman claims that the response to this letter should have been a public declaration that if Germany were to invade Belgium, England would immediately declare war on Germany. He claims that if this guarantee had been announced at the right time, then humanity would have been spared the spectacle of ten million deaths and the carnage of five years of war. To my great shame, I have to confess that these are my feelings also . . .
>
> I am one of those who believe that the friendship of the English is the cruellest gift the gods can bestow on any people. Whenever I see England, with the Bible in one hand and Covenant in the other, preaching the cause of the weak or the principles of justice, I can't help suspecting it's really about its special interests.
>
> I also believe that these interests, which have never changed, shape a policy as solid and as ancient as the throne of Edward the Confessor. This policy consists of ensuring instability on the Continent in order to maintain its overlordship of the seas. It entails buying the consciences of other people, enlisting mercenaries, sowing discord. It consists of preventing peace between the nations. It consists of planting clergymen on top of strong-boxes and getting them to preach the merits of deprivation to the world's poor. For that's the price of English comfort.
>
> Don't England's best friends keep telling us that control of the Red Sea is *indispensable* to Britain's foreign policy of safeguarding the route to India? That's quite possible. But one is bound to ask whether it's essential to the happiness of the human race for the route to India to be an *English* route.

And one can't help wondering whether the peace of the universe really requires that across the seven seas, an endless fleet of ships should transport as well as the playthings of the Vickers Company and the gentlemen of the Intelligence Service, a yapping cargo of ladies with big feet and pale, male virgins from Oxford. One would dearly like to know if the peasants of Europe are doomed to go on slaughtering each other till the end of time so that the people of John Lack-land can go on spreading on the bread from the richest cornfields the butter from the lushest meadows.

Envenomed though Béraud's words are, they are a model of rigorous reasoning compared to the impassioned invective of Louis Ferdinand Céline. Unlike most of the French Anglophobes, Céline had actually lived in England. In February 1909, he spent half a term at a boarding school in Rochester and freely transcribed his experiences into the more farcical scenes of his second novel, *Mort à Crédit* (1936). He then moved on to a happier school in Broadstairs, Pierremont Hall, which once housed the original of Dickens's Betsy Trotwood. In May 1915, having been invalided out of the army, he worked for six months in the French Passport Office in London. After being discharged from the Army and the Passport service, he stayed on in London, dividing his time between Leicester Square and the East End. He was by all accounts not unhappy, indeed, the official records at the Covent Garden Register Office reveal that he was married there on 16 January 1916. The wife, a Suzanne Nebout, has vanished without trace. What unhinged him over the next two decades is not entirely clear. Certainly he developed an intense loathing of the contemporary world but a central manifestation of it still defies explanation: his conviction that so many of Europe's ills derive from London and that the royal court, the English Government and the whole of the City are all controlled by Jews. A couple of extracts from the two most notorious of his pamphlets will suffice to convey the content and the savour. The first is from 'Bagatelles pour un Massacre', which appeared in 1937:

England as an ally? What bollocks! . . . One year to mobilise . . . another for training . . . We'll all be well and truly turned to maggots when the first queers from Oxford set foot in Flanders . . . and the jolly old Whisky Home Fleet fans out across the expectant Atlantic . . . Never forget that the City's ruled by Jews . . . With Wall Street and Moscow, it's one of their supreme citadels.

The second is from 'L'Ecole des Cadavres', which appeared in 1938:

> The City, the Secret Service and the Jewish royal court of England have been responsible, since Cromwell's time, for all our failures and all our humiliations in every single sphere . . . [On the forthcoming visit to Paris of the King and Queen of England] When you go down into the street to shout your heads off at the procession of George VI, half-Jewish, and his Queen Bowen-Lyon [*sic*], the Jewess, sent over by Chamberlain, half-Jewish, Eden, half-Jewish, Hoare-Belisha (Horeb Elisha, completely Jewish) . . . you'll certainly be able to pat yourselves on the back for having spent a marvellous afternoon.

For good measure, he adds that the Duke of Windsor's *inamorata* Mrs Simpson is Jewish, as is Pope Pius XI and his Secretary – shortly to become Pope Pius XII: 'You couldn't be more Jewish than the present Pope. His real name is Isaac Ratisch . . . The Vatican is a ghetto. The Christian religion? It's a Judeo-Talmudic-Communist gang! The Apostles? Jews, every one of them! All gangsters! The No. 1 Gang? The Church! Peter? The Al Capone of the New Testament! A Trotsky for Roman moujiks! The New Testament? A racketeer's handbook!'

He then proceeds to brand all France's leading left-wing politicians as members of an Israelite racket, all the leading right-wingers as demented juvenile delinquents and Pétain as a war-monger in the pay of international Jewry, speaking with a thick Central European accent. It is highly creditable – if annoying to the literary researcher – that for sixty years these pamphlets have been quite unobtainable in France.

★

While these rancorous Anglophobes were doing their best to whip themselves and their right-wing readers into a frenzy in France, Winston Churchill employed all his rhetorical skills to persuade his parliamentary colleagues to share his profound Francophilia. In the course of a foreign policy debate on 29 June 1931, he said in the House of Commons:

> I was, indeed, delighted to hear the Prime Minister making an appeal, addressed to his own party, to be fair to France. The Prime Minister, naturally, has to veil everything he says, but the significance of the few

words he dropped during the latter part of his speech in recognizing the anxieties and position of France were, I venture to think, much more important than all those well-turned phrases which will never miss their proper reception of cheers in this Island . . . It is not in the immediate interest of European peace that the French Army should be seriously weakened. It is certainly not in British interests to antagonize France, or all these small States associated with France, by pressing unreasonably for its reduction. We may well think France is over-insured, but it is certain that if we press at this [Disarmament] Conference too heavily in that direction, we shall not succeed in improving the relations between the countries. I must say that the French Army at the present moment is a stabilising factor, and one of the strongest, apart from the general hatred and fear of war. We should beware of deranging the situation which exists. It is not satisfactory, but it is one that might easily be replaced by a worse situation. The sudden disappearance or weakening of that factor of stability, the unquestioned superiority of French military power, might open floodgates of measureless consequence in Europe at the present time, might break the dyke and

> Let the boundless deep
> Down upon far-off cities while they dance –
> Or dream.

Apart from that, it would be the highest imprudence for our Government to cast reflections or disturb the good relations which prevail between us and the French.

Unfortunately for both countries, Churchill's was very much a voice crying in the political wilderness at this time. This speech attracted little attention when it was first delivered and the very fact that he was to produce numerous variations on it throughout the 1930s may even have been counterproductive. In political life, it is all too easy to marginalise a Member who insists on repeating the unpalatable truth and in the House of Commons there are none so deaf as those who choose not to listen.

For all Churchill's reassurances about the amicable relations still prevailing at high level between the England and France of his day, the truth of the matter was somewhat different. While one may be tempted to dismiss some French right-wing Anglophobic utterances as paranoia, there were occasions when French touchiness was justified. On 21 January 1930, for example, Admiral Darlan wrote to his wife about an official visit to the House of Lords before the opening of the International Naval Conference: 'At eleven a.m., wearing our top hats and dressed in morning coats, we presented ourselves at the great gallery of the House of Lords, a large, long room with faded gold decorations. On one of the walls, the Battle of Trafalgar. On the other, the Battle of Waterloo. Charming!' Writing to a friend about the Second Naval Conference in London, he complained, not unreasonably, about what he felt was characteristic special pleading by the English delegates and also about inter-service rivalry amongst the French:

> You ought to bear clearly in mind that for strictly personal reasons, England will argue that the English fleet should equal the French fleet *plus* the Italian fleet *plus* the German fleet, and that the total should not exceed 1,500,000 tons. The result will be that if France and Italy and Germany are all supposed to be equal, we will have to *reduce* a tonnage which is already inadequate for our needs while 'disarming' the others will actually mean an increase for them. None of this need come about if we keep our heads.
>
> Yet the French fondly believe they're protected because they've built themselves a new Wall of China and because they're mechanizing the Army!
>
> But the Wall needs its troops to be supplied with food and munitions, and machines have to run on petrol. All of these need to be transported across the seas and if we don't command those seas – we're well and truly buggered!

Churchill, in the meantime, had been seeking to influence whoever he could by whatever means at his disposal. In 1935, he button-holed André Maurois to enlist his support:

> One day toward the end of 1935 I had lunch in London at the home of Lady Leslie in company with Winston Churchill, my hostess's nephew. After the meal he took me by the arm and led me into a small room.
>
> 'Now, Mr Maurois,' he said brusquely, 'you must not write any more novels. No! And you must not write any more biographies. No!'
>
> I looked at him in some alarm.
>
> 'All you must do now,' he went on, 'is to write one article a day, a single article, and the *same* one every day. Articles in which you will express, in all the different ways you can think of, a single idea: the French air force, which used to be the best in the world, is slipping back to fourth or fifth place. The German air force, which used to be non-existent, is in the process of becoming the best in the world. Nothing else. And if you proclaim these truths in France, and if you force France to listen to them, you will have performed a much greater service than in describing a woman's loves or a man's ambitions.'
>
> I replied that, unfortunately, I was by no means an expert in aviation, that

I had no authority to talk about it, that no one would listen to me if I did, and that, consequently, despite his advice, I should continue to write novels and biographies.

'You will be wrong,' he said in his vigorous and ironic voice, to which from time to time a slight difficulty in enunciation gave a pleasant and characteristic flavour. 'You will be wrong. At this moment the threat embodied in the German air force is the *one* theme that should interest a Frenchman. For your own country may die because of it. Culture and literature, Mr Maurois, are all very well, but a culture without strength soon ceases to be a living culture.'

I never wrote the articles Winston Churchill advised me to write, and today I bitterly regret it.

Anthony Eden was another to sound the alarm when, on 26 March 1936, as Secretary of State for Foreign Affairs, he warned the House of Commons of the dangers of standing aloof from Western Europe:

I want to say one word to those who would argue that it is our duty at this time to keep free from all entanglements in Europe. With respect, I wonder whether those who say that are quite clear about what they mean. If they mean we must turn a blind eye to all that happens in Europe, I say that is to take no account at all of realities. We have never been able in all our history to disassociate ourselves from events in the Low Countries, neither in the time of Queen Elizabeth, nor in the time of Marlborough, nor in the time of Napoleon, and still less at the present day, when modern developments of science have brought a striking force so much nearer our shores. It is a vital interest of this country that the integrity of France and Belgium should be maintained and that no hostile force should cross their frontiers. The truth is . . . there was nothing very new in Locarno . . . It was a new label, but it was on old fact and that fact has been the underlying purpose of British foreign policy throughout history.

Like Churchill, he was unheeded.

Equally persuasive voices continued to counsel against involvement in European affairs and to express suspicion of France. When Germany reoccupied the demilitarised zone of the Rhineland in March 1936, Baldwin urged the French to show restraint. The Commonwealth continued to resent French 'vindictiveness' towards Germany. The rise to power of the left-wing 'Popular Front' in France in 1936 was unwelcome to British Conservatives. In his populist *Daily Express*, Beaverbrook extolled the virtues of the 'Empire and Splendid Isolation', declaring that the *Entente Cordiale* with France 'had brought only bloodshed and strife and sorrow'. On 16 January 1938, Neville Chamberlain promised an American friend that he would do everything in his power to promote understanding between Britain and the USA and then went on to complain that the instability of the French political system made planning difficult:

> Unhappily France keeps pulling her own house down about her ears. We are on excellent terms with her. With the Chautemps government which has just fallen we found ourselves in general agreement about all aims and objects. But France's weakness is a public danger just when she ought to be a source of strength and confidence, and as a friend she has two faults which destroy half her value. She never can keep a secret for more than half an hour, nor a government for more than nine months!

Relations between Britain and France, delicate ever since the end of the First World War, were further strained by the Czech crisis of 1938. With Hitler's reoccupation of the Rhineland in 1936 and his incorporation of Austria into the Third Reich in the spring of 1938, the threat he posed to the western democracies could no longer be disguised. The next item on his agenda was Czechoslovakia, the only European democratic state east of the Rhine, and bound to France by formal treaty since 1925. Czechoslovakia had a strong air force and could pit thirty-four Army divisions against the Germans' forty. What was at issue was whether France would honour its treaty obligations and go to war on the Czechs' behalf and whether Britain would fight too. In the event, neither France nor Britain proved able or willing to fight for a country that was geographically remote. Each wanted to secure peace without being seen to surrender. Each put pressure on Czechoslovakia to yield to Hitler's demands, which in the first instance meant handing over the Sudetenland with its three million Germans who were allegedly impatient to rejoin the Reich. Each sought to transfer the responsibility and the blame to the other. In mitigation, it should be said that the Western democratic chief negotiators, Chamberlain, Halifax, Daladier and Bonnet, like so many of their electorate, had a profound horror of war, and shrank from unleashing the holocaust that might well destroy the whole of Europe. France was torn with factional strife and, having built its Maginot Line, wholly wedded to a *defensive* military strategy. In 1938, Britain had neither the weaponry nor the will to fight. At the time, they were less than frank with one another.

Characteristic of the prevarication on each side was the exchange between the French and British Foreign Ministers on 12 September 1938. Bonnet asked: 'What answer would His Majesty's Government give to a question from the French Government, in the event of a German attack on Czechoslovakia: "We are going to march, will you march with us?" ' Halifax replied: 'The question itself, though plain in form, cannot be dissociated from the circumstances in which it might be posed, which are necessarily at this stage completely hypothetical.' Ironically, while Britain and France were seeking to bluff each other, Hitler was bluffing too. His armies were still only half-trained and his generals feared the consequences of a major war. Hitler kept his nerve throughout. On 18 June, he had stated in a General Strategic Directive: 'I shall only decide to take action against Czechoslovakia if, as in the occupation of the demilitarised zone and the entry into Austria, I am firmly convinced that France will not march and therefore Britain will not intervene either.' His judgement was entirely vindicated. The Western powers persuaded the Czechs to yield without a fight and not a shot was fired when the German columns moved in procession across the border. Daladier and Chamberlain have been excoriated ever since for their policy of appeasement, but one should not forget that when they returned to their capital cities at the beginning of October 1938, their citizens were delirious with delight.

Chamberlain's belief that he had won 'peace and honour' and that it would be 'peace for our time' proved cruelly mistaken. His was not the only mistake. Hitler declared to his generals on 14 August 1939: 'The men I got to know at Munich are not the kind to start a new world war.' Speaking to Churchill in 1942, and seeking to justify his signing of the Russo–German treaty on 24 August, Stalin conceded that he too had miscalculated: 'We formed the impression that the British and French Governments were not resolved to go to war if Poland were attacked, but that they hoped the diplomatic line-up of Britain, France, and Russia would deter Hitler. We were sure it would not.' 'How many divisions,' Stalin had asked, 'will France send against Germany on mobilisation? The answer was 'About a hundred.' He then asked, 'How many will England send? The answer was 'Two, and two more later.' 'Ah, two and two more later,' Stalin had repeated. 'Do you know,' he asked, 'how many divisions we shall have to put out on the Russian front if we go to war with Germany?' There was a pause. 'More than three hundred.' For all that, on 3 September 1939 the peace-loving Chamberlain declared war on Germany because it had invaded Poland, a country even more remote than Czechoslovakia. As a further irony, Britain, which ever since Versailles had preached conciliation with Germany, declared war at 11 a.m. on 3 September 1939, while France, which, for much of that time had incurred British odium for advocating armed resistance, sought delay right to the last and, against its better judgement, hurriedly declared war six hours afterwards.

★

From the beginning of the war, the Germans made a concerted attempt to demoralise the French and to intensify their ingrained resentment against the British. The Munich crisis had set a pernicious precedent. Nearly a million Frenchmen had been mobilised in 1938 and then stood down. When they were all mobilised again in 1939 and months passed by without military activity of any significance, they had ample time to observe that the British contingent was, once again, so small; that British troops were much better paid than the French (*les quinze francs des Anglais et les quinze sous des Français*); that while France had mobilised comprehensively, and its factories were working extra long hours, there were still more than a million registered unemployed in Britain and significantly under-used industrial capacity. In a notable 'Report on France' dated 1 January 1940, R. E. Balfour observed:

> The French feel, not without reason, that England is far too much concentrated on her own affairs. The ordinary men probably still thinks of the war as being primarily a British affair, though except for the black-out and the evacuees, English life has hardly been touched. There is no French citizen whose life has not been touched.

In his book *Why France Fell*, André Maurois described how the German propaganda machine tried to stir up Anglophobia amongst French serving soldiers:

> Each day it repeated to the French that the English had dragged them into the war; that the English themselves were not fighting and, moreover, never had fought; that the English were furnishing the machines and the French the cannon fodder. It distributed pictures showing a bath of blood toward which an English soldier was pushing a French soldier, and others

representing English officers in Paris fondling half-naked women while a French soldier kept watch on the Maginot Line.

As a committed Anglophile, Maurois said that he consistently tried to win support for his cause by evoking the *Entente Cordiale* of 1904 and the fact that 'England had fought at our side with perfect loyalty from 1914 to 1918' and that 'there were a million British dead reposing in the cemeteries of northern France'. For all that, he was forced to concede that 'the memory of nations is dreadfully retentive. In more than one French province, between 1919 and 1939, when I talked with confidence about British friendship, I encountered the vague, irritating and persistent memory of the Hundred Years War.'

In the autumn of 1939, the Germans showered pamphlets over the Maginot Line. Each pamphlet was shaped like a leaf and each was inscribed with the following poem:

> The leaves fall and we shall fall as they do.
> The leaves die because that is God's will.
> But when *we* fall, it is because the English will us to.
> When the springtime comes, no one will think any more
> Of the dead leaves or of the dead *poilus*.
> Life will pass by over our tombs.

The British were dismissive about this tactic. Air Marshal Arthur Harris commented:

> My personal view is that the only thing achieved was largely to supply the continent's requirement of toilet paper for the five long years of war. You have only to think of what any man of sense would do with an obviously enemy pamphlet, when he picked it up, how he would regard it, and how he would react to the statements in it. Our reaction to enemy pamphleteering had always been to jeer at it and at the most keep their leaflets as souvenirs.

Be that as it may, the principal activity of his own Bomber Command during the Phoney War was the dropping of similar – though less poetic – pamphlets over the Siegfried Line.

A British infantry officer made a more perceptive comment in his memoirs published anonymously in 1943:

> It has never surprised me that the French troops were in bad fettle when the

blow struck. The Frenchman lacked the phlegm of our soldier, to be so near home and at the same time so far away seemed senseless to him. The Hun was wise in aiming his propaganda mainly at the French – and very effective it was. Leaflets were dropped on us many times, our fellows just laughed at them. But the French took them seriously, which was bad, and what the Hun had expected.

In the higher reaches of the British Establishment, suspicion of and sometimes contempt for the French persisted. In March 1939, that influential figure Sir Henry 'Chips' Channon had noted in his diary on the occasion of a French State visit: 'Frog Week! ... Anthony, Winston, all the pro-Frog boys! . . . Faubourg Frogs at Covent Garden.' On 1 January 1940, a Ministry of Information official memorandum noted: 'We can never afford to relax our publicity work . . . The fact that France is our Ally and that her interests are as deeply at stake in the war as our own is irrelevant. There is always the possibility of a split between us.'

Nevertheless, in the spring of 1940, all manner of ideas were mooted to further Anglo–French unity: playing the *Marseillaise* as well as the National Anthem in cinemas and theatres: Anglo–French postage-stamps bearing the faces of the British King and the French President; the *tricolore* to be flown alongside the Union Jack; the study of English to be compulsory in French schools, the study of French in English schools. On 15 March 1940, Britain's Minister of Education proposed to Lord Halifax that as part of his contribution to furthering better relations, British schoolchildren should 'learn something about French food and I believe there are a number of unemployed French chefs in London whom we might get to go round the schools and cook French meals'. Halifax replied: 'I certainly think that the work you are doing will have most useful results.'

Rather more serious was the signing of a Franco–British trade agreement on 16 February 1940, the formation of an Anglo–French industrial council on 8 March, and the meeting of the Supreme War Council on 28 March, which issued the following communiqué:

The Government of the French Republic and His Majesty's Government in the United Kingdom and Northern Ireland mutually undertake that during the present war they will neither negotiate nor conclude an armistice or treaty of peace except by mutual consent.

They undertake not to discuss peace terms before reaching complete agreement on the conditions necessary to ensure to each of them an effective and lasting guarantee of their security.

Finally they undertake to maintain after the conclusion of peace, a community of action in all spheres for so long as may be necessary to effect the reconstruction, with the assistance of other nations, of an international order which will ensure the liberty of peoples, respect for the law and the maintenance of peace in Europe.

Within days of the unleashing of the German *Blitzkrieg* on the West on 10 May 1940, this portentous declaration was shown to be so much verbiage. The French Cabinet began to discuss the possibility of an Armistice as early as 25 May. The following day the British began to evacuate their shattered army from the beaches of Dunkirk. Why had the collapse been so comprehensive and so precipitate?

If one reason was the sheer brilliance of the German campaign, another was the total breakdown of communication between the French and English armies. As in the First World War, there was no unified command. Viscount Gort's divisions were not under the orders of Gamelin's Grand Quartier Général, and from 3 September 1939 his instructions had been to appeal to the British Government should any French order threaten to imperil his forces in the field. Wholly typical of the resulting confusion once battle had been joined, was General Franklyn's order to retreat his two divisions from Arras on 23 May just one day after the Allied Prime Ministers had agreed that their armies should mount a combined *attack*. On 25 May, the head of the Imperial General Staff, General Ironside, wrote in his diary: 'Gort has withdrawn from Arras . . . Why Gort has done this I don't know. He has never told us that he was going to do it or even that he had done it. He has used his discretion.' The British retreat at this particular juncture helped persuade General Weygand, the French Commander-in-Chief, to abandon his planned counter-offensive and to confirm the unreliability of the British.

This view was shared by Marshal Pétain who, on 4 June, told the American Ambassador:

The British intend to permit the French to fight without help until the last available drop of French blood . . . With quantities of troops on British soil and plenty of planes and a dominant fleet, the British, after a very brief resistance, or even without resistance, would make a compromise peace with Hitler which might evolve a British Government under a Fascist leader.

On 9 June, he told the French Cabinet: 'England has got us into this position. It is our duty not to put up with it but to get out of it.' On 10 June, the French Government left Paris for Tours.

In the meantime, during the closing stages of the futile battle, British senior officers continued to display a woeful ignorance of their French opposite numbers. On 11 June 1940, a telegram from French military headquarters reached a British military attaché: it was plainly signed Doumec. A translation of this document in the Air Ministry archives bears three comments in different hands: 1. a large question mark in red pencil; 2. 'A General?' . . . 'possibly opposite Italy'; 3. 'He's the man who went to Russia on the Joint Mission. I don't know what he's doing now.' General J. E. A. Doumec had indeed been head of the Anglo–French Mission in the summer of 1939. In June 1940, he was Chief Executive Officer of the Grand Quartier Général, directly responsible to Gamelin and Weygand. At that particular moment he was in charge of the whole catastrophic retreat.

On 12 June, General Weygand ordered a general retreat and advised his Government to seek an armistice. On 13 June, Churchill conferred with French cabinet ministers at Tours and refused to release France from its undertaking, made in March, not to negotiate a separate armistice. On 14 June, the French Government retreated to Bordeaux. On 16 June, the British Government granted France conditional release from the March agreement. It also issued a dramatic Declaration of Union, principally inspired by Jean Monnet, Chairman of the Anglo–French Co-ordinating Committee set up in December 1939, supported by Sir Robert Vansittart and hurriedly endorsed by the War Cabinet.

Declaration of Union

At this most fateful moment in the history of the modern world the Government of the United Kingdom and the French Republic make this declaration of indissoluble union and unyielding resolution in their common defence of justice and freedom against subjection to a system which reduces mankind to a life of robots and slaves.

The two Governments declare that France and Great Britain shall no longer be two nations, but one Franco–British Union.

The constitution of the Union will provide for joint organs of defence, foreign, financial and economic policies.

Every citizen of France will enjoy immediately citizenship of Great Britain; every British subject will become a citizen of France.

Both countries will share responsibility for the repair of the devastation of war, wherever it occurs in their territories, and the resources of both shall be equally, and as one, applied to that purpose.

During the war there shall be a single War Cabinet, and all the forces of Britain and France, whether on land, sea or in the air, will be placed under its direction. It will govern from wherever it best can. The two parliaments will be formally associated. The nations of the British Empire are already forming new armies. France will keep her available forces in the field, on the sea, and in the air. The Union appeals to the United States to fortify the economic resources of the Allies, and to bring her powerful material aid to the common cause.

The Union will concentrate its whole energy against the power of the enemy, no matter where the battle may be.

And thus we shall conquer.

The Declaration cut no ice with the French Government. On that same day, Reynaud, who was expected to be particularly sympathetic, ceased to be Prime Minister. He was replaced by Pétain who promptly asked for armistice terms. On 17 June, General de Gaulle flew to London, and next day made his first broadcast to his fellow countrymen asking them to join him in the Free French movement and appealing for continued resistance. Very few responded to his call.

What the British public made of the Declaration is hard to tell. News of it was published in the press only on 18 June after the French Government had chosen to ignore it. A number of key British Government ministers privately expressed dismay at the project and relief over its demise. On 17 June, Lord Simon, the Lord Chancellor, wrote to Chamberlain that he was 'simply staggered':

'No longer two nations' – what happens to the Dominions, or to the King? 'The constitution of the Union will provide for . . . joint finance!' What a squabble!

I well understand the need for boldness and imagination, but has the plan really been *examined*, however speedily, from the British point of view? I can appreciate that Monnet would approve it.

If the French are now seeking to come to terms with the Germans in their desperate situation, how can anyone feel confident that half the 'Franco–British Union' won't want us to give in later on? Surely, surely, *our* business is with the defence of this island, and I cannot believe that a half-and-half arrangement is going to serve us *now*: nothing will serve but a *British* resolve *never* to yield. Forgive me, but I am in great perplexity and of course knew nothing whatever of this.

Lord Hankey wrote to Chamberlain that same day:

> John Simon has sent me the enclosed letter to read. I confess I was so staggered when I heard the proposal that I broke out in a sweat.
> The more I reflect on the events of recent years the more clearly I realise that the French have been our evil genius from the Paris Peace Conference until today inconclusive. Heaven forbid that we should tie ourselves up with them in an indissoluble union!
> But when I thought about it I came to the conclusion that it was a tactical move in a terrible situation, with no real chance of acceptance.

On 22 June, he also wrote to Halifax: 'When the truth is realized I cannot believe that the British people will stand for a policy that merges our manhood, which for many people is our most precious possession, and that of France. They will not wish to bind themselves to a nation that has been so shattered.' To which Halifax replied next day: 'I am so sorry that this proposal should have caused you such anxiety, but I can assure you that it was only designed for the period of the war and is, in any case, completely dead. Nothing could be further now from reality than any idea of an indissoluble union with France, and I expect that many people will share your relief that this should be so.'

In the meantime, relations between Britain and France deteriorated still further. As it became increasingly evident that the war on land was irretrievably lost, the British grew more and more concerned about the fate of the powerful French Mediterranean fleet. They pressed the French either to join it with the Royal Navy or to move it to ports remote from German control. To such suggestions, France's Admiral Darlan was totally resistant. When, on 19 June, he received a delegation from Britain's First Lord of the Admiralty and the First Sea Lord, he wrote from Bordeaux to his wife to say that, 'They had the demeanour of heirs who'd come to make sure that the dying man really had made his will in their favour.' He maintained that Churchill should accept his solemn promise, as a naval officer and a gentleman, that France would never allow Germany to take possession of the French fleet and he later argued that had the surrender of their fleet been included among the

Armistice terms, the French would have resumed fighting. He further argued that by retaining control of its fleet, France ensured that its Mediterranean and North African coasts remained neutral and unavailable to Germany as submarine bases.

In the event, the Franco–German Armistice was signed on 24 June. On 25 June Britain declared France to be 'territory in the occupation of or under the control of the enemy.' On 28 June, de Gaulle was recognised as leader of 'all Free Frenchmen who rally to him in support of the Allied cause'. On 3 July, Britain unleashed Operation 'Catapult'. A number of French warships berthed in British ports were commandeered: these included two battleships, two light cruisers, eight destroyers and five submarines. The Royal Navy bombarded and effectively destroyed the French fleet anchored in the Algerian harbour of Mers-el-kebir: 1,297 French naval officers were killed and a further 351 wounded. On 4 July, other units of the British fleet disarmed the French fleet anchored in the Egyptian harbour of Alexandria. On 8 July, France broke off diplomatic relations with Britain.

French public opinion was understandably outraged. Darlan wrote to his son expressing bewilderment:

> Common sense will tell you that Hitler and Mussolini can only be delighted at the spectacle of the English striving so determinedly to destroy as many French warships as possible.
>
> Such attacks will inevitably cause Franco–English relations to deteriorate still further, leading to a complete break or even open conflict, and the very least of these possibilities will be of considerable benefit to the Axis powers.

There was a deal of bitterness on the British side over what was felt to be France's chauvinistic obstinacy in refusing to hand over its fleet, but over the Franco–German Armistice there was rather more relief than despair. As early as 26 May, Sir Alexander Cadogan noted in his diary that Britain would be better off without the French. When he heard that the Armistice had been signed, Air Marshal Dowding fell to his knees and thanked God. In his diary on 25 June, Hugh Dalton sneered at the refusal of the French Government to transfer itself overseas: 'Their insularity and non-travelling habits are coming out with a rush. They are too much attached to their mistresses, and their soup, and their little properties.' Lord Hankey wrote to his brother on 5 July 1940, 'We are fed to the teeth with the French. I have been all the war but have hesitated to say so. They never prepared properly for the war and never fought properly.' And, inevitably, the defeat of the French greatly encouraged those who all along had preferred Splendid Isolation. Following the final meeting of the Supreme War Council in France, Beaverbrook declared: 'We're all Splendid Isolationists now.' After the British attacks on units of the French Navy, *The Times* declared: 'The last vestige of reliance upon official France has been renounced', while the *Daily Mail* proclaimed: 'A new Britain has arisen. The days of nerveless fumbling are over.'

Eloquent English voices were certainly raised in the cause of France. On 21 October 1940, Churchill broadcast in French from London:

Frenchman! For more than thirty years in peace and war I have marched with you and I am marching still along the same road. Tonight I speak to you at your firesides wherever you may be, or whatever your fortunes are: I repeat the prayer around the *louis d'or: Dieu protège la France*. Here at home in England, under the fire of the Boche, we do not forget the ties and links that unite us to France, and we are persevering steadfastly and in good heart in the cause of European freedom and fair dealing for the common people of all countries, for which, with you, we drew the sword. When good people get into trouble, because they are attacked and heavily smitten by the vile and wicked, they must be careful not to get at loggerheads with one another. The common enemy is always trying to bring this about, and, of course, in bad luck a lot of things happen which play into the enemy's hands. We must just make the best of things as they come along.

Here in London, which Herr Hitler says he will reduce to ashes, and which his aeroplanes are now bombarding, our people are bearing up unflinchingly. Our Air Force has more than held its own. We are waiting for the long-promised invasion. So are the fishes . . .

Remember that we shall never stop, never weary and never give in, and that our whole people and Empire have vowed themselves to the task of cleansing Europe from the Nazi pestilence and saving the world from the new Dark Ages. Do not imagine, as the German-controlled wireless tells you, that we English seek to take your ships and colonies. We seek to beat the life and soul out of Hitler and Hilterism. That alone, that all the time, that to the end. We do not covet anything from any nation except their respect . . . To Frenchmen in the occupied regions . . . I say, when they think of the future, let them remember the words which Thiers, that great Frenchman, uttered after 1870 about the future of France and what was to come: 'Think of it always: speak of it never.'

Good night, then: sleep to gather strength for the morning. For the morning will come. Brightly will it shine on the brave and true, kindly upon all who suffer for the cause, glorious upon the tombs of heroes. Thus will shine the dawn. *Vive la France!* Long live also the forward march of the common people in all the lands towards their just and true inheritance, and towards the broader and fuller age.

Lord Vansittart, in an elegy entitled 'France: 1904–1940', grieved for his land of lost content in the accents of a bereaved lover:

> Was I not faithful to you from the first?
> When have I ever failed you since my youth?
> I loved without illusion, knew the worst,
> But felt the best was nearer to the truth.
>
> You were indulgent too and open-eyed
> To the shortcomings I was frank to own.
> So we were mingled, destined side by side
> To face a world we could not face alone.
>
> Did you keep faith with me? When all was well
> Yes; but I clave to you when all was not.
> And when temptation touched your citadel,
> Your weakness won again, and you forgot –
>
> Forgot your self, and freedom and your friends,
> Even interest; and now our vaunted glow
> Becomes a blush, as the long story ends
> In sorry separation at Bordeaux.
>
> You hate me now; you will not hate me less
> If I go on unshaken by your fall,
> If for your sake, devoid of bitterness,
> I face the world without you after all.

In 1942, in the same tone but at rather greater length, Charles Morgan published his 'Ode to France'. There can be no doubt that it was deeply felt but, like the similar odes addressed directly to France by Swinburne and Meredith, its rhetoric now seems embarrassingly windy. Yeats's well-known aphorism seems apposite here: 'Out of our quarrel with ourselves we make poetry; out of our quarrel with others, we make only rhetoric.'

What has worn rather better is Morgan's series of weekly articles commissioned by *The Times*, which appeared under the heading 'Menander's Mirror'. Several of these were translated and secretly circulated throughout France. Typical of these is a lecture he delivered on 25 February 1941, entitled 'France is an Idea Necessary to Civilisation':

A little before the collapse of France, my host at dinner, a good soldier and a country squire, having listened to what I had to say of the French, replied as follows: 'Well, I dunno. Sounds all right. Don't pretend to know the chaps myself. But what I say is "Never trust a Froggy." ' For this phrase there is a precise translation: 'Perfide Albion'. Among great sections of the two peoples mutual distrust is profound and hereditary, and this feeling was sharpened by the events of the summer of 1940. Our troops, and particularly our Air Force, believed that the French let us down in the field; the French, though the better informed among them acknowledged that we fulfilled our contract in the present war, that we did what we undertook to do, were nevertheless persuaded that, if we had stood by them firmly during the last twenty years, the German menace would not have revived and that, in any case, when the crisis arose, we ought to have been able to undertake more than we did. There is truth in both charges. All those who cry: 'Never trust a Froggy' or 'Perfide Albion' seem to themselves to have been justified.

Anyone who believes, as I do, that France is nevertheless an idea necessary to civilisation and that any victory which divides us from her is a defeat, must recognise these facts. A great number of English dislike the French; a great number of French dislike the English – with this result: that there are Frenchmen, represented by Laval, who look across the Rhine for their associates in a new European order, and there are Englishmen who, if they can win this war alone or in collaboration with America, rely for the future upon an Anglo-Saxon undertaking that shall exclude France. I hold and have long held a contrary view. Ever since the Treaty of Versailles, I have urged an active Anglo–French alliance as the only real core of a pacific system in Europe. In 1934, travelling through Europe for *The Times* newspaper on an unpolitical mission, I found everywhere that the men on the spot – diplomatic representatives or newspaper correspondents – were alive to the German intention to divide England from France and destroy each in turn. In November 1936, lecturing to a French audience at the Sorbonne, I urged them, if they were justifiably impatient with the hesitancies of our foreign policy, to remember the differences of temperament between our two peoples. The French liked every under-standing to be cut and dried, every treaty to be signed in ink and sealed with sealing-wax; the English stubbornly preferred a more elastic obligation. I asked my audience to remember the tablet set up in Notre Dame to the memory of our soldiers fallen in the earlier war. We were not bound by treaty to send across the Channel more than 200,000 men. Nevertheless the tablet was inscribed: '*A la mémoire du million de morts de l'Empire Britannique tombés dans la grande guerre, et qui pour la plupart reposent en France*'. I suggested that though it was not in ink that those signatures were written, we should honour them when the hour struck, and begged my hearers to believe in us, to be patient with us meanwhile, though our methods were different from theirs. '*Si nous nous divisons, le monde est perdu.*'

The equation between France and the noblest features of civilisation has been made from the Renaissance to the present and it was reformulated in the midst of the war in a lecture given by Cyril Connolly in June 1943. He sought to explain the presence in France of so many outstanding writers and painters. He answered:

I think it is largely due to its climate, or rather its combination of climates, Atlantic, Continental, and Mediterranean, and to its central position as a market for ideas; but I think it is also because in no other country is Art so highly considered, and artists left so benevolently alone. An English artist is always conscious of responsibilities – to his family, to his tutors, to his public, to society and to the State. We have produced the greatest poets, but somehow in spite of ourselves. That is why France must remain a place where everyone can go, and where everyone can, if he wishes, live, and without guilt and without a feeling of expatriation. The great blessing France confers on the artist is anonymity. When an English writer goes there, one by one the layers of his social personality peel off, he finds there are more and more things he can do without, and more and more he comes to be preoccupied with his central situation, his creative possibilities. For in France he is not an ordinary nobody. This nobody, who leaves behind his old social or academic skin, is offered all that is most rare and delightful in life: masterpieces of painting and architecture, natural beauty, congenial climate, cheap food, good wine, a room to write in, a café to talk in, and a well-wishing atmosphere in which everything is simplified. For the painter there is outdoor light at all seasons and the world's centre for pictures. For the writer, health and constant exhilaration. I don't think any writer can live in France without acquiring something of that serious and lucid power we have been discussing, and lacking which, so much English work is a salad without a dressing, a nostalgic left-over from the Victorian age.

Sweetly reasonable though these Francophile voices sound today, they were, at the time, the exception. While the war lasted and for long afterwards, the majority of the British Establishment spoke of France with anger and contempt rather than in sorrow. It was left to a distinguished Oxford don, R. B. McCallum, to express an alternative view in his book *Public Opinion and the Last Peace*, published in 1944 while France was still occupied. Observing that the English critics who accused the French of lacking back-bone in 1940 were the ones who had castigated them in the inter-war years for excessive militarism, he argued that a stricken ally should be given no less sympathy than a defeated enemy. His advice to his readers was 'remembering all that France has suffered in this war and has still to suffer, Englishmen should include among the many emotions with which they regard her, a sense of shame and deep humility'. Given the mood and circumstances of the time, his was a hopeless cause.

★

If, during the Occupation years, there was an increase in England's reputation for double-dealing with the French, there was, for once, ample cause. In his *History of the Second World War*, Churchill, a genuine Francophile, describes the dilemma with painful clarity and characteristic generosity:

> In spite of the Armistice and Oran and the ending of our diplomatic relations with Vichy, I never ceased to feel a unity with France. People who have not been subjected to the personal stresses which fell upon prominent Frenchmen in the awful ruin of their country should be careful in their judgments of individuals . . . I felt sure that the French nation would do its best for the common cause according to the facts presented to it. When they were told that their only salvation lay in following the advice of the illustrious Marshal Pétain, and that England, which had given them so little help, would soon be conquered or give in, very little choice was offered to the masses. But I was sure they wanted us to win, and that nothing would give them more joy than to see us continue the struggle with vigour. It was our first duty to give loyal support to General de Gaulle in his valiant constancy. On August 7 I signed a military agreement with him which dealt with practical needs. His stirring addresses were made known to France and the world by the British broadcast. The sentence of death which the Pétain Government passed upon him glorified his name. We did everything in our power to aid him and magnify his movement.
>
> At the same time it was necessary to keep in touch not only with France but even with Vichy. I therefore always tried to make the best of them . . . On July 25 I sent a minute to the Foreign Secretary in which I said: 'I want to promote a kind of collusive conspiracy in the Vichy Government whereby certain members of that Government, perhaps with the consent of those who remain, will levant to North Africa in order to make a better bargain for France from the North African shore and from a position of independence. For this purpose I would use both food and other

inducements, as well as the obvious arguments . . . Our consistent policy was to make the Vichy Government and its members feel that, so far as we were concerned, it was never too late to mend. Whatever had happened in the past, France was our comrade in tribulation, and nothing but actual war between us should prevent her being our partner in victory.

This mood was hard upon de Gaulle, who had risked all and kept the flag flying, but whose handful of followers outside France could never claim to be an effective French Government. Nevertheless we did our utmost to increase his influence, authority and power. He for his part naturally resented any kind of truck on our part with Vichy, and thought we ought to be exclusively loyal to him . . . He also felt it to be essential to his position before the French people that he should maintain a proud and haughty demeanour towards 'perfidious Albion', although an exile, dependent upon our protection and dwelling in our midst. He had to be rude to the British to prove to French eyes that he was not a British puppet. He certainly carried out this policy with perseverance. He even one day explained this technique to me, and I fully comprehended the extraordinary difficulties of his problem. I always admired his massive strength.

Britain's policy of dealing simultaneously with both Pétain's Vichy Government and de Gaulle's Free French was foredoomed to failure. From the outset, prominent members of the British government viewed Vichy with open contempt. Writing in his diary on 17 June 1940, Hugh Dalton described them as a 'most miserable lot of very old men', while the Foreign Office believed it was controlled by 'a crook' (Baudouin) and 'an old dotard' (Pétain). The official British view was that in signing the Armistice with Germany, France had reduced itself to 'a state of complete subjection to the enemy' and had deprived itself of 'all liberty and of all right to represent the French people'. The Foreign Office, always obsessed with protocol, remained distinctly uneasy about de Gaulle's direct radio appeal to the French people (though Churchill himself broadcast a similar appeal, in carefully rehearsed French, on 21 October 1940). If they disowned him, they ended the fiction that 'France' was somehow still in the war. By continuing to support him, they widened the gulf between Vichy and London.

The relationship between these two, embittered by what the French Establishment continued to feel was Britain's precipitate flight from Dunkirk in May 1940 and its cynical assault on the French fleet at the beginning of July, deteriorated still more when the Royal Navy intercepted three French cruisers sailing from Toulon to Dakar in mid September 1940 and forced them to return to neutral Casablanca. The

Vichy forces at Dakar rejected a personal appeal from de Gaulle himself. The British fleet shelled the French battleship *Richelieu* and bombarded Dakar's shore defences. The Vichy defenders lost 166 men and a further 340 were wounded.

Reaction in Vichy France was predictably scathing. Soon after the news broke, the following pamphlet was widely circulated over the signature of Pierre Constantini:

> Fellow Frenchmen,
> For those of you who've already forgotten the dead of Mers-el-Kebir, England has just refreshed your memories by killing a few hundred more of your sons. Can you still go on defending the cause of perfidious Albion?
> We're now going to do the honourable thing by taking up arms against this England which began by betraying us and has now set about slaughtering us.
> With all my mind, with all my heart, with all the anger of a Frenchman whose country and whose soul have been wounded
> I DECLARE WAR ON ENGLAND.
> It's for this war of liberation that I demand arms. It's for this honour that I ask my Air Force comrades to join me.
> France is at stake.
> Europe is at stake.
> Further delay is out of the question.
> Time is passing. Honour demands it.
> Where are you, Joan of Arc Squadron? Saint Helena Squadron? Fashoda Squadron? Shortly to be joined by Mers-el-Kebir Naval Squadron and Dakar Naval Squadron.
> Fill the sky of perfidious Albion with the vengeful lightning flashes of our reborn history. Our betrayed dead demand it.

His was not a lone voice. On 9 November 1940, the following appeared in the newspaper *L'Illustration*:

> We owe all our present misery, all the dead, all the destruction, all the ruins to the true and the unique hereditary enemy of our country: England. Fellow Frenchmen, it's fitting that we now thank England for having, over the centuries, ever since our colonies first began to make its mouth water, ceaselessly, tirelessly and always diabolically, plotted to sacrifice France to its insular and imperialistic interests.

Not all French commentators were hostile. Georges Bernanos was one such. A maverick of high distinction, he had been in the same form at the Jesuit College in Paris as Charles de Gaulle, and his wife, Jeanne Talbert d'Arc, was a direct descendant of one of Joan of Arc's brothers. He remains justly famous for his powerful novels – such as *Sous le soleil de Satan* (1926) or *Journal d'un curé de campagne* (1936) – which depict humble country priests confronted by implacably Godless communities. But he was also a fiery polemicist, who in *La Grande peur des bien pensants* (1931) mounted an eloquent defence of Edouard Drumont, a notorious anti-Semitic campaigner in the Dreyfus Affair; and in *Les Grands Cimetières sous la lune* (1937) conveyed his bitter disillusionment with the modern world occasioned by the Spanish Civil War. Disgusted even further by the events at Munich in 1938, he left with his family for Brazil. It was from there, in December 1940, that he wrote his *Lettre aux Anglais*:

> Englishmen! Englishmen! Men of England! these pages will probably reach you some day next December. I therefore wish you a Merry Christmas. Christmas is the festival of childhood! A Merry Childhood to the English people! Three cheers for the childhood of England! Unfortunately, we French people never tried hard to understand the English whom our fifteenth-century ancestors used to call 'Godons' and who they used to jeer at with the popular cry of 'You with the tail! You with the Tail!', because they suspected the English of concealing inside their breeches that diabolical appendage that had been stuck on them in punishment for their sins. But while we didn't know all that much about the English a fair number of us always knew that English children are some of the most beautiful in the world. Merry Christmas to the children of England! We assumed that you were all *milords* with high collars and fat bellies, made rich by sugar and cotton, who had invented the pound sterling, the racehorse and the umbrella, in a fit of bad temper while eating boiled leg of lamb served with some miserable potatoes. But, lo and behold! for six months now, day after day, you're telling us a marvellous story, totally incomprehensible to sober-sided people, to mature grown-ups, to the Worldly Wise and the Powers-that-Be, you're telling them all a children's story! Three cheers for the children of England!

He proceeded with a brief survey of the outlook in June 1940 when, for many observers, it appeared that to continue the war was mathematically impossible:

> . . . as if men were the tools of mathematics instead of mathematics being the tools of men. Some of them sniggered with joy but these weren't the most dangerous ones: hatred is a salt which, for a brief while, at least,

preserves old men from corruption. Others threatened us with the contagion of their crocodile tears, they decomposed before our eyes, they dissolved in floods of futile weeping which gave off a nasty smell. 'Standing alone against all the odds?' they said 'That's just a children's story!' Three cheers for the children of England!

Men of England, at the present time you're writing – as orators might say in their special language – one of the great pages of History. I'd like to put that more simply, in plainer words. But perhaps there aren't any plainer words just as there's no longer any genuine bread. Too bad! If the best words have been used too often, then, all right, we'll make use of different ones: we'll use free words for free men! At the present time, you're writing one of the great pages of History. You English are the ones who are writing it, but it was surely for your children that you began to write it '*Once upon a time, on a little island, there was a great nation alone against all the odds . . .*' At the sound of an opening like that, which wily old fox of politics or business would not have shrugged his shoulders and snapped the book shut? Your victory is a child's dream which men have made come true.

The voice of Bernanos was, in more respects than one, exceptional. While Britain fought on alone in the early 1940s, a clamorous chorus of Anglophobic commentators scoffed at the notion of a British victory and revelled in the news of their defeats. The catalogue of grievances grew longer and was tirelessly repeated. In October 1941, an Anglophobic pamphlet was extensively circulated. It bore the title 'Entente Cordiale'. An ex-soldier, wounded in the First World War, tries to reason with his son who has been quoting Gaullist speeches at him. He compares the consequences of the Versailles Treaty for France with those for England:

They gained fifteen times more territory. They lost a mere tenth of our dead. That's the balance-sheet of the last war . . .

Who stopped France from picking herself up and from growing again after 1918?

Who held back our recovery by infiltrating our political life, favouring the Marxist parties, the strikes, the pseudo-socialism?

Who allowed the evacuation of the Rhineland?

Who prevented the rebirth of our Navy?

Who wanted to limit our armaments?

And now, under the pretext that it will help their cause, here we are, after Fashoda, after Suez, after Egypt, robbed blind by our allies – of the French Congo, of Central Africa, of Syria, of Tahiti, of French India.

As if we hadn't lost enough, now they're trying to finish us off.

That's what's meant by the so-called *Entente Cordiale* . . .

And before they raise the subject of torn-up treaties, as London puts it, just let England remind itself that it was General Gort, in the first instance, who tore up the war treaty right in the middle of the battle, when he deserted the Front with his troops, and opened the gates of Paris to the Germans so that he could scuttle off to guard the vaults of the City of London . . .

If I have a longing to express for your arms, it is that I wish with all my heart that these Frenchmen who have lost their way could fiercely, heroically and totally, go on fighting till the last Englishman.

While Charles Morgan and Cyril Connolly were deploying their elegant arguments in support of French civilisation, the Vichy spokesmen for that same civilisation poured out a malodorous stream of anti-English, anti-Semitic and anti-Gaullist invective almost till the end of the German Occupation. The three most accomplished performers were Lucien Rebatet, Jean-Hérold Paquis and Philippe Henriot. Rebatet's articles, which appeared in the right-wing paper *Je suis partout*, were published in book-form in 1942 under the title *Les Décombres* – 'the ruins' to which French civilisation was being reduced by Anglo–Jewish Big Business interests directed from the City and from Wall Street (the inclusion of America amongst the world-conspirators was something of a novelty). He denounced the *Entente Cordiale* as a fraud:

Friendship with our insular neighbours has become one of our sacred cows. The indissoluble marriage between our two empires now forms part of the catechism. We're all invited to show enthusiasm for the pompous prelude to the shooting-match, the pow-wows, the trips of the Lord Admirals and the Sir Marshals, the parades of the Scotch [*sic*] Guards and the Home Fleet, the Jew Hore Belisha, London's Minister of War, coming to Paris on 14 July to conduct the supreme review of French troops to check whether they're fit to serve His Gracious Majesty. A dazzled Thierry Maulnier finds the war effect of John Bull awe-inspiring. At the sound of the tons of shipping over which the Union Jack is going to fly, the Frenchman's heart is supposed to burst with joy. The most militant of France's awkward squad, those who write for *Je suis partout*, must use their most flowery language in timidly reminding these magnificent gentlemen that war has also to be waged by the poor bloody infantry.

And he dismissed the supporters of de Gaulle as deluded Anglophile snobs:

As far as high society and its acolytes were concerned, they went in for De Gaullism because compared with the English fashion scene, the simplicity and austerity of the Third Reich provided no opportunities for snobbery. People believed in Churchill because of the golf, the horseracing and Scottish tweed. To side with the English was to side with the *gentlemen* [*sic*]. It was reckoned to be bad form forever to be evoking Dunkirk and Mers-el-Kebir when there was Oxford and Piccadilly. The younger generation looked to America for their salvation because of Hollywood and 'swing' and the Marx Brothers and Duke Ellington. They thought themselves no end of a hero just by shouting 'Bye! Bye!'

Philippe Henriot was a gifted broadcaster. When it became apparent that Britain was likely to end on the winning side, one of his regular jeremiads was how the Liberation armies would ravage France. This supplied the title for the collection of his broadcast scripts that were published in 1944 as *Et s'ils débarquaient?* ('What if they landed?'). He too linked Gaullism with social snobbery in a broadcast on 18 April 1943 called 'Le Trahison des Snobs':

An interesting chapter needs to be written about certain acts of desertion now taking place and the way certain high Civil Servants have become dissidents. A good title for it would be: the role of snobbery in high treason. To be sure, I'm not so naïve as to underestimate the role played by money in these lamentable episodes. But when I see the great *bourgeois* of our Tax Inspectorate and the Diplomatic Service departing with their aristocratic titles and all their elegance to lands that have been colonised by the pound sterling and the American dollar, I find it hard to take such escapades too tragically. At least these characters have an excuse: they have been fashioned by their background, their education and their profession into embracing a form of Anglomania which is quite incurable. This Anglomania began with their mode of dressing and their outward appearance. It then went deeper, went right through them, moulded them. Gradually, they adopted all manner of Anglo-Saxon attitudes, and it was the British belief that money is King that proved particularly appealing to these financiers, these manipulators of money, these experts in political economics. Their world-view oscillated between Ascot race-course and the London Stock Exchange. British shirt-makers and British tailors clothed these mannequins. So why shouldn't they have done the same thing for their personalities. They are all po-faced, self-satisfied, strait-laced theoreticians who seek the remedy for all ills by consulting the Stock Exchange. Life for them means penetrating the innermost recesses of international finance, knowing when to buy and sell or where to make the best investments. But there are still millions of people who don't play the markets, who don't speculate, who don't hob-

nob with the Mannheimers, the Kreugers, the Staviskys or the Loewen-
steins. These people try to earn their living by hard work. They're creatures
of flesh and blood who are of scant concern to the speculators in the money-
markets or the wheeler-dealers in business, or the capitalist robots
programmed and controlled by London and Washington.

Symptomatically, when the Allied armies occupied Tunisia in the
spring of 1943, Henriot construed this not as as preliminary to the
invasion of Europe but as one more move by the English in their age-
old plan to take over the French Empire. On 16 May 1943, he spelled
this out in a broadcast entitled 'La France partout perdante' ('France
losing out all round'):

> How could we ever have forgotten that England has never ceased to look
> on the Mediterranean as its private game preserve? In the eighteenth
> century, across the western end of this inner lake, it drew the bolt of
> Gibraltar. In the nineteenth century, when de Lesseps cut through the
> isthmus at Suez, it didn't rest until it had pocketed the key to this second
> door which others had proceeded to open. In order to oversee and control
> the interior of this maritime fief, it stole Malta from us, swore to hand it
> back in 1802, then kept it. In a mood of black rage, it gave up Corsica which
> it had temporarily occupied. It took up position in Cyprus. It mounted
> guard at the feet of the Sphinx while repeatedly promising it would
> decamp. It bullies or buys or enslaves the rulers of Arabia and Transjordan.
> Its Secret Service sends Lawrence into these regions where, over the years,
> he will fight with every weapon – guile, brute strength, assassination,
> bribery – to undermine the French influence that so alarms the Foreign
> Office . . . But yet, after all that, there still remains the splendid block,
> patiently built up over a hundred years of diplomacy and conquest, from the
> Duke of Aumale to Lyautey, of those three prodigious territories, that new
> France which began as an outlying branch and was then united with the
> mother country in an indissoluble union. England did all it could to impede
> this expansion. Having organised the Fashoda incident, it then proceeds to
> exploit the Agadir incident as soon as it happens. It plans to act the role of
> mediator in the Franco–German dispute and pick up its commission as an
> honest broker through a compromise which will deprive France of the
> sovereignty of her conquest. This scheme doesn't come off and the genius
> of Lyautey, so subtle, so bold and so dazzling, wins the admiration of the
> whole world and universal respect.
> It is that failure which England has just avenged by effectively excluding
> France from the Mediterranean. In stealing these lands and these provinces,
> England is not striking a blow against Germany – but against France!

Jean-Hérold Paquis also made broadcasts and contributed to *Je suis partout*. A comprehensive collection of these was published in 1944 under the title *L'Angleterre comme Carthage* ... His readers were presumed to be sufficiently cultured to complete the classical quotation with the words *delenda est* (must be destroyed) and no doubt to recognise that to compare England with the great trading city of the ancient Roman world had been the crowning insult regularly hurled by Anglophobic demagogues during the French Revolutionary wars. In this characteristic broadcast, of 16 June 1943, entitled 'Dieu sauve notre bon roi Georges!' his cruel sarcasm, masquerading as extreme servility, is at the expense of George VI's mild and homely demeanour and the speech-defect which became pronounced when he was called upon to perform in public:

Sire, this is the first time that as a humble subject of Your Crown, I am daring to speak to Your Majesty without laughing. Up till now I have never been anything other than a bad subject, may Your Majesty make of that what he can or what he will. Nevertheless, I have always remained a faithful subject of Your Majesty, the subject of all the thoughts of Your Majesty, of all the worries of Your Majesty. I'm well aware, indeed, that at this very moment, Your Graciousness is reviewing thousands and thousands of future corpses, thousands and thousands of soldiers, sailors and airmen, who are soon going to try, I believe, in your name, in the name of ever faithful England, and of your former American colonies which were set free through the wicked stupidity of the French, who are going to try, in the name of the Free Hindus, the Free Canadians, the Free Irish, the Free Australians, the Free New Zealanders, the Free French, the Free Blacks, the Free Mexicans, the Free Brazilians, in the name of all the nations so harmoniously assembled by Your unselfish Majesty, in the same hotel and in the same camp, who are going to try to give back to us that precious liberty which England has never yet given to anybody. Sire, I give tongue to our great joy because it cannot be doubted that it is to your personal intelligence, your personal politics and your very special friendship that we are all indebted for that spectacle which has been promised time and time again but never yet delivered: the spectacle absolutely unheard of and never yet seen, the spectacle of British troops at long last fighting for somebody and for something, something which isn't Your Sovereign Crown, something which isn't England's interest. Because we know that Your Majesty is totally detached from the things of this world, is as poor as Gandhi and for that reason, is completely uninterested in the profits of war. Your unforgettable smile, Your Majesty, is the smile of a saint. And we're not about to forget, we have never once forgotten the dazzling glitter of your glance, the marvellous vivacity of your expression, we haven't forgotten the virility of your graciousness, or your formidable powers of seduction. Sire, let us hold nothing back, many a shop-girl sits dreaming at nightfall in front of your picture. Sire, for reasons I cannot fathom, there are young men who keep your portrait next to their heart. Sire, you are indeed the saviour for whom we've been waiting. And you *speak* so well and we do so love people who speak well. Your Majesty is so kind, he will have several tries at saying the same word. So we hear you three times over and our pleasure is therefore tripled. But we've been missing your gracious presence. So today, you're the admired guest of the Fourth Republic of Algeria. Permit me, Sire, as a confirmed monarchist to here publicly express mild regret that it has fallen to the Republicans to cry 'Long live the King! Long live good King George!' and that we aren't there ourselves, we who admire and love you so, so we can't recall to your failing memory that your visit proved fatal to the Third Republic, and that there's both fear and joy in our hearts at the thought that since you're present there, the Algerian régime could already be in danger.

None of France's professional Anglophobes prospered after the Liberation. The pamphleteer Pierre Constantini was certified insane. Philippe Henriot was shot in 1944. Paquis tried to escape, was captured, and also shot. Rebatet and Béraud each received death-sentences, which were commuted to life-imprisonment. Rebatet was eventually murdered in Paris in the 1970s. Céline was under darkest suspicion for some time and all his books were kept out of print for many years but he was finally amnestied. The father-figure, Maurras, after a protracted trial, was sentenced to life-imprisonment at the age of seventy-six. As he was led away from the court, he shouted, 'Dreyfus has had his revenge.' He kept his sense of history and his sense of grievance till the last.

The fortunes of Charles Morgan, as befitted a spokesman for the winning side, could not have been more different. Just two weeks after Paris was liberated on 25 August 1944, Morgan and just three other Englishmen were flown to Paris in a Dakota bomber. He included a graphic record of the scene in an essay later published under the title 'On Transcending the Age of Violence':

> The enemy had but recently been driven out, and Paris was happy as I have never known a city be happy before or since, not with wild rejoicing but with profound and passionate relief. I was, I believe, the only civilian and unofficial Englishman to have reached France so early, and the French, expecting nothing but soldiers and more soldiers, looked at any English writer in plain clothes as though he were a visitor from another world.
>
> Memory of these re-encounters will never fade while I live: how eyes

widened and held their gaze like the eyes of children; how hand clung to hand, feeling with incredulous avidity the living flesh and bones; how even the sun and wine in the glass, were as wine and sun had never been before. There was the shiver of renaissance in the air. Little more than two months later, when I came to Paris again for the reopening of the Comédie-Française, the sense of relief remained, but the French were already settling down to the business of existence. They had resumed their eternal task of analysis and self-criticism; they were correcting and re-correcting the prose of life; the freshness, the lyricism of the early days was gone.

How wonderful it had been then to ask after an old friend and to receive not the common answer: 'He is well,' but the August answer: 'He is alive'! I for my friends, my friends for me, were all in that hour young again and newly risen from the grave. There before our eyes was Paris, a French Paris, and there, as astonishing evidence of how Germans hope to conciliate those whom they mean to destroy, was L'Aiglon beside his father in the Invalides; it was pleasant to watch a Frenchman smile at that . . . And there was the river and the Ile St-Louis and the rue Bonaparte and the rue de Seine and the little house at Vanves and no Germans. The river flowed down to Mantes, to La Roche Guyon, to Vernon, to Rouen, to the Sea, and there was ruins, but no Germans. The air was sweet with their absence. It was French air. One might talk above a whisper with one's friends.

But Morgan was not in Paris to sight-see. He was there, quite specifically, to be hailed and fêted. A party of distinguished French dignitaries was summoned to meet him including Paul Valéry with whom he discussed George Meredith. Shortly afterwards, he attended the reopening of the Comédie-Française where he recited his 'Ode to France' to the assembled company. He described the occasion to Mrs Belloc Lowndes who was born in Paris during the siege of 1870:

> It was very exciting – the most exciting day of my life. I care desperately for French honour. The programme consisted of poems of the Resistance – Claudel, Eluard, Vercors etc. The National Guard in helmets and plumes. De Gaulle in the stagebox . . . My Ode came last . . . When I bowed to the audience I suddenly heard a noise like the wings of angels and then I saw that the whole audience of the *Comédie-Française* had risen . . . An Englishman can't ask much more of life.

Next day, he reported that he had attended a lecture on his works at the Sorbonne 'with the young almost crawling up the walls'. Honours continued to be showered on him: honorary doctorates from St Andrews in 1947 and, a year later, from the Universities of Caen and Toulouse. There were also civic receptions, speeches and *vins d'honneur*

for him that same year in Paris, Bordeaux, Montpellier and Carcas-
sonne, where the mayor presented him with an antique lamp. In Paris,
the bookshops all put on lavish displays of his works. His novel on the
French Resistance, *The River Line* (1949), was very well received as was
its stage-adaptation three years later. Between 1953 and 1956, he was
President of International PEN. He died in February 1958. In France,
his works are studied still; in Britain, they have nearly all been out of
print for years. No fall from literary grace in the twentieth century has
been more spectacular. It is a phenomenon not only of interest in itself
but as being emblematic of a whole range of differences in perception
that have characterised Anglo–French relations from the outset. In this
respect, the fifty years following the Liberation of France were to prove
no different from the centuries that preceded it.

8 : *De Gaulle and After*

I love France: and I am glad I saw it first when I was young. For if an Englishman has understood a Frenchman, he has understood the most foreign of foreigners. The nation that is nearest is now the furthest away. Italy and Spain, and rather especially Poland, are much more like England than that square stone fortress of equal citizens and Roman soldiers.

G. K. Chesterton, *Autobiography* (1936)

De Gaulle's relationship with Britain was, like Napoleon's, seriously misrepresented by populist English journalists and cartoonists, as well as by politicians who ought to have known – and, in some cases, probably did know – better. It is wrong to classify him, as many commentators have been wont to do, as a dyed-in-the-wool Anglophobe and attribute this to the French professional military background that also produced Admiral Darlan, or to personal pique occasioned by the slights, real or imaginary, that he experienced as leader of the Free French in London. There is abundant evidence to show how his single-minded dedication to the cause of France made him both a formidable adversary and a difficult ally: Churchill's quip that the greatest cross he had to bear was the Cross of Lorraine was, in important respects, amply justified. But it is by no means the whole story. As with Napoleon, the reality of de Gaulle's relationship with Britain was more complex.

In June 1940, he greeted the plan for a full-blown Anglo–French Union with an enthusiasm that would seem to have been entirely genuine. Cynics might dismiss this as a mere gesture on his part, as opportunistic and as empty as it was on the part of the British politicians who made the offer, but the charge can surely not be made of the speech he made on 25 November 1941 at the University of Oxford. His theme was the past, present and future of Anglo–French relations and he treated it with all the elegance and erudition that the subject and the setting demanded:

Barrès used to speak of *lieux où souffle l'esprit* (places where the Spirit bloweth). I do not think that there can be a formulation better than this evocative phrase to convey the character of your illustrious home. But if, for that reason, I am all the more aware of the honour paid me by the University French club, I am at the same time encouraged in tackling such a difficult subject. What I have to talk about is the collaboration of the English and French nations if we are to derive the maximum benefit from victory once it's won. As the study of such a subject implies some impartiality in thought and feeling, I feel encouraged in evoking it here in this place where disinterested thinking has been long traditional.

When people used to talk to Monsieur Thiers of Anglo–French relations, he was in the habit of listening in silence to the words of his interlocutor. Then he would look over the top of his spectacles and say: 'How very interesting! But wouldn't it have been enough just to say that England is an island?' Monsieur Thiers held that this simple geographical aphorism provided the complete explanation of everything that had happened in the past, everything that was happening in the present and everything that would happen in the future between the French and English nations.

Perhaps Monsieur Thiers was right at the time he spoke. It is, in point of fact, now commonplace to develop the theory that Great Britain's insular position has pre-determined its belief that the sea is its surest bulwark, its nearest neighbour, the vital route for all its supplies and, therefore, has made the command of the seas its principal national concern and virtually its second nature. At the same time, England's maritime and commercial vocation inspired it to found its Empire and to insist on ruling over the seas which led to it. Albion could not accept the establishment of any sort of hegemony on the continent of Europe because the country which succeeded in achieving it would have immediately sought the command of the seas. This, quite clearly, explains the frequent tensions in the foreign policies of London and Paris in the seventeenth, eighteenth and nineteenth centuries. It also explains the frequent conflicts between the two countries. And it also brings home how dramatic was the upheaval of centuries old traditional nature of the inter-relationship thanks to the initiative of your King Edward VII. The Entente Cordiale was born, almost overnight, from the moment that Germany, driven on by Prussia, unfurled the banner of Pan-Germanism, threatened the balance of power by its triumphant expansion and cried through the mouth of Wilhelm II, 'Our future is on the Ocean!'

Moving from the past to the present, de Gaulle indicated the manifold ways in which the mutual enemies of Britain and the Free French were seeking to drive a wedge between them, ticking off the points persistently being made by the Vichyite Anglophobes but without their rancour. He insisted that his fellow Frenchmen across the Channel did not share these views:

> The Reich loses no opportunity of forcing its collaborators to commit as many hostile or spiteful acts as possible against England with the intention of arousing its hostility against a nation which, if truth be told, is still sincerely its friend.
>
> One of the most remarkable facts of these tragic times is that none of these numerous artificial pretexts for discord have in any way diminished the confidence and the friendship the French people feel for the British. More remarkable still, the English are more popular in France today that they have ever been. There is a total contrast between what seems to be the attitude of the official Establishment and the true feelings of the French people at every level . . . Let me cite three examples. In July, at Lens, an RAF raid on a factory killed some French workers. An English plane was brought down close by. The French were buried first and the whole population attended the ceremony. Next day, the British airmen. The same crowd followed their bodies to the cemetery and in the front row marched the mourning widows of the workers who had been killed.
>
> On 2 November last year, the Day of the Dead, French families went as they always do to pray by the graves of their dead relatives. I want you to know that throughout France, there wasn't a single English war grave that wasn't visited, and that of all the graves in all the cemeteries across France, the British graves were decorated with more flowers than any others.
>
> As for the third fact, over which I shan't linger but is perhaps worth your consideration, not a single day goes by without several young Frenchmen from every region and every class getting to England in order to fight beside their English comrades. In order to get here, they have to accomplish prodigious deeds of courage and cunning, the narration of which will sound wholly astonishing when the day comes when books can be written about them.

De Gaulle then looked towards the future, graphically and movingly unveiling his vision of the New Order:

> I remain convinced that . . . if we win this year, it is of the utmost importance that we set up an Anglo–French alliance more open and more soundly based than it has ever been before. While there are excellent practical and emotional reasons for such a union, in my view, a much more

compelling reason is a responsibility which must be shared by our two great and ancient nations: I mean the well-being of civilisation itself . . .

However complete one day may be the victory won for the democratic nations by its armies, its fleets and its air squadrons, and however wise and far-sighted may their policies turn out to be towards those whom it once again will have conquered, nothing will prevent the menace from re-emerging even more dangerous than before, nothing will guarantee the peace, nothing will safeguard the order of the world, if the party of freedom . . . does not succeed in constructing a new order in which the liberty, security and dignity of its members are so exalted and assured that they will seem so much more desirable than whatever it is that threatens to replace them. There is no other way to ensure the definitive victory of the spirit over matter. Because, in the final analysis, this is what it's really all about.

But how can one conceive such a programme of renovation – spiritual, social and moral, just as much as political – if our two peoples remain divided? For centuries now, France and England have been the homes for – and the champions of – human freedom. Liberty will perish if those homes don't conjoin and those champions don't unite. All the resources of the mind and the will which, for far too long, have been pouring out of each country separately in the name of the same great cause of Civilisation, should surely be united since our enemies have joined together to destroy it. Now, this open and passionate collaboration of minds and wills of all those who in your country and in mine, are marching towards the same light, isn't, henceforth, conceivable unless our two nations are in alliance.

Various reasons might be adduced to explain why this noble vision has not yet been translated into reality. De Gaulle's faith in that Anglo–French future must have been sorely tested by the British Government's insistence on trying to further a relationship with Vichy, a regime whose proponents were no less scathing about the Free French than they were about the English. In one of his broadcasts in 1943, Henriot chose as his subject La France 'libre et combattante':

They've given the name of 'fighting France' to the most amazing rag-bag, the most ill-assorted collection of hotheads, crazy egg-heads, embittered malcontents, frustrated place-seekers and greedy mercenaries that has ever been assembled. Among their ranks, you can number incompetent generals, genuine officer adventurers, youthful enthusiasts alongside precocious go-getters, discredited politicians cheek by jowl with pretentious imbeciles. How can any Frenchmen not throw up when presented with a bunch of characters like this and is supposed to accept that they're great men?

I ask you! We're asked to believe that these grotesque farces, these displays of buffoonery, these generals who beg for absolution and offer to demonstrate their prowess in treachery after they've already proved it in incompetence, these venal politicians, these hired hacks, these pseudo-nationalists who've drifted off into Gaullist hysteria, these Catholics touched by Stalinist grace – all these are the true face of France! the France of Vercingetorix, Joan of Arc, Bayard, Colbert, Richelieu, Louis XIV, Napoleon, Charles X, Lyautey and Foch!

A further contributory factor might conceivably have been the lack of true sympathy between Churchill and de Gaulle. In their writings and on those public occasions when formality required it of them, they paid fulsome tribute to each other, but their contrasting temperaments precluded a deep or durable relationship. Churchill was sentimental, gregarious, romantic, occasionally petty but fundamentally magnani-mous. De Gaulle was aloof, much more self-contained, inflexible when it came to France's interests and more realistic, to the point of being cynical, in assessing character and motive. Like Churchill, he was a superb orator and a magnificent writer. He establishes this, and at the same time demonstrates why he proved so implacable an ally, with the opening paragraph of his war memoirs:

My whole life long I have cherished a particular idea of France. It has been inspired by sentiment as well as reason. The emotional side of my nature instinctively visualises France as the princess in a fairy story or the Madonna of a wall-fresco, meant for some eminent and exceptional destiny. I have the instinctive belief that Providence has created her for outstanding successes or exemplary disasters. If it should, however, happen that her words or deeds are marked with mediocrity, then I feel in the presence of some absurd anomaly which is attributable to the defects of Frenchmen but in no way to the spirit of the country itself. At the same time, the rational part of me is convinced that France can be true to herself only in the front rank: that only vast enterprises have the power to compensate for the temptations towards disunity that are part of her people's nature; that our country, such as it is, when set beside other countries, such as they are, must, because its very life is at stake, aim high and always stand tall. To put it simply, I believe that if it cannot be great, France cannot be France.

De Gaulle and Churchill should have been closer allies than they turned out to be. Churchill was the most Francophile of the British War Cabinet. In a speech to the House of Commons on 2 August 1944, he declared: 'All my life, I have been grateful for the contribution France has made to the glory and culture of Europe – above all for the sense of personal liberty and the rights of man that has radiated from the soul of France.' De Gaulle, for his part, could, on occasion, be no less generous in his praise of Britain but he became convinced that it harboured secret designs on the French overseas empire in the Middle East and in Africa. Anthony Eden, another authentic Francophile, was later to say in his memoirs:

> The fervour of his faith made him at times too suspicious of the intentions of others . . . The schemes and greed not infrequently attributed to Britain . . . were many of them insubstantial myths. We did not want Madagascar, or Jibuti, nor to succeed to the French position there or elsewhere . . . but I doubt if General de Gaulle ever believed this.

Be that as it may, de Gaulle had grounds for feeling increasingly resentful. After America entered the war in December 1941, he was pointedly excluded from top-level planning sessions and from the military operations that followed. No Free French forces were allowed to participate in Operation 'Torch', the Allied invasion of French North Africa, which was launched on 7–8 November 1942. The Americans, who never trusted de Gaulle, and who had maintained full diplomatic relations with Vichy since the Armistice, planned to instal either Admiral Darlan or General Giraud as head of French North Africa once it was liberated; Churchill acquiesced. In the event, their choice fell on Darlan, who was conveniently on an official tour of North Africa at the time. On 11 November he was disavowed by Vichy, and on 24 December he was assassinated by Bonnier de la Chapelle, a young man sent over by the French Resistance. Even when it came to replacing Darlan, de Gaulle was excluded. General Giraud was appointed High Commissioner for French North Africa and, on 4 June 1943, he was made Joint President, alongside de Gaulle, of the French Committee of National Liberation. He proved to be vain and politically inept and he was forced to resign five months later, leaving de Gaulle, once again, as undisputed leader of the Free French. Despite this, the Americans continued to exclude him from all the top-level discussions in Teheran, Yalta and Potsdam. In doing so, they incurred de Gaulle's undying antagonism: what wounded him even more than their distrust of him personally was the fact that they rejected the notion of France as a Great Power.

In November 1944, de Gaulle was convinced that Europe's future equilibrium would be best guaranteed through a Franco–British pact. He believed that America and Russia would be 'hobbled by their rivalries' and would be unlikely to raise objections. In his war memoirs, he described how Churchill and Eden reacted to his plan, which he unveiled on the eve of a fresh Allied offensive:

> During the entire day of November 13, under ceaselessly falling snow, Mr Churchill saw the newborn French Army, its major units in position, its services functioning, its general staffs at their work, its generals confident; all were prepared for offensive, which was, in fact, to be launched the next day. Churchill appeared deeply impressed, and declared that he felt more justified than ever in placing his confidence in France.
>
> Churchill's confidence, however, was insufficient for him to adopt, in our regard, that policy of frank solidarity which might have re-established Europe and maintained Western prestige in the Middle East, in Asia, and in Africa. The visit he paid to us was perhaps the last possible occasion to bring him to a change of heart. I took every opportunity to do so during the conversations we had together.

His arguments failed to command English support:

> The Prime Minister departed on November 14 to inspect the British sector of the front. Eden had already returned to London. From the statements both had made, it was apparent that England was in favour of France's political re-emergence, that she would go on doing so for reasons of equilibrium, tradition and security, that she wanted a formal alliance with us, but would not agree to linking her strategy with ours . . . The peace we French hoped to build in harmony with what we regarded as logic and justice, the British found it expedient to view in terms of pragmatism and compromise. Furthermore, they were pursuing certain specific goals, which, in areas where the positions of states and the balance of power had not yet been settled, offered to Britain's ambitions all manner of opportunities to manipulate and expand.

De Gaulle's scepticism over Churchill's personal commitment to France was unfounded. Churchill had genuinely admired France and the French when he rode with his father through Paris in 1883, and that admiration lasted his whole life. He expressed it particularly eloquently in a speech he delivered at Metz on 15 July 1946 when France was still in political turmoil in the aftermath of the Second World War:

> There can be no revival of Europe, with its culture, its charm, its tradition

and its mighty power, without a strong France. Many nations in the past have wished and tried to be strong. But never before has there been such a clear need for one country to be strong as there is now for France. When I think of the young Frenchmen growing into manhood in this shattered and bewildered world, I cannot recall any generation in any country before whose eyes duty is written more plainly or in more gleaming characters.

Two hundred years ago in England, the Elder and the greater Pitt addressed this invocation to his fellow-countrymen, torn, divided and confused by faction as they then were. 'Be one people.' That was his famous invocation. And in our island, for all its fog and muddles, we are one people today, and dangers if they threaten will only bind us more firmly together.

Using my privilege as your old and faithful friend, I do not hesitate to urge upon all Frenchmen, worn and worried though they may be, to unite in the task of leading Europe back in peace and freedom to broader and better days. By saving yourselves you will save Europe and by saving Europe you will save yourselves.

These were Churchill's personal views, however. They were shared neither by members of his own party, which was, in any event, in Opposition at that time, nor by the ruling Labour Party. If any 'special relationships' were going to be formed in the post-war world, it soon became clear that they were not going to be between Britain and France. While British eyes looked westward across the Atlantic, France once again looked to the east, as it had felt obliged to do in the 1920s. The consequences for contemporary Europe have been momentous.

★

In his memoirs, de Gaulle relates that shortly before the total collapse of Germany, he received a memorandum from Himmler. The German leader accepted that his own cause was irretrievably lost and then asked, 'But what will *you* do now? Rely on the Americans and the British? They will simply treat you as a satellite . . . In point of fact, the only road that can lead on to greatness, and to independence is an *entente* with defeated Germany.' Opportunistic or not, the sentiments were impeccable: only the timing was wrong. The time was still inopportune in September 1946, when, in the course of a major speech at Zurich, Churchill declared: 'I am now going to say something which will astonish you. The first step in the recreation of the European family must be a partnership between France and Germany. In this way only, can France recover the moral and cultural leadership of Europe. There can be no revival of Europe without a spiritually great France and a spiritually great Germany.' Whether they achieved 'spiritual greatness' must remain debatable, but just over a decade later the first major steps towards Franco–German partnership were taken. Britain remained aloof.

In the immediate post-war years, the French needed some convincing that Britain's attitude to European security had in any way changed. They were uneasy over Britain's traditional reluctance to commit land-forces to the Continent; they were unenthusiastic at the prospect of a European defence force to which Britain would contribute the sailors, America the airmen and France the bulk of the soldiers. President Auriol expressed his misgivings in his diary on 5 August 1950: 'I am petrified by the attitude of the English. The British people really have no sense of international or European solidarity.'

The extent to which Britain's Labour Government resented the French attitude is recorded in the diary of Sir George Mallaby. He describes a Cabinet meeting on this issue:

> The discussion was about the French, their political instability, the deficiencies of their armed forces, etc. Someone was suggesting that the French were very critical of us, that they expected us to do far more for the defence of Western Europe than we were doing, and so on. 'What the hell right have they got to criticize us?' [Attlee] shouted. 'Tell them to go and clear up their own bloody mess. They haven't got any decent generals. They haven't had a good general since Prince Eugène – and he served their enemies.'

The point of Attlee's quip was that during the War of the Spanish Succession Prince Eugène of Savoy had fought brilliantly for the English against Louis XIV. Just a few years later, History had a further irony in store. It was as dark as any in this long chronicle of Anglo–French involvement in warfare. It came as a consequence of one of the most outstanding operations Britain and France fought together as allies; it earned international obloquy for both countries and it indelibly stained the reputation of the one British politician to resign from Chamberlain's cabinet in 1938 over his Czechoslovak policy, Sir Anthony Eden.

It was curiously fitting that the end of a chapter should be enacted in Egypt, because the *Entente Cordiale* of 1904 was in large measure fashioned out of the need to resolve Anglo–French rivalries there. The *casus belli* was the Suez Canal, which itself was an example of Anglo–French enterprise. Built in 1869 by a Frenchman, Ferdinand de Lesseps, its headquarters remained in Paris throughout the Suez Company's life; though Britain had been the major shareholder since 1875. Britain was in the process of disengaging relatively peacefully from Egypt in the 1950s, after seventy years of military occupation, when what was perceived as a particularly potent menace to the peace of the Middle East arrived in the person of General Nasser. Egyptian nationalism was already inflamed with the setting-up in 1947 of the new state of Israel, and Arab states throughout the region were in the process of flexing their muscles. On 1 March 1956, the youthful King Hussein of Jordan dismissed the British General Sir John Glubb as head of his army, and on 26 July Nasser nationalised the Suez Canal. The French and British Governments, conscious of the dangers of appeasing dictators, resolved to topple Nasser without delay but were aware that the United Nations would be unlikely to give them permission to intercede. In October 1956, they secretly conspired with Israel to fashion a pretext: Israel would invade Egypt and make for the Suez Canal. England and France would intervene to 'separate the combatants', regain control of the Canal and the humiliated Nasser would inevitably fall from power. The final details were agreed at Sèvres, in the salon of the home of the Bonnier de la Chapelle family, who had supplied the assassin of Admiral Darlan in 1943. Israel attacked on 29 October; on 31 October British and French planes bombed Egypt's main airfields; on 2 November the United Nations General Assembly called for a cease-fire; on 4 November Egypt blocked the Canal; on 5 November British and French paratroops were dropped on Port Said to be followed next day by further troops from amphibious landing-craft. That same day, a cease-fire was ordered and fighting ceased. It was a much less costly action than the Anglo–French campaign in the Crimean War but decidedly more inglorious.

The action was called off less because of the unanimous disapproval of the United Nations or the Russian threat to launch rocket attacks against Paris and London than because of a major run on the pound and American refusal to sanction support from the International Monetary Fund unless Britain and France promptly withdrew. Eden, a chronically sick man, resigned in January 1957, his reputation grievously damaged by his persistent refusal to admit that any plot with the French and Israelis had ever been hatched. His obituary writer was to say in *The Times* in January 1977: 'He was the last Prime Minister to believe Britain was a great power and the first to confront a crisis which proved she was not.'

Thereafter, Britain was to forge ever closer links with the USA, while France pursued a radically different policy. Unwilling to become an American satellite, France proceeded to develop its own nuclear *force de frappe* and it resolutely stood outside NATO. It did something even more radical and in so doing found the best possible way of insuring against yet another invasion from a renascent Germany. In 1957, France and Germany signed the Treaty of Rome thereby implementing what Himmler and Churchill had each advocated in the mid 1940s. On the very day that the Suez operation was stopped in its tracks, Germany's President Adenauer is said to have consoled France's Prime Minister Guy Mollet with the words 'Europe will be your revenge.' Euro-phobes and Euro-fantatics, on either side of the Channel, have had ample opportunity to ponder the consequences ever since.

★

While the momentous Franco–German negotiations were in train, de Gaulle was out of office. In 1947, frustrated by the party bickering between the political leaders of the Fourth Republic, he had retired into private life at Colombey-les-deux-Eglises, in anticipation of the national crisis that he felt only he would be considered competent to resolve. The urgent summons came in the spring of 1958 when the increasingly bloody civil war in Algeria, still technically part of mainland France, threatened to spread to the mother country itself. With consummate statesmanship, de Gaulle ended the deadlock. He was the one French leader of sufficient stature to take the crucial action of clearing the road towards Algerian independence and of ensuring that his decision – intolerable to a large and vociferous minority – was enforced.

In Paris, on 6 November 1958, amid the pomp and panache of a French State occasion, he presented the Croix de la Libération to Churchill, who had retired from active political life. Churchill, now in his eighty-fourth year, showed that he had lost none of his wit or his love of France:

> I am going to speak English today. I have often made speeches in French, but that was wartime, and I do not wish to subject you to the ordeals of darker days.
>
> I am particularly happy that it should be my old friend and comrade, General de Gaulle, who should be paying me this honour. He will always be remembered as the symbol of the soul of France and of the unbreakable integrity of her spirit in adversity. I remember, when I saw him in the sombre days of 1940, I said, 'Here is the Constable of France.' How well he lived up to that title!
>
> Now he is back again in a position of the greatest and gravest responsibility for his country. The problems which confront us are no less important than our struggle for survival eighteen years ago. Indeed, in some ways they may be more complicated, for there is no clear-cut objective of victory in our sight. It is harder to summon, even among friends and allies, the vital unity of purpose amidst the perplexities of a world situation which is neither peace nor war.
>
> I trust that I may be permitted these observations of a very general character. I think that I can claim always to have been a friend of France. Certainly your great country and your valiant people have held a high place in my thoughts and affection in all the endeavours and great events with which we have been associated in the last half-century. Some of these events have been terrible: they have brought great suffering on the world and on our peoples. The future is uncertain, but we can be sure that if Britain and France, who for so long have been the vanguard of the Western civilization, stand together, with our Empires, our American friends, and our other allies and associates, then we have grounds for sober confidence and high hope.
>
> I thank you all for the honour you have done me.
> *Vive la France!*

The speech suited the occasion admirably: the sentences as beautifully fashioned as his listeners would have expected of a legendary orator who had been awarded the Nobel Prize for Literature in 1953. But one can clearly see, with the advantages of hindsight, that the resounding peroration indicates why Britain's applications to join the European Common Market in the 1960s were twice rejected. Just as in November 1944 Churchill had shown de Gaulle that rather than the general's vision of an even-closer Anglo–French alliance the British envisaged a much wider partnership with members of the English-speaking world, so, again, in November 1958, with his references to 'our Empires' and 'our American friends', he effectively demonstrated that Britain and France were setting off down diverging roads.

When, belatedly, in 1963 Britain made its first formal request to join the European Common Market, President de Gaulle's veto was applied not, as Francophobes were quick to allege, in pique or with rancour, but for what can be seen to be cogent and well-argued reasons. After stressing that agriculture was an essential element within the French economy, de Gaulle went on:

> When Great Britain applied for membership of the Common Market, it did so after earlier refusing to participate in the community that was being built, after having set up a Free Trade area with six other states, and, finally – I can say this, the negotiations conducted for so long on this subject can still be recalled – after putting pressure on the Six to prevent the work of the Common Market from getting under way. Later, Britain, in its turn, applied to join – but on its own conditions.
>
> This undoubtedly raises – for each of the six member States and for England – problems of great dimensions.
>
> England is, in effect, insular and maritime. It is linked through its trade, its markets and its food supply to very diverse and often very distant countries. Its activities are essentially industrial and commercial, and only slightly agricultural. In short, the nature, structure and economic context of England differ profoundly from those of the other States of Europe.
>
> What is to be done so that Britain – in the way it lives, the way it produces, the way it trades – may be incorporated into the Common Market in the way it has been conceived and in the way it now functions? As an example, the way in which the people of Great Britain feed themselves is in fact by importing foodstuffs purchased at low prices in the two Americas or in the former Dominions, while still granting large subsidies to British farmers. This is obviously quite incompatible with the system the Six have quite naturally set up for themselves . . .

After deciding that the different approaches between Britain and the Six were too great to reconcile, de Gaulle concluded:

> What Britain has done over the centuries and throughout the world is recognised as gigantic, even though there have often been conflicts with France. The glorious participation of Great Britain in the victory that crowned the First World War, we French will always admire. As for the role played by Britain at the most dramatic and decisive moment of the Second World War, no one has the right to forget it.
>
> Truly, the fate of the free world, and first of all our own and even that of the United States and of Russia, has depended to a large extent on the

resolution, the steadfastness and the courage of the British people such as Churchill gave them the will to be. Even today no one can dispute the worth and the valour of the British.

I therefore repeat that even if the Brussels negotiations do not succeed at the present time, nothing would prevent the signing of an agreement between the Common Market and Britain that would safeguard trade. Neither would anything prevent the maintenance of the close relations between Britain and France and the continuation and development of their co-operation in all fields, especially those of science, technology and industry as, indeed, the two countries have just demonstrated by their decision to join forces in constructing the Concorde supersonic aircraft.

It was not until 1 January 1994 that it became apparent that – not for the first time in his political career – de Gaulle was here delivering a coded message. With the lifting of the thirty-year embargo on sensitive classified documents, it was revealed that, in an attempt to weaken his resolve, the British Government offered to share some of the secrets of its nuclear weaponry. In the event, he stuck to his principles, an attitude described by Foreign Office representatives as a characteristic 'fit of the sulks'. The British press ran true to form. Little or none of de Gaulle's solidly argued speech was relayed across the Channel. In populist editorials and cartoons, he was portrayed as stubborn and spiteful, paying back his one-time hosts for not treating him with the deference that he – quite misguidedly, of course – believed to be his due. And since all French politicians were assumed to sing the same Gaullist song no publicity was ever accorded a speech made on 21 November 1963 in the French Senate by Pierre Marcilhacy. It was during a debate on foreign affairs at a time when the French populist press had been making much capital out of the misfortunes of the British Cabinet Minister John Profumo, who felt obliged to resign for lying to the House of Commons over the liaison he had had with Christine Keeler, a young woman of easy virtue:

> I propose to indulge myself by speaking about England. For France, England is a constant preoccupation, a sort of mirror, an association we either love or loathe. France veers between Anglomania and Anglophobia. And what's worth noting is that it's not unknown for our Government's hostility towards England to co-exist with Anglomania in certain sections of French society. All this comes and goes and – my God! – relations between us aren't as bad as all that. This is why I deplore the fact that quite recently, people have been sounding those familiar anti-English chords

and, indeed, organising a whole concert because – let's not beat about the bush – of an incident involving a British Cabinet Minister, an incident involving what we could term the oldest sin in the world, which, on other occasions, we French have often treated with a benevolent if not guilty indulgence.

Thereafter, a certain number of criticisms have been orchestrated, which some French people, including your humble servant, have found rather disagreeable. We've borne them with some discomfort and we could prefer it all to be quickly forgotten and that we concentrate instead on something that shows Great Britain in its true glory. Because after the ordeal I've just mentioned, what other country would have dared to submit such a case to an impartial inquiry for the report on that inquiry to be published without Her Majesty's Government's changing a single word? What an example of true democracy in action! How desirable it would be for inquiries of that nature to be held in other countries and – why not say it? – sometimes in our own country too.

Yes, Great Britain is the land of democracy. I readily recognise that there are detestable aspects of the English character. I know that the British often consider that 'fair play' is a concept that should apply to others less than to themselves. I know that they have the great drawback, a grave one in my view, of speaking English [*laughter*] and that their taste in food is abominable and that they have the major defect of driving on the left. All the same, when conflict breaks out and when Great Britain sends its boys to the battlefields, they – in the magnificent words of an English author – they know how to die well: and they often die for us [*applause*].

If I cast a quick glance over the history of Anglo–French relations, I observe with some astonishment that the more authoritarian France is the worse those relations become, and that when our country is incontrovertibly on the side of liberty and democracy – those two words are inseparable – then we're on good terms with our neighbours. Ladies and gentlemen, I'm a parliamentarian whom nobody can accuse of being an Anglomaniac – I can scarcely understand English, I hardly ever speak it and that I much regret – but for me, Great Britain is the country where, after Holland, I'd like best to live because for four years, it was over the British radio that I heard the heartbeat of Liberty: that is something I shall never forget.

To end on a slightly less serious note, I'll say, paraphrasing the English national anthem, on behalf of freedom, for democracy and for France, in equal measure: God save England! [*Applause from the left, from the centre and from various benches on the right.*]

Senator Marcilhacy's encomium was challenged head-on by André Avice who, in 1964, published a 400-page diatribe against what he alleged were the unrivalled iniquities of the English. It bore the title *La Mésentente Cordiale* and demonstrated that twenty years after the execution of Henriot and Paquis, their baleful spirit – and their paranoia – was alive and spitting:

> We're not taken in by what you say, sir, because those of us who've lived long lives have regretfully to remind you that England's heroism has only ever been available for its own causes . . .
>
> It's because this is something we've never forgotten – even if it makes the ignorant fairly burst with indignation – that we've decided to illustrate the cover of our book with the 1899 cartoon by Willette which has as its caption the words: 'The day when perfidious Albion finally kicks the bucket will be a day of universal rejoicing.'
>
> Yes, that caption provides the best possible reply to Field Marshal Douglas Haig's private diary . . . published in 1964 in the Gaullist weekly *Candide* (which is not as candid as people think). It's a diary full of bad faith, typically English, which is one long insult to the French Army . . .
>
> Yes, that caption will also act as the ideal riposte to the declaration made in June 1940 over London radio, with the backing of the English Government, by the South African Smuts, a British Field Marshal, when he told the whole world 'France is definitely dead!'
>
> Yes, that caption can serve as a comment on Churchill's cowardice, who, when he wanted to announce a victory, no matter over whom, to the British people and to enlist their whole-hearted support for the war, got the whole of the English Navy, on 3 July 1940, to destroy the French fleet, which had been disarmed after the Armistice and at anchor off Mers-el-Kebir. 1,300 French sailors were victims of that odious act of aggression. England was not at war with France and that ignoble act was a flagrant violation of international law.
>
> And finally, that caption will serve as judgement on that further example of English cowardice when, in the course of the case brought against Marshal Pétain by the first government of de Gaulle, on the subject of the secret agreement between George VI and Pétain, which, eventually, was completely authenticated, the British Government – with Churchill still at its head – decided that by keeping silent, it could have condemned for alleged dealings with the Germans, the man who had made an agreement with its own king. As complete silence was the *sine qua non* condition of that agreement, negotiations over which began on the very day the Armistice was signed with Germany, the Marshal, true to his word, let himself be condemned and didn't mention George VI.
>
> This was how England rewarded our country, this was its response to those who still believed they could rely on it to keep its word. The case rests.

Mercifully, Avice's weighty tome, illustrated with a selection of scurrilous anti-English cartoons, passed unnoticed on this side of the

Channel. One can only speculate at the feelings it might have aroused given the execration President de Gaulle earned for himself when, for the second time, he vetoed Britain's second application to join the European Common Market, submitted four years after the first. On 27 November 1967, at a packed press conference, after giving a long and by no means inaccurate account of Britain's evolving attitude towards membership, he speculated why it now seemed so keen to join, and why it should, at one and the same time, be promising to become a model partner yet be insisting on major concessions:

> This attitude can fairly easily be explained. The English people doubtless see more and more clearly that in face of the great movements which are now sweeping the world – the huge power of the United States, the growing power of the Soviet Union, the renascent power of the Continental countries of Europe, the newly emerging power of China – its own structures, its traditions, its activities and even its national character are from now on all at risk. This is brought home to her, day after day, by the grave economic, financial and currency problems with which she is currently contending. This is why she feels the profound need to find some sort of framework, even a European one if need be, which would enable her to safeguard her own identity, to play a leading role, and at the same time, to lighten some of her burden.

He concluded it was Britain that should change its outlook and its practices, not the Six foundation-members: 'If the British Isles are to be truly linked to the Continent, we are talking about the need for vast and profound changes. What is required is not negotiations (which, for the Six, would be the road to chaos if not the destruction of their Community) but the good will and positive action of the great English people which would make their country into one of the pillars of the European community.' It will be for posterity to judge whether President de Gaulle was on this, as on the previous occasion, being casuistic or speaking with the voice of cool reason. For the present, the least that one might suggest after the variety of spirited rearguard actions mounted by British politicians over the first two decades of our membership of the European Community, is that his original misgivings were not altogether misplaced.

★

While French and British negotiators failed to reach agreement in the 1960s and xenophobes in the media of each country loosed off the occasional poisoned barb at the other, there were clear indications in parts of Paris that a fresh wave of Anglomania was breaking. The Sir Winston Churchill Pub opened as did the Bedford Arms and the Gaff, where guests enthusiastically consumed *le sausage and match* [*sic*] or *club sandwish à la milord*. Before Britain was finally admitted to the Common Market in 1973, Paris branches of Jaeger, Burberrys and The White House were already trading with success and style. Their clientèle was the same as it had been at the time of the Bourbon restoration or in the Age of Worth: what the English would call *la crème de la crème* and the French, varying the culinary metaphor, *le gratin*. The new arrivals on the scene, wielding as much power and influence because of their formidable spending-power, were the teenagers (in French *les teens* or *les yé-yé*). Their addiction to pop music, to blue jeans and to fast food affected not only their appearance and their general lifestyle but also their modes of writing and speaking. 1964, the same year as Avice published *La Mésentente Cordiale*, saw the appearance of René Etiemble's *Parlez-vous franglais?* It is rich in hilarious examples of the bizarre Newspeak but the underlying tone is almost as envenomed as that of Avice. For Etiemble, however, the enemy is not England. He is motivated by the same spirit that drove President de Gaulle to keep France outside NATO and develop his own independent nuclear *force de frappe*. It comes across as outspoken, often truculent anti-American-ism but it is essentially the dogged denial, in spite of all the evidence, that France has ceased to be a major power. Consider Etiemble's attack on French restaurateurs who, to demonstrate that they are in the fashionable swim, set out their notices and menu-cards in what they imagine to be English:

Particularly serious is the servility of our shopkeepers who, to attract the punters and indulge their indolence, cover their signs and shop-fronts with English and American words – or their own version of them. When some clever-dick called Louis attracts the GIs and the tourists by naming his establishment Loui's, when our restaurants, so as not to frighten the Yankees off, plaster American over half their menus, when a caterer in Maine advertises *grapefruit cocktail, turtle soup, toasts, mixed grill, lobster cocktail* and *chicken à la king* without supplying a French translation, when a 'restoroute' offers me a *cheeseburger steack* [*sic*], *hot-dogs, club sandwich* and a *steack garni*, without a translation, when Odette Panier, while recommending a hundred Paris restaurants, employs a hundred English words including *eggburger* and *baby cochon de lait*, I can tell you that France is indeed close to becoming the famous *France éternelle*: it's very close indeed finally to popping its clogs.

Thirty years on since Etiemble uttered this *cri de cœur*, the situation would seem, from his point of view, to have deteriorated still further. Fast-food outlets abound, abbreviated, like many imported Anglo–American words, to '*les fasts*', and the McDonald's Empire, on which the sun never sets, is as entrenched in Paris and other major cities as it is everywhere else. Etiemble might, however, find consolation in the knowledge that in England, all the keyterms in the catering industry – for every dish and recipe, for all the employees from *commis-chef* to *maître d'hôtel* – are, like the words *restaurant* and *menu* themselves, still French. As long as discerning English diners seeks *haute cuisine* or *cordon bleu* cooking in establishments that have been awarded their Michelin stars, the spirit if not the names of France will continue to be *de rigueur*.

Another form of Francophilia that has shown no sign of fading is the preference of some English people for living in France rather than in England, either on a permanent basis or for many months of the year. Winston Churchill himself spent lengthy periods of his declining years in the South of France, writing and painting. In 1948, with a bankdraft of a million francs from Time-Life International, he stayed in Aix-en-Provence at the Hôtel du Roy René, working on the second volume of his history of the Second World War, which covers the Fall of France and the Battle of Britain. Thereafter, he stayed regularly with friends: at Lord Beaverbrook's villa, La Capponcina, at Cap d'Ail near Monte Carlo, in Lord Rothermere's villa, La Dragonière, on Cap Martin, or at La Pausa, the villa of Emery Reves. He also made frequent cruises on Aristotle Onassis's yacht *Christina*, which was based on the Riviera. Grahame Greene spent his last years in his seaside villa at Antibes though he allowed his peace to be disturbed when he mounted a personal campaign against the criminal mafia of Nice for persecuting the daughters of close friends of his.

Other English expatriates equally appreciative of the southern French climate but preferring greater seclusion, have elected to settle further inland, in Provence or Languedoc. After living in Corfu, Athens and Alexandria, Lawrence Durrell settled firstly just outside the small medieval village of Sommières, between Nîmes and Montpellier, then in a peasant farmhouse at Engances, near Nîmes. Other writers who found peace in Provence and not a little profit from the books recounting their expatriate experiences have been the actor Dirk Bogarde, in *An Orderly Man*, and Peter Mayle, in two books incorporating the name Provence as a talisman in the title. Whether their fame proves as transient as that of Charles Morgan remains to be seen. It would seem to rest on foundations less solid than that of two other notable English Francophiles who preferred Paris as their alternative home: Nancy Mitford moved there when the war ended, wrote all her best books there and remained there until her death in 1973; Richard Cobb, Emeritus Professor of Modern History of the University of Oxford and our most eminent authority on the French Revolution, has conducted a life-long love-affair with Paris, which has given him, to quote the title of his delightful memoir devoted to it, *A Second Identity*.

Another form of English Francophilia not seen in full flower since the middle of the nineteenth century manifested itself in the high summer of 1968. This is the view, sometimes expressed by intellectual observers, themselves uninvolved in the event in question, that there is something 'special' about the Paris mob in full cry. In the nineteenth century, writers as diverse as George Eliot, Matthew Arnold and Walter Bagehot had felt their adrenalin flowing faster at the spectacle and the same was true of some left-wing journalists reporting on the spectacular demonstrations in Paris in May and June 1968. What began as a student protest at the University of Nanterre, over the need to reform the syllabus and relax campus regulations, quickly mushroomed into a general strike involving nine million workers, which appeared, for a brief period, to threaten the very existence of the Republic itself. Paul Johnson's editorial in the *New Statesman* on 24 May 1968 was positively dithyrambic. He found that in the courtyard of the Faculty of Letters at the Sorbonne 'the heart and brain of the movement, a thousand flowers not only bloom but load the spring air with intellectual incense'. Noting that every conceivable topic was being passionately debated by young and old of every colour and creed, he perceived a 'pentecostal mood in which those speaking different tongues evoke a common understanding'. And displaying the standard left-wing contempt for de Gaulle, he claimed that, in his rage, the President had fallen back on the vernacular of a young subaltern, and called the student demonstrations 'a dog's breakfast'. De Gaulle's dismissive phrase was, in fact, rather more pungent: it was *chie-en-lit* and meant that they had fouled their own nest or shat in their bed. Anyone who has had to clear up after a student sit-in would agree that de Gaulle's barb was not far wide of the mark.

Mervyn Jones, also writing in the *New Statesman*, on 7 June 1968, was, if anything, even more starry-eyed than Paul Johnson:

> I push my way into the Sorbonne. The vast courtyard is filled with the same endlessly talking groups. Total tolerance is the unbroken rule: Maoists offer their intellectual wares side by side with upholders of Yugoslav self-management, Trotskyists with anarchists, Zionists with advocates of Arab liberation. Victor Hugo presides benevolently, red flag strapped to his stone hand.
>
> The young men are intense but strangely calm with a fine inner confidence; eyes red from sleepless nights, but mostly with freshly shaven cheeks or trimmed beards. The girls are lovely with their pale faces, long hair, big serious eyes, and those who aren't intrinsically beautiful are rendered beautiful by their faith and their vivacity. Love is incorporated into discussion by means of squeezed hands and rapid kisses. A pair of militant lesbians, both dazzling, embrace boldly.

That euphoria, conveyed rather more memorably by Wordsworth when evoking the dawn of the French Revolution, proved even more transient in the summer of 1968 than it had been in the early 1790s. While President de Gaulle was uncharacteristically indecisive during the middle part of May, he regained the initiative with consummate political skill. When it began to look as though a Communist-dominated Popular Front was a distinct possibility, he made a magisterial broadcast to the French nation proclaiming an imminent General Election in which the stark choices were represented either as Gaullist order or Red Revolution. The Left and Centre parties lost heavily and the Gaullist vote increased by a clear 20 per cent.

Two years later, British undergraduates, studying in conditions that, in 1968, French students would have given their eye-teeth to acquire, organised a series of sit-ins of their own. The issue, the purely factitious allegation that their teachers were compiling secret files on their political affiliations for onward transmission to Government intelligence agencies or the American CIA, was greeted with blank incomprehension by British Trade Unions whose taxes contributed, in no small measure, to students' maintenance grants. The workers did not, therefore, take to the city streets to show solidarity, and no hard evidence of a single 'political file' was ever unearthed. As de Gaulle observed of the May 1968 events in Paris, half ironically and wholly gnomically: 'As always, France has led the way.'

★

Whether the English like or dislike the French would seem, in the twentieth century, to be as much a matter of social status as of artistic temperament. One is strongly tempted to agree with M. Maurice Druon, at one time French Minister for Cultural Affairs, who observed in an interview in *The Times* on 20 July 1973: 'The élites tend to admire one another and the peoples to despise one another. This means that the first run the risk of disappointing one another and the second of not wanting to know one another.' A significant reservation that might, however, be made is the remarkable number of twinning arrangements that have been established over the post-war years between French and English communities large and small: the committees who manage these tend to be run neither by the social nor the intellectual élite and seem none the less effective for that.

But over the twentieth century as a whole, the most dedicated of English Francophiles have, more often than not, been the artistically creative and the well-to-do, though it was left to Nancy Mitford's relatively well-heeled Uncle Matthew in *The Pursuit of Love* to speak for all xenophobes with his reverberating pronouncement that 'Abroad is unutterably bloody and foreigners are fiends.' The big battalions of English Francophobes read the tabloid newspapers and are avid watchers of television soap-operas and feature films that pander to their prejudices. Their knowledge of France and the French derives principally from media images rather than direct contact: when they venture abroad on holiday, they make for the southern coast of Spain, for Majorca or Ibiza. All of this makes for striking differences between French Anglophobes and English Francophobes. The former have regularly enlisted high intelligence and broad culture to convey their powerful loathing of all things English. The style of the latter has been populist rather than sophisticated and the mood they have most commonly expressed has been contempt rather than active malevolence. Sometimes, the insults traded have seemed mere echoes of each other as when each side attributed the fall of France in 1940 to the cowardice and military incompetence of its ally or, in the post-war years, suspected each other of bad faith and double-dealing over the unravelling of their overseas Empires. And sometimes, the popular stereotypes each has fashioned of the other seem polar opposites: the French popular image of the cold and supercilious English officer, unruffled though the heavens fall, contrasts with the stereotypical Frenchman as an over-excitable, beret-wearing, under-sized buffoon or as an inordinately suave, irresistible gallant capable of incredible feats of sexual athleticism. Their feminine counterparts are the eccentric English spinster with protruding teeth and over-large feet and the pert and provocative piece of French fluff only too ready to translate into action some of the more whimsical game-plans of the *Kama Sutra*.

It matters not that such images have only tenuous connections with reality, that Soho long provided sexual displays much more outrageous than the *Folies Bergères* or that Verlaine and Rimbaud chose to spend their homosexual honeymoon in London while Gide and Marc Allegret spent theirs in Cambridge: in the populist English view, Paris remains the capital of sexual licence while 'French kissing' and 'French knickers' continue to enjoy a *cachet* they may not altogether deserve. The populist English view that the French are both unreliable and immoral dies hard: it can be demonstrated in quips such as Noël Coward's refrain from *Conversation Piece*, 'There's always something fishy about the French' (amended in 1941 by Ivor Novello to 'There's always something Vichy about the French') and in all manner of films, plays and popular jokes right up to the present day from *French without Tears* to *Allo! Allo!* or *The Darling Buds of May*. However, the belief that the French have attitudes to sexual matters more advanced than our own is not confined to regular readers of English tabloid newspapers. When the Wolfenden Bill to relax English laws against male homosexuals was being debated, Field Marshal Montgomery observed on 27 May 1965: 'This sort of thing may be tolerated by the French but *we* are British − thank God!' In much the same spirit, an anonymous patriot once wrote underneath a British Rail poster that proclaimed 'HARWICH FOR THE CONTINENT' the pencilled afterthought 'AND PARIS FOR THE INCONTINENT'. And, reporting in the *Sunday Telegraph* on 16 January 1994, on contrasting attitudes to the marital infidelity of prominent public figures on either side of the Channel, its Paris correspondent declared: 'Adultery is not eulogised but it is considered normal at a certain level of society: indeed, a sophisticated man in Paris who did *not* have affairs, would be considered feeble, even suspect.'

By and large, since Britain was finally admitted to the Common Market in 1973 it would not seem to have done much to revive the *Entente Cordiale*. On the contrary, our membership of the Common Market so far seems to have been characterised primarily by a series of rearguard actions mounted by anti-European English MPs, occasional demonstrations against imports of English lamb by militant French farmers and outbursts of Francophobic spleen in the populist English press.

In the mid 1960s, Sir William Connor, 'Cassandra' of the *Daily Mirror*, could write with grace, wit and erudition in response to an anti-English article that had just appeared in the popular French newspaper *Paris-Jour*. This had called for a ban on drinking Scotch whisky and total silence throughout the forthcoming (separate) visits of Queen Elizabeth and the Beatles. 'If all these things are taken away from England, what is left? Three times nothing – a little island facing our coasts where they eat boiled beef with mint sauce.' This was to 'Cassandra' the crowning insult. He retorted that he could forgive their ban on whisky, their threat to boycott the Beatles and Her Majesty. 'We might even ask to be forgiven for having burnt Mademoiselle d'Arc and for forcing Monsieur Napoleon on St Helena. But not, repeat not, the charge of eating boiled beef with mint sauce! Longbowmen of Crécy! Archers of Agincourt! Arise from your honourable graves and we will teach these French dogs the lessons of 1346 and 1415 once more!'

In the 1980s, the Francophobic campaigns orchestrated by the *Sun* were decidedly more puerile. In January 1984, in one of their periodic protests against the importing of foreign produce – a tactic first put into practice in 1786, with the implementation of the Anglo–French Commercial Treaty – French farmers seized and destroyed a consignment of British lamb. On 13 January, the *Sun* produced a blistering editorial deploring the absence of activity from the Ministry of Agriculture, the Foreign Office and the whole of Whitehall. To make up for this, it urged the British people not to buy 'a single item of French produce, nothing from camembert to their rotten Golden Delicious apples': 'If you want wine, choose German, Italian, Spanish – even

315

Chateau Dorking. Nothing – not even l'amour – is as close to a Frenchman's heart as his wallet. *Let's hit him there and go on hitting until he stops behaving like some evil robber baron out of the darkest pages of history.*' The humour is perceptibly cruder than 'Cassandra's' and the historical reference a great deal less precise: such 'robber barons' as there were in the saga of Anglo–French relations were, almost invariably, English, such as the henchmen of the Black Prince who enriched their estates, still extant today, with the plunder amassed during their *chevauchées* across the French countryside.

The *Sun* followed this with an anti-French joke competition: prize-winning entries ranged from the openly offensive (Q. Why are French roads ranged with poplar trees? A. So that German armies can walk in the shade – this in *1984*!) to the demonstrably inaccurate (Q. What do you call a pretty girl in France? A. A tourist). Claude Sarraute, one of the star-columnists of *Le Monde*, replied in kind on 4 February 1984 with a nosegay of jokes about the English. 'Do you know how to save an Englishman from drowning? – You don't? – Well, good for you!' Or 'What's the difference between an accident and a catastrophe? An accident is when a liner full of English people sinks. A catastrophe is if they can swim.'

Subsequently, the *Sun* offered free lapel-badges to its readers which bore the legend 'Hop off, you Frogs!' and, on another occasion, it invited its readers to assemble on the Channel coast in order to chant in unison at the then President of the European Commission 'Up yours, Delors!' Confronted by antics of this sort, and by the prospect of ever-larger hordes of Union Jack-waving lager louts, almost as intimidating as the invading *godons* of the Hundred Years War, it came as no surprise that a French observer, rather than a Little Englander, should have commented: 'When the Channel Tunnel is opened, England will finally cease to be an island. What a pity!'

*

The opening of the Channel Tunnel restores the physical link between Britain and the European mainland that was severed in prehistoric times when the intervening land was submerged as the northern ice-cap melted in the course of the Holocene Age. And other, less spectacular parallels, can diffidently be drawn between our Anglo–French present and the times when the two nations were still not fully fashioned: between the modern English fashion of setting up second homes in France and the English settlements around Calais and across Aquitaine at the start of the Hundred Years War; between the medieval university system open to French and English students alike and the still expanding 'Erasmus' programme of exchanges between higher educational establishments throughout the Community; between the Plantagenet Kingdom, stretching from the Pentlands to the Pyrenees, in which merchandise could move with minimal interference, and the promises held out by the progenitors of the Single European Market.

For all that, and in spite of the plethora of 'twinning' arrangements between French and British municipalities, and the inauguration of *Le Shuttle*, John Bull and Marianne remain separated by their gender, temperament, social class and political allegiances. As has already been noted (see pages 87–8), the early history of John Bull has been well documented: his prototype was the early eighteenth-century English gentleman farmer, gruff, bluff, plain-dealing and set in his ways. Marianne's origins are still the subject of speculation but the most persuasive hypothesis locates them in the last decade of that same century, in a rural fête at Montpellier during the Terror, when the part of the Goddess of Reason was played by a local 'Marianne', a regional term for a prostitute. The name achieved national prominence soon after Louis-Napoleon's *coup* of 1851 when the question '*Connaissez-vous Marianne?*' was part of the membership ritual for those seeking to join the secret society plotting to replace the Bonapartist regime with a Republic. Anglophobes had their ingrained suspicions confirmed by the revelation that the conspirators' headquarters was in London. For the first decades of her life, therefore, until the Republic was finally established, Marianne was a political subversive, ready to take to the barricades like her bare-breasted cousin, Liberty, as depicted in Delacroix's famous painting. From first to last, John Bull has stood for the Establishment and for Law and Order. As long as these two figures retain their emblematic significance, therefore, *entente* between them is unlikely to be either *cordiale* or durable.

As the twentieth century nears its end, the governments of each country continue to view each other with considerable circumspection. The French remain convinced that the British have a special and fundamentally anti-French understanding with the Americans; the

British strongly suspect that the French have an equally special and essentially anti-British understanding with the Germans. Each suspects – and not infrequently accuses – the other of being bad Europeans: the British believe that French are covertly running the European Community as a latter-day version of the Napoleonic Empire; the French, noting Britain's crab-wise approach to entering the Community and the vociferous opposition of both right- and left-wing British politicians, are all too ready to perceive the machinations of *l'Albion perfide*, and to conclude *plus, ça change, plus c'est la même chose . . .*

While one can only speculate about the ultimate shape and constitution of the European Community and the status within it of Britain and France, it is surely unthinkable that either will ever go to war with one another again or be reduced to the status of mere provincials. Though they no longer bestride the world's stage as the major imperial powers that once they were, they still have enduring claims to greatness. Other countries can advance the claims of outstanding artists and thinkers or point to a particular period when, in one area of cultural achievement or another, they were pre-eminent. But no two other countries have a heritage that has been enriched over so long a period of time as England and France. And no two countries have made so powerful and protracted an impact as these two have upon the lives of one another. Over a span of almost a thousand years, no nation has had so many dealings with the English as the French. In that same time, no people have exerted so important an influence on the French consciousness as the English. And not on the French consciousness alone: more English dead lie buried beneath the killing fields of northern France than anywhere else on earth. Because of the history and the geography they share, they seem likely, whatever the future holds, to go on viewing each other with that mixture of resentment and respect that has characterised their relationship over the centuries. Because of each country's shortcomings and misdemeanours, the other will, on occasion, see it as fit subject for censure and self-congratulation. Because of each country's unique merits, it will remain, for the other, the one nation to which it can never feel quite superior. If only for those two reasons, it is to be hoped that whatever the success of Europe's bureaucrats in standardising its law and its currency, the English and the French will continue to cultivate the fundamental differences between each other and to relish their effect.

Bibliography

Unless otherwise stated, all English titles were published in London and all French titles were published in Paris.

General

N. Calder, *The English Channel*, Chatto & Windus, 1989.

C. Campos, *The Image of France*, Oxford University Press, 1965.

I. F. Clarke, *Voices Prophesying War: 1763–1984*, Oxford University Press, 1966.

C. Crossley & I. Small (eds.), *Studies in Anglo–French Cultural Relations: Imagining France*, Macmillan, 1988.

F. Crouzet, 'Problèmes de la communication franco–britanniques aux xixe et xxe siècles', in *Revue historique*, 1975, pp. 105–134.

P. Fussell, *Abroad*, Oxford University Press, 1980.

S. Harrison, *The Channel*, Collins, 1989.

J. Joll, *Britain and Europe – Pitt to Churchill: 1793–1940*, Nicholas Kaye, 1950.

D. Johnson, F. Crouzet & F. Bedarida (eds.), *Britain and France: Ten Centuries*, Dawson, 1980.

J. J. Jusserand, *Shakespeare en France sous l'ancien régime*, Armand Colin, 1898.

P.-O. Lapie, *Les Anglais à Paris de la Renaissance à l'Entente Cordiale*, Fayard, 1976.

N. Legrand & R. Grant, *Mésentente cordiale*, Jarrolds, 1952.

C. Mackworth, *English Interludes*, Routledge, 1974.

W. E. Mann, *Robinson Crusoe en France*, Davy, 1916.

C. Maxwell, *The English Traveller in France: 1698–1815*, Routledge, 1932.

S. Osgood, 'Le mythe de la "perfide Albion" en France', in *Cahiers d'histoire*, 1975, pp. 5–20.

R. E. Palmer (ed.), *French Travellers in England: 1600–1900*, Hutchinson, 1960.

R. Postgate & A. Vallance, *Those Foreigners*, Harrap, 1937.

E. J. Rathery, *Des relations sociales et intellectuelles entre la France et l'Angleterre*, Brière, 1855.

F. C. Roe, *French Travellers in Britain: 1800–1926*, Nelson, 1928.

H. D. Schmidt, 'The idea and slogan of "Perfidious Albion" ', in *Journal of the History of Ideas*, 1953, pp. 604–616.

R. W. Seton-Watson, *Britain in Europe: 1789–1914. A survey of foreign policy*, Cambridge University Press, 1945.

E. Starkie, *From Gautier to Eliot: The Influence of France on English Literature*, Hutchinson, 1960.

G. Tabouis, *Albion perfide ou loyale: de la guerre de cent ans à nos jours*, Payot, 1938.

A. J. P. Taylor, *The Troublemakers: Dissent Over Foreign Policy – 1792–1939*, Hamish Hamilton, 1957.

P. Van Tieghem, *Les influences étrangères sur la littérature française: 1550–1880*, Presses Universitaires de France, 1961.

Sir A. W. Ward & G. P. Gooch (eds.), *The Cambridge History of British Foreign Policy*, 3 vols, Cambridge University Press, 1923.

F. M. Wilson (ed.), *Strange Island: Britain through Foreign Eyes: 1395–1940*, Longmans, 1955.

T. Zeldin, *France: 1848–1945*, 2 vols, Clarendon Press, Oxford, 1973–77.

Chapter 1: The Growth of Nationalism in the Middle Ages

C. T. Allmand (ed.), *Society at War: The Experience of England and France During the Hundred Years War*, Barnes & Noble, 1973.

—— (ed.), *War, Literature and Politics in the Late Middle Ages*, Liverpool University Press, 1976.

G. Ascoli, *La Grande Bretagne devant l'opinion française: depuis la guerre de cent ans jusqu'à la fin du xviᵉ siècle*, Gamber, 1947.

I. S. T. Aspin (ed.), *Anglo–Norman Political Songs*, Oxford, 1953.

J. Barnie, *War in Medieval Society: Social Values in the Hundred Years War*, Weidenfeld & Nicolson, 1974.

E. Bourassin, *La France anglaise: 1415–1453*, Tallandier, 1981.

G. Doncieux (ed.), *Le Romancero populaire de la France*, 1904.

K. Fowler, *The Hundred Years War*, Macmillan, 1971.

J. Froissart, *Chronicles* (Lord Berners' translation), 6 vols, Nutt, 1901–3.

E. Freeman, *History of the Norman Conquest*, 5 vols, 1867–79.

D. Howarth, *1066: the Year of the Conquest*, Collins, 1977.

J. Huizinga, *The Waning of the Middle Ages*, Arnold, 1924.

—— *Men and Ideas*, Eyre & Spottiswoode, 1960.

F. Hutchinson, *Henry V*, Eyre & Spottiswoode, 1967.

R. L. Kilgour, *The Decline of Chivalry as shown in French Literature of the Late Middle Ages*, Cambridge, Massachusetts, 1937.

M. D. Legge, *Anglo–Norman Literature and its Background*, Oxford University Press, 1963.

P. S. Lewis, 'War, Propaganda and Historiography in Fifteenth-Century France and England', in *Transactions of the Royal Historical Society*, 1964, pp. 1–21.

R. Neillands, *The Hundred Years War*, Routledge, 1990.

J. J. N. Palmer, *England, France and Christendom: 1377–99*, Routledge, 1972.

E. Perroy, *The Hundred Years War*, Eyre & Spottiswoode, 1951.

P. Rickard, *Britain in Medieval French Literature: 1100–1500*, Cambridge University Press, 1956.

T. Rowley, *The Norman Heritage*, Routledge, 1983.

V. J. Scattergood, *Politics and Poetry in the Fifteenth Century*, Blandford Press, 1971.

D. Seward, *The Hundred Years War*, Constable, 1978.

J. Sumption, *The Hundred Years War: (Vol. 1) Trial by Battle*, Faber, 1990.

T. F. Tout, *France and England: Their Relations in the Middle Ages and Now*, Manchester University Press, 1922.

M. Vale, *The Angevin Legacy and the Hundred Years War*, Blackwell, Oxford, 1990.

T. Wright, *Political Poems and Songs*, 2 vols, 1859–61.

*Chapter 2: The Religious and Cultural Divide in the Sixteenth
and Seventeenth Centuries*

P. Allen, *The Plays of Shakespeare and Chapman in relation to French History*, Denis Archer, 1933.

G. Ascoli, *La Grande Bretagne devant l'opinion française au xviie siècle*, Gamber, 1930.

C. Bastide, *Anglais et Française de xviie siècle*, Alcan, 1912.

M. De Béthune, duc de Sully, *Mémoires*, 1638.

L. Charlanne, *L'Influence française en Angleterre au XVIIe siècle*, Société française de l'imprimerie, 1906.

A. F. B. Clarke, *Boileau and French Classical Critics in England: 1660–1830*, Champion, 1925.

R. Dallington, *The View of France*, 1604.

S. Gunn, 'The French Wars of Henry VIII', in J. Black (ed.), *The Origins of War in Early Modern Europe*, J. Donald, Edinburgh, 1987.

J. R. Hale, *War and Society in Renaissance Europe: 1450–1620*, Fontana, 1985.

J. Howell, *Instructions for Forreine Travel*, 1642.

G. Kipling, *The Triumph of Honour*, Leiden University Press, The Hague, 1977.

K. Lambley, *The Teaching of French in England in Tudor and Stuart Times*, Manchester University Press, 1920.

S. Lee, *The French Renaissance in England*, Oxford, 1910.

Dr M. Lister, *A Journey to Paris in the Year 1698*, 1698.

J. Lough (ed.), *Locke's Travels in France: 1675–1679*, Cambridge University Press, 1953.

—— *France Observed in the Seventeenth Century by British Travellers*, Oriel Press, 1984.

R. K. Marshall, *Queen of Scots*, H.M.S.O., 1986.

M. Mission, *Mémoires et observations faites par un voyageur en Angleterre*, 1698.

E. Perlin, *Description des Royaulmes d'Angleterre et d'Ecosse*, 1558.

D. L. Potter, 'The Duc de Guise and the fall of Guise', in *English Historical Review*, 1983.

J. G. Russell, *The Field of Cloth of Gold*, Routledge, 1969.

S. Sorbière. *Relation d'un voyage en Angleterre*, 1666.

D. R. Starkey, *The Reign of Henry VIII*, G. Philip, 1985.

M. Strachey, *The Life and Adventures of Thomas Coryate*, Oxford University Press, 1962.

Chapter 3: *Cosmopolitanism and Xenophobia in the Eighteenth Century*

F. Acomb, *Anglophobia in France: 1763–1789*, Duke University Press, N. Carolina, 1950.

J. Arbuthnot, *The History of John Bull* (1712), ed. A. W. Bower and R. A. Erickson, Oxford University Press, 1976.

G. Bonno, *La constitution britannique devant l'opinion française de Montesquieu à Bonaparte*, Champion, 1931.

—— 'La Culture et la civilisation britannique devant l'opinion française de la Paix d'Utrecht aux *Lettres Philosophiques*', in *Transactions of the American Philosophical Society*, 1948.

J. S. Bromley, 'Britain and Europe in the Eighteenth Century', in *History*, 1981, pp. 394–412.

Lord Chesterfield, *Letters to His Son,* ed. B. Dobrée, Oxford University Press, 1932.

Revd W. Cole, *Journal of my Journey to Paris in the year 1765*, 1765.

J. Churton Collins, *Voltaire, Montesquieu and Rousseau in England*, 1908.

S. Foote, *The Englishman in Paris*, 1753.

—— *The Englishman Returned from Paris*, 1756.

W. B. Fryer, 'Mirabeau in England', in *Renaissance and Modern Studies*, Nottingham, 1966.

P. Gay, *Voltaire's Politics,* Princeton University Press, 1959.

G. P. Gooch, *French Profiles: Prophets and Pioneers*, Longmans, 1961.

P. Gosse, *Dr Viper: The Querulous Life of Philip Thicknesse*, Cassell, 1952.

G. R. Havens, *The Abbé Prévost and English Literature*, Princeton University Press, 1921.

D. B. Horn, *Great Britain and Europe in the Eighteenth Century*, Oxford, 1967.

D. Jarrett, *The Begetters of Revolution: England's Involvement with France 1759–89*, Longmans, 1973.

F. duc de la Rochefoucauld, *Mélanges sur l'Angleterre*, 1784.

Abbé le Blanc, *Lettres d'un Français*, 1745.

D. McKay & H. M. Scott, *The Rise of the Great Powers 1648–1815*,

Longmans, 1983.

J. Millard, *The Gentleman's Guide in his Tour through France*, 1770.

M. Miller, 'The English People as portrayed in certain French journals', in *Modern Philology*, 1937.

C. de Montesquieu, *Notes sur l'Angleterre*, 1728–31.

—— *De l'Esprit des Lois*, 1748.

B. L. de Muralt, *Lettres sur les Anglais et les Française et sur les Voyages*, first pub. 1728.

B. Saurin, *L'Anglomane ou l'orpheline léguée*, 1772.

T. Smollett, *Travels through France and Italy* (ed. F. Felsenstein), Oxford University Press, 1979.

L. Sterne, *A Sentimental Journey through France and Italy*, 1768.

P. Thicknesse, *Observations on the Customs and Manners of the French Nation*, 1766.

—— *Useful Hints to Those Who Make the Tour of France*, 1768.

—— *A Year's Journey through France and part of Spain*, 1777.

F. M. A. de Voltaire, *Lettres philosophiques*, 1734.

H. Walpole, *Correspondence*, 42 vols (ed. W. S. Lewis), Oxford University Press, 1937–81.

A. Young, *Travels in France during the Years 1787, 1788 and 1789* (ed. C. Maxwell), Cambridge University Press, 1950.

Chapter 4: The French Revolution

B. T. Bennett, *British War Poetry in the Age of Romanticism*, Garland Publications, New York, 1976.

T. C. W. Blanning, *The Origins of the French Revolutionary Wars*, Longmans, 1986.

E. Burke, *Reflections on the Revolution in France*, 1790.

M. Butler, *Burke, Paine, Godwin and the Revolution Controversy*, Cambridge University Press, 1984.

A. Cobban, *Edmund Burke and the Revolt Against the Eighteenth Century*, Allen & Unwin, 1929.

—— *The Debate on the French Revolution: 1789–1800*, A & C Black, 1960.

—— *The Social Interpretation of the French Revolution*, Cambridge University Press, 1964.

C. Emsley, *British Society and the French Wars 1793–1815*, Macmillan,

1979.

N. Hampson, *A Social History of the French Revolution,* Routledge, 1963.

A. D. Harvey, 'European Attitudes to Britain during the French Revolutionary and Napoleonic Era', in *History,* 1978.

M. Hutt, 'Spies in France 1793–1808', in *History Today,* 1962, pp. 158–167.

D. Johnson (ed.), *French Society and the Revolution,* Cambridge University Press, 1976.

C. Jones (ed.), *Britain and Revolutionary France,* Exeter University Press, 1983.

G. Lefebvre, *The French Revolution: From its Origins to 1793,* Routledge, 1962.

—— *The French Revolution: From 1793 to 1799,* Routledge, 1964.

J. M. Roberts, *The French Revolution,* Oxford University Press, 1978.

G. Rudé, *The Crowd in the French Revolution,* Oxford University Press, 1959.

A. Soboul, *The French Revolution 1789–99,* N.L.B., 1974.

J. M. Thompson, *English Witnesses of the French Revolution,* Blackwell, Oxford, 1938.

—— *Robespierre,* Blackwell, Oxford, 1939.

H. M. Stephens, *Speeches of the Statesmen and Orators of the French Revolution,* 2 vols, Clarendon Press, Oxford, 1892.

P. Vansittart, *Voices of the Revolution,* Collins, 1989.

W. Wordsworth, *The Prelude,* 1805 edition.

Chapter 5: Napoleon

F. Burney, *Selected Letters and Journals* (ed. J. Hemlow), Clarendon Press, Oxford, 1986.

R. Coupland (ed.), *The War Speeches of William Pitt the Younger,* Clarendon Press, Oxford, 1940.

V. Cronin, *Napoleon,* Penguin Books, 1983.

H. T. Dickinson, *British Radicalism and the French Revolution: 1789–1815,* Blackwell, Oxford, 1985.

J. Fiévée, *Lettres sur l'Angleterre,* 1802.

P. Geyl, *Napoleon, For and Against,* Peregrine Books, 1965.

R. B. Holtman, *Napoleonic Propaganda,* Louisiana State University

Press, Baton Rouge, 1950.

F. Markham, *Napoleon*, Mentor Books, New York, 1966.

J. M. Sherwig, *Guineas and Gunpowder. British Foreign Aid in the Wars with France: 1793–1815*, Harvard University Press, 1969.

Chapter 6: Love, Hate and Suspicion: 1814–1914

L. Blanc, *Lettres sur l'Angleterre*, 4 vols, 1866–67.

R. Boutet de Monvel, *Les Anglais à Paris: 1800–1850*, Plon, 1911.

J. M. Carré, 'Michelet et l'Angleterre', in *Revue de littérature comparée*, 1924.

R. de Chateaubriand, *De l'Angleterre et des Anglais*, 1800.

—— *Mémoires d'outre-tombe*, 1848–50.

J. P. Cobbett, *A Ride of 800 miles in France*, 1824.

F. Delattre, *Dickens et la France*, Gamber, 1927.

E. Demolins, *A quoi tient la supériorité des Anglo-Saxons?*, Firmin-Didot, 1897.

A. Esquiros, *L'Angleterre et la vie anglaise*, Hetzel, 1869.

W. C. Frierson, 'The English controversy over Realism in France', in *Publications of the Modern Language Association of America*, 1928, pp. 533–550.

Mrs E. Gaskell, 'My French Master', in *Household Words*, 1853.

—— 'French Life', in *Fraser's Magazine*, April/June 1864.

T. Gautier, *Caprices et Zigzags*, Victor Lecou, 1852.

Capt. R. H. Gronow, *Reminiscences and Recollections – Anecdotes of the Camp, Court, Clubs and Society: 1810–1860*, new abridged edn., Bodley Head, 1964.

D. Gunnell, *Stendhal et l'Angleterre*, Bosse, 1909.

W. Hazlitt, *Notes of a Journey through France and Italy* (ed. P. P. Howe), Dent, 1930–34.

R. Kipling, *Souvenirs of France*, Macmillan, 1933.

A. Ledru-Rollin, *De la décadence en Angleterre*, 1850.

K. McWatters & C. Thompson (eds.), *Stendhal et l'Angleterre*, Liverpool University Press, 1987.

P. Mérimée, *Lettres à une Inconnue*, 2 vols, Lévy, 1874.

S. Pakenham, *Sixty Miles from England – the English at Dieppe: 1814–1914*, Macmillan, 1967.

P. Reboul, 'Chateaubriand et les Anglais', in *Revue de littérature comparée*, 1949.

—— *Le mythe anglais dans la littérature française sous la restauration*, Lille, 1962.

F. C. Roe, *Taine et l'Angleterre*, Champion, 1923.

R. L. Stevenson, *An Inland Voyage*, 1878.

—— *Travels with a Donkey in the Cévennes*, 1879.

R. S. Surtees, *Jorrocks's Jaunts and Jollities*, 1838.

H. Taine, *Notes sur l'Angleterre*, 1872.

W. M. Thackeray, *The Paris Sketch-book*, 1840.

—— *The Book of Snobs*, 1848.

A. de Tocqueville, *Journeys to England and Ireland* (ed. J. P. Mayer), Faber, 1958.

Mrs F. Trollope, *Paris and the Parisians*, 1835.

J. Vallès, *La Rue à Londres* (ed. L. Scheler), Editions Françaises réunies, 1951.

Vermont, Marquis de, & Darnley, Sir Charles (pseudonyms), *London and Paris or Comparative Sketches*, 1823.

J. Verne, *Le tour du monde en 80 jours*, 1873.

Chapter 7: Uneasy Entente in the Two World Wars

M. Beloff, 'The Anglo–French Union Project of June 1940', in *Mélanges Pierre Renouvin*, 1966.

H. Béraud, *Faut-il réduire l'Angleterre en esclavage?*, Editions de France, 1935.

G. Bernanos, *Lettre aux Anglais*, Gallimard, 1946.

R. Boucard, *Les Dessous de l'espionnage anglais*, Editions de France, 1929.

J. C. Cairns, 'Great Britain and the Fall of France: A Study in Allied Disunity', in *Journal of Modern History*, December 1955.

—— 'A Nation of Shopkeepers in Search of a Suitable France', in *American Historical Review*, 1974.

L. Cazamian, *Ce qu'il faut connaître de l'âme anglaise*, Boivin, 1927.

L. F. Céline, *Bagatelles pour un massacre*, Denoël & Steele, 1937.

—— *L'Ecole des Cadavres*, Denoël & Steele, 1938.

W. S. Churchill, *The Second World War*, 6 vols, Collins, 1948–54.

A. Darlan, *L'Amiral Darlan parle*, Amiot et Dumont, 1952.

J.-B. Duroselle, *Politique étrangère de la France: la décadence 1932–39*,

Point-Seuil, 1983.

M.-F. Guyard, 'Charles Morgan en France', in *Revue de littérature comparée*, 1949, pp. 71–79.

—— *La Grande Bretagne dans le roman français – 1914–40*, Didier, 1954.

P. Henriot, *Et s'ils débarquaient?*, Agence Inter-France, 1944.

D. Johnson, 'Britain and France in 1940', in *Transactions of the Royal Historical Society*, 1972.

J. M. Keynes, *Essays in Biography*, Hart-Davis, 1951.

R. B. McCallum, *Public Opinion and the Last Peace*, Oxford University Press, 1944.

A. Maurois, *Conseils à un jeune Français partant pour l'Angleterre*, Grasset, 1938.

P. Morand, *Londres*, Plon, 1933.

E. D. Morel, *The Horror on the Rhine*, Union of Democratic Control Pamphlet No. 44, 1921.

C. Morgan, *Ode to France*, 1942.

—— *Reflections in a Mirror*, Macmillan, 1944.

K. L. Nelson, 'The Black Horror on the Rhine. Race as a Factor in Post-World War I Diplomacy', in *Journal of Modern History*, December 1955.

J.-H. Paquis, *L'Angleterre comme Carthage . . .* , Editions Inter-France, 1944.

L. Rebatet, *Les Décombres*, Denoël & Steele, 1942.

R. C. Reinders, 'Racialism on the Left: E. D. Morel and the Black Horror on the Rhine', in *International Review of Social History*, 1968.

G. B. Shaw, *What I Really Wrote About the War*, Constable, 1931.

R. T. Thomas, *Britain and Vichy: The Dilemma of Anglo–French Relations 1940–42*, Macmillan, 1979.

G. Warner, *Pierre Laval and the Eclipse of France*, Eyre & Spottiswoode, 1968.

N. Waites (ed.), *Troubled Neighbours: Franco–British Relations in the Twentieth Century*, Weidenfeld & Nicolson, 1971.

H. G. Wells, *A Year of Prophesying*, Fisher Unwin, 1924.

Sir E. L. Woodward, *British Foreign Policy in the Second World War*, 5 vols, H.M.S.O., 1970–76.

Chapter 8: De Gaulle and After

J. Ardagh, *France in the 1980's*, Penguin, 1986.

P. Daninos, *Les Carnets du Major Thompson*, Hachette, 1954.

—— *Le Secret du Major Thompson*, Hachette, 1956.

C. de Gaulle, *Discours aux Français: 18 June 1940 – 2 January 1944*, Office française d'édition, 1944.

—— *Major Addresses, Statements and Press-Conferences of General Charles de Gaulle*, French Embassy Press & Information Service.

—— *Mémoires de Guerre*, 3 vols, Plon, 1954.

Etiemble, *Parlez-vous franglais?*, Gallimard, 1964.

J. Lacoutre, *De Gaulle* (3 vols: I: *Le Rebelle*, 1984; II: *Le Politique*, 1985; III: *Le Souverain*, 1986), Seuil.

K. A. Reader, *The May 1968 Events in France*, Macmillan, 1993.

A. Williams, *Britain and France in the Middle East and North Africa: 1914–67*, Macmillan, 1968.

Index